Adobe®
Photoshop® 6.0

User Guide

Adobe®

Contents

Working with Color

Chapter 3

Producing Consistent
Color (Photoshop)

Chapter 4

Selecting

Chapter 5

Drawing and Editing

Chapter 6

Using Channels and Masks

Chapter 7

Using Layers

Chapter 8

Using Type

Chapter 9

Designing Web Pages

Chapter 10

Getting Started

Welcome to the Adobe® Photoshop® 6.0 application, the world-standard image-editing, photo-retouching, and Web-graphics solution. With its integrated Web tool application, Adobe ImageReady™ 3.0, Photoshop delivers a comprehensive environment for professional designers and graphics producers to create sophisticated images for both print and the Web. Moreover, Photoshop 6.0 expands the definition of desktop image-editing by adding new support for vector-based drawing and editing, improved tools for producing Web graphics, and an enhanced user interface, all to your creative advantage.

Registration

Adobe is confident you will find that its software greatly increases your productivity. So that Adobe can continue to provide you with the highest quality software, offer technical support, and inform you about new Photoshop software developments, please register your application.

When you first start the Photoshop or ImageReady application, you're prompted to register online. You can choose to submit the form directly or fax a printed copy. You can also register by filling out and returning the registration card included with your software package.

Installing Adobe Photoshop and ImageReady

You must install the Photoshop and ImageReady applications from the Adobe Photoshop CD onto your hard drive; you cannot run the program from the CD.

Follow the on-screen installation instructions. For more detailed information, see the *Install-ReadMe* file on the CD. The single installer installs both the Photoshop and ImageReady applications.

Learning Adobe Photoshop and ImageReady

Adobe provides a variety of options for you to learn Photoshop, including printed guides, online Help, and tool tips. Using the Adobe Online feature, you can easily access a host of continually updated Web resources for learning Photoshop, from tips and tutorials to tech support information.

Adobe Acrobat® Reader™ software, included on the Photoshop CD, lets you view PDF files. Acrobat Reader or Adobe Acrobat is required to view many documents included on this CD.

Using the printed documentation

Two printed documents are included with the application.

Using online Help

The Adobe Photoshop and ImageReady applications include complete documentation in an HTML-based help system. The help system includes all of the information in the *Adobe Photoshop 6.0 User Guide* plus information on additional features, keyboard shortcuts, and full-color illustrations.

For more detailed information about using online Help, click the Help on Help button next to the Content tab.

To properly view online Help topics, you need Netscape Communicator 4.0 (or later) or Microsoft® Internet Explorer 4.0 (or later). You must also have JavaScript active.

To start online Help:

Do one of the following:

• Choose Help > Help Contents (Photoshop) or Help > Help Topics (ImageReady).

• Press F1 (Windows).

Adobe Photoshop 6.0 User Guide Contains essential information on using Photoshop and ImageReady commands and features. Complete information on all topics is available in online Help. The printed guide and help also indicate when a topic, procedure, or command pertains specifically to Photoshop or ImageReady, for example, "Choose View > Actual Pixels (Photoshop) or View > Actual Size (ImageReady)."

The user guide assumes you have a working knowledge of your computer and its operating conventions, including how to use a mouse and standard menus and commands. It also assumes you know how to open, save, and close files. For help with any of these techniques, please see your Microsoft Windows® or Mac® OS documentation.

Adobe Photoshop Quick Reference Card
Contains basic information about the Adobe Photoshop and ImageReady tools and palettes, and shortcuts for using them. Shortcuts are also included in the online Help.

Using tool tips

The tool tips feature lets you display the name of tools, or buttons and controls in palettes.

To identify a tool or control:

Position the pointer over a tool or control and pause. A tool tip appears showing the name and keyboard shortcut (if any) for the item.

If tool tips don't appear, the preference for displaying them may be turned off.

To display tool tips:

1 Choose Edit > Preferences > General.

2 Select Show Tool Tips, and click OK.

Note: Tool tips are not available in most dialog boxes.

Using Web resources

If you have an Internet connection and a Web browser installed on your system, you can access additional resources for learning Photoshop and ImageReady located on the Adobe Systems home page on the World Wide Web. These resources are continually updated.

To access the Adobe home page for your region:

1 Open the Adobe U.S. home page at www.adobe.com.

2 From the Adobe Sites menu, choose your geographical region. The Adobe home page is customized for several geographical regions.

About Adobe Online

Adobe Online provides access to the latest tutorials, quicktips, and other Web content for Photoshop and other Adobe products. Using Adobe Online, you can also download and view the current version of the Photoshop Top Issues document containing the latest Photoshop technical support solutions. Bookmarks are also included to take you quickly to noteworthy Adobe- and Photoshop-related sites.

Using Adobe Online

Adobe Online is constantly changing, so you should refresh before you use it. Refreshing through Adobe Online updates bookmarks and buttons so you can quickly access the most current content available. You can use preferences to automatically refresh Adobe Online daily, weekly, or monthly.

When you set up Adobe Online to connect to your Web browser, Adobe can either notify you whenever new information is available through the Downloadables feature or automatically download that information to your hard disk. If you choose not to use the automatic download feature, you can still view and download new files whenever they are available using the Downloadables command in the Help menu.

To use Adobe Online:

1 In Photoshop or ImageReady, choose Help > Adobe Online, or click the icon at the top of the toolbox.

Note: You must have an Internet connection and an Internet browser installed. Adobe Online will launch your browser using your default Internet configuration.

2 Do any of the following:

• Click Refresh to make sure you have the latest version of the Adobe Online window and its buttons, as well as the latest bookmarks. It is important to refresh the screen so that the current options are available for you to choose from.

• Click Preferences to specify connection options. General preferences affect how Adobe Online interacts with all Adobe products installed on your system, and Application preferences affect how

Adobe Online interacts with Photoshop and ImageReady. To see an explanation of each preference option, click Setup and follow the prompts. You also can set up an automatic refresh using the Update Options.

Note: *You can also set Adobe Online preferences by choosing Edit > Preferences > Adobe Online.*

• Click any button in the Adobe Online window to open the Web page to which the button is linked.

• Click the bookmark button (🐾) to view suggested Web sites related to Photoshop and Adobe. These bookmarks are automatically updated as new Web sites become available.

• Click Close to return to Photoshop or ImageReady.

Accessing Adobe Online through the Help menu

The Help menu includes options to view and download information from the Adobe Web site.

To view updated articles or documents:

Click Help and choose the topic you want to view.

To view and download information from the Adobe Web site using the Help menu:

1 In Photoshop or ImageReady, choose Help > Downloadables.

2 Select a View Option:

• Select Show Only New Files to view only the files that are new since the last time you viewed downloadable files or were notified of them.

• Select Show All Files to view all the files on the Adobe Web site that are currently available for download.

3 Select Download Options:

• Select Auto Install Downloaded Components if you want Adobe to start the component's installer (if available) as soon as the download is complete. You can then follow the prompts to install the files.

• Select Download in Background if you want to continue working in Photoshop, ImageReady, and other applications while the file downloads.

• Select Notify When Download Complete if you want Adobe to display a message when the files have been transferred to your computer.

4 To view a list of files, open the Downloadables folder and any other folder listed.

5 To see a description of a file, position the mouse cursor over a filename and view its description in the Item Description section.

6 To see the location where a file will be installed if downloaded, select a file and view its location in the Download Directory section. To change the location, click the Folder button (📁).

7 To download a file, select it and click Download.

8 To close the Downloadables dialog box, click Close.

Other learning resources

Other Adobe learning resources are available but are not included with your application.

Classroom in a Book Is the official training series for Adobe graphics and publishing software. This book is developed by experts at Adobe and published by Adobe Press. The *Adobe Photoshop Classroom in a Book* includes lessons about using Photoshop. For information on purchasing *Adobe Photoshop Classroom in a Book*, visit the Adobe Web site at www.adobe.com, or contact your local book distributor.

Official Adobe Print Publishing Guide

Provides in-depth information on successful print production, including topics such as color management, commercial printing, constructing a publication, imaging and proofing, and project management guidelines. For information on purchasing the *Official Adobe Print Publishing Guide*, visit the Adobe Web site at www.adobe.com.

Official Adobe Electronic Publishing Guide

Tackles the fundamental issues essential to ensuring quality online publications in HTML and PDF. Using simple, expertly illustrated explanations, design and publishing professionals tell you how to design electronic publications for maximum speed, legibility, and effectiveness. For information on purchasing the *Official Adobe Electronic Publishing Guide*, visit the Adobe Web site at www.adobe.com.

The Adobe Certification program Offers users, instructors, and training centers the opportunity to demonstrate their product proficiency and promote their software skills as Adobe Certified Experts, Adobe Certified Instructors, or Adobe Authorized Learning Providers. Certification is available for several different geographical regions. Visit the Partnering with Adobe Web site at www.partners.adobe.com to learn how you can become certified.

Customer support

When you register your product, you may be entitled to technical support for up to 90 days from the date of your first call. Terms may vary depending on the country of residence. For more information, refer to the technical support card provided with the Photoshop documentation.

Customer support on Adobe Online

Adobe Online provides access to FAQs (Frequently Asked Questions) and trouble-shooting information that provides solutions to common problems.

Additional customer support resources

Adobe Systems provides several forms of automated technical support:

• See the ReadMe and ReadMe First! files installed with the program for information that became available after this guide went to press.

• Explore the extensive customer support information on Adobe's World Wide Web site (www.adobe.com). To access the Adobe Web site from Photoshop, choose Help > Adobe Online or click the icon at the top of the toolbox. (See "Using Web resources" on page 3.)

• Read the Top Issues PDF that is available from the Help menu.

Adobe Photoshop Basics

This interactive overview of Adobe Photoshop offers a number of short lesson modules designed to introduce the key features of the program. You can complete the modules in sequence, or select individual ones to design your own program introduction. If you are an experienced Photoshop user, you may want to quickly review sections of this overview and then skip to "What's New in Adobe Photoshop 6.0."

Setting up the work area

Using tools and palettes

The Photoshop or ImageReady work area consists of the image window, the toolbox, the options bar, and a set of floating palettes. This module shows you the basics of navigating the work area, from selecting tools and tool options to customizing the display and arrangement of palettes.

Select a tool To select a tool, click its icon in the toolbox. Some tools in the toolbox have additional hidden tools, as indicated by the small triangle to the lower right of the tool icon. To select a hidden tool, position the pointer on the visible tool and hold down the mouse button until the tools list appears. Then, click the tool you want.

Choose tool options When you first start the application, the options bar appears docked to the top of your screen. This options bar contains option settings for the currently selected tool.

- To display the options bar if it is hidden, click a tool in the toolbox, or choose Window > Show Options.
- To move the options bar to a different location, drag the title bar on the left edge of the bar. You can move the options bar anywhere in the work area and dock it to the top or bottom of the screen.

Options bar

Display the palettes When you first start the application, the floating palettes appear stacked in default groups. Use the following techniques to show and hide palettes:

- To bring a palette to the front of its group, click the palette's tab.

- To show or hide a palette as you work, choose the appropriate Window > Show or Window > Hide command.

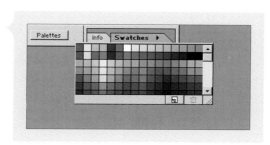

Palette group with Color palette at front

- (ImageReady) To show or hide options for palettes that include hidden options, click the Show Options button (◆) on the palette tab to cycle through palette displays.

- To hide or display all open palettes and the toolbox, press Tab. To hide or display palettes only, press Shift+Tab.

Arrange the palettes Depending on your available screen area and work needs, you may want to reposition and regroup the palettes. Use the following techniques to change palette arrangements:

- To move an entire palette group, drag its title bar.

- To rearrange or separate a palette from its group, drag the palette's tab. Dragging a palette outside of an existing group creates a new group.

Click a tab to display a palette stored in the palette well.

- To dock palettes together, drag a palette's tab to the bottom of another palette so that the bottom of the second palette is highlighted. You can move an entire docked group by dragging its title bar. You cannot dock existing palette groups together.

- To store an undocked palette in the palette well at the options bar's right edge, drag the palette's tab into the palette well so that the palette well is highlighted. To display a palette in the well, click the palette's tab. This technique is useful for providing quick and compact access to palettes.

Display a palette menu Most palettes have menus that contain additional commands and options. To display a palette menu, click the black triangle at the upper right of the palette. (For palettes stored in the options bar, first display the palette and then click the black triangle in the palette's tab.)

Opening images in Photoshop and ImageReady

Photoshop and ImageReady let you open or import a variety of source images. You can create new images, import digital images saved in various formats, and scan or capture images from an imaging device.

(Photoshop) Specify color management settings Before opening or creating new images, specify the color management settings you want to use. Photoshop color management features are designed to help keep colors in your image consistent as the image is transferred between different users, systems, and display and output devices. To set up color management, choose Edit > Color Settings, choose a predefined configuration from the Settings menu, and click OK.

The configuration you choose defines the specific color spaces that Photoshop uses when working with images in RGB, CMYK, and Grayscale modes. For complete information on setting up color management, see the online help section on producing consistent color.

Scan the image at the correct size and resolution If you are scanning an image to be opened in Photoshop or ImageReady, it's a good idea to scan the image as close as possible to the size dimensions and resolution that you want. When in doubt, scan at a higher resolution than what is needed. You can always reduce the image later in Photoshop or ImageReady by cutting down the resolution or pixel dimensions.

Open or create an image Do one of the following:

- Choose File > Open, and locate and select the desired image file. Depending on your color management settings and the color profile associated with the file, you may be prompted to specify how to handle color information in the file.

- Choose File > New. Enter a name for the image, and specify its dimensions, resolution (Photoshop only), and color mode (Photoshop only). In addition, specify whether to fill the image with white, the current background color, or transparency.

Set rulers, guides, and the grid To help position and align elements accurately in the image, use rulers, guides, and grid lines:

• To display rulers along the top and left side of the document window, choose View > Show Rulers. (In Photoshop, you can change the ruler units by choosing Edit > Preferences > Units & Rulers.)

• To place a horizontal or vertical guide, drag from either the horizontal or vertical ruler.

• (Photoshop) To display grid lines throughout the document window, choose View > Show > Grid. (You can control the color, style, and spacing of the grid and guide lines by choosing Edit > Preferences > Guides & Grid.)

You can toggle the display of guides and grid lines at any time by choosing the appropriate command from the View > Show submenu. Checked items are visible; unchecked items are hidden.

Adjust the image view Photoshop and ImageReady offer several tools for navigating and magnifying the view of your image:

Drag with the zoom tool to magnify.

• To move a different area of the image into view, drag with the hand tool (🖑) in the image. You can use the hand tool while another tool is selected by holding down the spacebar.

• To magnify the view, select the zoom tool (🔍), and click in the image or drag over the part of the image you want to magnify. To reduce the view magnification, Alt-click (Windows) or Option-click (Mac OS) with the zoom tool in the image.

• (Photoshop) To adjust the image view using the Navigator palette, choose Window > Show Navigator. In the Navigator palette, drag the view box in the image thumbnail to move the view, or click the area of the thumbnail that you want to display in the window.

• To display the same image in multiple windows, choose View > New View. Multiple windows let you display different views of the same image.

Monitor your work status As you experiment with different tools, commands, and image views, check out the status bar at the bottom edge of the document window. This area displays useful information about your work status, such as the current magnification percentage or the name of the currently selected tool. You can specify the type of information displayed by using the pop-up menu in the status bar.

Status bar

Display the Info palette For convenient access to additional information about your image, display the Info palette by choosing Window > Show Info. The Info palette displays information about the color values in the image beneath the pointer and, depending on the tool in use, other useful measurements.

Streamlining your workflow

Photoshop and ImageReady provide a number of convenient features to help your work flow more smoothly. The Jump To button makes it easy to work on the same image seamlessly in both Photoshop and ImageReady. The Undo command and History palette let you correct editing mistakes. And the Actions palette lets you save sequences of commonly used tasks so that you can perform them automatically on an image or batch of images.

Switch between Photoshop and ImageReady

You can easily jump between Photoshop and ImageReady when working on an image to use the full feature sets of both applications. To switch to either application, click the Jump To button in the toolbox.

Jump To button in Photoshop and ImageReady

Undo the last performed operation If you make a mistake while working, simply choose Edit > Undo to reverse the effect of the last operation. Most, but not all, operations can be reversed this way.

Undo multiple operations If you need to undo more than one operation, choose Window > Show History to display the History palette. This palette lists all the different states that the image has undergone as a result of the recent edits you've made. To revert the image to a previous state, click the name of the state in the History palette.

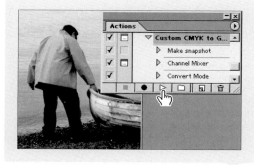

History palette

Playing an action

Automate repeated tasks To automatically apply a sequence of operations to your image, choose Window > Show Actions to display the Actions palette. This palette includes a default list of common tasks, or *actions*. You can perform a desired action automatically by selecting it and clicking the Play button (▷) at the bottom of the Actions palette. Or, you can record your own sequence of operations as a stored action in the palette for future playback on a single image or batch of images.

Adjusting and retouching images

Making tonal and color adjustments

Upon first opening a scanned image or digital photograph in Photoshop or ImageReady, it's common to notice some problems with color quality and tonal range. The image may appear washed out, for example, or appear too dark or too light in certain areas.

Open the Levels dialog box When making tonal adjustments to an image in Photoshop, it's a good idea to use adjustment layers. You can limit the application of flexible and reversible adjustments to an adjustment layer, so that underlying layers show the effects of the adjustment without being permanently altered. (You can even block areas from being adjusted by painting the adjustment layer with black.) To create an adjustment layer that adjusts the tonality of an image, choose Layer > New Adjustment Layer > Levels. Name the layer and click OK.

In ImageReady, you do not have the option of adjustment layers, so choose Image > Adjust > Levels.

Adjust tonal levels The Levels dialog box displays a graph representing the tonal distribution of the image—from shadows (on the left) to midtones (in the middle) to highlights (on the right). To achieve good tonal range, drag the black and white sliders to where the graph begins at either end. Then drag the middle slider to adjust midtones to the desired level.

Adjusting tonal levels

The Levels dialog box provides a useful way to adjust your image's overall tonal range. The Curves dialog box represents another, more precise method, letting you adjust any point along a 0–255 tonal scale.

Make other adjustments If needed, you can use other adjustment features to correct for color casts and sharpen details in the final image.

Retouching images

Many of the retouching tools in Photoshop and ImageReady are modeled after traditional photo-studio techniques for correcting blemishes and faulty exposures in images. However, with the power of digital technology you can use these tools to apply all sorts of creative effects beyond basic photo retouching.

Dodge or burn the image The dodge tool ( ) and burn tool ( ) let you respectively lighten and darken a localized area in your image. With either tool selected, choose a brush from the brushes menu in the options bar. In addition, choose the range of tones you want to affect from the range menu in the options bar. Then drag over the part of the image that you want to lighten.

Remove imperfections The clone stamp tool ( ) lets you paint over an area of your image using a sample taken from the same image or another image. With the clone stamp tool selected, choose a brush from the options bar. Alt-click (Windows) or Option-click (Mac OS) the image area you want to sample. Release Alt/Option, and then drag to paint with the sample.

Removing areas with the clone stamp tool

For best results, use short strokes when painting, and Alt/Option-click to take updated samples frequently between strokes. This helps to produce a smoother, more natural effect.

Editing images

Making pixel selections

Before you can edit an area of an image, you must first select the image area. This type of selection is called a pixel selection because you are selecting an area that contains pixel information. If you experience trouble selecting the image area you want, you may need to check that you are working on the proper layer.

Select with a marquee tool The marquee tools let you select image areas by dragging to define a shaped selection border. First, select the rectangular marquee (⬚) or the elliptical marquee (◯) from the toolbox. Then drag over the area you want to select.

Reposition a selection border At times, you may want to adjust the position of a selection border to enclose a different area of the image. To reposition a selection border using any selection tool, move the pointer inside the border and drag to the desired location. Or, use the arrow keys to move the selection border in gradual increments.

Select with a lasso tool The lasso (⌇) and polygon lasso (⌇) tools let you select areas by dragging and clicking, respectively, to define the boundary of the selected area. (In Photoshop, you can also use the magnetic lasso tool (⌇) to find the edges of the desired area automatically.) These tools are especially useful for selecting irregularly shaped areas.

Selecting with the magnetic lasso tool

Select with the magic wand The magic wand tool (✎) lets you select a consistently colored area without having to trace its outline. To use the magic wand, first enter a tolerance value in the options bar. (A higher tolerance selects a broader range of colors.) Then click the area in the image you want to select.

Modify a selection border The selection tools come with several options for enhancing or modifying an existing selection border. These options can help you select areas that are difficult to define with a single selection. First, make a selection. Then, using any selection tool, specify an option in the options bar:

- The Add to Selection option (▣) adds the new selection to the first selection.

- The Subtract from Selection option (▣) subtracts the new selection from the first selection.

- The Restrict Selection option (▣) selects only the intersection of the two selections.

(Photoshop) Quick Mask mode A quick mask lets you refine an existing selection border with the aid of painting tools. This technique is useful for selecting areas that are more easily defined with a painting brush. Use any selection tool to select the desired image area, and then click the Quick Mask mode button (▣) in the toolbox. In Quick Mask mode, everything outside the selection appears masked by a color overlay. Do any of the following to modify the selection border:

- To add to the selection, use a painting tool to paint with white. (See "Painting" on page 26 for more information.)

- To subtract from the selection, paint with black.

- To create a semitransparent selection area, paint with gray. This is useful for creating a selection with feathered edges.

Click the Standard mode button (▣) to turn off the quick mask and display the modified selection border.

Making edits

Photoshop and ImageReady are equipped with a rich collection of editing tools and commands that you can use to modify your images. In addition to basic edits such as repositioning or applying geometric changes to a selection, you can create an unlimited variety of special effects using the Filter commands.

Resize the image To change the dimensions or resolution of your image, choose Image > Image Size and specify values for the image:

* For an image intended for the Web or online display, enter values for the pixel dimensions and click OK.

* (Photoshop) For an image intended for printed output, enter values for the physical output size. Enter the resolution value recommended for your press or desktop printer, and click OK.

Move a selection To move a selected pixel area, select the move tool (▶₊) in the toolbox. Position the pointer inside the selection, and drag the selection to a new location.

Duplicate a selection You can also use the move tool to duplicate a selection. With the move tool selected, simply Alt-drag (Windows) or Option-drag (Mac OS) the selection to copy it.

Duplicating a selection

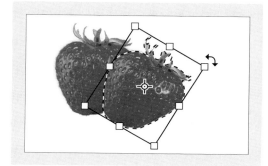

Rotating a selection

Apply a transformation The transformation commands let you make geometric changes—such as resizing, rotations, shears, distortions, and reflections—to a selection. To apply a transformation, do one of the following:

- Choose the desired command from the Edit > Transform menu. (In Photoshop, this menu changes to Edit > Transform Path if a vector shape is selected.)

- Select the move tool (▸⊹), and select Show Bounding Box in the options bar.

If applicable, drag the handles that appear around the selection to achieve the desired effect. Then press Enter or Return to apply the transformation. You can even choose additional transformation commands before you press Enter or Return, adjusting the handles for each command to achieve a cumulative effect.

Apply a filter Photoshop and ImageReady provide a generous array of filters for creating all kinds of special effects—from blurs and ripples to mosaics, brushlike patterns, and other artistic effects. To apply a filter to a pixel selection, select a command from a submenu in the Filter menu. (If no selection exists, the filter is applied to the entire layer.)

Using layers

Layers provide a powerful way for you to organize and manage the various components of your image. For example, by placing an element on a separate layer, you can easily edit and arrange the element without interfering with other parts of the image. Layers also provide the basis for managing and defining advanced features such as Web animations and rollovers.

Display the list of layers If needed, choose Window > Show Layers to display the Layers palette. This palette shows the list of layers that have been created in the image. The thumbnail previews help you monitor the contents of each layer. Layers may be grouped under layer sets to aid in organizing complex images. To toggle between the expanded and collapsed displays of a layer set, click the triangle to the left of the layer set's name.

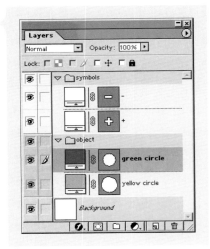

Layers palette with expanded display

Change the visibility of a layer To help focus your work on individual layers in the image, you can toggle the visibility of one or more layers:

• To make a single layer invisible, click the eye icon next to that layer in the Layers palette.

• To display just a single layer and make all other layers invisible, Alt-click (Windows) or Option-click (Mac OS) the eye icon next to the layer you want to show.

Select a layer Often you will need to target a specific layer for further editing in Photoshop or ImageReady. For instance, many tasks—such as transformations or filters—can be applied to entire layers as well as to individual selections. In addition, you must first target a layer in order to select an area or shape that sits on that layer. To select or target a layer, click its name in the Layers palette.

Create a selection based on the contents of a layer To select all the opaque contents of a layer, Ctrl-click (Windows) or Command-click (Mac OS) the layer in the Layers palette. The resulting selection border represents the boundaries of the layer.

Adjust opacity and blending mode For each layer, you can specify an opacity percentage (to control how much layers beneath show through) and blending mode (to control how the colors in the layer are blended with the colors of underlying layers). To specify the opacity of a selected layer, enter a value for Opacity or drag the slider at the upper right of the Layers palette. To specify a blending mode for a selected layer, choose an option from the menu at the upper left of the Layers palette.

Move a layer's stacking order The Layers palette displays layers in the order that they are stacked in the image, with the topmost layer appearing at the top of the list. To move a layer (or layer set) to a different level in the stacking order, simply drag the layer up or down in the palette. You can also move a layer into a layer set by dragging the layer over the layer set icon.

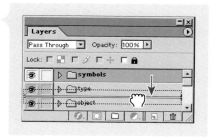

Reordering a layer set

Move a layer's contents To move all the contents of a layer to a different position in the image, first select the layer in the Layers palette. Then use the move tool (▶₊) to drag in the image. Only the contents of the selected layer are affected.

Apply a layer style You can apply predefined styles to the contents of a layer to produce instant graphic effects. This feature is especially useful for creating Web buttons and rollover states. You can also define your own layer styles.

To apply a style, choose Window > Show Styles to display the Styles palettes. Select the desired layer in the Layers palette, and then select the style you want to apply from the Styles palette.

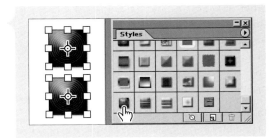

Applying a layer style

Compositing images

You can use various features in Photoshop and ImageReady to combine several images or parts of images to produce creative compositions. For example, by isolating the foreground area of an image and placing it against the background of another image, you can create unlimited composite effects.

Copy a layer between images To copy a layer with all its contents from one image to another, make sure that both images are open. In the Layers palette for the source image, select the layer that you want to copy. Then select the move tool (⤧), and drag from the source image to the destination image until a border highlights the destination window. (If you have made a selection, only the selected area is copied to the destination image.)

(Photoshop) Erase the background area of a layer The background eraser tool (⌗) lets you erase similarly colored areas of a layer. This is useful for extracting a foreground object that is surrounded by a consistently colored background. First select the desired layer in the Layers palette. Select the background eraser tool, and set the Tolerance option to a low value. Then drag in the area that you want to remove.

(Photoshop) Extract part of an image The Extract Image command provides controls for isolating image areas with wispy or intricate edges. First, duplicate the layer containing the desired area, and select the duplicate layer in the Layers palette. Then choose Image > Extract.

In the Extract dialog box, drag with the edge highlighter tool (✐) in the image preview to highlight the edges of the desired area. Then click inside the highlighted area with the fill tool (⬗). Click OK to perform the extraction. All areas on the layer outside the extracted area are erased to transparency.

Extracting an image area

Mask part of a layer Layer masks let you selectively hide parts of a layer without permanently altering the layer. For example, you can create a mask that reveals a certain area of detail on a layer; the rest of the layer is hidden but still available behind the mask. In the Layers palette, select the layer that you want to mask, and click the New Layer Mask button (▣) at the bottom of the palette. Create the mask:

- To add to the mask and hide more of the layer, use a painting tool to paint with black. (See "Painting" on page 26 for more information.)

- To subtract from the mask and reveal more of the layer, paint with white.

- To create a semitransparent mask, paint with gray. This is useful for partially hiding areas of the layer.

Painting and drawing

Painting

Painting in Photoshop or ImageReady is as easy as choosing a color, selecting a tool, choosing a brush tip, and dragging in the image to paint. The various painting tools are modeled after styles of traditional paint media.

Choose a foreground color Before painting an image, you need to specify the foreground color that will be used to paint. Click the top color selection box in the toolbox, and choose a color in the color picker. You can select the Only Web Colors option to confine your range of choices to Web-safe colors.

You can also use the Color or Swatches palette to choose colors.

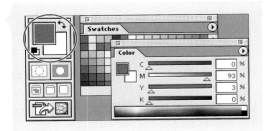

Choosing a foreground color

Select a painting tool Select a painting tool from the toolbox and drag in the image to paint:

- The paintbrush tool (✐) creates soft strokes of color.

- The pencil tool (✐) creates hard-edged freehand lines.

- The airbrush tool (✐) lets you apply gradual tones and sprays of color. You can build up color (as with a traditional airbrush) by holding down the mouse in a stationary position.

- The eraser tool (✐) lets you erase areas to transparency or, if you're working in the background layer or in a layer with locked transparency, to the background color. (You set the background color by clicking the bottom color selection box in the toolbox.)

Choose a brush The Brush option in the options bar lets you specify the brush tip used by many painting and editing tools. With a painting tool selected, click the triangle to the right of the Brush option in the options bar to display the brushes. Then click to select the desired brush tip. (Larger brushes are indicated by numeric size rather than representative preview.) You can customize the specified brush by clicking its preview in the options bar.

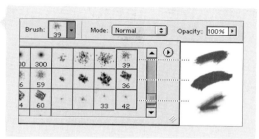

Sample brushes

Specify opacity and blending mode In the options bar for each painting tool, you can also specify an opacity (to control how much the underlying image shows through the paint) and a blending mode (to control how the paint is blended with the colors of the underlying image).

Drawing shapes

The shape tools let you draw crisp-edged shapes of various dimensions and colors. Unlike pixel data such as a scanned photograph, these shapes are defined using the mathematical principle of vectors. Used in drawing applications such as Adobe Illustrator® and now Photoshop and ImageReady, vectors describe shape, size, and boundary properties of graphics with clean, resolution-independent precision.

Select a shape tool and set options Select the rectangle tool (□), rounded rectangle tool (◯), ellipse tool (◯), or polygon tool (◇) from the toolbox. Then select one of the following drawing options from the options bar:

- The Create Shape Layer option (□) creates a vector shape filled with the current foreground color. The shape is created on a new layer containing a layer clipping path.

- The Create Work Path option (▨) creates an unfilled vector path with shaped boundaries. The shape appears as a new work path in the Paths palette.

- The Fill Region option (□) creates a rasterized shape filled with the current foreground color on the active layer. Selecting this option creates a shape based on pixel, rather than vector, information.

You can also specify other settings in the options bar, such as layer style, opacity, and blending mode.

Draw a vector shape Drag in the image to draw the specified shape.

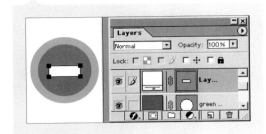

Drawing a shape on a shape layer

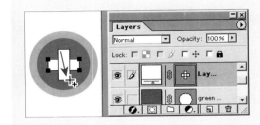

Adding to an existing shape

Select a shape To select a vector shape for editing, you must first target the layer or path containing the shape. Do one of the following:

- If the shape is part of a layer, click the shape thumbnail in the Layers palette. (The path associated with the shape is automatically selected in the Paths palette.) In ImageReady, the shape is automatically selected in the image with a bounding box for repositioning or transforming.

- (Photoshop) If the shape is stored in the Paths palette, select that path in the palette.

After you have targeted the layer or path in Photoshop, select the path component selection tool (▶) in the toolbox, and click anywhere inside the shape in the artwork. To help make the selected shape more visible, select Show Bounding Box in the options bar.

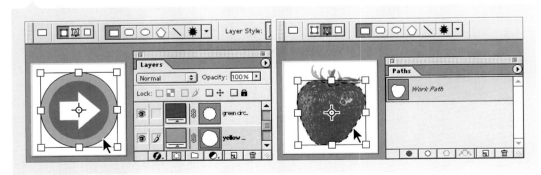

Selecting a shape on a shape layer

Selecting a shape on a work path

(Photoshop) Create a custom shape When the shape layer or work path option is selected in the options bar, you can use the basic shape tools in combination with one another to create more complex shapes. Select the shape you want to modify, and then select the shape tool you want to use to add variations to the first shape. Then select one of the following from the options bar:

- The Add Path Area option (⊡) adds the new shape on top of the first shape.
- The Subtract Path Area option (⊡) subtracts the overlapping area of the two shapes.
- The Restrict Path Area option (⊡) keeps only the overlapping area of the two shapes.
- The Invert Path Area option (⊡) reverses the fill of the overlapping area of the two shapes and the background.

Drag with the shape tool to draw a shape that interacts with the first shape in the manner specified. You can continue to add more variations to the custom shape using the different shape tools and options.

(Photoshop) Define a custom shape You can simplify the process of recreating a custom shape by storing it in the custom shape library. You can then redraw the shape automatically at any time using the custom shape tool. Select the shape that you just created and choose Edit > Define Custom Shape.

(Photoshop) Draw with the custom shape tool Select the custom shape tool (✳), and choose your custom shape from the Shape list in the options bar. Then drag in the image to draw the shape.

Working with type

Creating type

Photoshop and ImageReady provide excellent support for adding graphic type and text to images. You can enter and preview type directly in an image, as well as specify a full range of formatting options. Type is automatically added to a new layer.

Set a type insertion point Select the type tool (T) in the toolbox, and do one of the following:

- To enter type at a point, click in the image to set an insertion point. The type is added starting from the point you click.

- To enter type inside a bounding box, drag in the image to define the box. The type automatically wraps to fit inside the bounding box.

Set type attributes You can use the options bar, Character palette, or Paragraph palette to specify various type attributes, such as orientation, font, style, color, and alignment.

Enter text Enter the desired text using the keyboard, pressing Enter or Return to start new paragraphs. You can continue to change type attributes in the options bar, the Character palette, or the Paragraph palette as you enter additional text.

In Photoshop, you must commit the type to its type layer before you can perform other operations. Click the Commit button (☑) in the options bar to commit the type.

Editing type

Using the type tool in conjunction with the options bar, the Character palette, and the Paragraph palette, you can edit type directly as it appears in an image. In addition, you can apply special warp effects to the shape of type and make global edits to type layers.

Edit type content and attributes Select the type tool (T), and click inside the desired type to set an insertion point or drag to highlight the characters you want to edit. Then change the type content and attributes as desired. In Photoshop, click the Commit button (✔) in the options bar to commit the changes.

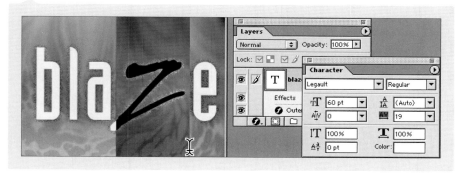

Changing the font of a single character

Warp the shape of type The warp feature lets you creatively stretch and distort the shape of type. Use the type tool to click inside the type you want to warp, and click the warp icon (工) in the options bar. For Style, choose a warp effect. Specify whether to apply the warp horizontally or vertically, drag the sliders to adjust the intensity of the effect, and click OK.

Apply layer edits to type Because type resides on its own type layer, you can apply all sorts of layer-specific edits to type—from changing the opacity and blending mode to adding layer styles. (See "Using layers" on page 22.)

Preparing Web graphics

Designing Web graphics

Photoshop and ImageReady provide a rich set of tools for adding Web features to your images. Among other benefits, you can divide an image into download-efficient slices, define image maps directly in the image, and add interactive rollover effects.

Slice an image When you slice an image, each rectangular slice downloads individually so that users can view parts of the image as the downloading progresses. You can also use slices to help keep file sizes down and define Web features such as links, rollovers, and animations. To slice an image, select the slice tool ( ) and drag in the image to define the slice areas. Photoshop or ImageReady automatically generates slices for the remaining areas of the image.

Slicing an image

Another way to define slices is by using the boundaries of layers. See "Enhanced slicing capabilities" on page 45 for more information.

Assign a URL link to a slice Assigning a URL to a slice makes the entire slice area a hotspot in the Web page, with a link to the specified URL. Select the slice select tool ( ), and double-click the desired slice to display the Slice Options dialog box (Photoshop) or the Slice palette (ImageReady). Then enter the desired URL destination and, if needed, the target frame.

For information on setting other slice options such as message text and Alt tags, see "Enhanced slicing capabilities" on page 45.

(ImageReady) Create an image map Image maps let you add URL links to different areas of an image. Select the rectangle image map tool ( ), and drag in the image to define the image map. Then select the image map selection tool ( ) and double-click the desired image map to display the Image Map palette. Enter a name and URL link destination for the image map. If desired, enter a target frame destination and text for an Alt tag.

(ImageReady) Add a rollover effect Rollover effects display different states of an image when a viewer performs a mouse action—such as rolling or clicking—over an area of the Web page. Layers provide an efficient way to store different image states for rollovers.

Select the slice or image map to which you want to add the rollover, and choose Window > Show Rollover. The Rollover palette shows a single thumbnail representing the normal, inactivated state. Click the New State button (🖫) at the bottom of the palette. From the pop-up menu above the new rollover thumbnail, choose the mouse action that you want to trigger the rollover. Then hide and show appropriate layers in the Layers palette to define the appearance of the new rollover state. (The rollover thumbnail updates to reflect the new appearance, which applies only to this rollover state.)

Creating animations (ImageReady)

With ImageReady, it's easy to create multiple-frame animations from a single image. The key is to use the Animation palette in conjunction with the Layers palette to set up the composition of animation frames. To output your animated image for Web use, optimize the image in GIF format.

Set up the starting frame Choose Window > Show Animation to display the Animation palette. Show and hide appropriate layers in the Layers palette to set up the contents of the starting animation frame. (The frame thumbnail updates to reflect the current image state, which applies only to this animation frame.)

Set up additional frames Click the New Frame button (🖫) at the bottom of the Animation palette, and do one of the following:

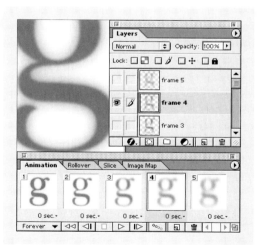

Setting up animation frames

• Using the Layers palette, modify the image to create the state of the second animation frame. For example, you can show and hide appropriate layers and layer effects, reposition a layer in the image, or change a layer's opacity or blending mode. Click the New Frame button and repeat this step to set up more frames.

- Using the Layers palette, adjust the position, opacity, or layer effects of desired layers to create the state of the final animation frame. Then choose Tween from the Animation palette menu to have ImageReady generate intermediate frames from the starting and ending states you've defined. Specify which layers and parameters to tween, enter the number of frames to generate, and click OK. The Tween feature is useful for generating a variety of animations, such as making a single layer move across the canvas or fade in or out.

Preview the animation ImageReady offers the convenience of previewing your animation directly in the image window. In the Animation palette, select the first animation frame and then click the Play button (▷) at the bottom of the palette.

Optimizing Web graphics

Optimization involves compressing the file size while optimizing the display quality of an image for Web output. Photoshop and ImageReady let you optimize images in several Web file formats— GIF, JPEG, and PNG—and provide you with both basic and advanced controls for fine-tuning the quality and compression level of the optimization. Because live previews of the optimized image are regenerated whenever an optimization setting is adjusted, you are free to experiment with different settings before committing to final changes.

Compare original and optimized images Choose File > Save for Web (Photoshop) or Window > Show Optimize (ImageReady) to display the Web optimization settings. Click the Optimized tab above the image preview (Photoshop) or in the image window (ImageReady) to display how the image will appear on the Web using the current optimization settings. To display original and optimized previews side by side, click the 2-Up tab.

Choose an optimization set Photoshop and ImageReady provide a number of predefined optimization settings. To apply a predefined optimization set, choose the desired set from the Settings menu in the Save for Web dialog box (Photoshop) or the Optimize palette (ImageReady).

View optimized file information In Photoshop, you can view optimized file information—such as file size and projected download time for various modem speeds—below the optimized preview in the Save for Web dialog box. In ImageReady, you can display two sets of file information in the status bar along the bottom edge of the image window. Click the triangle next to either information set to choose one of the optimized information display options.

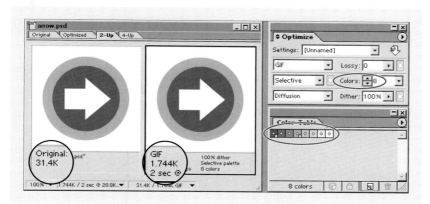

Optimizing a GIF image with 8 colors, shifted to Web-safe values

Fine-tune optimization settings You can further customize the optimization by adjusting individual optimization settings. You can even name and save your customized settings as a new optimization set.

Save the optimized image Click OK in the Save for Web dialog box (Photoshop) or choose File > Save Optimized As (ImageReady). For Format, choose one of the following options:

• Images Only generates only the optimized image files. If you have defined slices in your image, an optimized file is generated for each slice.

• HTML and Images generates an HTML file along with the optimized image files. If you have defined slices in your image, this HTML file contains code for the table that assembles the slices. If you are saving the image from ImageReady, the HTML file also contains code for any Web features—such as image maps, animations, or rollovers—that you have added to the image.

What's New in Adobe Photoshop 6.0

Adobe Photoshop 6.0, along with the dedicated Web tool ImageReady 3.0, delivers powerful image-editing capabilities with a range of new features that offer something for every user. New capabilities include integrated vector-drawing tools to extend your creative range, expanded tools and features for Web-production tasks, and numerous interface enhancements to help you get to work quickly and use the Photoshop and ImageReady features more fully.

Expand beyond pixels

Superb vector support

Photoshop 6.0 provides integrated tools for creating and outputting crisp, editable vector shapes and text. With these new tools, you can incorporate resolution-independent, vector-based graphics and type along with pixel-based images to achieve an unparalleled range of design effects. You can save vector data in EPS, DCS, TIFF, and PDF formats.

Shape tools The new rectangle, rounded rectangle, ellipse, polygon, custom shape, and line tools let you create a wide variety of vector-based shapes. These tools let you create shapes in three forms: as work paths, as shape layers, or as painted pixels.

Shape editing Photoshop 6.0—like Adobe Illustrator and other Adobe programs—also provides pathfinder operations for quickly combining basic vector shapes into hard-to-draw shapes. These operations include add, subtract, restrict, and invert. You can edit the segments of any basic or combined shape by using the direct selection, add anchor point, delete anchor point, and convert anchor point tools.

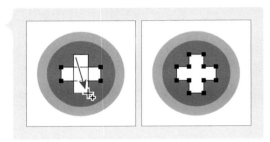

Adding to a basic shape and result after combining

Storage of custom shapes Once you've created shapes that you want to use over again or share with colleagues, you can save them as custom shapes. Photoshop stores custom shapes in a shape library that's available from the options bar when you select the custom shape tool. Alternatively, you can use the Preset Manager to save custom shapes in separate shape libraries. Shape libraries are portable, so workgroups can easily design, share, and add to them.

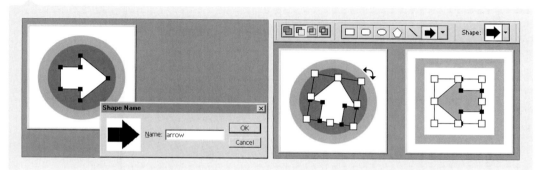

Defining and working with a custom shape

Resolution-independent type With Photoshop 6.0, you can easily combine crisp, resolution-independent type with pixel-based images and then output sharp type edges with your image to produce high-quality results.

Vector-based masks One powerful new vector feature involves using editable shapes to clip out or mask image areas. Known as *layer clipping paths,* these shapes can be modified just like any other vector shapes using the direct selection, add anchor point, and delete anchor point tools. To produce a mix of hard and soft masking edges, simply combine layer clipping paths and layer masks on the same layer.

Enhanced vector output

Creating vector graphics and type to incorporate into your images is only part of a complete workflow. Photoshop 6.0 provides complete support for outputting vector-based graphics along with your pixel-based images—all with the highest-quality printed results.

PostScript vector output You can print images containing resolution-independent shapes and text directly to any PostScript output device.

Advanced PDF output Photoshop 6.0 extends its integration with Adobe products by offering enhanced support for Adobe PDF, including the ability to save transparency, layers, and vector objects in PDF files. Any service provider with Adobe Acrobat® InProduction™ (or other Acrobat prepress plug-ins) can then prepare those PDF files for high-end printing.

Layer styles

Photoshop 6.0 presents an intuitive new layer effects interface, new effect options, and new support for saving combinations of layer effects as layer styles for ongoing use. Layer effects and styles update automatically as you edit your image and are particularly useful for designing type, buttons, and banners.

New and enhanced layer effects Photoshop 6.0 introduces a number of new and enhanced features for layer effects, including the new stroke, overlay, and satin layer effects; a new contour option; advanced blending and transparency options; and enhancements to the drop shadow, inner shadow, glow, and bevel and emboss effects.

New layer styles The new Layer Styles dialog box shows at a glance which effects are applied to the currently selected layer. To add effects to a layer, you simply check each one you want in the list and specify appropriate settings.

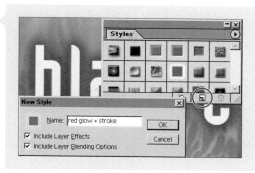

Once you've designed a custom layer style, you can save it in the Styles palette for future use. Layer styles work just like layer effects, applying nondestructive changes that update automatically when you change layer contents. You can store styles in a default styles library or in your own style libraries using the Preset Manager. Style libraries are

Defining a new layer style

portable, so you can share them with colleagues. Plus, Photoshop layer styles are compatible with ImageReady—you can open a Photoshop layer style library in ImageReady, and vice versa.

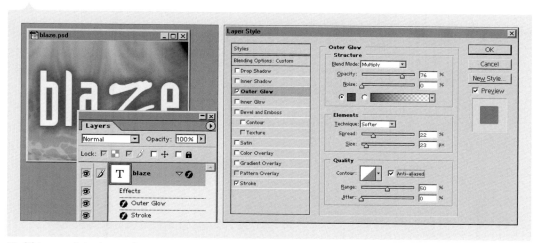

Modifying an existing layer style

Easy application of layer styles Applying layer styles is easy: You create type, shapes, and other artwork elements on a layer, and then click a style in the Styles palette to apply it. Or, select a shape tool, select the shape layer option and choose a layer style in the options bar, and then start drawing; the style is applied as you draw. The combination of layer styles and the new shape tools opens up a wide array of creative opportunities for print and Web designers alike.

Interactive image warping

With the new Liquify command in Photoshop 6.0, you can quickly distort or warp an image by interactively pushing, pulling, rotating, enlarging, and shrinking different image areas. These distortion controls are ideal for a wide range of tasks from making fine warping adjustments to a small image area to making sweeping adjustments for a wildly warped-out effect. When you open the Liquify dialog box, you can display a fine mesh over the image to help you achieve precise adjustments. To prevent unwanted changes, freeze certain parts of the image and zero in on the areas you want to modify. To switch between large-scale changes and finer adjustments, vary the size of the brush you're using. The Liquify command also provides options for reconstructing the original image as needed.

Warping in Amplitwist mode

Produce superb Web graphics

Enhanced slicing capabilities

Slicing images is the key to incorporating large or complex image files into your Web site because browsers can download and display sliced images more efficiently. You can also use slices as a basis for creating rollovers or setting up animations. Or, you can generate HTML pages directly from Photoshop, including the HTML table code necessary to reassemble the sliced image.

Direct Photoshop slicing With the new slice tool and slice select tool, you can now define and edit slices directly in Photoshop 6.0. Create user-defined slices by dragging over different image areas with the slice tool; Photoshop defines slices automatically for the areas you don't define. You can modify many attributes of user-slices, including size, position, stacking order, and visibility.

Slices created with slice tool

Slice-specific formatting and optimization Sliced images give you more control over how optimization options are applied because you can select separate slices and apply appropriate settings. An image that includes solid colors, text, and photographic images, for example, looks best with different settings applied to different areas. You can also assign a separate file name, URL link, Alt tag, and message to each slice. In ImageReady, you can link multiple slices together in a set, so you can quickly select, optimize, output, and delete only those slices.

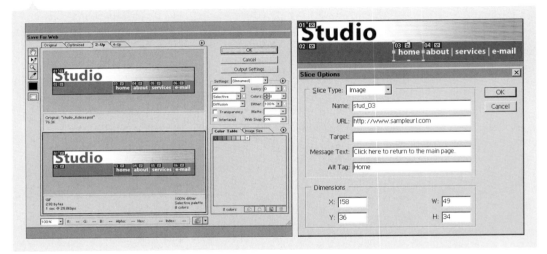

Setting optimization options for an individual slice; assigning a URL, message text, and an Alt tag to a slice

Dynamic layer-based slices Photoshop 6.0 introduces a new way to slice images: Set up your slice content on separate layers and then let Photoshop or ImageReady generate layer-based slices for you. When you slice images this way, each slice is bound to the outermost pixels on each layer. If you then reposition or edit the content of the layer, the slice adjusts dynamically to accommodate the changes. This technique is particularly useful for generating precise slices for rollovers.

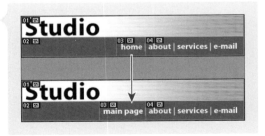

Slice updates automatically when source layer is modified.

Enhanced support for image maps and rollovers

ImageReady 3.0 provides new and enhanced support for creating image maps and rollover effects directly in an image.

Image map creation Using the new image map tools in conjunction with the new Image Map palette, you can define image map areas in your image, complete with URL, target frame, and Alt text options. You can also define an image map based on the boundaries of a layer.

Rollover enhancements You can now save a rollover as a style in the Styles palette. All of the rollover's attributes, including its effects, slices, and states, are saved in the style, which you can reapply easily with a single click. Other enhancements include the sharing of color palettes between rollover states and the ability to preview rollovers directly in ImageReady.

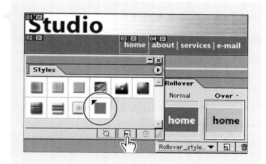

Creating a new rollover style

Weighted optimization

Photoshop 6.0 incorporates new weighted optimization controls that let you use 8-bit alpha channels to smoothly vary compression settings across an image. This technique produces higher-quality results in critical image areas without sacrificing file size. In the past, you would have made harder trade-offs, either favoring image quality in a complex image over smaller files sizes, or vice versa. Using channels, you can produce gradual variations in GIF dithering, lossy GIF settings, and JPEG compression. Weighted optimization controls also let you favor colors in selected image areas as you generate custom color palettes.

Improved Web workflow

Photoshop 6.0 and the built-in Web-production tool, ImageReady 3.0, are now more tightly integrated than ever, resulting in a powerful new tool combination for creating your Web graphics from start to finish. Adobe Photoshop 6.0 also offers improved integration with Adobe GoLive™ 5.0.

Integrated optimization with Adobe GoLive 5.0 Adobe Photoshop 6.0 and Adobe GoLive 5.0 integrate tightly to support your Web production process. Now you can add native Photoshop (PSD) files directly to the Adobe GoLive application without having to optimize them first. Instead, you can use the built-in image optimization tools in the Adobe GoLive application to perform those steps.

Automated updates with Adobe GoLive 5.0 Any URLs written by Photoshop or ImageReady are accessible in Adobe GoLive for management and editing. You can even update edited URLs in the original Photoshop (PSD) file. You can also set up a sliced file, complete with rollovers and image maps, in ImageReady or Photoshop and then add the single PSD file to Adobe GoLive. Adobe GoLive automatically calls ImageReady or Photoshop to compile the sliced pieces and update edits you make to the image. Adobe GoLive also goes back to the original PSD file to generate the final GIF or JPEG file for the Web page.

HTML integration with Adobe GoLive 5.0 When exporting sliced images, Photoshop and ImageReady both generate a set of named image files and an HTML file with the table code necessary to reassemble the image. Alternatively, you can save sliced image files as CSS-based (cascading style sheet) objects. The high-quality HTML code produced is ready to be copied into Adobe GoLive or another HTML editor. When exporting rollovers from ImageReady, select the Include GoLive Code option in the Save Optimized As dialog box for optimal results.

Master Photoshop more quickly

Streamlined interface

Photoshop 6.0 introduces numerous interface enhancements designed to make it easier and more efficient to use its powerful features.

Options bar Now, when you select a tool in the toolbox, all the options that control its behavior are easily accessible in a context-sensitive options bar. For example, when you're working with the shape or selection tools, you have access to modifiers such as add, subtract, restrict, and invert, which were previously available only by keyboard shortcuts. You can dock the options bar to the top or bottom of your screen or let it float anywhere on your screen.

Palette docking and storage In Photoshop 6.0, you can dock palettes to each other. You can also store the palettes you use most often in the palette well in the options bar, where they are readily available when you need them but out of your way when you're focused on a task. When you want to display a palette in the well, click the palette's tab; click again and the palette tucks out of sight.

Improved color management and proofing The new Edit > Color Settings command simplifies ICC-based color management by gathering controls in a single dialog box and offering a choice of predefined color management settings based on common press and Web conditions. Based on Adobe Color Engine (ACE) technology, this color management workflow encompasses much of the RGB, CMYK, and Grayscale setup controls of previous Photoshop versions and offers improved integration with Adobe Illustrator 9.0 and other upcoming Adobe products. In addition, Photoshop 6.0 provides new controls for generating soft proofs of images on-screen and for printing hard proofs based on ICC color profiles.

Enhanced layer management

Layers are more flexible than ever in Photoshop 6.0. Now you can create hundreds of layers in an image to help arrange elements in an intricate composition. In addition, you can use an array of new features to help organize and manage layers more efficiently.

Layer sets You can organize layers into sets to keep better track of related parts. You can then toggle the visibility of layer sets, hiding or showing them as you work, or move a layer set in the stacking order by dragging it in the Layers palette. And you can specify the opacity of an entire layer set.

Layer identification and locking Color-coding layers in the Layers palette lets you quickly identify layer relationships. Once your layers are set as desired, you can lock them to prevent accidental edits.

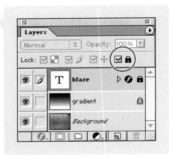

Locking the selected layer

Layers palette enhancements The enhanced Layers palette helps you handle layer effects more efficiently. If you assign a layer effect to one layer and want to reuse it on another, just drag and drop it on the target layer. All of the settings are preserved and instantly copied to the target layer.

Fill layers You can now experiment with color, gradient, or pattern fills by adding them to a new type of layer, called a *fill layer*. Like adjustment layers, fill layers apply nondestructive changes to the underlying image and can be modified or discarded at any time.

Expanded text features

Photoshop 6.0 offers an expanded range of formatting options for both Roman and Asian text, as well as direct, on-canvas text editing. The new Character and Paragraph palettes make it easy to choose formatting options for your type.

Direct text editing in the image You can enter text and modify style directly in the image, without having to toggle back and forth from a dialog box. If you rotate, scale, or skew your text in the image, the text remains editable.

Type warping The new type-warping feature lets you distort type layers in the form of special shapes such as arcs and waves.

Warping type using Arc style

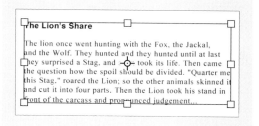

Setting paragraph formatting options

New paragraph options Extensive new options for styling paragraphs now appear in the new Paragraph palette, which operates similarly to the Paragraph palette in Adobe InDesign™ and Adobe Illustrator. You can specify alignment, auto-leading, space before and after, hanging punctuation, and left-, right-, and first-line indents on a per-paragraph basis.

Hyphenation, justification, and composition controls Photoshop provides professional-quality hyphenation settings with control over the minimum word size, minimum number of characters before and after a hyphen, number of consecutive hyphens, and hyphenation zone. Photoshop also fully supports paragraph justification with various option settings. Photoshop even supports the next generation of Adobe composition engines, offering you a choice of the every-line and single-line composers. The every-line composer sets multiple lines of text in relation to each other to ensure optimal line breaks, while the single-line composer handles one line of text at a time.

New character options With the controls in the new Character palette, you can apply color on a per-character basis, scale characters vertically and horizontally, and set baseline shift. Plus, Photoshop fully supports OpenType fonts and their related features, such as all caps, small caps, superscript, and subscript. (Photoshop produces faux versions of these text options for non-OpenType fonts.) A new no-break option controls whether or not a range of characters wraps as a single word.

Formatting options for Asian type Photoshop 6.0 includes extensive Asian formatting controls such as the following: Tsume for manual kerning and tracking; Tate-chu-yoko for setting horizontal text within vertical text; Kinsoku shori for setting word breaks; Burasagari for hanging punctuation; and Mojikumi for auto-kerning, tracking, and justification.

Preset Manager

The new Preset Manager centralizes management of your custom brushes, gradients, shapes, contours, patterns, and layer styles and offers instant access to extensive libraries of these elements included with Photoshop 6.0. When you create your own custom element, save it in a library file so that it can be accessed through the Preset Manager. Once you load a library in the Preset Manager, it becomes available whenever its elements are used in Photoshop—in the options bar, the Styles palette, the Gradient Editor dialog box, and other locations. Libraries can also be shared with colleagues to streamline their creative work.

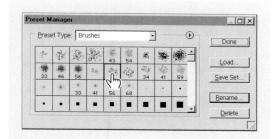

Using the Preset Manager

Other new and enhanced features

Annotations The new notes and audio annotation tools let you attach text and voice comments to images. These annotations are supported in both Photoshop and Adobe Acrobat. You can also import annotations from a PDF document into a Photoshop image.

Control of nonprinting elements The new View > Show Extras and Hide Extras commands let you globally control the display of nonprinting elements such as guides, grids, target paths, selection edges, slices, image maps, text bounding boxes, text selections, and annotations. Commands for controlling the display and snapping behavior of specific nonprinting element types are grouped under the new View > Show and View > Snap To submenus.

Perspective cropping The crop tool offers a new Perspective option, which lets you correct perspective distortions as you crop an image.

WebDAV workflow management New commands under the File > Manage Workflow submenu let you manage files using the Web Distributed Authoring and Versioning (WebDAV) server technology.

Cascading style sheets You can now generate a cascading style sheet along with an HTML file when saving an optimized image.

Expanded file format support You can now preserve layers, transparency, and multiresolution pyramid data in exported TIFF files and choose from more TIFF compression options. The File > Import > PDF Image command lets you import specific images into Photoshop from a PDF document.

Reorganized and expanded print options The new File > Print Options command gathers together many of the output and color management options that once only appeared in the Page Setup and Print dialog boxes. In addition, you can now adjust and preview the position and scale of an image before printing.

Photoshop droplets In Photoshop, the new File > Automate > Create Droplet command lets you create a droplet from an action.

Gradient Map adjustment The new Gradient Map adjustment layer lets you map the tonal range of an image to the colors of a gradient fill.

Expanded support for 16-bit-per-channel images In Photoshop, the following tools and commands are now available for images containing 16 bits per channel: the history brush, slice, and shape tools, and the Canvas Size, Auto Contrast, Gradient Map, Gaussian Blur, Add Noise, Median, Unsharp Mask, High Pass, and Dust & Scratches commands.

Easy measurement switching Now you can switch the units of measurement for your rulers on the fly. Just right-click (Windows) or Control-click (Mac OS) the rulers and choose the measurement unit you want from the context menu. In addition, whenever you are asked to enter measurement values for a tool or dialog box, you can use any combination of units you want—for example, 2 inches by 45 pixels for a rectangle.

Enhanced multiple-image options The Contact Sheet II command offers more label options, the Picture Package command offers an enhanced set of layout options, and the Web Photo Gallery lets you choose from a variety of customizable HTML templates.

Moved preferences The preference commands now appear under the Edit menu.

1

Chapter 1: Looking at the Work Area

The Adobe Photoshop and Adobe ImageReady work area includes the command menus at the top of your screen and a variety of tools and palettes for editing and adding elements to your image. You can also add commands and filters to the menus by installing third-party software known as plug-in modules.

Using the toolbox

The first time you start the application, the toolbox appears on the left side of the screen. Some tools in the toolbox have options that appear in the context-sensitive tool options bar. (See "Using the tool options bar" on page 59.) These include the tools that let you use type, select, paint, draw, sample, edit, move, annotate, and view images. Other tools in the toolbox allow you to change foreground/background colors, go to Adobe Online, work in different modes, and jump between Photoshop and ImageReady applications.

For an overview of each tool, see the "Toolbox overview" topics in online Help. For information on the foreground and background color controls, see "Choosing foreground and background colors" in online Help.

Displaying and working with tools

You select a tool by clicking its icon in the toolbox. A small triangle at the lower right of a tool icon indicates hidden tools. Positioning the pointer over a tool displays a tool tip with the tool's name and keyboard shortcut.

To show or hide the toolbox:

Choose Window > Show Tools or Window > Hide Tools.

To move the toolbox:

Drag the toolbox by its title bar.

To select a tool:

Do one of the following:

• To select a visible tool, click its icon or press its keyboard shortcut.

• To select a hidden tool, position the pointer on the visible tool and hold down the mouse button until the tools list appears. Then, click the tool you want.

To cycle through a set of hidden tools, hold down Shift and press the visible tool's shortcut key. To enable or disable this option, choose Edit > Preferences > General, then select or deselect Use Shift Key for Tool Switch.

To view or move a hidden tools list (ImageReady):

1 Position the pointer on the visible tool and hold down the mouse button until the hidden tools list appears.

2 Select the small downward-pointing triangle at the bottom of the hidden tools list. A hidden tools list appears and remains open until you click the close box. You can view more than one hidden tools list simultaneously.

3 Drag the hidden tools list by its title bar to move it anywhere on your desktop.

To display or hide tool tips:

1 Choose Edit > Preferences > General, then select or deselect Show Tool Tips. Show Tool Tips is the default.

To enable or disable cycling through a set of hidden tools:

Choose Edit > Preferences > General, then select or deselect Use Shift Key for Tool Switch.

Using the tool pointers

When you select most tools, the mouse pointer matches the tool's icon. The marquee pointer appears by default as cross-hairs, the text tool pointer as an I-beam, and painting tools default to the Brush Size icon.

Each default pointer has a different *hot spot*, where an effect or action in the image begins. With all tools except the move tool, annotation tools, and the type tool, you can switch to precise cursors, which appear as cross-hairs centered around the hot spot.

To set the tool pointer appearance:

1 Do one of the following:

• (Photoshop) Choose Edit > Preferences > Display & Cursors.

• (ImageReady) Choose Edit > Preferences > Cursors.

2 Choose a tool pointer setting:

• Click Standard under Painting Cursors, Other Cursors, or both to display pointers as tool icons.

• Click Precise under Painting Cursors, Other Cursors, or both to display pointers as cross-hairs.

• Click Brush Size under Painting Cursors to display the painting tool cursors as brush shapes representing the size of the current brush. Brush Size cursors may not display for very large brushes.

3 Click OK.

The Painting Cursors options control the pointers for the following tools:

• (Photoshop) Eraser, pencil, airbrush, paintbrush, rubber stamp, pattern stamp, smudge, blur, sharpen, dodge, burn, and sponge tools.

• (ImageReady) Paintbrush, pencil, and eraser tools.

The Other Cursors options control the pointers for the following tools:

• (Photoshop) Marquee, lasso, polygon lasso, magic wand, crop, slice, eyedropper, pen, gradient, line, paint bucket, magnetic lasso, magnetic pen, measure, and color sampler tools.

• (ImageReady) Marquee, lasso, magic wand, eyedropper, paint bucket, and slice tools.

To toggle between standard and precise cursors in some tool pointers, press Caps Lock. Press Caps Lock again to return to your original setting.

Using the tool options bar

Most tools have options that are displayed in the tool options bar. The options bar is context sensitive and changes as different tools are selected. Some settings in the options bar are common to several tools (such as painting modes and opacity), and some are specific to one tool (such as the Auto Erase setting for the pencil tool).

You can move the options bar anywhere in the work area. In Photoshop, you can dock it at the top or bottom of the screen.

(Photoshop) The options bar includes a palette well for storing other palettes, providing quick access to palettes such as Swatches and Actions that you reference briefly while using the application. The palette well is only available when using a screen resolution greater than 800 pixels x 600 pixels (a setting of at least 1024 x 768 is recommended).

To display the tool options bar:

Do one of the following:

• Choose Window > Show Options.

• Single-click a tool in the toolbox.

Note: *You can double-click the title bar at the left edge to collapse the options bar, showing only the tool icon.*

Lasso options bar

To return a tool or all tools to the default settings:

Do one of the following:

• Click the tool icon on the options bar, then choose Reset Tool or Reset All Tools from the context menu.

• Choose Edit > Preferences > General, then click Reset All Tools.

To move the options bar:

Do one of the following:

• Drag the title bar at the left edge of the options bar.

• (Photoshop) Grab the gripper bar at the left edge of the options bar. The gripper bar will only appear if the options bar is docked at the top or bottom of your screen.

To store other palettes in the options bar (Photoshop):

Drag the desired palette's tab into the palette well so that the palette well is highlighted.

Palettes are considered hidden when stored in the options bar. The Window menu item associated with a stored palette will say Show when it is stored. Clicking on the title of a palette stored in the well shows the palette until you click outside the palette.

Using palettes

Palettes help you monitor and modify images. By default, palettes appear stacked together in groups.

Displaying palettes

You can display or hide palettes as you work.

To show or hide palettes:

Do one of the following:

• To show or hide all open palettes, the options bar, and the toolbox, press Tab.

• To show or hide all palettes, press Shift+Tab.

To show or hide one palette:

Choose Window > Show to display the selected palette at the front of its group. Or, choose Window > Hide to conceal the entire group of which the selected palette is a part.

Changing the palette display

You can rearrange your palettes to make better use of your work area by using the following techniques:

• To make a palette appear at the front of its group, click the palette's tab, or choose Window > Show.

• To move an entire palette group, drag its title bar.

• To rearrange or separate a palette group, drag a palette's tab. Dragging a palette outside of an existing group creates a new group.

• To move a palette to another group, drag the palette's tab to that group.

• To display a palette menu, position the pointer on the triangle (⊙) in the upper right corner of the palette, and press the mouse button.

• To change the size of a palette, drag any corner of the palette (Windows) or drag the size box at its lower right corner (Mac OS). Not all palettes can be resized.

• To collapse a group to palette titles only, click the Minimize/Maximize box (Windows) or the Zoom box (Mac OS), or double-click a palette's tab. You can still access the menu of a collapsed palette.

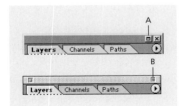

Click to collapse or expand palette.
A. *Windows* **B.** *Mac OS*

• (ImageReady) To show or hide options for palettes that include hidden options (the Optimize, Color, Type, Layer Options, and Slice palettes), click the Show Options button (⬍) on the palette tab to cycle through palette displays, or choose Show Options or Hide Options from the palette menu.

Docking palettes together

Docking palettes together lets you view multiple palettes at the same time and move them as a group. Entire palette groups cannot be docked together at once, but you can dock the palettes from one group to another, one at a time.

In Photoshop, you can also store palettes in the palette well of the tool options bar. (See "Using the tool options bar" on page 59.)

To dock palettes together:

Drag a palette's tab to the bottom of another palette so that the bottom of the target palette is highlighted.

To move an entire docked group, drag its title bar.

Setting the positions of palettes and dialog boxes

The positions of all open palettes and moveable dialog boxes are saved when you exit the application. Alternatively, you can always start with default palette positions or restore default positions at any time.

To reset palettes to the default positions:

Do one of the following:

• (Photoshop) Choose Edit > Preferences > General, and select Save Palette Locations.

• (Photoshop) Choose Window > Reset Palette Locations.

• (ImageReady) Choose Window > Arrange > Reset Palettes.

To always start with the default palette and dialog box positions:

1 Choose Edit > Preferences > General.

2 Deselect Save Palette Locations. The change takes effect the next time you start the application.

Using pop-up sliders

A number of palettes and dialog boxes contain settings that use pop-up sliders (for example, the Opacity option in the Layers palette).

To use a pop-up slider:

Do one of the following:

• Position the pointer over the triangle next to the setting, hold down the mouse, and drag the slider or angle radius to the desired value.

• Click the triangle next to the setting to open the pop-up slider box, and drag the slider or angle radius to the desired value. Click outside the slider box or press Enter or Return to close the slider box. To cancel changes, press the Escape key (Esc).

To increase or decrease values in 10% increments when the pop-up slider box is open, hold down Shift and press the Up or Down arrow key.

Using pop-up palettes

Pop-up palettes provide easy access to libraries of brushes, swatches, gradients, styles, patterns, contours, and shapes. You can customize pop-up palettes by renaming and deleting items and by loading, saving, and replacing libraries. You can also change the display of a pop-up palette to view items by their names, as thumbnail icons, or with both names and icons.

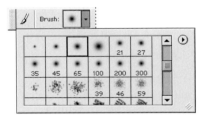

The Brush pop-up palette in the options bar.

To select an item in a pop-up palette:

1 Click the triangle next to the thumbnail image of the current item. Be careful not to click the thumbnail image—doing so will display the settings editor for the item.

2 Click an item in the pop-up palette.

To rename an item in a pop-up palette:

1 Do one of the following:

• Double-click an item.

• Select an item, click the triangle (⊙) in the upper right corner of the pop-up palette, and choose the Rename command from the palette menu.

2 Enter a new name in the provided dialog box, and click OK.

To delete an item in a pop-up palette:

Do one of the following:

• Select an item, click the triangle (⊙) in the upper right corner of the pop-up palette, and choose the Delete command from the palette menu.

• Hold down Alt (Windows) or Option (Mac OS) and click an item.

To customize the list of items in a pop-up palette:

1 Click the triangle (⊙) in the upper right corner of the pop-up palette to view the palette menu.

2 To return to the default library, choose the Reset command. You can either replace the current list or append the default library to the current list.

3 To load a different library, do one of the following:

• Choose the Load command to add a library to the current list. Then select the library file you want to use, and click Load.

• Choose the Replace command to replace the current list with a different library. Then select the library file you want to use, and click Load.

• Choose a library file (displayed at the bottom of the palette menu). Then click OK to replace the current list, or click Append to append the current list.

4 To save the current list as a library for later use, choose the Save command. Then enter a name for the library file, and click Save.

You can specify that a file extension is always appended to a library file by choosing Edit > Preferences > Saving Files, and setting Append File Extension to Always. You should put the extension on a library filename so that you can easily share the libraries across operating systems.

To change the display of items in a pop-up palette:

1 Click the triangle (⊙) in the upper right corner of the pop-up palette to view the palette menu.

2 Select a view option: Text Only, Small Thumbnail, Large Thumbnail, Small List, and Large List.

Using the Info palette

The Info palette displays information about the color values beneath the pointer and, depending on the tool in use, other useful measurements.

To display the Info palette:

Choose Window > Show Info.

(Photoshop) The Info palette displays the following information:

• When displaying CMYK values, the Info palette displays an exclamation point next to the CMYK values if the color beneath the pointer or color sampler is out of the printable CMYK color gamut.

For more information, see "Identifying out-of-gamut colors (Photoshop) in online Help.

• When you use the marquee tool, the Info palette displays the x- and y-coordinates of the pointer position and the width (W) and height (H) of the marquee as you drag.

• When you use the crop tool or zoom tool, the Info palette displays the width (W) and height (H) of the marquee as you drag. The palette also shows the angle of rotation of the crop marquee.

• When you use the line tool, pen tool, or gradient tool or when you move a selection, the Info palette displays the x- and y-coordinates of your starting position, the change in X (DX), the change in Y (DY), the angle (A), and the distance (D) as you drag.

• When you use a two-dimensional transformation command, the Info palette displays the percentage change in width (W) and height (H), the angle of rotation (A), and the angle of horizontal skew (H) or vertical skew (V).

• When you use any color adjustment dialog box (for example, Curves), the Info palette displays the before and after color values of the pixels beneath the pointer and beneath color samplers.

For more information, see "Seeing the color values of pixels (Photoshop)" in online Help.

(ImageReady) The Info palette displays the following information:

• The RGB numeric values for the color beneath the pointer.

• The Opacity value for the pixels beneath the pointer.

• The hexadecimal value for the color beneath the pointer.

• The index color table position for the color beneath the pointer.

• The x- and y-coordinates of the pointer.

• The x- and y-coordinates of your starting position (before you click in the image) and your ending position (as you drag in the image) when you use the marquee tool, the shape tools, the crop tool, and the slice tool.

• The width (W) and height (H) of the selection as you drag when you use the crop tool, the shape tools, the slice tool, or the zoom tool.

• The percentage change in width (W) and height (H), the angle of rotation (A), and the angle of horizontal skew (H) or vertical skew (V) when you use a Transform or Free Transform command.

To change the Info palette options:

1 Choose Palette Options from the Info palette menu.

2 For First Color Readout, choose one of the following display options:

• Actual Color to display values in the current color mode of the image.

• Total Ink to display the total percentage of all CMYK ink at the pointer's current location, based on the values set in the CMYK Setup dialog box.

• Opacity to display the opacity of the current layer. This option does not apply to the background.

• Any other option to display the color values in that color mode.

3 For Second Color Readout, choose a display option listed in step 2.

4 For Ruler Units, choose a unit of measurement.

5 Click OK.

To change measurement units, click the cross-hair icon in the Info palette for a menu of options. To change color readout modes, click the eyedropper icon.

Using context menus

In addition to the menus at the top of your screen, context-sensitive menus display commands relevant to the active tool, selection, or palette.

To display context menus:

1 Position the pointer over an image or palette item.

2 Click with the right mouse button (Windows) or hold down Control and press the mouse button (Mac OS).

Viewing images

The hand tool, the zoom tools, the Zoom commands, and the Navigator palette let you view different areas of an image at different magnifications. You can open additional windows to display several views at once (such as different magnifications) of an image. You can also change the screen display mode to change the appearance of the Photoshop or ImageReady work area.

Changing the screen display mode

The window controls let you change the screen display mode, including menu bar, title bar, and scroll bar options.

To change the screen display mode:

Click a screen mode button in the toolbox:

• The left button (⊡) displays the default window with a menu bar at the top and scroll bars on the sides.

• The center button (▭) displays a full-screen window with a menu bar and a 50% gray background, but no title bar or scroll bars.

• The right button (▭) displays a full-screen window with a black background, but no title bar, menu bar, or scroll bars.

Using the document window

The document window is where your image appears. Depending on the screen display mode (see "Changing the screen display mode" on page 65), the document window may include a title bar and scroll bar.

In ImageReady, the document window allows you to switch easily between original and optimized views of an image using tabs, and to view the original image and multiple versions of an optimized image simultaneously. For information on changing the view in the document window, see "Viewing images during optimization" on page 316.

You can open multiple windows to display different views of the same file. A list of open windows appears in the Window menu. Available memory may limit the number of windows per image.

To open multiple views of the same image:

Do one of the following:

• Choose View > New View.

• (ImageReady) Drag any tab away from the document window.

To arrange multiple windows (Windows only):

Do one of the following:

• Choose Window > Cascade (Photoshop) or Window > Arrange > Cascade (ImageReady) to display windows stacked and cascading from the upper left to the lower right of the screen.

• Choose Window > Tile (Photoshop) or Window > Arrange > Tile (ImageReady)to display windows edge to edge.

• Choose Window > Arrange Icons (Photoshop) or Window > Arrange > Arrange Icons (ImageReady) to align minimized images along the bottom of the work area.

To close windows:

Choose a command:

• Choose File > Close to close the active window.

• (Windows) Choose Window > Close All to close all windows.

Navigating the view area

If the entire image is not visible in the document window, you can navigate to bring another area of the image into view.

In Photoshop, you can also use the Navigator palette to quickly change the view of an image.

To view another area of an image:

Do one of the following:

• Use the window scroll bars.

• Select the hand tool (🖑) and drag to pan over the image.

> 💡 *To use the hand tool while another tool is selected, hold down the spacebar as you drag in the image.*

To move the view of an image using the Navigator palette (Photoshop):

1 Choose Window > Show Navigator.

2 Do one of the following:

• Drag the view box in the thumbnail of the image, which represents the boundaries of the image window.

• Click in the thumbnail of the image. The new view includes the area you click.

To change the color of the Navigator palette view box (Photoshop):

1 Choose Palette Options from the Navigator palette menu.

2 Choose a color:

• To use a preset color, choose an option for Color.

• To specify a different color, click the color box, and choose a color.

> 📖 For more information on choosing colors, see "Using the Adobe Color Picker" in online Help.

3 Click OK.

Magnifying and reducing the view

You can magnify or reduce your view using various methods. The window's title bar displays the zoom percentage (unless the window is too small for the display to fit), as does the status bar at the bottom of the window.

Note: *The 100% view of an image displays an image as it will appear in a browser (based on the monitor resolution and the image resolution). (See "About image size and resolution" on page 92.)*

To zoom in:

Do one of the following:

• Select the zoom tool (🔍). The pointer becomes a magnifying glass with a plus sign in its center (🔍). Click the area you want to magnify. Each click magnifies the image to the next preset percentage, centering the display around the point you click. When the image has reached its maximum magnification level of 6400%, the magnifying glass appears empty.

• Choose View > Zoom In to magnify to the next preset percentage. When the image has reached its maximum magnification level, the command is dimmed.

• (Photoshop) Enter a magnification level in the Zoom text box at the lower left of the window.

• (ImageReady) Click on the Zoom Level pop-up menu at the bottom left of the document window, and choose a zoom level.

To zoom out:

Do one of the following:

• Select the zoom tool. Hold down Alt (Windows) or Option (Mac OS) to activate the zoom-out tool. The pointer becomes a magnifying glass with a minus sign in its center (⊖). Click the center of the area of the image you want to reduce. Each click reduces the view to the previous preset percentage. When the file has reached its maximum reduction level so that only 1 pixel is visible horizontally or vertically, the magnifying glass appears empty.

• Choose View > Zoom Out to reduce to the previous preset percentage. When the image reaches its maximum reduction level, the command is dimmed.

• (Photoshop) Enter a reduction level in the Zoom text box at the lower left of the window.

• (ImageReady) Click on the Zoom Level pop-up menu at the lower left of the document window, and choose a zoom level.

To magnify by dragging:

1 Select the zoom tool.

2 Drag over the part of the image you want to magnify.

The area inside the zoom marquee is displayed at the highest possible magnification. To move the marquee around the artwork in Photoshop, begin dragging a marquee and then hold down the space bar while dragging the marquee to a new location.

To display an image at 100%:

Do one of the following:

• Double-click the zoom tool.

• Choose View > Actual Pixels (Photoshop) or View > Actual Size (ImageReady).

To change the view to fit the screen:

Do one of the following:

• Double-click the hand tool.

• Choose View > Fit on Screen.

These options scale both the zoom level and the window size to fit the available screen space.

To automatically resize the window when magnifying or reducing the view:

With the Zoom tool active, select Resize Windows to Fit in the options bar. The window resizes when you magnify or reduce the view of the image.

When Resize Windows to Fit is deselected (the default), the window maintains a constant size regardless of the image's magnification. This can be helpful when using smaller monitors or working with tiled views.

To automatically resize the window when magnifying or reducing the view using keyboard shortcuts:

Choose Edit > Preferences > General, then select the Keyboard Zoom Resizes Windows preference.

Correcting mistakes

Most operations can be undone if you make a mistake. Alternatively, you can restore all or part of an image to its last saved version. But available memory may limit your ability to use these options.

For information on how to restore your image to how it looked at any point in the current work session, see "Reverting to any state of an image" on page 69.

To undo the last operation:

Choose Edit > Undo.

If an operation can't be undone, the command is dimmed and changes to Can't Undo.

To redo the last operation:

Choose Edit > Redo.

💡 *You can set the Redo keystroke preference to be the same for Photoshop and ImageReady. Choose Edit > Preferences > General and select a preference for the Redo key. You can also set the key to toggle between Undo and Redo.*

To free memory used by the Undo command, the History palette, or the Clipboard:

Choose Edit > Purge, and choose the item type or buffer you want to clear. If already empty, the item type or buffer is dimmed.

Important: *The Purge command permanently clears from memory the operation stored by the command or buffer; it cannot be undone. For example, choosing Edit > Purge > Histories deletes all history states from the History palette. Use the Purge command when the amount of information held in memory is so large that Photoshop's performance is noticeably diminished.*

To revert to the last saved version:

Choose File > Revert.

Note: *Revert is added as a history state in the History palette and can be undone.*

To restore part of an image to its previously saved version (Photoshop):

Do one of the following:

• Use the history brush tool (🖌) to paint with the selected state or snapshot on the History palette.

[?] For more information, see "Painting with a state or snapshot of an image (Photoshop)" in online Help.

• Use the eraser tool (✐) with the Erase to History option selected.

[?] For more information, see "Using the eraser tool" in online Help.

• Select the area you want to restore, and choose Edit > Fill. For Use, choose History, and click OK.

For more information, see "Filling and stroking selections and layers" in online Help.

Note: *To restore the image with a snapshot of the initial state of the document, choose History Options from the Palette menu and make sure that the Automatically Create First Snapshot option is on.*

Reverting to any state of an image

The History palette lets you jump to any recent state of the image created during the current working session. Each time you apply a change to an image, the new state of that image is added to the palette.

For example, if you select, paint, and rotate part of an image, each of those states is listed separately in the palette. You can then select any of the states, and the image will revert to how it looked when that change was first applied. You can then work from that state.

About the History palette

Note the following guidelines when using the History palette:

• Program-wide changes, such as changes to palettes, color settings, actions, and preferences, are not changes to a particular image and so are not added to the History palette.

• By default, the History palette lists the previous 20 states. Older states are automatically deleted to free more memory for Photoshop. To keep a particular state throughout your work session, make a snapshot of the state. (See "Making a snapshot of an image (Photoshop)" on page 72.)

• Once you close and reopen the document, all states and snapshots from the last working session are cleared from the palette.

• By default, a snapshot of the initial state of the document is displayed at the top of the palette.

• States are added from the top down. That is, the oldest state is at the top of the list, the most recent one at the bottom.

• Each state is listed with the name of the tool or command used to change the image.

• By default, selecting a state dims those below. This way you can easily see which changes will be discarded if you continue working from the selected state. For information on customizing the history options, see "Setting history options (Photoshop)" on page 71.

• By default, selecting a state and then changing the image eliminates all states that come after.

• If you select a state and then change the image, eliminating the states that came after, you can use the Undo command to undo the last change and restore the eliminated states.

• By default, deleting a state deletes that state and those that came after it. If you choose the Allow Non-Linear History option, deleting a state deletes just that state. (See "Setting history options (Photoshop)" on page 71.)

Using the History Palette

You can use the History palette to revert to a previous state of an image, to delete an image's states, and in Photoshop, to create a document from a state or snapshot.

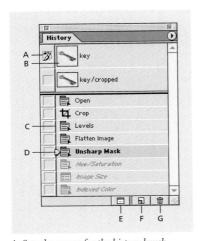

A. Sets the source for the history brush
B. Thumbnail of a snapshot C. History state
D. History state slider E. Create new document
from current state button F. Create new
snapshot button G. Trash button

To display the History palette:

Choose Window > Show History, or click the History palette tab.

To revert to a previous state of an image:

Do any of the following:

• Click the name of the state.

• Drag the slider at the left of the state up or down to a different state.

• (Photoshop) Choose Step Forward or Step Backward from the palette menu or the Edit menu to move to the next or previous state.

To delete one or more states of the image (Photoshop):

Do one of the following:

• Click the name of the state, and choose Delete from the History palette menu to delete that change and those that came after it.

• Drag the state to the Trash button (🗑) to delete that change and those that came after it.

• Choose Clear History from the palette menu to delete the list of states from the History palette, without changing the image. This option doesn't reduce the amount of memory used by Photoshop.

• Hold down Alt (Windows) or Option (Mac OS), and choose Clear History from the palette menu to purge the list of states from the History palette without changing the image. If you get a message that Photoshop is low on memory, purging states is useful, since the command deletes the states from the Undo buffer and frees up memory.

Important: This action cannot be undone.

• Choose Edit > Purge > Histories to purge the list of states from the History palette for all open documents.

Important: This action cannot be undone.

To delete all of an image's states (ImageReady):

Choose Clear Undo/Redo History from the History palette menu.

Important: This action cannot be undone.

To create a new document from the selected state or snapshot of the image (Photoshop):

Do one of the following:

• Drag a state or snapshot onto the New Document button (🗔).

• Select a state or snapshot, and click the New Document button.

• Select a state or snapshot, and choose New Document from the History palette menu.

The history list for the newly created document will be empty.

🔎 *To save one or more snapshots or image states for use in a later editing session, create a new file for each state you save, and save each in a separate file. When you reopen your original file, plan to open the other saved files also. You can drag each file's initial snapshot to the original image and thus access the snapshots again from the original image's History palette.*

To replace an existing document with a selected state (Photoshop):

Drag the state onto the document.

Setting history options (Photoshop)

You can specify the maximum number of items to include in the History palette and set other options that customize the way you work with the palette.

To set history options:

1 Choose History Options from the History palette menu.

2 Select an option:

• Automatically Create First Snapshot to automatically create a snapshot of the initial state of the image when the document is opened.

• Automatically Create New Snapshot When Saving to generate a snapshot every time you save.

• Allow Non-Linear History to make changes to a selected state without deleting the states that come after. Normally, when you select a state and change the image, all states that come after the selected one are deleted. This enables the History palette to display a list of the editing steps in the order you made them. By recording states in a nonlinear way, you can select a state, make a change to the image, and delete just that state. The change will be appended at the end of the list.

• Show New Snapshot Dialog By Default to force Photoshop to prompt you for snapshot names even when using the buttons on the palette.

3 Click OK.

Making a snapshot of an image (Photoshop)

The Snapshot command lets you make a temporary copy (or *snapshot*) of any state of the image. The new snapshot is added to the list of snapshots at the top of the History palette. Selecting a snapshot lets you work from that version of the image.

Important: Snapshots are not saved with the image—closing an image deletes its snapshots. Also, unless you select the Allow Non-Linear History option, selecting a snapshot and changing the image deletes all of the states currently listed in the History palette.

Snapshots let you do the following:

• Switch repeatedly between several states. By taking a temporary snapshot of a state, you can keep that state for the entire work session, even if the original state is deleted from the list of states in the History palette.

• Give a unique name to states to make them easier to identify.

• Experiment more freely. For example, you may want to compare two different techniques for achieving a similar effect. You can take a snapshot before and after trying the first technique. You can then select the first snapshot, try the second technique on it, and then compare snapshots of each technique.

• Take a snapshot before creating or applying an action. Then you can recover your work more easily if you decide later you don't like the action. Each step in an action is added to the list of states on the History palette. An action with many steps could scroll the current states off the palette, so that you could not return to any of them. Using the Undo command lets you undo only one step and state. By making a snapshot first, you can select and redisplay the pre-action image.

To create a snapshot:

1 Select a state.

2 To automatically create a snapshot, click the New Snapshot button ( ) on the History palette, or if Automatically Create New Snapshot When Saving is selected in the history options, choose New Snapshot from the History palette menu.

3 To set options when creating a snapshot, choose New Snapshot from the History palette menu, or Alt-click (Windows) or Option-click (Mac OS) the New Snapshot button.

4 Enter the name of the Snapshot in the Name text box.

5 For From, select the snapshot contents:

• Full Document to make a snapshot of all layers in the image at that state.

• Merged Layers to make a snapshot that merges all layers in the image at that state.

• Current Layer to make a snapshot of only the currently selected layer at that state.

6 Click OK.

To select a snapshot:

Do any of the following:

• Click the name of the snapshot.

• Drag the slider at the left of the snapshot up or down to a different snapshot.

To rename a snapshot:

Double-click the snapshot and enter a name.

To delete a snapshot:

Do one of the following:

• Select the snapshot, and choose Delete from the palette menu.

• Select the snapshot, and click the Trash button (🗑).

• Drag the snapshot to the Trash button.

For more information, see "Painting with a state or snapshot of an image (Photoshop)" in online Help.

Duplicating images

You can duplicate an entire image (including all layers, layer masks, and channels) into available memory without saving to disk. In ImageReady, you can also duplicate optimized versions of an image.

Using duplicates in ImageReady lets you experiment and then compare several versions of the optimized image to the original.

To duplicate an image (Photoshop):

1 Open the image you want to duplicate.

2 Choose Image > Duplicate.

3 Enter a name for the duplicated image.

4 To duplicate the image without layers, select Duplicate Merged Layers Only.

5 Click OK.

To duplicate an image in Photoshop and automatically append the name "copy" to its filename, hold down Alt (Windows) or Option (Mac OS) when you choose Image > Duplicate.

To duplicate an original image (ImageReady):

1 Open the image you want to duplicate.

2 Select the Original tab at the top of the image window.

3 Hold down Alt (Windows) or Option (Mac OS), and drag the Original tab from the image window, or choose Image > Duplicate.

4 Name the duplicate, specify whether to flatten the layers, and click OK.

To duplicate an optimized image (ImageReady):

1 Open the image you want to duplicate.

2 Select the Optimized tab at the top of the image window.

3 Hold down Alt (Windows) or Option (Mac OS), and drag the Optimized tab from the image window, or choose Image > Duplicate Optimized.

4 Name the duplicate, and click OK.

Note: *When you duplicate an image in Optimized, 2-Up, or 4-Up view, the duplicate image appears in the Original view in the duplicate image window. If you want a duplicate optimized image to appear in the Optimized, 2-Up, or 4-Up view, duplicate the original image, and then select the Optimized, 2-Up, or 4-Up tab in the duplicate image window.*

Using rulers, the measure tool, guides, and the grid

Rulers, the measure tool, guides, and the grid help you position images or elements precisely across the width or length of an image.

Note: You can also align and distribute parts of an image using the Layers palette. (See "Moving and aligning the contents of layers" on page 214.)

Using rulers

When visible, rulers appear along the top and left side of the active window. Markers in the ruler display the pointer's position when you move it. Changing the ruler origin (the (0, 0) mark on the top and left rulers) lets you measure from a specific point on the image. The ruler origin also determines the grid's point of origin.

To display or hide rulers:

Choose View > Show Rulers or View > Hide Rulers.

To change the rulers' zero origin:

1 To snap the ruler origin to guides, slices, or Document bounds, choose View > Snap To, then choose any combination of options from the submenu. (See "Working with snap" on page 152.)

(Photoshop) You can also snap to a grid in addition to guides, slices, and Document bounds.

2 Position the pointer over the intersection of the rulers in the upper left corner of the window, and drag diagonally down onto the image. A set of cross hairs appears, marking the new origin on the rulers.

To make the ruler origin snap to the ruler ticks (Photoshop), hold down Shift as you drag.

Note: To reset the ruler origin to its default value, double-click the upper left corner of the rulers.

To change the rulers' settings (Photoshop):

1 Do one of the following:

• Double-click a ruler.

• Choose Edit > Preferences > Units & Rulers.

2 For Rulers, choose a unit of measurement.

Note: Changing the units on the Info palette automatically changes the units on the rulers.

3 For Width and Gutter, enter values for the column size. You can also change the units.

Some layout programs use the column width setting to specify the display of an image across columns. The Image Size and Canvas Size commands also use this setting. (See "Changing the print dimensions and resolution of an image (Photoshop)" on page 97.)

For more information, see "Changing the size of the work canvas" in online Help.

4 For Point/Pica Size, choose from the following options:

• PostScript (72 points per inch) if you are printing to a PostScript device.

• Traditional to use printer's 72.27 points per inch.

5 Click OK.

Using the measure tool (Photoshop)

The measure tool calculates the distance between any two points in the work area. When you measure from one point to another, a nonprinting line is drawn and the options bar and Info palette show the following information:

• The starting location (X and Y).

• The horizontal (W) and vertical (H) distances traveled from the *x*- and *y*-axes.

• The angle measured relative to the axis (A).

• The total distance traveled (D1).

• When using a protractor, you can view two distances traveled (D1 and D2).

All measurements except the angle are calculated in the unit of measure currently set in the Units & Rulers preference dialog box. For information on setting the unit of measure, see "Using rulers" on page 74.

To display an existing measuring line:

Select the measure tool (✐).

To measure between two points:

1 Select the measure tool (✐).

2 Drag from the starting point to the ending point. Hold down the Shift key to constrain the tool to multiples of 45°.

3 To create a protractor from an existing measuring line, Alt-drag (Windows) or Option-drag (Mac OS) at an angle from one end of the measuring line, or double-click the line and drag. Hold down the Shift key to constrain the tool to multiples of 45°.

To edit a measuring line or protractor:

1 Select the measure tool (✐).

2 Do one of the following:

• To resize the line, drag one end of an existing measuring line.

• To move the line, place the pointer on the line away from either endpoint, and drag the line.

• To remove the line, place the pointer on the line away from either endpoint, and drag the line out of the image.

Note: *You can drag out a measure line on an image feature that should be horizontal or vertical, then choose Image > Rotate Canvas > Arbitrary and the correct angle of rotation required to straighten the image will already be entered into the Rotate Canvas dialog box.*

Using guides and the grid

Guides appear as lines that float over the entire image and do not print. You can move, remove, or lock a guide to avoid accidentally moving it.

In Photoshop, a grid appears by default as nonprinting lines but can also be displayed as dots. The grid is useful for laying out elements symmetrically.

Guides and grids behave in similar ways:

• Selections, selection borders, and tools snap to a guide or the grid when dragged within 8 screen (not image) pixels. Guides also snap to the grid when moved. You can turn this feature on and off.

• Guide spacing, along with guide and grid visibility and snapping, is specific to an image.

• Grid spacing, along with guide and grid color and style, is the same for all images.

To show or hide a grid or guides:

Do one of the following:

• (Photoshop) Choose View > Show > Grid.

• Choose View > Show > Guides.

• Choose View > Show Extras. This command also shows or hides: (Photoshop) selection edges, target path, slices, and notes, or (ImageReady) selection edges, slices, image maps, text bounds, text baseline, and text selection. (See "Working with Extras" on page 77.)

To place a guide:

1 If the rulers are not visible, choose View > Show Rulers.

Note: For the most accurate readings, view the image at 100% magnification or use the Info palette.

2 Create a guide:

• Choose View > New Guide. In the dialog box, select Horizontal or Vertical orientation, and enter a position.

• Drag from the horizontal ruler to create a horizontal guide.

• Hold down Alt (Windows) or Option (Mac OS), and drag from the vertical ruler to create a horizontal guide.

• Drag from the vertical ruler to create a vertical guide.

• Hold down Alt (Windows) or Option (Mac OS), and drag from the horizontal ruler to create a vertical guide.

• Hold down Shift and drag from the horizontal or vertical ruler to create a guide that snaps to the ruler ticks.

The pointer changes to a double-headed arrow (⁑) when you drag a guide.

To move a guide:

1 Select the move tool ( ), or hold down Ctrl (Windows) or Command (Mac OS) to activate the move tool. (This option does not work with the hand ( ), zoom ( ), and slice ( ) tools.)

2 Position the pointer over the guide (the pointer turns into a double-headed arrow).

3 Move the guide:

• Drag the guide to move it.

• Change the guide from horizontal to vertical, or vice versa, by holding down Alt (Windows) or Option (Mac OS) as you click or drag the guide.

• (Photoshop) Align the guide with the ruler ticks by holding down Shift as you drag the guide. The guide will snap to the grid if the grid is visible and View > Snap To > Grid is selected.

To lock all guides:

Choose View > Lock Guides.

To remove guides from the image:

Do one of the following:

• To remove a single guide, drag the guide outside the image window.

• To remove all guides, choose View > Clear Guides.

To turn snapping to guides on or off:

Choose View > Snap To > Guides. (See "Working with snap" on page 152.)

To turn snapping to the grid on or off (Photoshop):

Choose View > Snap To > Grid. (See "Working with snap" on page 152.)

To set guide and grid preferences (Photoshop):

1 Choose Edit > Preferences > Guides & Grid.

2 For Color, choose a color for the guides, the grid, or both. If you choose Custom, click the color box, choose a color, and click OK.

For more information on choosing colors, see "Using the Color palette" in online Help.

3 For Style, choose a display option for guides or the grid, or both.

4 For Gridline Every, enter a value for the grid spacing. For Subdivisions, enter a value to subdivide the grid.

If desired, change the units for this option. The Percent option creates a grid that divides the image into even sections. For example, choosing 25 for the Percent option creates an evenly divided 4-by-4 grid.

5 Click OK.

Working with Extras

Guides, grid, target paths, selection edges, slices, image maps, text bounds, text baselines, text selections, and annotations are nonprinting *Extras* that help you select, move, or edit images and objects. You can turn on or off an Extra or any combination of Extras without affecting the image. You can also show or hide Extras by choosing the Show Extras command in the View menu.

For a description of using specific Extras, see "Using guides and the grid" on page 75; "Annotating images (Photoshop)" on page 80; "Making pixel selections" on page 139; "Using the marquee tools" on page 140; "Selecting paths (Photoshop)" on page 173; "Entering paragraph type" on page 252; "Formatting characters" on page 258; "Creating and viewing slices" on page 272; and "Creating and viewing image maps (ImageReady)" on page 286.

Note: Show Extras also shows or hides color samplers, even though color samplers are not an option in the Show submenu.

To show Extras:

Choose View > Show Extras. A check mark appears next to all shown Extras in the Show submenu.

To hide Extras:

With Extras showing, choose View > Show Extras. A dot (Windows) or a dash (Mac OS) appears next to all hidden Extras in the Show submenu.

Note: Hiding only suppresses the display of Extras. It does not turn off these options.

To show one Extra from a list of hidden Extras:

Choose View > Show and choose an Extra from the submenu. Choosing one of the hidden Extras will cause it to show, and turn off all other Extras.

To Turn on and off a group of Extras:

Choose View > Show > All to turn on and show all available Extras. Choose View > Show > None to turn off all Extras.

Displaying status information

The status bar at the bottom of the window displays useful information—such as the current magnification and file size of the active image, and brief instructions for using the active tool.

To show or hide the status bar (Windows only):

Choose Window > Show Status Bar or Window > Hide Status Bar.

Displaying file and image information

Information about the current file size and other features of the image is displayed at the bottom of the application window (Windows) or document window (Mac OS).

Note: In ImageReady, if the document window is wide enough, two image information boxes appear, enabling you to view two different information options for the image at the same time. For more information about original and optimized images, see "Viewing images during optimization" on page 316.

You can also view copyright and authorship information that has been added to the file. This information includes standard file information and Digimarc® watermarks. Photoshop automatically scans opened images for watermarks using the Digimarc Detect Watermark plug-in. If a watermark is detected, Photoshop displays a copyright symbol in the image window's title bar and updates the Copyright & URL section of the File Info dialog box.

To display file information in the document window (Photoshop):

1 Click the triangle in the bottom border of the application window (Windows) or document window (Mac OS).

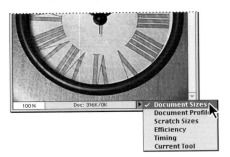

2 Select a view option:

• Document Size to display information on the amount of data in the image. The number on the left represents the printing size of the image—approximately the size of the saved, flattened file in Adobe Photoshop format. The number on the right indicates the file's approximate size including layers and channels. For more information on how layers affect file size, see "Using layer styles" on page 226.

• Document Profile to display the name of the color profile used by the image.

• Scratch Sizes to display information on the amount of RAM and scratch disk used to process the image. The number on the left represents the amount of memory that is currently being used by the program to display all open images. The number on the right represents the total amount of RAM available for processing images.

• Efficiency to display the percentage of time actually doing an operation instead of reading or writing the scratch disk. If the value is below 100%, Photoshop is using the scratch disk and, therefore, is operating more slowly.

• Timing to display the amount of time it took to complete the last operation.

• Current Tool to view the name of the active tool.

To display image information in the document window (ImageReady):

1 Click an image information box at the bottom of the document window.

2 Select a view option:

• Original/Optimized File Size to view the original and optimized file size images. The first value indicates the original image file size. The second value (present if the original image has been optimized) indicates the optimized image file size and file format based on the current settings in the Optimize palette.

• Optimized Information to view the file format, file size, number of colors, and dither percentage for the optimized image.

• Image Dimensions to view the image's pixel dimensions.

• Watermark Strength to view the strength of the Digimarc digital watermark in the optimized image, if present.

For more information on using digital watermarks, see "Adding digital copyright information" in online Help.

• Undo/Redo Status to view the number of undos and redos that are available for the image.

• Original in Bytes to view the size of the original, flattened image expressed in bytes.

• Optimized in Bytes to view the size of the optimized image expressed in bytes.

• Optimized Savings to view the percentage of the optimized image file size reduction, followed by the difference in bytes between the original and optimized sizes.

• Size/Download Time (14.4 Kbps/28.8 Kbps/ 56.6 Kbps) to view the file size for the optimized image and estimated download time using the selected modem speed.

Note: Download times may vary based on Internet traffic and modem compression schemes. The value displayed is an approximation.

To view additional file information:

Do one of the following:

• (Photoshop) Choose File > File Info. For section, choose the attribute you want to view.

• (ImageReady) Choose File > Image Info.

To read a Digimarc watermark:

1 Choose Filter > Digimarc > Read Watermark. If the filter finds a watermark, a dialog box displays the Creator ID, copyright year (if present), and image attributes.

2 Click OK, or for more information, choose from the following:

• If you have a Web browser installed, click Web Lookup to get more information about the owner of the image. This option launches the browser and displays the Digimarc Web site, where contact details appear for the given Creator ID.

• Call the phone number listed in the Watermark Information dialog box to get information faxed back to you.

For more information on adding digital watermarks to an image, see "Adding digital copyright information with the Digimarc filter" in online Help.

Annotating images (Photoshop)

You can attach note annotations (notes) and audio annotations to an image in Photoshop. This is useful for associating review comments, production notes, or other information with the image. Because Photoshop annotations are compatible with Adobe Acrobat, you can use them to exchange information with Acrobat users as well as Photoshop users.

To circulate a Photoshop document for review in Acrobat, save the document in Portable Document Format (PDF) and ask reviewers to use Acrobat to add notes or audio annotations. Then import the annotations into Photoshop.

Notes and audio annotations appear as small nonprintable icons on the image. They are associated with a location on the image rather than with a layer. You can hide and show annotations, open notes to view or edit their contents, and play audio annotations. You can also add audio annotations to actions, and set them to play during an action or during a pause in an action. (See "Setting playback options (Photoshop)" on page 400.)

Adding notes and audio annotations

You can add notes and audio annotations anywhere on a Photoshop image canvas. When you create a note, a resizable window appears for entering text. When you record an audio annotation, you must have a microphone plugged into the audio-in port of your computer.

You can import both kinds of annotations from Photoshop documents saved in PDF or from Acrobat documents saved in PDF or Form Data Format (FDF).

To create a note:

1 Select the notes tool ( ).

2 Set options as needed:

• Enter an author name. The name appears in the title bar of the notes window.

• Choose a font and size for the note text.

• Select a color for the note icon and the title bar of note windows.

3 Click where you want to place the note, or drag to create a custom-sized window.

4 Click inside the window, and type the text. If you type more text than fits in the note window, the scroll bar becomes active.

Edit the text as needed:

• You can use the standard editing commands for your system (Undo, Cut, Copy, Paste, and Select All). In Windows, right-click in the text area and choose the commands from the context menu. In Mac OS, choose the commands from the Edit and Select menus. You can also use standard keyboard shortcuts for these editing commands.

• If you have the required software for different script systems (for example, Roman, Japanese, or Cyrillic) installed on your computer, you can switch between the script systems. Right-click (Windows) or Control-click (Mac OS) to display the context menu, and then choose a script system.

5 To close the note to an icon, click the close box.

To create an audio annotation:

1 Select the audio annotation tool ( ).

2 Set options as needed:

• Enter an author name.

• Select a color for the audio annotation icon.

3 Click where you want to place the annotation icon.

4 Record and save the audio annotation:

• (Windows) Click Start and then speak into the microphone. When you're finished, click Stop.

• (Mac OS) Click Record and then speak into the microphone. You can click Pause to temporarily stop the recording, and then click Record to resume. When you're finished, click Stop and then click Save.

To import annotations:

1 Choose File > Import > Annotations.

2 Select a PDF or FDF file that contains annotations, and then click Load. The annotations appear in the locations where they were saved in the source document.

Opening and editing annotations

A note or audio annotation icon marks the location of an annotation on an image. When you move the pointer over an annotation icon and pause, a message displays the author name. You use the icons to open notes or play audio annotations. You can show, hide, or move the icons, and edit the contents of notes.

Note: Resizing an image does not resize the annotation icons and note windows. The icons and note windows keep their locations relative to the image. Cropping an image removes any annotations in the cropped area; you can recover the annotations by undoing the Crop command.

To open a note or play an audio annotation:

Double-click the icon:

• If you are opening a note, a window appears, displaying the note text.

• If you are playing an audio annotation and have a sound card installed, the audio file begins to play.

To show or hide annotation icons:

Do one of the following:

• Choose View > Show > Notes.

• Choose View > Show Extras. This command also shows or hides grids, guides, selection edges, target paths, and slices.

To edit annotations:

Do any of the following:

• To move an annotation icon, move the pointer over the icon until it turns into an arrow, and then drag the icon. You can do this with any tool selected. Moving a note icon does not move its note window.

• To move a note window, drag it by the title bar.

• To delete a selected annotation, press Delete.

• To edit the contents of a note, open the note, change any options, and add, delete, or change the text. You can use the same editing commands that you use when creating a note. (See "Adding notes and audio annotations" on page 81.)

• To delete all annotations, right-click (Windows) or Control-click (Mac OS) an annotation icon to display the context menu, and choose Delete All Annotations. You can also delete all annotations by clicking Clear All in the options bar for notes or audio annotations.

Jumping between applications

You can jump between Photoshop and ImageReady to transfer an image between the two applications for editing without closing or exiting the originating application. In addition, you can jump from ImageReady to other graphics editing applications and HTML editing applications installed on your system.

Jumping to an application saves you from having to close the file in one application and reopen it in another application.

Jumping between Photoshop and ImageReady

You can easily jump between Photoshop and ImageReady to use features in both applications when preparing graphics for the Web or other purposes. Jumping between the applications allows you to use the full feature sets of both applications while maintaining a streamlined workflow. Files and documents updated in one application can be automatically updated in the other application by choosing a preference.

To jump between Photoshop and ImageReady:

Do one of the following:

• Click the Jump To button (⧉) in the toolbox.

• Choose File > Jump To > Photoshop or File > Jump To > ImageReady.

When jumping between Photoshop and ImageReady, the applications use a temp file for transferring changes.

To automatically update files or documents when jumping between Photoshop and ImageReady:

Do one of the following:

• (Photoshop) Choose Edit > Preferences > General, then select Auto-update open documents.

• (ImageReady) Choose Edit > Preferences > General, then select Auto-Update Files.

Jumping to other applications (ImageReady)

You can jump to graphics-editing applications and HTML-editing applications from within ImageReady.

When you install ImageReady, Adobe graphics-editing and HTML-editing applications currently on your system are added to the Jump To submenu. You can add more applications, including non-Adobe applications, to the Jump To submenu.

When you jump to a graphics-editing application, the original file is opened in the destination application. When you jump to an HTML editor, the optimized file and the HTML file are saved and opened in the destination application. If the image contains slices, all filesfor the full image are included. A preference enables files updated in another application to be automatically updated in ImageReady, when jumping back to ImageReady.

To jump to another application from ImageReady:

1 Choose a method for jumping to the destination application:

• Choose File > Jump To > Other Graphics Editor or File > Jump To > Other HTML Editor, and select an application by navigating through the Jump To dialog.

2 If the file has been modified since the last save, choose an option in ImageReady for saving the file:

• Click Save, and save the file with its current name and location.

• Click Save As, and save the file with a new name, a new location, or both.

To add an application to the Jump To submenu:

1 Create a shortcut (Windows) or an alias (Mac OS) for the application you want to add to the menu.

2 Drag the icon for the shortcut or alias into the Jump To Graphics Editor or the Jump To HTML Editor folder in the Helpers folder in the Photoshop folder.

3 Restart ImageReady to view the application in the Jump To submenu.

To automatically update a file when jumping back to ImageReady from another application:

Choose Edit > Preferences > General, then select Auto-Update Files.

Previewing an image in a browser

You can open a browser and preview an optimized image. You can preview the image in any browser installed on your system. The browser displays the image with a caption listing the image's file type, pixel dimensions, file size, and compression specifications in the first paragraph, and filename and other HTML information in the second paragraph.

When you install Photoshop and ImageReady, all browsers currently on your system are added to the Preview In menu. You can add additional browsers to the menu, and specify which browser will be launched when using a keyboard shortcut.

To preview an optimized image in a browser:

Do one of the following:

• (Photoshop) Choose File > Save for Web, then select a browser from the Preview In button at the bottom right area of the Save for Web window.

• (ImageReady) Choose File > Preview In, then choose an option from the submenu. (Choose Other to select a browser not listed in the submenu.)

• (ImageReady) Select a browser from the Preview in Default Browser tool in the toolbox.

To add a browser to the Preview In menu:

1 Create a shortcut (Windows) or an alias (Mac OS) for the browser you want to add to the menu.

2 Drag the icon for the shortcut or alias into the Preview In folder, located in the Helpers folder in the Photoshop program folder.

3 Restart Photoshop and ImageReady to view the browser in the Preview In menu.

(ImageReady) To specify a browser to be launched by the Preview In keyboard shortcut:

Do one of the following:

• Choose File > Preview In, then choose an option from the submenu.

• Select a browser from the Preview in Default Browser tool in the toolbox.

The shortcut specification takes effect immediately and will persist the next time you launch ImageReady.

Managing libraries with the Preset Manager (Photoshop)

You can use the Preset Manager to manage libraries of preset brushes, swatches, gradients, styles, patterns, contours, and custom shapes. This lets you easily reuse or share libraries of presets. Each type of library has its own file extension and default folder. You can always restore the default presets. Note that you cannot create new presets using the Preset Manager, as each preset is created in its own type of editor. The Preset Manager lets you create a library composed of multiple presets of a single type.

Any new preset brush, swatch, and so on, automatically displays in the Preset Manager. Prior to saving it into a preset library, the new brush, swatch, and so on, is saved in the Preferences file so that it persists between editing sessions. To permanently save the new item as a preset, you need to save it in the editor used to create it. Otherwise, it will be lost if you create a new one, or if you replace (rather than append) a new library of the same type.

To create, load, save, or delete libraries:

1 Choose Edit > Preset Manager.

2 Choose a preset type from the Preset Type menu.

3 Do one of the following:

• Choose Save Set, then enter a name for the library. If you want to save it to a folder other than the default, navigate to the new folder before saving.

• Choose Load, then select a library from the list. If you want to load a library located in another folder, navigate to that folder, then select the library. Or select a library from the pop-up menu.

• Choose Delete to delete the selected presets in the library. You can delete the default presets, but they can always be restored.

To reset or replace libraries:

1 Choose Edit > Preset Manager.

2 Select the preset type you want to reset or replace in the Preset Type menu. Any unsaved presets in the list will be lost. You may want to save the current library before you continue.

3 From the Preset Manager pop-up menu do one of the following:

• Choose Reset to restore the default library for that type. Select Append to append the default presets to the current set, OK to replace the current presets with the default presets, or Cancel.

• Choose Replace to replace the current library with the contents of another libraryloaded from a file.

To save a subset of a library:

1 Choose Edit > Preset Manager.

2 Choose a preset type from the Preset Type menu.

3 Shift-click to select multiple presets. Only the selected presets will be saved to the new library.

4 Choose Save Set, then enter a name for the library. If you want to save the library to a folder other than the default, navigate to the new folder before saving.

To rename presets contained in a library:

1 Choose Edit > Preset Manager.

2 Choose a preset type from the Preset Type menu.

3 Select a preset in the list.

4 Choose Rename, then enter a new name for the brush, swatch, and so on. If you selected multiple presets, you will be prompted to enter multiple names.

Changing views of the Preset Manager

You can change the view of the Preset Manager to display presets by name, by thumbnail, or for some preset types, you can choose to show both the name and thumbnail of each item. Only the available choices for each type of preset display when you change the view for that preset type.

To change the view of the Preset Manager:

In the Preset Manager dialog box, choose one of the available views from the pop-up menu:

• Text Only to display the name of each preset item.

• Small Thumbnail or Large Thumbnail to display a thumbnail of each preset item.

• Small List or Large List to display the name and thumbnail of each preset item.

Setting preferences

Numerous program settings are stored in Adobe Photoshop 6 Prefs.psp file (Windows) or the Adobe Photoshop 6 Prefs file (Mac OS) in the Adobe Photoshop 6 Settings folder. Among the settings stored in this file are general display options, file-saving options, cursor options, transparency options, and options for plug-ins and scratch disks. Most of these options are set in dialog boxes that can be opened through the Preferences submenu in the Edit menu. Preference settings are saved each time you exit the application.

Note: The default location of the Adobe Photoshop 6 Settings folder varies by operating system; use your operating system's Find command to locate this folder.

Unexpected behavior may indicate damaged preferences. By removing damaged preferences, you can restore preferences to their default settings.

To open a preferences dialog box:

1 Choose the desired preference set from the Edit > Preferences submenu.

2 To switch to a different preference set, do one of the following:

• Choose the preference set from the menu at the top of the dialog box.

• Click Next to display the next preference set in the menu list; click Prev to display the previous preference set.

For information on a specific preference option, see the Index.

To restore all preferences to their default settings:

In Windows, press and hold Alt+Control+Shift immediately after launching Photoshop or ImageReady. Click Yes to (Photoshop) delete the Adobe Photoshop settings file or (ImageReady) erase all ImageReady preferences.

In Mac OS, do one of the following:

• Hold down the Shift, Option, and Command keys at the startup of Photoshop to reset preferences to their default settings.

• Open the Preferences folder in the System Folder, and drag the following files to the Trash: (Photoshop) Adobe Save For Web 2.0 prefs, and, located in the Adobe Photoshop 6 Settings folder, Adobe Photoshop 6 Prefs, Actions Palette (prefs), Color Settings (prefs), Contours.psp, Custom Shape.psp, Patterns.psp, Shape Curves.psp, and Styles.psp; (ImageReady) Adobe ImageReady 3.0 Prefs.

New Preferences files will be created the next time you start Photoshop or ImageReady.

Resetting all warning dialogs

Sometimes messages containing warnings or prompts regarding certain situations are displayed. You can disable the display of these messages by selecting the Don't Show Again option in the message. You can also globally reset the display of all messages that have been disabled.

To reset the display of all warning messages (Photoshop):

1 Choose Edit > Preferences > General.

2 Click Reset All Warning Dialogs, and click OK.

To turn on or off warning messages (ImageReady):

1 Choose Edit > Preferences > General.

2 Deselect or select Disable Warnings, and click OK.

Monitoring operations

A progress bar indicates that an operation is in process. You can interrupt the process or have the program notify you when it has finished.

To cancel operations:

Hold down Esc until the operation in progress has stopped. In Mac OS, you can also press Command+period.

To set notification for completion of operations:

1 Choose Edit > Preferences > General.

2 Do one of the following:

• (Photoshop) Select Beep When Done.

• (ImageReady) Select Notify When Done and choose (Mac OS only): System Alert to use your system alert for notification or Text to Speech to use a spoken notification.

3 Click OK.

Closing files and quitting

To close a file:

1 Choose File > Close (Windows and Mac OS) or File > Close All (Mac OS).

2 Choose whether or not to save the file:

• Click Yes (Windows) or Save (Mac OS) to save the file.

• Click No (Windows) or Don't Save (Mac OS) to close the file without saving it.

To exit Photoshop or ImageReady:

1 Choose File > Exit (Windows) or File > Quit (Mac OS).

2 Choose whether or not to save any open files:

• Click Yes (Windows) or Save (Mac OS) for each open file to save the file.

• Click No (Windows) or Don't Save (Mac OS) for each open file to close the file without saving it.

For information on using Adobe and third-party plug-in modules, see "Using plug-in modules" in online Help.

2

Chapter 2: Getting Images into Photoshop and ImageReady

You can get digital images from a variety of sources—you can create new images, import them from another graphics application, or capture them using a digital camera. Often you will begin by scanning a photograph, a slide, or an image. To create effective artwork, you must understand some basic concepts about how to work with digital images, how to produce high-quality scans, how to work with a variety of file formats, and how to adjust the resolution and size of images.

About bitmap images and vector graphics

Computer graphics falls into two main categories—*bitmap* and *vector*. You can work with both types of graphics in Photoshop and ImageReady; moreover, a Photoshop file can contain both bitmap and vector data. Understanding the difference between the two categories helps as you create, edit, and import artwork.

Bitmap images Bitmap images—technically called *raster images*—use a grid of colors known as pixels to represent images. Each pixel is assigned a specific location and color value. For example, a bicycle tire in a bitmap image is made up of a mosaic of pixels in that location. When working with bitmap images, you edit pixels rather than objects or shapes.

Bitmap images are the most common electronic medium for continuous-tone images, such as photographs or digital paintings, because they can represent subtle gradations of shades and color. Bitmap images are resolution-dependent—that is, they contain a fixed number of pixels. As a result, they can lose detail and appear jagged if they are scaled on-screen or if they are printed at a lower resolution than they were created for.

3:1

24:1

Bitmap images are good for reproducing subtle gradations of color, as in photographs. They can have jagged edges when printed at too large a size or displayed at too high a magnification.

Vector graphics Vector graphics are made up of lines and curves defined by mathematical objects called *vectors*. Vectors describe an image according to its geometric characteristics. For example, a bicycle tire in a vector graphic is made up of a mathematical definition of a circle drawn with a certain radius, set at a specific location, and filled with a specific color. You can move, resize, or change the color of the tire without losing the quality of the graphic.

Vector graphics are resolution-independent—that is, they can be scaled to any size and printed at any resolution without losing detail or clarity. As a result, vector graphics are the best choice for representing bold graphics that must retain crisp lines when scaled to various sizes—for example, logos.

Vector graphics are good for reproducing crisp outlines, as in logos or illustrations. They can be printed or displayed at any resolution without losing detail.

Because computer monitors represent images by displaying them on a grid, both vector and bitmap data is displayed as pixels on-screen.

About image size and resolution

In order to produce high-quality images, it is important to understand how the pixel data of images is measured and displayed.

Pixel dimensions The number of pixels along the height and width of a bitmap image. The display size of an image on-screen is determined by the pixel dimensions of the image plus the size and setting of the monitor.

For example, a 15-inch monitor typically displays 800 pixels horizontally and 600 vertically. An image with dimensions of 800 pixels by 600 pixels would fill this small screen. On a larger monitor with an 800-by-600-pixel setting, the same image (with 800-by-600-pixel dimensions) would still fill the screen, but each pixel would appear larger. Changing the setting of this larger monitor to 1024-by-768 pixels would display the image at a smaller size, occupying only part of the screen.

When preparing an image for online display (for example, a Web page that will be viewed on a variety of monitors), pixel dimensions become especially important. Because your image may be viewed on a 15-inch monitor, you may want to limit the size of your image to 800-by-600 pixels to allow room for the Web browser window controls.

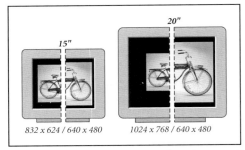

How large an image appears on-screen depends on a combination of factors—the pixel dimensions of the image, the monitor size, and the monitor resolution setting. The examples above show a 620-by-400-pixel image displayed on monitors of various sizes and resolutions.

Image resolution The number of pixels displayed per unit of printed length in an image, usually measured in pixels per inch (ppi). In Photoshop, you can change the resolution of an image; in ImageReady, the resolution of an image is always 72 ppi. This is because the ImageReady application is tailored to creating images for online media, not print media.

In Photoshop, image resolution and pixel dimensions are interdependent. The amount of detail in an image depends on its pixel dimensions, while the image resolution controls how much space the pixels are printed over. For example, you can modify an image's resolution without changing the actual pixel data in the image—all you change is the printed size of the image. However, if you want to maintain the same output dimensions, changing the image's resolution requires a change in the total number of pixels.

72-ppi and 300-ppi images; inset zoom 200%

When printed, an image with a high resolution contains more, and therefore smaller, pixels than an image with a low resolution. For example, a 1-by-1-inch image with a resolution of 72 ppi contains a total of 5184 pixels (72 pixels wide x 72 pixels high = 5184). The same 1-by-1-inch image with a resolution of 300 ppi contains a total of 90,000 pixels. Higher-resolution images usually reproduce more detail and subtler color transitions than lower-resolution images. However, increasing the resolution of a low-resolution image only spreads the original pixel information across a greater number of pixels; it rarely improves image quality.

Using too low a resolution for a printed image results in *pixelation*—output with large, coarse-looking pixels. Using too high a resolution (pixels smaller than the output device can produce) increases the file size and slows the printing of the image; furthermore, the device will be unable to reproduce the extra detail provided by the higher resolution image.

Monitor resolution The number of pixels or dots displayed per unit of length on the monitor, usually measured in dots per inch (dpi). Monitor resolution depends on the size of the monitor plus its pixel setting. Most new monitors have a resolution of about 96 dpi, while older Mac OS monitors have a resolution of 72 dpi.

Understanding monitor resolution helps explain why the display size of an image on-screen often differs from its printed size. Image pixels are translated directly into monitor pixels. This means that when the image resolution is higher than the monitor resolution, the image appears larger on-screen than its specified print dimensions.

For example, when you display a 1-by-1 inch, 144-ppi image on a 72-dpi monitor, it appears in a 2-by-2 inch area on-screen. Because the monitor can display only 72 pixels per inch, it needs 2 inches to display the 144 pixels that make up one edge of the image.

Printer resolution The number of ink dots per inch (dpi) produced by all laser printers, including imagesetters. Most desktop laser printers have a resolution of 600 dpi and imagesetters have a resolution of 1200 dpi or higher. To determine the appropriate resolution for your image when printing to any laser printer, but especially to imagesetters, see "screen frequency."

Ink jet printers produce a spray of ink, not actual dots; however, most ink jet printers have an approximate resolution of 300 to 600 dpi and produce good results when printing images up to 150 ppi.

Screen frequency The number of printer dots or halftone cells per inch used to print grayscale images or color separations. Also known as screen ruling or line screen, screen frequency is measured in lines per inch (lpi)—or lines of cells per inch in a halftone screen.

The relationship between image resolution and screen frequency determines the quality of detail in the printed image. To produce a halftone image of the highest quality, you generally use an image resolution that is from 1.5 to at most 2 times the screen frequency. But with some images and

output devices, a lower resolution can produce good results. To determine your printer's screen frequency, check your printer documentation or consult your service provider.

Note: Some imagesetters and 600-dpi laser printers use screening technologies other than halftoning. If you are printing an image on a nonhalftone printer, consult your service provider or your printer documentation for the recommended image resolutions.

A. 65 lpi: Coarse screen typically used to print newsletters and grocery coupons. B. 85 lpi: Average screen typically used to print newspapers. C. 133 lpi: High-quality screen typically used to print four-color magazines. D. 177 lpi: Very fine screen typically used for annual reports and images in art books.

File size The digital size of an image, measured in kilobytes (K), megabytes (MB), or gigabytes (GB). File size is proportional to the pixel dimensions of the image. Images with more pixels may produce more detail at a given printed size, but they require more disk space to store and may be slower to edit and print. For instance, a 1-by-1-inch, 200-ppi image contains four times as many pixels as a

1-by-1-inch, 100-ppi image and so has four times the file size. Image resolution thus becomes a compromise between image quality (capturing all the data you need) and file size.

Another factor that affects file size is file format—due to varying compression methods used by GIF, JPEG, and PNG file formats, file sizes can vary considerably for the same pixel dimensions. Similarly, color bit-depth and the number of layers and channels in an image affect file size.

Photoshop supports a maximum file size of 2 GB and maximum pixel dimensions of 30,000 by 30,000 pixels per image. This restriction places limits on the print size and resolution available to an image.

Changing image size and resolution

Once you have scanned or imported an image, you may want to adjust its size. In Photoshop, the Image Size command lets you adjust the pixel dimensions, print dimensions, and resolution of an image; in ImageReady, you can only adjust the pixel dimensions of an image.

For assistance with resizing and resampling images in Photoshop, choose Help > Resize Image. This interactive wizard helps you scale your images for print or online media.

Keep in mind that bitmap and vector data can produce different results when you resize an image. Bitmap data is resolution-dependent; therefore, changing the pixel dimensions of a bitmap image can cause a loss in image quality and sharpness. In contrast, vector data is resolution-independent; you can resize it without losing its crisp edges.

Displaying image size information

You can display information about the current image size using the information box at the bottom of the application window (Windows) or the document window (Mac OS). (See "Displaying file and image information" on page 78.)

To display the current image size:

Do one of the following:

• (Photoshop) Press Alt (Windows) or Option (Mac OS), position the pointer over the file information box, and hold down the mouse button. The box displays the width and height of the image (both in pixels and in the unit of measurement currently selected for the rulers), the number of channels, and the image resolution.

• (ImageReady) Click an image information box, and select Image Dimensions from the pop-up menu. The box displays the width and height of the image in pixels.

About resampling

Resampling refers to changing the pixel dimensions (and therefore display size) of an image. When you *downsample* (or decrease the number of pixels), information is deleted from the image. When you *resample up* (or increase the number of pixels), new pixels are added based on color values of existing pixels. You specify an *interpolation* method to determine how pixels are added or deleted. (See "Choosing an interpolation method" on page 96.)

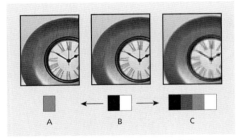

A. Downsampled *B.* Original *C.* Resampled up
(Selected pixels displayed for each image.)

Keep in mind that resampling can result in poorer image quality. For example, when you resample an image to larger pixel dimensions, the image will lose some detail and sharpness. Applying the Unsharp Mask filter to a resampled image can help refocus the image's details.

 For more information, see "Sharpening images" in online Help.

You can avoid the need for resampling by scanning or creating the image at a high enough resolution. If you want to preview the effects of changing pixel dimensions on-screen or print proofs at different resolutions, resample a duplicate of your file.

Choosing an interpolation method

When an image is resampled, an *interpolation method* is used to assign color values to any new pixels it creates, based on the color values of existing pixels in the image. The more sophisticated the method, the more quality and detail from the original image are preserved.

The General Preferences dialog box lets you specify a default interpolation method to use whenever images are resampled with the Image Size or transformation commands. The Image Size command also lets you specify an interpolation method other than the default.

To specify the default interpolation method:

1 Choose Edit > Preferences > General.

2 For Interpolation, choose one of the following options:

• Nearest Neighbor (Jagged) for the fast but less precise method. This method is recommended for use with illustrations containing non-anti-aliased edges, to preserve hard edges and produce a smaller file. However, this method can result in jagged effects, which become apparent when distorting or scaling an image or performing multiple manipulations on a selection.

• (Photoshop) Bilinear for a medium-quality method.

• Bicubic (Smooth) for the slow but more precise method, resulting in the smoothest tonal gradations.

Changing the pixel dimensions of an image

When preparing images for online distribution, it's useful to specify image size in terms of the pixel dimensions. Keep in mind that changing pixel dimensions affects not only the size of an image on-screen but also its image quality and its printed characteristics—either its printed dimensions or its image resolution. (See "About image size and resolution" on page 92.)

To change the pixel dimensions of an image (Photoshop):

1 Choose Image > Image Size.

2 Make sure that Resample Image is selected, and choose an interpolation method. (See "Choosing an interpolation method" on page 96.)

3 To maintain the current proportions of pixel width to pixel height, select Constrain Proportions. This option automatically updates the width as you change the height, and vice versa.

4 Under Pixel Dimensions, enter values for Width and Height. To enter values as percentages of the current dimensions, choose Percent as the unit of measurement.

The new file size for the image appears at the top of the Image Size dialog box, with the old file size in parentheses.

5 Click OK to change the pixel dimensions and resample the image.

For best results in producing a smaller image, downsample and apply the Unsharp Mask filter. To produce a larger image, rescan the image at a higher resolution.

To change the pixel dimensions of an image (ImageReady):

1 Choose Image > Image Size.

2 To maintain the current proportions of pixel width to pixel height, select Constrain Proportions.

3 Under New Size, enter values for Width, Height, or Percent. The New Size text field displays the new file size for the image.

4 Select a resampling method from the Quality pop-up menu.

5 Click OK to change the pixel dimensions and resample the image.

For information on setting action options, see "Recording image size options (ImageReady)" on page 398.

Changing the print dimensions and resolution of an image (Photoshop)

When creating an image for print media, it's useful to specify image size in terms of the printed dimensions and the image resolution. These two measurements, referred to as the *document size*, determine the total pixel count and therefore the file size of the image; document size also determines the base size at which an image is placed into another application. You can further manipulate the scale of the printed image in the Print Options dialog box; however, changes you make in the Print Options dialog box affect only the printed image, not the document size of the image file. (See "Positioning and scaling images" on page 377.)

If you turn on resampling for the image, you can change print dimensions and resolution independently (and change the total number of pixels in the image). If you turn resampling off, you can change either the dimensions or the resolution—Photoshop adjusts the other value automatically to preserve the total pixel count. For the highest print quality, it's generally best to change the dimensions and resolution first without resampling. Then resample only as necessary.

To change the print dimensions and resolution of an image:

1 Choose Image > Image Size.

2 Change the print dimensions, image resolution, or both:

• To change only the print dimensions or only the resolution and adjust the total number of pixels in the image proportionately, make sure that Resample Image is selected. Then choose an interpolation method. (See "Choosing an interpolation method" on page 96.)

• To change the print dimensions and resolution without changing the total number of pixels in the image, deselect Resample Image.

3 To maintain the current proportions of image width to image height, select Constrain Proportions. This option automatically updates the width as you change the height, and vice versa.

4 Under Document Size, enter new values for the height and width. If desired, choose a new unit of measurement. Note that for Width, the Columns option uses the width and gutter sizes specified in the Units & Rulers preferences. (See "Using rulers, the measure tool, guides, and the grid" on page 74.)

5 For Resolution, enter a new value. If desired, choose a new unit of measurement.

6 Click OK.

To return to the original values displayed in the Image Size dialog box, hold down Alt (Windows) or Option (Mac OS), and click Reset.

To view the print size on-screen:

Do one of the following:

• Choose View > Print Size.

• Select the hand tool or zoom tool, and click Print Size in the options bar.

The magnification of the image is adjusted to display its approximate printed size, as specified in the Document Size section of the Image Size dialog box. Keep in mind that the size and resolution of your monitor affect the on-screen print size.

Determining a recommended resolution for an image (Photoshop)

If you plan to print your image using a halftone screen, the range of suitable image resolutions depends on the screen frequency of your output device. You can have Photoshop determine a recommended resolution for your image based on your device's screen frequency. (See "About image size and resolution" on page 92.)

Note: If your image resolution is more than 2.5 times the screen ruling, an alert message appears when you try to print the image. This means that the image resolution is higher than necessary for the printer. Save a copy of the file, and then reduce the resolution.

To determine a suggested resolution for an image:

1 Choose Image > Image Size.

2 Click Auto.

3 For Screen, enter the screen frequency for the output device. If desired, choose a new unit of measurement. Note that the screen value is used only to calculate the image resolution, not to set the screen for printing.

Important: To specify the halftone screen ruling for printing, you must use the Halftone Screens dialog box, accessible through the Print Options dialog box. (See "Selecting halftone screen attributes" on page 379.)

4 For Quality, select an option:

• Draft to produce a resolution the same as the screen frequency (no lower than 72 pixels per inch).

• Good to produce a resolution 1.5 times the screen frequency.

• Best to produce a resolution 2 times the screen frequency.

5 Click OK.

Scanning images

Before you scan an image, make sure that the software necessary for your scanner has been installed. To ensure a high-quality scan, you should predetermine the scanning resolution and dynamic range your image requires. These preparatory steps can also prevent unwanted colors casts from being introduced by your scanner.

Scanner drivers are provided and supported by the manufacturers of the scanners, not Adobe Systems Incorporated. If you have problems with scanning, make sure that you are using the latest version of the appropriate scanner driver.

Importing scanned images

You can import scanned images directly from any scanner that has an Adobe Photoshop-compatible plug-in module or that supports the TWAIN interface. To import the scan using a plug-in module, choose the scanner name from the File > Import submenu. See your scanner documentation for instructions on installing the scanner plug-in.

 For more information, see "Using plug-in modules" in online Help.

If your scanner does not have an Adobe Photoshop-compatible scanner driver, import the scan using the TWAIN interface. (See "Importing an image using the TWAIN interface" on page 100.)

If you can't import the scan using the TWAIN interface, use the scanner manufacturer's software to scan your images, and save the images as TIFF, PICT, or BMP files. Then open the files in Photoshop or ImageReady.

Importing an image using the TWAIN interface

TWAIN is a cross-platform interface for acquiring images captured by certain scanners, digital cameras, and frame grabbers. The manufacturer of the TWAIN device must provide a Source Manager and TWAIN Data source for your device to work with Photoshop and ImageReady.

You must install the TWAIN device and its software, and restart your computer, before you can use it to import images into Photoshop and ImageReady. See the documentation provided by your device manufacturer for installation information.

To import an image using the TWAIN interface (Photoshop):

Choose File > Import, and choose the device you want to use from the submenu.

To import an image using the TWAIN interface (ImageReady):

1 If you're using the TWAIN device for the first time with ImageReady, choose File > Import > TWAIN Select. Then select the device you want to use. You do not need to repeat this step for subsequent use of the TWAIN module.

If more than one TWAIN device is installed in your system and you want to switch devices, use the TWAIN Select command.

2 To import the image, choose File > Import > TWAIN Acquire.

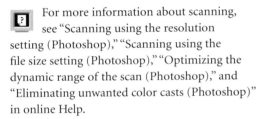 For more information about scanning, see "Scanning using the resolution setting (Photoshop)," "Scanning using the file size setting (Photoshop)," "Optimizing the dynamic range of the scan (Photoshop)," and "Eliminating unwanted color casts (Photoshop)" in online Help.

Creating new images

The New command lets you create a blank image.

To create a new image:

1 Do one of the following:

• To base the image dimensions and resolution (Photoshop) on the Clipboard contents, choose File > New. If the Clipboard does not contain image data, the image dimensions and resolution are based on the last image you created.

• (Photoshop) To base the image size on the default dimensions and resolution or the last entered settings, hold down Alt (Windows) or Option (Mac OS) when you choose File > New.

2 If desired, type a name for the image, and set the width and height.

(Photoshop) To match the width and height of the new image to that of any open image, choose a filename from the bottom section of the Windows menu.

3 (Photoshop) Set the resolution and mode. (See "About image size and resolution" on page 92 and "About color modes and models (Photoshop)" on page 109.)

4 Select an option for the contents of the background layer (Photoshop) or first layer (ImageReady) of the image:

• White to fill the background or first layer with white, the default background color.

• Background Color to fill the background or first layer with the current background color.

 For more information, see "Choosing foreground and background colors" in online Help.

• Transparent to make the first layer transparent, with no color values. The resulting document will have a single, transparent layer as its contents.

5 Click OK.

Opening and importing images

You can open and import images in various file formats. The available formats appear in the Open dialog box, the Open As dialog box (Windows), or the Import submenu.

 For more information, see "About file formats" in online Help.

Note: *Photoshop and ImageReady use plug-in modules to open and import many file formats. If a file format does not appear in the Open dialog box or in the File > Import submenu, you may need to install the format's plug-in module.*

 For more information, see "Using plug-in modules" in online Help.

Opening files

The Open dialog box provides controls for locating and previewing files. To bypass the Open dialog box, use the Open Recent command.

There may be instances when Photoshop cannot determine the correct format for a file. For example, transferring a file between Mac OS and Windows can cause the format to be mislabeled. In such cases, you must specify the correct format in which to open the file.

To open a file:

1 Choose File > Open.

2 Select the name of the file you want to open. If the file does not appear, select the option for showing all files from the Files of Type (Windows) or Show (Mac OS) pop-up menu.

3 (Mac OS) Click Show Preview to preview the selected file. This option requires the Apple QuickTime extension.

Note: Previews display faster if they are saved with the file. In Photoshop, select Always Save for Image Previews in the Saving Files preferences to always save a preview; select Ask When Saving to save previews on a file-per-file basis.

4 Click Open. In some cases, a dialog box appears, letting you set format-specific options. (See "Opening and importing PDF files" on page 102 and "Opening PostScript artwork" on page 104.)

Note: If a color profile warning message appears, specify whether to convert the pixels based on the file's color profile. (See "Specifying color management policies" on page 128.)

 For more information on opening and importing Photo CD files, see "Opening Photo CD files," "Opening Raw files (Photoshop)," "Importing anti-aliased PICT files (Mac OS)," and "Importing PICT Resources (Mac OS)" in online Help.

To open a recently used file:

Choose File > Open Recent, and select a file from the submenu.

To specify the number of files that are available in the Open Recent submenu, choose Edit > Preferences > Saving Files, and enter a number in the Recent File List Contains text box.

To specify the file format in which to open a file (Photoshop):

Do one of the following:

• (Windows) Choose File > Open As, and select the file you want to open. Then choose the desired format from the Open As pop-up menu, and click Open.

• (Mac OS) Choose File > Open, and choose All Documents from the Show pop-up menu. Then select the file you want to open, choose the desired file format from the Format pop-up menu, and click Open.

Important: If the file does not open, then the chosen format may not match the file's true format, or the file may be damaged.

Opening and importing PDF files

Portable Document Format (PDF) is a versatile file format that can represent both vector and bitmap data and can contain electronic document search and navigation features. PDF is the primary format for Adobe Illustrator 9.0 and Adobe Acrobat.

 For more information, see "PDF" in online Help.

Some PDF files contain a single image. Other PDF files (called Generic PDF files) may contain multiple pages and images. When you open a Generic PDF file, you can choose which page to open and specify rasterization options. If you want to open an image (versus a page) from a PDF file, you can use the File > Import > PDF Image command.

You can also bring PDF data into Photoshop or ImageReady using the Place command, the Paste command, and the drag-and-drop feature. (See "Placing files" on page 104, "Using drag and drop to copy between applications" on page 151, and "Using the Clipboard to copy between applications" on page 152.)

To open a PDF file:

1 Choose File > Open.

2 Select the name of the file, and click Open. You can change which types of files show by selecting an option from the Files of Type (Windows) or Show (Mac OS) pop-up menu.

3 If you are opening a Generic PDF file, do the following:

• If the file contains multiple pages, select the page you want to open, and click OK.

• Indicate the desired dimensions, resolution, and mode. If the file has an embedded ICC profile, you can choose the profile from the mode pop-up menu.

• Select Constrain Proportions to maintain the same height-to-width ratio.

• Select Anti-aliased to minimize the jagged appearance of the artwork's edges as it is rasterized.

• Click OK.

To import images from a PDF file:

1 Choose File > Import > PDF Image, select the file you want to import images from, and click Open.

2 Select the image you want to open:

• To open a specific image, select it and click OK. You can use the arrows to scroll through the images, or click Go to Image to enter an image number.

• To open each image as a separate file, click Import All Images.

💡 *Press Esc to cancel the import operation before all images are imported.*

To create a new Photoshop file for each page of a multiple-page PDF file (Photoshop):

1 Choose File > Automate > Multi-Page PDF to PSD.

2 Under Source PDF, click the Choose button, and select the file you want to import images from.

3 Under Page Range, specify a range of pages to import.

4 Under Output Options, specify a resolution, choose a color mode, and set the Anti-alias option for rasterizing each page of the PDF file. (To blend edge pixels during rasterization, select the Anti-alias option. To produce a hard-edged transition between edge pixels during rasterization, deselect the Anti-alias option.)

5 Under Destination, enter a base name for the generated files. (When Photoshop creates the new files, the base name is appended with a number that corresponds to the page number of the PDF file.) Then click the Choose button, and select the location where you want to save the generated files.

6 Click OK.

Opening PostScript artwork

Encapsulated PostScript® (EPS) can represent both vector and bitmap data and is supported by virtually all graphic, illustration, and page-layout programs. Adobe applications that produce PostScript artwork include Adobe Illustrator, Adobe Dimensions, and Adobe Streamline. When you open an EPS file containing vector art, it is *rasterized*—the mathematically defined lines and curves of the vector artwork are converted into the pixels or bits of a bitmap image.

You can also bring PostScript artwork into Photoshop or ImageReady using the Place command, the Paste command, and the drag-and-drop feature. (See "Placing files" on page 104, "Using drag and drop to copy between applications" on page 151, and "Using the Clipboard to copy between applications" on page 152.)

To open an EPS file:

1 Choose File > Open.

2 Select the file you want to open, and click Open.

3 Indicate the desired dimensions, resolution, and mode. To maintain the same height-to-width ratio, select Constrain Proportions.

4 Select Anti-aliased to minimize the jagged appearance of the artwork's edges as it is rasterized.

5 Click OK.

Turning off anti-aliasing for PDF and EPS files (ImageReady)

The Anti-alias PostScript option removes jagged edges from a pasted or placed selection by making a subtle transition between the edges of the selection and its surrounding pixels. Turning off this option produces a hard-edged transition between pixels—and therefore the appearance of jagged edges—when vector artwork is rasterized.

Note: In Photoshop, you can deselect the Anti-alias option when you open or place a PDF or EPS file.

To turn off the Anti-alias Postscript option:

1 Choose Edit > Preferences > General.

2 Deselect Anti-alias PostScript. Clearing this option can decrease the time it takes to import the file.

Placing files

You can use the File > Place command to place artwork into a new layer in an image. In Photoshop, you can place PDF, Adobe Illustrator, and EPS files; in ImageReady, you can place files in any supported format, with the exception of Photoshop (PSD) files containing CMYK images.

When you place a PDF, Adobe Illustrator, or EPS file, it is rasterized; you cannot edit text or vector data in placed artwork. Keep in mind that artwork is rasterized at the resolution of the file into which it is placed.

To place a PDF, Adobe Illustrator, or EPS file (Photoshop):

1 Open the Photoshop image into which you want to place the artwork.

2 Choose File > Place, select the file you want to place, and click Place.

3 If you are placing a PDF file that contains multiple pages, select the page you want to place in the provided dialog box, and click OK.

The placed artwork appears inside a bounding box at the center of the Photoshop image. The artwork maintains its original aspect ratio; however, if the artwork is larger than the Photoshop image, it is resized to fit.

4 If desired, reposition the placed artwork by doing one or more of the following:

• Position the pointer inside the bounding box of the placed artwork, and drag.

• In the options bar, enter a value for X to specify the distance between the center point of the placed artwork and the left edge of the image. Enter a value for Y to specify the distance between the center point of the placed artwork and the top edge of the image.

• To adjust the center point of the placed artwork, drag the center point to a new location, or click a handle on the center point icon (▦) in the options bar.

5 If desired, scale the placed artwork by doing one or more of the following:

• Drag one of the handles at the corners or sides of the bounding box. Hold down Shift as you drag a corner handle to constrain the proportions.

• In the options bar, enter values for W and H to specify the width and height of the artwork. By default, these options represent scale as a percentage; however, you can enter another unit of measurement (in, cm, or px). To constrain the proportions of the artwork, click the Constrain Proportions icon (▯); the option is on when the icon has a white background.

6 If desired, rotate the placed artwork by doing one or more of the following:

• Position the pointer outside the bounding box of the placed artwork (the pointer turns into a curved arrow), and drag.

• In the options bar, enter a value (in degrees) for the Rotation option (∠).

The artwork rotates around the center point of the placed artwork. To adjust the center point, drag it to a new location, or click a handle on the Center Point icon (▦) in the options bar.

7 If desired, skew the placed artwork by holding down Ctrl (Windows) or Command (Mac OS), and dragging a side handle of the bounding box.

8 Set the Anti-alias option in the options bar as desired. To blend edge pixels during rasterization, select the Anti-alias option. To produce a hard-edged transition between edge pixels during rasterization, deselect the Anti-alias option.

9 To commit the placed artwork to a new layer, do one of the following:

• Click the OK button (☑) in the options bar.

• Press Enter or Return.

To cancel the placement, click the Cancel button (☒) in the options bar, or press Esc.

To place a file (ImageReady):

1 Open the ImageReady image into which you want to place the file.

2 Choose File > Place, select the file you want to place, and click Open.

3 Select offset options:

• From the Horizontal pop-up menu, choose an option for placing the file horizontally with respect to the ImageReady image. In the Pixels text box, enter the number of pixels to offset the placed image horizontally.

• From the Vertical pop-up menu, choose an option for placing the file vertically with respect to the ImageReady image. In the Pixels text box, enter the number of pixels to offset the placed image vertically.

Note: To enter a negative number (and offset the placed file to the left or below the ImageReady image), type a hyphen (-) before the number.

4 Click OK.

5 If you are placing a PDF file that contains multiple pages, select the page you want to place, and click OK.

6 If you are placing a PDF or EPS file, select Rasterize options, and click OK:

• Enter Width and Height values for Image Size.

• Select Anti-aliased to minimize the jagged appearance of the artwork's edges as it is rasterized.

• Select Constrain Proportions to maintain the same height-to-width ratio.

Managing files with WebDAV

Photoshop and ImageReady offer support for a server technology known as Web Distributed Authoring and Versioning (WebDAV). You can easily connect to a WebDAV server, download and upload files, lock files so others cannot work on them at the same time as you are, and add additional files (called *assets*) to the server. Using a WebDAV server lets you work in a collaborative environment without fear that files will be accidentally overwritten or updates lost.

 For more information, see "Managing files with WebDAV" in online Help.

3

Chapter 3: Working with Color

Familiarity with color theory and termi-nology can help you understand how color is measured and how Adobe Photoshop and Adobe ImageReady use this information to define, display, and print color values.

After you determine the appropriate color mode for your image, you can apply colors and make color and tonal adjustments.

About color modes and models (Photoshop)

A color mode determines the color model used to display and print images. Photoshop bases its color modes on established models for describing and reproducing color. Common models include HSB (hue, saturation, brightness); RGB (red, green, blue); CMYK (cyan, magenta, yellow, black); and CIE L*a*b*. Photoshop also includes modes for specialized color output such as Indexed Color and Duotone. ImageReady uses RGB mode to work with images.

In addition to determining the number of colors that can be displayed in an image, color modes affect the number of channels and the file size of an image.

You can set up the Info palette so that you can select any tool, position the pointer over any part of an image, and determine the color value under the pointer. You can customize the Info palette and color samplers to express color values using HSB, RGB, CMYK, Lab, or Grayscale modes without changing the mode of the image itself. (See the procedure to change Info palette options in "Using the Info palette" on page 63.)

For more information, see "Seeing the color values of pixels (Photoshop)" in online Help.

HSB model

Based on the human perception of color, the HSB model describes three fundamental characteristics of color:

• *Hue* is the color reflected from or transmitted through an object. It is measured as a location on the standard color wheel, expressed as a degree between 0° and 360°. In common use, hue is identified by the name of the color such as red, orange, or green.

• *Saturation*, sometimes called *chroma*, is the strength or purity of the color. Saturation represents the amount of gray in proportion to the hue, measured as a percentage from 0% (gray) to 100% (fully saturated). On the standard color wheel, saturation increases from the center to the edge.

• *Brightness* is the relative lightness or darkness of the color, usually measured as a percentage from 0% (black) to 100% (white).

Although you can use the HSB model in Photoshop to define a color in the Color palette or Color Picker dialog box, there is no HSB mode available for creating and editing images.

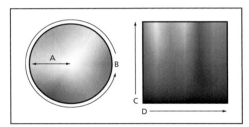

A. *Saturation* **B.** *Hue* **C.** *Brightness* **D.** *All hues*

RGB model

A large percentage of the visible spectrum can be represented by mixing red, green, and blue (RGB) colored light in various proportions and intensities. Where the colors overlap, they create cyan, magenta, yellow, and white.

Because the RGB colors combine to create white, they are also called *additive colors*. Adding all colors together creates white—that is, all light is transmitted back to the eye. Additive colors are used for lighting, video, and monitors. Your monitor, for example, creates color by emitting light through red, green, and blue phosphors.

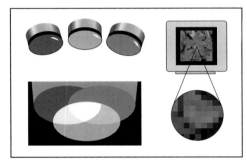

Additive colors (RGB)

RGB mode

Photoshop's RGB mode uses the RGB model, assigning an intensity value to each pixel ranging from 0 (black) to 255 (white) for each of the RGB components in a color image. For example, a bright red color might have an R value of 246, a G value of 20, and a B value of 50. When the values of all three components are equal, the result is a shade of neutral gray. When the value of all components is 255, the result is pure white; when the value is 0, pure black.

RGB images use three colors, or channels, to reproduce up to 16.7 million colors on-screen; the three channels translate to 24 (8 x 3) bits of color information per pixel. (In 16-bit-per-channel images, this translates to 48 bits per pixel, with the ability to reproduce many more colors.) In addition to being the default mode for new Photoshop images, the RGB model is used by computer monitors to display colors. This means that when working in color modes other than RGB, such as CMYK, Photoshop temporarily uses RGB mode for display on-screen.

Although RGB is a standard color model, the exact range of colors represented can vary, depending on the application or display device. Photoshop's RGB mode varies according to the working space setting that you have specified in the Color Settings dialog box. (See "About working spaces" on page 125.)

CMYK model

The CMYK model is based on the light-absorbing quality of ink printed on paper. As white light strikes translucent inks, part of the spectrum is absorbed and part is reflected back to your eyes.

In theory, pure cyan (C), magenta (M), and yellow (Y) pigments should combine to absorb all color and produce black. For this reason these colors are called *subtractive* colors. Because all printing inks contain some impurities, these three inks actually produce a muddy brown and must be combined with black (K) ink to produce a true black. (*K* is used instead of B to avoid confusion with blue.) Combining these inks to reproduce color is called *four-color process printing*.

The subtractive (CMY) and additive (RGB) colors are *complementary colors*. Each pair of subtractive colors creates an additive color, and vice versa.

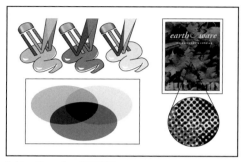

Subtractive colors (CMYK)

CMYK mode

In Photoshop's CMYK mode, each pixel is assigned a percentage value for each of the process inks. The lightest (highlight) colors are assigned small percentages of process ink colors, the darker (shadow) colors higher percentages. For example, a bright red might contain 2% cyan, 93% magenta, 90% yellow, and 0% black. In CMYK images, pure white is generated when all four components have values of 0%.

Use the CMYK mode when preparing an image to be printed using process colors. Converting an RGB image into CMYK creates a *color separation*. If you start with an RGB image, it's best to edit first and then convert to CMYK. In RGB mode, you can use the Proof Setup commands to simulate the effects of a CMYK conversion without changing the actual image data. (See "Soft-proofing colors" on page 131.) You can also use CMYK mode to work directly with CMYK images scanned or imported from high-end systems.

Although CMYK is a standard color model, the exact range of colors represented can vary, depending on the press and printing conditions. Photoshop's CMYK mode varies according to the working space setting that you have specified in the Color Settings dialog box. (See "About working spaces" on page 125.)

L*a*b model

The L*a*b color model is based on the model proposed by the Commission Internationale d'Eclairage (CIE) in 1931 as an international standard for color measurement. In 1976, this model was refined and named CIE L*a*b.

L*a*b color is designed to be *device independent*, creating consistent color regardless of the device (such as a monitor, printer, computer, or scanner) used to create or output the image.

L*a*b color consists of a *luminance* or lightness component (L) and two chromatic components: the *a* component (from green to red) and the *b* component (from blue to yellow).

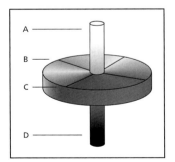

A. Luminance=100 (white)
B. Green to red component
C. Blue to yellow component
D. Luminance=0 (black)

Lab mode

In Photoshop, Lab mode (the asterisks are dropped from the name) has a lightness component (L) that can range from 0 to 100. The *a* component (green-red axis) and the *b* component (blue-yellow axis) can range from +120 to −120.

You can use Lab mode to work with Photo CD images, edit the luminance and the color values in an image independently, move images between systems, and print to PostScript® Level 2 and Level 3 printers. To print Lab images to other color PostScript devices, convert to CMYK first.

Lab color is the intermediate color model Photoshop uses when converting from one color mode to another.

Bitmap mode

This mode uses one of two color values (black or white) to represent the pixels in an image. Images in Bitmap mode are called bitmapped 1-bit images because they have a bit depth of 1.

 For more information, see "Specifying 8-bit color display (Photoshop)" in online Help.

Grayscale mode

This mode uses up to 256 shades of gray. Every pixel of a grayscale image has a brightness value ranging from 0 (black) to 255 (white). Grayscale values can also be measured as percentages of black ink coverage (0% is equal to white, 100% to black). Images produced using black-and-white or grayscale scanners typically are displayed in Grayscale mode.

Although Grayscale is a standard color model, the exact range of grays represented can vary, depending on the printing conditions. In Photoshop, Grayscale mode uses the range defined by the working space setting that you have specified in the Color Settings dialog box. (See "About working spaces" on page 125.)

These guidelines apply to converting images to and from Grayscale mode:

• You can convert both Bitmap-mode and color images to grayscale.

• To convert a color image to a high-quality grayscale image, Photoshop discards all color information in the original image. The gray levels (shades) of the converted pixels represent the luminosity of the original pixels.

You can mix information from the color channels to create a custom grayscale channel by using the Channel Mixer command.

• When converting from grayscale to RGB, the color values for a pixel are based on its previous gray value. A grayscale image can also be converted to a CMYK image (for creating process-color quadtones without converting to Duotone mode) or to a Lab color image.

Duotone mode

This mode creates duotone (two-color), tritone (three-color), and quadtone (four-color) grayscale images using two to four custom inks. (See "Printing duotones" on page 384.)

Indexed Color mode

This mode uses at most 256 colors. When converting to indexed color, Photoshop builds a color lookup table (CLUT), which stores and indexes the colors in the image. If a color in the original image does not appear in the table, the program chooses the closest one or simulates the color using available colors.

By limiting the palette of colors, indexed color can reduce file size while maintaining visual quality—for example, for a multimedia animation application or a Web page. Limited editing is available in this mode. For extensive editing you should convert temporarily to RGB mode. (See "Converting to indexed color (Photoshop)" on page 118.)

Multichannel mode

This mode uses 256 levels of gray in each channel. Multichannel images are useful for specialized printing—for example, converting a duotone for printing in Scitex CT format.

These guidelines apply to converting images to Multichannel mode:

• Channels in the original image become spot color channels in the converted image.

• When you convert a color image to multichannel, the new grayscale information is based on the color values of the pixels in each channel.

• Converting a CMYK image to multichannel creates cyan, magenta, yellow, and black spot channels.

• Converting an RGB image to multichannel creates cyan, magenta, and yellow spot channels.

• Deleting a channel from an RGB, CMYK, or Lab image automatically converts the image to Multichannel mode. (See "About color channels" on page 116 for more information on channels.)

• To export a multichannel image, save it in Photoshop DCS 2.0 format.

Color gamuts (Photoshop)

A *gamut* is the range of colors that a color system can display or print. The spectrum of colors seen by the human eye is wider than the gamut available in any color model.

Among the color models used in Photoshop, L*a*b has the largest gamut, encompassing all colors in the RGB and CMYK gamuts. Typically, the RGB gamut contains the subset of these colors that can be viewed on a computer or television monitor (which emits red, green, and blue light). Therefore, some colors, such as pure cyan or pure yellow, can't be displayed accurately on a monitor.

The CMYK gamut is smaller, consisting only of colors that can be printed using process-color inks. When colors that cannot be printed are displayed on-screen, they are referred to as out-of-gamut colors—that is, outside the CMYK gamut.

 For more information, see "Identifying out-of-gamut colors (Photoshop)" in online Help.

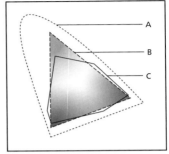

A. Lab color gamut B. RGB color gamut C. CMYK color gamut

Adjusting the monitor display

Although the RGB color model used by computer monitors is capable of displaying much of the visible spectrum, the video system sending data to a given monitor often limits how many colors can be displayed at once. By understanding how color data is measured in digital files and on-screen, you can better adjust color display settings to offset the limitations of your video system.

 For more information, see "Specifying 8-bit color display (Photoshop)" in online Help.

Making previews display more quickly (Photoshop)

The Use Pixel Doubling preference option speeds up the preview of a tool or command's effects by temporarily doubling the size of the pixels (halving the resolution) in the preview. This option has no effect on the pixels in the file; it simply provides faster previews with the tools and commands.

To speed up previews:

1 Choose Edit > Preferences > Display & Cursors.

2 Select Use Pixel Doubling, and click OK.

Adjusting color display for cross-platform variations

RGB color display on a computer monitor varies with the operating system used by the computer. For example, an image appears darker on a Windows system than on a Mac OS computer (because the standard RGB color space is darker in Windows than in Mac OS). The Preview commands in ImageReady enable you to compensate for cross-platform differences in RGB color display during image preview. In Photoshop, you can simulate cross-platform differences by using the Macintosh RGB, Windows RGB, and Monitor RGB commands in the View > Proof Setup menu. (See "Soft-proofing colors" on page 131.)

RGB color display can also vary between Photoshop and ImageReady. In Photoshop, you can select from several RGB color spaces when editing images. As a result, images created in Photoshop may use an RGB color space that differs from the monitor RGB color space used by ImageReady. You can adjust the RGB color display during image preview to compensate for differences between Photoshop and ImageReady.

To adjust RGB color display for cross-platform variations (ImageReady):

Choose View > Preview and choose an option for adjusting the color display:

• Uncompensated Color (the default option) to view the image with no color adjustment.

• Standard Macintosh Color (Windows) to view the image with color adjusted to simulate a standard Macintosh monitor.

• Standard Windows Color (Mac OS) to view the image with color adjusted to simulate a standard Windows monitor.

Note: *These options adjust color display only. No changes are made to pixels in the image.*

To adjust RGB color display to match Photoshop color display (ImageReady):

Choose View > Preview > Use Embedded Color Profile.

Note: In order to use the Use Embedded Color Profile command in ImageReady, you must save the original image, with color profile embedded, in Photoshop.

Channels and bit depth (Photoshop)

A working knowledge of color channels and bit depth is key to understanding how Photoshop stores and displays color information in images.

About color channels

Every Adobe Photoshop image has one or more *channels,* each storing information about color elements in the image. The number of default color channels in an image depends on its color mode. For example, a CMYK image has at least four channels, one each for cyan, magenta, yellow, and black information. Think of a channel as analogous to a plate in the printing process, with a separate plate applying each layer of color.

In addition to these default color channels, extra channels, called *alpha channels,* can be added to an image for storing and editing selections as masks, and spot color channels can be added to add spot color plates for printing. (See "Storing masks in alpha channels" on page 199 and "Adding spot colors (Photoshop)" on page 191.)

An image can have up to 24 channels. By default, Bitmap-mode, grayscale, duotone, and indexed-color images have one channel; RGB and Lab images have three; and CMYK images have four. You can add channels to all image types except Bitmap-mode images.

About bit depth

Bit depth—also called pixel depth or color depth—measures how much color information is available to display or print each pixel in an image. Greater bit depth (more bits of information per pixel) means more available colors and more accurate color representation in the digital image. For example, a pixel with a bit depth of 1 has two possible values: black and white. A pixel with a bit depth of 8 has 2^8, or 256, possible values. And a pixel with a bit depth of 24 has 2^{24}, or roughly 16 million, possible values. Common values for bit depth range from 1 to 64 bits per pixel.

In most cases, Lab, RGB, grayscale, and CMYK images contain 8 bits of data per color channel. This translates to a 24-bit Lab bit depth (8 bits x 3 channels); a 24-bit RGB bit depth (8 bits x 3 channels); an 8-bit grayscale bit depth (8 bits x 1 channel); and a 32-bit CMYK bit depth (8 bits x 4 channels). Photoshop can also read and import Lab, RGB, CMYK, and grayscale images that contain 16 bits of data per color channel.

Converting between bit depths

A 16-bit-per-channel image provides finer distinctions in color, but it can have twice the file size of an 8-bit-per-channel image. In addition, only the following Photoshop tools and commands are available for 16-bit-per-channel images:

• The marquee, lasso, crop, measure, zoom, hand, pen, eyedropper, history brush, slice, color sampler, and clone stamp tools, as well as the pen and shape tools (for drawing work paths only).

• The Duplicate, Feather, Modify, Levels, Auto Levels, Auto Contrast, Curves, Histogram, Hue/Saturation, Brightness/Contrast, Color Balance, Equalize, Invert, Channel Mixer, Gradient Map, Image Size, Canvas Size, Transform Selection, and Rotate Canvas commands, and a limited set of filters.

 For more information, see "Using filters" in online Help.

To take full advantage of Photoshop features, you can convert a 16-bit-per-channel image to an 8-bit-per-channel image.

To convert between 8 bits per channel and 16 bits per channel:

1 To convert to a 16-bit-per-channel image, first flatten the image. (See "Flattening all layers" on page 248.)

2 Choose Image > Mode > 16 Bits/Channel or 8 Bits/Channel.

Converting between color modes (Photoshop)

When you choose a different color mode for an image, you permanently change the color values in the image. For example, when you convert an RGB image to CMYK mode, RGB color values outside the CMYK gamut (defined by the CMYK working space setting in the Color Settings dialog box) are adjusted to fall within gamut. Consequently, before converting images, it's best to do the following:

• Do as much editing as possible in the image's original mode (usually RGB from most scanners, or CMYK from traditional drum scanners or if imported from a Scitex system).

• Save a backup copy before converting. Be sure to save a copy of your image that includes all layers in order to edit the original version of the image after the conversion.

• Flatten the file before converting it. The interaction of colors between layer blending modes will change when the mode changes.

To convert an image to another mode:

Choose Image > Mode and the mode you want from the submenu. Modes not available for the active image appear dimmed in the menu.

Images are flattened when converted to Multichannel, Bitmap, or Indexed Color mode, because these modes do not support layers.

 For more information, see "Converting between Grayscale and Bitmap modes (Photoshop)" in online Help.

Converting to indexed color (Photoshop)

Converting to indexed color reduces the number of colors in the image to at most 256—the standard number of colors supported by the GIF and PNG-8 formats and many multimedia applications. This conversion reduces file size by deleting color information from the image.

To convert to indexed color, you must start with either a grayscale or RGB image.

To convert a grayscale or RGB image to indexed color:

1 Choose Image > Mode > Indexed Color.

Note: *The image must be flattened first, or you will lose layers.*

For grayscale images, the conversion happens automatically. For RGB images, the Indexed Color dialog box appears.

2 Select Preview the Indexed Color dialog box to display a preview of the changes.

3 Specify conversion options.

For information on conversion options and customizing indexed color tables, see "Conversion options for indexed-color images (Photoshop)" in online Help.

4 Click OK.

Applying colors

Once you have set up the color mode for an image, you can specify a foreground and background color by using the eyedropper tool, the Color palette, the Swatches palette, or a color picker. Photoshop uses the foreground color to paint, fill, and stroke selections and the background color to make gradient fills and fill in erased areas of an image. The foreground and background colors are also used by some special-effects filters.

For information on specifying foreground and background colors; using the painting, erasing, art history, and gradient tools; and filling and stroking selections and layers, see "Painting" in online Help. For information on filters, see "Applying filters for special effects" in online Help.

Making color and tonal adjustments

When you photograph, scan, or resample images, you can often introduce problems involving color quality and tonal range. Photoshop provides a comprehensive set of tools for making color and tonal corrections and sharpening the overall focus of an image. ImageReady provides many of the basic correction tools.

 For more information, see "Making color and tonal adjustments" in online Help.

4

Chapter 4: Producing Consistent Color (Photoshop)

When your document must meet color standards set by clients and designers, viewing and editing color consistently becomes critical, all the way from scanning source images to creating final output. A color management system reconciles color differences among devices so that you can be reasonably certain of the colors your system ultimately produces.

Why colors sometimes don't match

No device in a publishing system is capable of reproducing the full range of colors viewable to the human eye. Each device operates within a specific color space, which can produce a certain range, or *gamut*, of colors.

The RGB (red, green, blue) and CMYK (cyan, magenta, yellow, black) color modes represent two main categories of color spaces. The gamuts of the RGB and CMYK spaces are very different; while the RGB gamut is generally larger (that is, capable of representing more colors) than CMYK, some CMYK colors still fall outside the RGB gamut. (See "Color gamuts (Photoshop)" on page 114 for an illustration.) In addition, different devices produce slightly different gamuts within

the same color mode. For example, a variety of RGB spaces can exist among scanners and monitors, and a variety of CMYK spaces can exist among printing presses.

Because of these varying color spaces, colors can shift in appearance as you transfer documents between different devices. Color variations can result from different image sources (scanners and software produce art using different color spaces), differences in the way software applications define color, differences in print media (newsprint paper reproduces a smaller gamut than magazine-quality paper), and other natural variations, such as manufacturing differences in monitors or monitor age.

About color management

Because color-matching problems result from various devices and software using different color spaces, one solution is to have a system that interprets and translates color accurately between devices. A color management system (CMS) compares the color space in which a color was created to the color space in which the same color will be output, and makes the necessary adjustments to represent the color as consistently as possible among different devices.

Note: Don't confuse color management with color adjustment or color correction. A CMS won't correct an image that was saved with tonal or color balance problems. It provides an environment where you can evaluate images reliably in the context of your final output.

Photoshop follows a color management workflow based on conventions developed by the International Color Consortium (ICC). The following elements and concepts are integral to such a color-managed workflow.

Color management engine Different companies have developed various ways to manage color. To provide you with a choice, a color management system lets you choose a *color management engine* that represents the approach you want to use. Sometimes called the *color management module (CMM)*, the color management engine is the part of the CMS that does the work of reading and translating colors between different color spaces.

Color numbers Each pixel in an image document has a set of *color numbers* that describe the pixel's location in a particular color mode—for example, red, green, and blue values for the RGB mode. However, the actual appearance of the pixel may vary when output or displayed on different devices, because each device has a particular way of translating the raw numbers into visual color. (See "Why colors sometimes don't match" on

page 121.) When you apply color and tonal adjustments or convert a document to a different color space, you are changing the document's color numbers.

Color profiles An ICC workflow uses *color profiles* to determine how color numbers in a document translate to actual color appearances. A profile systematically describes how color numbers map to a particular color space, usually that of a device such as a scanner, printer, or monitor. By associating, or *tagging,* a document with a color profile, you provide a definition of actual color appearances in the document; changing the associated profile changes the color appearances. (For information on displaying the current profile name in the status bar, see "Displaying file and image information" on page 78.) Documents without associated profiles are known as *untagged* and contain only raw color numbers. When working with untagged documents, Photoshop uses the current working space profile to display and edit colors. (See "About working spaces" on page 125.)

Do you need color management?

Use the following guidelines to determine whether or not you need to use color management:

• You might not need color management if your production process is tightly controlled for one medium only, for example, if you're using a closed system where all devices are calibrated to the same specifications. You or your prepress service provider may prefer to tailor CMYK images and specify color values for a known, specific set of printing conditions.

• You also might not need color management if you are producing images for the Web or other screen-based output, since you cannot control the color management settings of monitors displaying your final output. It is helpful, however, to use the Web Graphics Defaults setting when preparing such images, because this setting reflects the average RGB space of many monitors. (See "Using predefined color management settings" on page 124.)

• You can benefit from color management if you have more variables in your production process (for example, if you're using an open system with multiple platforms and multiple devices from different manufacturers). Color management is recommended if you anticipate reusing color graphics for print and online media, if you manage multiple workstations, or if you plan to print to different domestic and international presses. If you decide to use color management, consult with your production partners—such as graphic artists and prepress service providers—to ensure that all aspects of your color management workflow integrate seamlessly with theirs.

Creating a viewing environment for color management

Your work environment influences how you see color on your monitor and on printed output. For best results, control the colors and light in your work environment by doing the following:

• View your documents in an environment that provides a consistent light level and color temperature. For example, the color characteristics of sunlight change throughout the day and alter the way colors appear on your screen, so keep shades closed or work in a windowless room. To eliminate the blue-green cast from fluorescent lighting, consider installing D50 (5000 degree Kelvin) lighting. Ideally, view printed documents using a D50 lightbox or using the ANSI PH2.30 viewing standard for graphic arts.

• View your document in a room with neutral-colored walls and ceiling. A room's color can affect the perception of both monitor color and printed color. The best color for a viewing room is polychromatic gray. Also, the color of your clothing reflecting off the glass of your monitor may affect the appearance of colors on-screen.

• Match the light intensity in the room or variable lightbox to the light intensity of your monitor. View continuous-tone art, printed output, and images on-screen under the same intensity of light.

• Remove colorful background and user-interface patterns on your monitor desktop. Busy or bright patterns surrounding a document interfere with accurate color perception. Set your desktop to display neutral grays only.

• View document proofs in the real-world conditions under which your audience will see the final piece. For example, you might want to see how a housewares catalog looks under the incandescent light bulbs used in homes, or view an office furniture catalog under the fluorescent lighting used in offices. However, always make final color judgements under the lighting conditions specified by the legal requirements for contract proofs in your country.

Setting up color management

Photoshop simplifies the task of setting up a color-managed workflow by gathering most color management controls in a single Color Settings dialog box. You can choose from a list of predefined color management settings, or you can adjust the controls manually to create your own custom settings. You can even save customized settings to share them with other users and other Adobe applications, such as Illustrator 9.0, that use the Color Settings dialog box.

Photoshop also uses color management policies, which determine how to handle color data that does not immediately match your current color management workflow. Policies provide guidelines on what to do when you open a document or import color data into an active document.

To specify color management settings:

1 Choose Edit > Color Settings.

To display helpful descriptions of the options that appear in the dialog box, position the pointer over a section heading or menu item. These descriptions appear in the lower area of the dialog box.

2 Do one of the following:

• To set up a predefined color management workflow, see "Using predefined color management settings" on page 124.

• To customize your own color management settings, see "Customizing color management settings" on page 126.

3 Click OK.

Using predefined color management settings

Photoshop offers a collection of predefined color management settings designed to produce consistent color for a common publishing workflow, such as preparation for Web or offset press output. In most cases, the predefined settings will provide sufficient color management for your needs. These settings can also serve as starting points for customizing your own workflow-specific settings.

To choose a predefined color management setting, choose one of the following options from the Settings menu in the Color Settings dialog box.

Color Management Off Uses passive color management techniques to emulate the behavior of applications that do not support color management. Although working space profiles are considered when converting colors between color spaces, Color Management Off does not tag documents with profiles. Use this option for content that will be output on video or as on-screen presentations; do not use this option if you work mostly with documents that are tagged with color profiles.

Emulate Photoshop 4 Emulates the color workflow used by the Mac OS version of Adobe Photoshop 4.0 and earlier.

U.S. Prepress Defaults Manages color for content that will be output under common press conditions in the U.S.

Europe Prepress Defaults Manages color for content that will be output under common press conditions in Europe.

Japan Prepress Defaults Manages color for content that will be output under common press conditions in Japan.

Web Graphics Defaults Manages color for content that will be published on the World Wide Web.

ColorSync Workflow (Mac OS only) Manages color using the ColorSync CMS with the profiles chosen in the ColorSync control panel. Use this option if you want to use color management with a mix of Adobe and non-Adobe applications. This color management configuration is not recognized by Windows systems, or by versions of ColorSync earlier than 3.0.

When you choose a predefined configuration, the Color Settings dialog box updates to display the specific color management settings associated with the configuration.

About working spaces

Among other options, predefined color management settings specify the color profiles to be associated with the RGB, CMYK, and Grayscale color modes. The settings also specify the color profile for spot colors in a document. Central to the color management workflow, these profiles are known as *working spaces*. The working spaces specified by predefined settings represent the color profiles that will produce the best color fidelity for several common output conditions. For example, the U.S. Prepress Defaults setting uses a CMYK working space that is designed to preserve color consistency under standard Specifications for Web Offset Publications (SWOP) press conditions.

A working space acts as the color profile for untagged documents and newly created documents that use the associated color mode. For example, if Adobe RGB (1998) is the current RGB working space, each new RGB document that you create will use colors within the Adobe RGB (1998) color space. Working spaces also define the destination color space of documents converted to RGB, CMYK, or Grayscale color mode.

About color management policies

When you specify a predefined color management setting, Photoshop sets up a color management workflow that will be used as the standard for all documents and color data that you open or import. For a newly created document, the color workflow operates relatively seamlessly: the document uses the working space profile associated with its color mode for creating and editing colors.

However, it is common to encounter the following exceptions to your color-managed workflow:

• You might open a document or import color data (for example, by copying and pasting or dragging and dropping) from a document that is not tagged with a profile. This is often the case when you open a document created in an application that either does not support color management or has color management turned off.

• You might open a document or import color data from a document that is tagged with a profile different from the current working space. This may be the case when you open a document that has been created using different color management settings, or a document that has been scanned and tagged with a scanner profile.

In either case, Photoshop must decide how to handle the color data in the document. A *color management policy* looks for the color profile associated with an opened document or imported color data, and compares the profile (or lack of profile) with the current working space to make default color management decisions. If the profile is missing or does not match the working space, Photoshop displays a message that indicates the default action for the policy. In many cases you will also be provided with the opportunity to choose

another action. For detailed information on the color management decisions associated with different policies, see "Specifying color management policies" on page 128.

Working with policy warnings and messages

The predefined color management workflows are set to display warning or option messages when a default color management policy is about to be used. Although you can disable the repeated display of some warning and messages by selecting the Don't Show Again option, it is highly recommended that you continue to display all policy messages, to ensure the appropriate color management of documents on a case-by-case basis. (See "Resetting all warning dialogs" on page 87.) You should only turn off message displays if you are very confident that you understand the default policy decision and are willing to accept it for all documents that you open. You cannot undo the results of a default policy decision once a document has been saved.

Customizing color management settings

Although the predefined settings should provide sufficient color management for many publishing workflows, you may sometimes want to customize individual options in a configuration. For example, you might want to change the CMYK working space to a profile that matches the proofing system used by your service bureau.

It's important to save your custom configurations so that you can reuse and share them with other users and Adobe applications that use the same color management workflows. The color management settings that you customize in the Color Settings dialog box have an associated preferences file called Color Settings.csf, found in the Adobe Photoshop 6 Settings folder.

Note: *The default location of the Adobe Photoshop 6 Settings folder varies by operating system; use your operating system's Find command to locate this folder.*

To customize color management settings:

1 Choose Edit > Color Settings.

2 To use a preset color management configuration as the starting point for your customization, choose that configuration from the Settings menu.

3 Specify the desired color settings. As you make adjustments, the Settings menu option changes to Custom by default.

For detailed customization instructions, see "Specifying working spaces" on page 127, "Specifying color management policies" on page 128, and "Customizing advanced color management settings" on page 130.

4 Save your custom configuration so that it can be reused. (See "Saving and loading color management settings" on page 130.)

5 Click OK.

Specifying working spaces

In a color-managed workflow, each color mode must have a working space profile associated with it. (See "About working spaces" on page 125.) Photoshop ships with a standard set of color profiles that have been recommended and tested by Adobe Systems for most color management workflows. By default, only these profiles appear in the working space menus.

To display additional color profiles that you have customized or installed on your system, select Advanced Mode in the Color Settings dialog box. To appear in a working space menu, a color profile must be bidirectional, that is, contain specifications for translating both into and out of color spaces. You can also create a custom RGB, CMYK, Grayscale, or Spot working space profile to describe the color space of a particular output or display device.

For more information, see "Creating custom RGB profiles," "Creating custom CMYK profiles," and "Creating custom grayscale and spot-color profiles" in online Help.

For information about a specified RGB or CMYK working space profile, see the Description area of the Color Settings dialog box. (See "Setting up color management" on page 124.) The following information can help you specify an appropriate Gray or Spot working space:

• You can specify a Gray or Spot working space profile that is based on the characteristics of a particular dot gain. *Dot gain* occurs when a printer's halftone dots change as the ink spreads and is absorbed by paper. Photoshop calculates dot gain as the amount by which the expected dot increases or decreases. For example, a 50% halftone screen may produce an actual density of 60% on the printed page, exhibiting a dot gain of 10%. The Dot Gain 10% option represents the color space that reflects the grayscale characteristics of this particular dot gain.

Proof (no dot gain), and printed image (with dot gain)

• You can also specify a Gray working space profile that is based on the characteristics of particular gamma. A monitor's *gamma setting* determines the brightness of midtones displayed by the monitor. Gray Gamma 1.8 matches the default grayscale display of Mac OS computers and is also the default grayscale space for Photoshop 4.0 and earlier. Gray Gamma 2.2 matches the default grayscale display of Windows computers.

Specifying color management policies

Each predefined color management configuration sets up a color management policy for the RGB, CMYK, and Grayscale color modes and displays warning messages to let you override the default policy behavior on a case-by-case basis. If desired, you can change the default policy behavior to

reflect a color management workflow that you use more often. For more information on policies, see "About color management policies" on page 125.

To customize color management policies:

1 In the Color Settings dialog box, under Color Management Policies, choose one of the following to set the default color management policy for each color mode:

• Off if you do not want to color-manage imported or opened color data.

• Preserve Embedded Profiles if you anticipate working with a mix of color-managed and non-color-managed documents, or with documents that use different profiles within the same color mode.

• Convert to Working Space if you want to force all documents to use the current working space.

For detailed descriptions of the default behaviors associated with each policy option, see the table following this procedure.

2 For Profile Mismatches, select either, both, or neither of the following:

• Ask When Opening to display a message whenever you open a document tagged with a profile other than the current working space. You will be given the option to override the policy's default behavior.

• Ask When Pasting to display a message whenever color profile mismatches occur as colors are imported into a document (via pasting, drag-and-drop, placing, and so on). You will be given the option to override the policy's default behavior.

The availability of options for Profile Mismatches depends on which policies have been specified.

3 For Missing Profiles, select Ask When Opening to display a message whenever you open an untagged document. You will be given the option to override the policy's default behavior.

The availability of options for Missing Profiles depends on which policies have been specified.

It is strongly recommended that you keep the Ask When Opening and Ask When Pasting options selected.

Policy option	Default color management behavior
Off	• New documents and existing untagged documents remain untagged. • Existing documents tagged with a profile other than the current working space become untagged. • Existing documents tagged with the current working space profile remain tagged. • For color data imported into a document using the same color mode, color numbers are preserved. • For all other import cases, colors are converted to the document's color space.

Policy option	Default color management behavior
Preserve Embedded Profiles	• New documents are tagged with the current working space profile. • Existing documents tagged with a profile other than the current working space remain tagged with the original embedded profile. • Existing untagged documents use the current working space for editing but remain untagged. • For color data imported within the same color mode between either a non-color-managed source or destination, or from a CMYK document into a CMYK document, color numbers are preserved. • For all other import cases, colors are converted to the document's color space.
Convert to Working Space	• New documents are tagged with the current working space profile. • Existing documents tagged with a profile other than the current working space are converted to and tagged with the working space profile. • Existing untagged documents use the current working space for editing but remain untagged. • For color data imported within the same color mode between either a non-color-managed source or destination, color numbers are preserved. • For all other import cases, colors are converted to the document's color space.

Customizing advanced color management settings

When you select Advanced Mode at the top of the Color Settings dialog box, you have the option of further customizing settings used for color management.

For detailed information on advanced color management settings, see "Specifying a color management engine," "Specifying a rendering intent," "Using black-point compensation," "Using dither," "Desaturating monitor colors," and "Blending RGB colors" in online Help.

Saving and loading color management settings

When you create a custom color management configuration, you should name and save the configuration to ensure that it can be shared with other users and applications that use the Color Settings dialog box, such as Adobe Illustrator 9.0. You can also load previously saved color management configurations into the Color Settings dialog box.

To save a custom color management configuration:

1 In the Color Settings dialog box, click Save.

2 Name your color settings file, and click Save.

To ensure that the saved configuration appears in the Settings menu of the Color Settings dialog box, save the file in one of the following recommended locations:

• (Windows) Program Files/Common Files/ Adobe/Color/Settings.

• (Mac OS) System Folder/Application Support/ Adobe/Color/Settings.

3 Enter any comments that you want to associate with the configuration, and click OK.

The comments that you enter will appear in the Description area of the Color Settings dialog box when the pointer is positioned over the configuration in the Settings menu.

To load a color management configuration:

1 In the Color Settings dialog box, click Load.

2 Locate and select the desired color settings file, and click Load.

When you load a custom color settings file, it appears as the active choice in the Settings menu of the Color Settings dialog box. If you load a settings file that has been saved outside the recommended location, it temporarily replaces the Other option in the Settings menu until another settings file is loaded.

Synchronizing color management between applications

The Color Settings dialog box represents the common color management controls shared by several Adobe applications, including Photoshop 6.0 and Illustrator 9.0. If you modify and save over the current color settings file in any application other than Photoshop, you may be prompted to synchronize the common color settings upon starting Photoshop or upon reopening the Color Settings dialog box in Photoshop.

Synchronizing the color settings helps to ensure that color is reproduced consistently between Adobe applications that use the Color Settings dialog box. To share custom color settings between applications, be sure to save and load the settings file in the desired applications. (See "Saving and loading color management settings" on page 130.)

Soft-proofing colors

In a traditional publishing workflow, you print a hard proof of your document to preview how the document's colors will look when reproduced on a specific output device. In a color-managed workflow, you can use the precision of color profiles to *soft-proof* your document directly on the monitor—to display an on-screen preview of the document's colors as reproduced on a specified device. In addition, you can use your printer to produce a hard-proof version of this soft proof. (See "Using color management when printing" on

page 382.) The following diagram shows how the source document profile, proof profile, and monitor profile are used to represent colors in a soft proof.

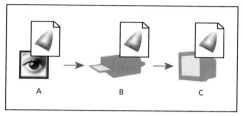

A. Document space B. Proof space C. Monitor space

Keep in mind that the reliability of the soft proof is highly dependent upon the quality of your monitor, your monitor profile, and the ambient lighting conditions of your work station. (See "Creating an ICC monitor profile" on page 136.)

To display a soft proof:

1 Choose View > Proof Setup, and choose the proof profile space that you want to simulate:

• Custom soft-proofs colors using the color profile of a specific output device. Follow the instructions after this procedure to set up the custom proof.

• Working CMYK soft-proofs colors using the current CMYK working space as defined in the Color Settings dialog box.

• Working Cyan Plate, Working Magenta Plate, Working Yellow Plate, Working Black Plate, or Working CMY Plates soft-proofs specific CMYK ink colors using the current CMYK working space.

• Macintosh RGB or Windows RGB soft-proofs colors in an image using either a standard Mac OS or Windows monitor as the proof profile space to simulate. Neither option is available for CMYK documents.

• Monitor RGB soft-proofs colors in an RGB document using your current monitor color space as the proof profile space. This option is unavailable for CMYK documents.

• Simulate Paper White previews the specific shade of white exhibited by the print medium defined by a document's profile. This option is not available for all profiles and is available only for soft-proofing, not printing.

• Simulate Ink Black previews the actual dynamic range defined by a document's profile. This option is not available for all profiles and is available only for soft-proofing, not printing.

2 Choose View > Proof Colors to turn the soft-proof display on and off. When soft proofing is on, a checkmark appears next to the Proof Colors command.

When soft proofing is on, the name of the current proof profile appears in the document's title bar.

To create a custom proof setup:

1 Choose View > Proof Setup > Custom.

💡 *If you want the custom proof setup to be the default proof setup for documents, close all document windows before choosing the View > Proof Setup > Custom command.*

2 Select Preview to display a live preview of the proof settings in the document while the Proof Setup dialog box is open. This preview appears only when you enable the Proof Colors command.

3 To use an existing proof setup as a starting point, choose it from the Setup menu. If the desired setup does not appear in the menu, click Load to locate and load the setup.

4 For Profile, choose the color profile for the device for which you want to create the proof.

5 If the proof profile you chose uses the same color mode as the document, do one of the following:

• Select Preserve Color Numbers to simulate how the document will appear without converting colors from the document space to the proof profile space. This simulates the color shifts that may occur when the document's color values are interpreted using the proof profile instead of the document profile.

• Deselect Preserve Color Numbers to simulate how the document will appear if colors are converted from the document space to their nearest equivalents in the proof profile space in an effort to preserve the colors' visual appearances. Then specify a rendering intent for the conversion.

🖰 For more information, see "Specifying a rendering intent" in online Help.

6 If needed, select any of the following:

• Simulate Paper White to preview, in the monitor space, the specific shade of white exhibited by the print medium described by the proof profile. Selecting this option automatically selects the Simulate Ink Black option.

• Simulate Ink Black to preview, in the monitor space, the actual dynamic range defined by the proof profile.

The availability of these options depends on the proof profile chosen. Not all profiles support both options.

7 To save your custom proof setup as a preset proof setup, click Save. To ensure that the new preset appears in the View > Proof Setup menu, save the preset in the Program Files/Common Files/Adobe/Color/Proofing folder (Windows) or the System Folder/Application Support/Adobe/Color/Proofing folder (Mac OS).

8 Click OK.

Changing the color profile of a document

In some cases you may want to convert a document's colors to a different color profile, tag a document with a different color profile without making color conversions, or remove the profile from a document altogether. For example, you may want to prepare the document for a different output destination, or you may want to correct a policy behavior that you no longer want implemented on the document. The Assign Profile and Convert to Profile commands are recommended only for advanced users.

When using the Assign Profile command, you may see a shift in color appearance as color numbers are mapped directly to the new profile space. Convert Profile, however, shifts color numbers before mapping them to the new profile space, in an effort to preserve the original color appearances.

To reassign or discard the profile of a document:

1 Choose Image > Mode > Assign Profile.

2 Select one of the following:

• Don't Color Manage This Document to remove the profile from a tagged document. Select this option only if you are sure that you want the document to become untagged.

• Working *color mode: working space* to tag the document with the current working space profile.

• Profile to reassign a different profile to a tagged document. Choose the desired profile from the menu. Photoshop tags the document with the new profile without converting colors to the profile space. This may dramatically change the appearance of the colors as displayed on your monitor.

3 To preview the effects of the new profile assignment in the document, select Preview.

4 Click OK.

To convert colors in a document to another profile:

1 Choose Image > Mode > Convert to Profile.

2 Under Destination Space, choose the color profile to which you want to convert the document's colors. The document will be converted to and tagged with this new profile.

3 Under Conversion Options, specify a color management engine, a rendering intent, and black point and dither options.

🖥️❓ For more information, see "Customizing advanced color management settings" in online Help.

4 To flatten all layers of the document onto a single layer upon conversion, select Flatten Image.

5 To preview the effects of the conversion in the document, select Preview. This preview becomes more accurate if you select Flatten Image.

6 Click OK.

Embedding profiles in saved documents

By default, a tagged document will have its profile information embedded upon saving in a file format that supports embedded ICC profiles. Untagged documents are saved by default without embedded profiles.

You can specify whether or not to embed a profile as you save a document; you can also specify to convert colors to the proof profile space and embed the proof profile instead. However, changing the profile-embedding behavior is recommended only for advanced users who are familiar with color management.

To change the embedding behavior of a profile in a document:

1 Choose File > Save As.

2 Do one of the following:

• To toggle the embedding of the document's current color profile, select or deselect ICC Profile (Windows) or Embed Color Profile (Mac OS). This option is available only for the native Photoshop format (.psd) and PDF, JPEG, TIFF, EPS, DCS, and PICT formats.

• To toggle the embedding of the document's current proof profile, select or deselect Use Proof Setup (available for PDF, EPS, DCS 1.0, and DCS 2.0 formats only). Selecting this option converts the document's colors to the proof profile space and is useful for creating an output file for print. For information on setting up a proof profile, see "Soft-proofing colors" on page 131.

3 Name the document, choose other save options, and click Save.

Obtaining, installing, and updating color profiles

Precise, consistent color management requires accurate ICC-compliant profiles of all of your color devices. For example, without an accurate scanner profile, a perfectly scanned image may appear incorrect in another program, simply due to any difference in color space between the scanner and the program displaying the image. This misleading representation may cause you to make unnecessary, time-wasting, and potentially damaging "corrections" to an already satisfactory image. With an accurate profile, a program importing the image can correct for any gamut differences and display a scan's actual colors.

Once you obtain accurate profiles, they will work with all applications that are compatible with your color-management system. You can obtain profiles in the following ways, with the most precise methods listed first:

• Generate profiles customized for your specific devices using professional profiling equipment.

• Use the settings in the Custom CMYK dialog box to describe your device, and then save the settings as a color profile.

For more information, see "Creating custom CMYK profiles" in online Help.

• Obtain a profile created by the manufacturer. Unfortunately, such profiles do not account for individual variations that naturally occur among machines (even identical modes from the same manufacturer) or from age.

• Substitute an available profile that may be appropriate for the device's color space. For example, many Mac OS scanners have been optimized for an Apple RGB monitor color space, so you might try using an Apple monitor profile for these devices; for a non-profiled Windows scanner, try substituting the sRGB color space. Be sure to proof images created with the profile before using the profile in production.

Adding device profiles to the color management system

You can add color profiles to your system so that they appear as choices in the Color Settings dialog box. To minimize confusion when working with profiles, delete any profiles for devices not used by you or your workgroup. Once you have added a profile to the recommend location on your system, you may need to load it or restart Photoshop so that the profile appears in the Color Settings dialog box.

Note: *In Mac OS, you can organize the ColorSync Profiles folder by creating additional folders within it, or adding aliases to other folders. However, nested folders may cause conflicts with some applications, such as Adobe PressReady.*

To add profiles to your system:

Copy profiles to one of the following recommended locations:

• (Windows 2000) WinNT/System/Spool/ Drivers/Color.

• (Windows NT) WinNT/System32/Color.

• (Windows 98) Windows/System/Color.

• (Mac OS) System Folder/ColorSync Profiles.

Note: *If you use ColorSync 2.5 but have used earlier versions, some profiles may still be stored in the System Folder/Preferences/ColorSync™ Profiles folder on your hard disk. For compatibility with ColorSync 2.5 or later, store profiles in the ColorSync Profiles folder in the System Folder.*

Updating profiles

The color reproduction characteristics of a color device change as it ages, so recalibrate devices periodically and generate updated profiles. Profiles should be good for approximately a month depending on the device. Some monitors automatically compensate for phosphor aging.

Also, recalibrate a device when you change any of the factors that affect calibration. For example, recalibrate your monitor when you change the room lighting or the monitor brightness setting.

Creating an ICC monitor profile

Your monitor will display color more reliably if you use color management and accurate ICC profiles. The Adobe Gamma utility, which is automatically installed into your Control Panels folder, lets you calibrate and characterize your monitor to a standard and then save the settings as an ICC-compliant profile available to any program that uses your color management system.
This calibration helps you eliminate any color cast in your monitor, make your monitor grays as neutral as possible, and standardize image display across different monitors.

Although Adobe Gamma is an effective calibration and profiling utility, hardware-based utilities are more precise. If you have a hardware-based utility that can generate an ICC-compliant profile, you should use that instead of Adobe Gamma. Also, be sure to use only one calibration utility to display your profile; using multiple utilities can result in incorrect color.

For more information, see "Calibrating versus characterizing a monitor," "About monitor calibration settings," "Guidelines for creating an ICC monitor profile," and "Calibrating with Adobe Gamma" in online Help.

5

Chapter 5: Selecting

To modify part of an image in Adobe Photoshop or Adobe ImageReady, you first select the area you want to edit. A selected area is indicated by a dotted selection border, also called a selection marquee. The area outside the selection border is protected while you move, copy, paint, or apply special effects to the isolated area.

You can choose from a variety of specialized tools for creating selection borders.

About selections

Since there are two different types of data in your image—bitmap and vector—you need to use separate sets of tools to make selections of each type. You can use selection borders to select pixels. When you select pixels, you are selecting resolution dependent information in the image. For more information about bitmap images and vector graphics, see "About bitmap images and vector graphics" on page 91.

You can also create selections using the pen or shape tools, which produce precise outlines called *paths*. A path is a vector shape that contains no pixels. (See "Moving, copying, and pasting selections and layers" on page 149.) You can convert paths to selections or convert selections to paths. (See "Converting between paths and selection borders (Photoshop)" on page 180.)

In Photoshop, you can use the Extract command to isolate an object from its background and erase the background to transparency. You can also make sophisticated selections using masks. (See "Saving a mask selection" on page 200.)

Making pixel selections

You can select pixels in an image by dragging with the marquee tools or lasso tools, or by targeting color areas with the magic wand tool. In Photoshop, you can also use the Color Range command. Making a new selection replaces the existing one. Additionally, you can create selections that add to a selection, subtract from a selection, select an area intersected by other selections, or select the union of a new selection and the current selection.

Using the Select menu

You can use commands in the Select menu to select all pixels, to deselect, or to reselect.

To select all pixels on a layer within the canvas boundaries:

1 Select the layer in the Layers palette.

2 Choose Select > All.

To deselect selections:

Do one of the following:

• Choose Select > Deselect.

• If you are using the rectangle marquee, rounded rectangle marquee (ImageReady), elliptical marquee, or lasso tool, click anywhere in the image outside the selected area.

To reselect the most recent selection:

Choose Select > Reselect.

Using the marquee tools

The marquee tools let you select rectangles, ellipses, rounded rectangles (ImageReady), and 1-pixel rows and columns. By default, a selection border is dragged from its corner.

To use the marquee tools:

1 Select a marquee tool:

• Rectangle marquee (⬚) to make a rectangular selection.

• Rounded rectangle marquee (⬚) to select a rounded rectangle such as a Web-page button (ImageReady).

• Elliptical marquee (◯) to make an elliptical selection.

• Single row (⬚) or single column (⬚) marquee to define the border as a 1-pixel-wide row or column.

2 In the options bar, specify whether to add a new selection (■), add to a selection (■), subtract from a selection (■), or select an area intersected by other selections (■).

3 Specify a feathering setting in the options bar. Turn anti-aliasing on or off for the rounded rectangle or elliptical marquee. (See "Softening the edges of a selection" on page 147.)

4 For the rectangle, rounded rectangle, or elliptical marquee, choose a style in the options bar:

• Normal to determine marquee proportions by dragging.

• Constrained Aspect Ratio to set a height-to-width ratio. Enter values (decimal values are valid) for the aspect ratio. For example, to draw a marquee twice as wide as it is high, enter 2 for the width and 1 for the height.

• Fixed Size to specify set values for the marquee's height and width. Enter pixel values in whole numbers. Keep in mind that the number of pixels needed to create a 1-inch selection depends on the resolution of the image. (See "About image size and resolution" on page 92.)

5 For aligning your selection to guides, a grid, slices, or document bounds, do one of the following to snap your selection:

• (Photoshop) Choose View > Snap or View > Snap To then choose a command from the submenu. The marquee selection can snap to a document bound and more than one Photoshop Extra. This is controlled in the Snap To menu. (See "Working with snap" on page 152.)

• (ImageReady) Choose View > Snap To > Guides.

6 Do one of the following to make a selection:

• With the rectangle, rounded rectangle, or elliptical marquee, drag over the area you want to select. Hold down Shift as you drag to constrain the marquee to a square or circle. To drag a marquee from its center, hold down Alt (Windows) or Option (Mac OS) after you begin dragging.

• With the single row or single column marquee, click near the area you want to select, and then drag the marquee to the exact location. If no marquee is visible, increase the magnification of your image view.

To reposition a rectangle, rounded rectangle, or elliptical marquee, first drag to create the border, keeping the mouse button depressed. Then hold down the spacebar and continue to drag. If you have finished drawing the border, drag from inside the selection.

Using the lasso, polygonal lasso, and magnetic lasso tools

The lasso and polygonal lasso tools let you draw both straight-edged and freehand segments of a selection border. With the magnetic lasso tool (Photoshop), the border snaps to the edges of defined areas in the image.

The magnetic lasso tool is especially useful for quickly selecting objects with complex edges set against high-contrast backgrounds.

To use the lasso tool:

1 Select the lasso tool (), and select options. (See "Setting options for the lasso, polygonal lasso, and magnetic lasso tools" on page 142.)

2 Drag to draw a freehand selection border.

3 To draw a straight-edged selection border, hold down Alt (Windows) or Option (Mac OS), and click where segments should begin and end. You can switch between drawing freehand and straight-edged segments.

4 To erase recently drawn segments, hold down the Delete key until you've erased the fastening points for the desired segment.

5 To close the selection border, release the mouse without holding down Alt (Windows) or Option (Mac OS).

To use the polygonal lasso tool:

1 Select the polygonal lasso tool (), and select options. (See "Setting options for the lasso, polygonal lasso, and magnetic lasso tools" on page 142.)

2 Click in the image to set the starting point.

3 Do one or more of the following:

• To draw a straight segment, position the pointer where you want the first straight segment to end, and click. Continue clicking to set endpoints for subsequent segments.

• To draw a freehand segment, hold down Alt (Windows) or Option (Mac OS), and drag. When finished, release Alt or Option and the mouse button.

• To erase recently drawn straight segments, press the Delete key.

4 Close the selection border:

• Position the polygonal lasso tool pointer over the starting point (a closed circle appears next to the pointer), and click.

• If the pointer is not over the starting point, double-click the polygonal lasso tool pointer, or Ctrl-click (Windows) or Command-click (Mac OS).

To use the magnetic lasso tool (Photoshop):

1 Select the magnetic lasso tool (⬚), and select options. (See "Setting options for the lasso, polygonal lasso, and magnetic lasso tools" on page 142.)

2 Click in the image to set the first fastening point. Fastening points anchor the selection border in place.

3 To draw a freehand segment, move the pointer along the edge you want to trace. (You can also drag with the mouse button depressed.)

The most recent segment of the selection border remains active. As you move the pointer, the active segment snaps to the strongest edge in the image, based on the detection Width set in the options bar. Periodically, the magnetic lasso tool adds fastening points to the selection border to anchor previous segments.

4 If the border doesn't snap to the desired edge, click once to add a fastening point manually. Continue to trace the edge, and add fastening points as needed.

5 To switch temporarily to the other lasso tools, do one of the following:

• To activate the lasso tool, hold down Alt (Windows) or Option (Mac OS), and drag with the mouse button depressed.

• To activate the polygonal lasso tool, hold down Alt (Windows) or Option (Mac OS), and click.

6 To erase recently drawn segments and fastening points, press the Delete key until you've erased the fastening points for the desired segment.

7 Close the selection border:

• To close the border with a freehand magnetic segment, double-click, or press Enter or Return.

• To close the border with a straight segment, hold down Alt (Windows) or Option (Mac OS), and double-click.

• To close the border, drag back over the starting point and click.

Setting options for the lasso, polygonal lasso, and magnetic lasso tools

The lasso tool options let you customize how the different lasso tools detect and select edges.

To set options for the lasso tools:

1 If needed, select the tool.

2 In the options bar, specify whether to add a new selection (⬚), add to an existing selection (⬚), subtract from a selection (⬚), or select an area intersected by other selections (⬚).

3 Specify feather and anti-aliasing options. (See "Softening the edges of a selection" on page 147.)

4 For the magnetic lasso tool (Photoshop), set any of these options:

• To specify a detection width, enter a pixel value between 1 and 40 for Width. The magnetic lasso detects edges only within the specified distance from the pointer.

• To specify the lasso's sensitivity to edges in the image, enter a value between 1% and 100% for Edge Contrast. A higher value detects only edges that contrast sharply with their surroundings; a lower value detects lower-contrast edges.

• To specify the rate at which the lasso sets fastening points, enter a value between 0 and 100 for Frequency. A higher value anchors the selection border in place more quickly.

On an image with well-defined edges, try a higher width and higher edge contrast, and trace the border roughly. On an image with softer edges, try a lower width and lower edge contrast, and trace the border more precisely.

• To change the lasso cursor to indicate the lasso Width value in the options bar, press the Caps Lock key on the keyboard. Change the cursor while the tool is selected but not in use.

• If you are working with a stylus tablet, select or deselect the Stylus Pressure option. When the option is selected, an increase in stylus pressure will cause the edge width to decrease.

While creating a selection, you can press] to increase the magnetic lasso edge width by 1 pixel; press [to decrease the width by 1 pixel.

Using the magic wand tool

The magic wand tool lets you select a consistently colored area (for example, a red flower) without having to trace its outline. You specify the color range, or *tolerance*, for the magic wand tool's selection.

Note: You cannot use the magic wand tool on an image in Bitmap mode.

To use the magic wand tool:

1 Select the magic wand tool (✎).

2 In the options bar, specify whether to add a new selection (◪), add to an existing selection (◪), subtract from a selection (◪), or select an area intersected by other selections (◪). The magic wand cursor changes depending on which option is selected.

3 For Tolerance, enter a value in pixels, ranging from 0 to 255. Enter a low value to select colors very similar to the pixel you click, or enter a higher value to select a broader range of colors.

4 To define a smooth edge, select Anti-aliased. (See "Softening the edges of a selection" on page 147.)

5 To select only adjacent areas using the same colors, select Contiguous. Otherwise, all pixels using the same colors will be selected.

6 To select colors using data from all the visible layers, select Use All Layers. Otherwise, the magic wand tool selects colors from the active layer only.

7 In the image, click the color you want to select. If Contiguous is selected, all adjacent pixels within the tolerance range are selected. Otherwise, all pixels in the tolerance range are selected.

Using the Color Range command (Photoshop)

The Color Range command selects a specified color or color subset within an existing selection or an entire image. If you want to replace a selection, be sure to deselect everything before applying this command.

To refine an existing selection, use the Color Range command repeatedly to select a subset of colors. For example, to select the green areas in a cyan selection, select Cyans in the Color Range dialog box, and click OK. Then reopen the Color Range dialog box, and select Greens. (The results are subtle because the technique selects parts of colors within a color mix.)

To select a color range using sampled colors:

1 Choose Select > Color Range.

2 For Select, choose the Sampled Colors tool (✒).

3 Select one of the display options:

• Selection to preview only the selection as you build it.

• Image to preview the entire image. For example, you might want to sample from a part of the image that isn't on-screen.

> 💡 *To toggle between the Image and Selection previews in the Color Range dialog box, press Ctrl (Windows) or Command (Mac OS).*

4 Position the pointer over the image or preview area, and click to sample the colors you want included.

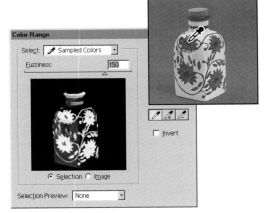

Sampling color

5 Adjust the range of colors using the Fuzziness slider or by entering a value. To decrease the range of colors selected, decrease the value. The Fuzziness option partially selects pixels by controlling the degree to which related colors are included in the selection (whereas the Tolerance option for the magic wand and paint bucket options increases the range of colors that are fully selected).

Increasing Fuzziness expands selection.

6 Adjust the selection:

• To add colors, select the plus eyedropper, and click in the preview area or image.

• To remove colors, select the minus eyedropper, and click in the preview area or image.

To activate the plus eyedropper temporarily, hold down Shift. Hold down Alt (Windows) or Option (Mac OS) to activate the minus eyedropper.

7 To preview the selection in the image window, choose an option for Selection Preview:

• Grayscale to display the selection as it would appear in a grayscale channel.

• Black Matte to display the selection in color against a black background.

• White Matte to display the selection in color against a white background.

• Quick Mask to display the selection using the current quick mask settings. (See "Creating temporary masks in Quick Mask mode (Photoshop)" on page 197.)

8 To revert to the original selection, hold down Alt (Windows) or Option (Mac OS), and click Reset.

9 Click OK to make the selection.

To select a color range using preset colors:

1 Choose Select > Color Range.

2 For Select, choose a color or tonal range. The Out-of-Gamut option works only on RGB and Lab images. (An out-of-gamut color is an RGB or Lab color that cannot be printed using process color printing. See "Color gamuts (Photoshop)" on page 114.)

3 Click Selection to display the selected areas in the preview area.

4 To preview the selection in the image window, choose an option for Selection Preview:

• None to display no preview in the image window.

• Grayscale to display the selection as it would appear in a grayscale channel.

• Black Matte to display the selection in color against a black background.

• White Matte to display the selection in color against a white background.

• Quick Mask to display the selection using the current quick mask settings. (See "Creating temporary masks in Quick Mask mode (Photoshop)" on page 197.)

5 To revert to the original selection, hold down Alt (Windows) or Option (Mac OS), and click Reset.

6 Click OK to make the selection.

Note: *If a message appears stating "No pixels are more than 50% selected," the selection border will not be visible. You may have selected a color, such as red, when the image didn't contain the fully saturated color.*

To save and load color range settings:

Use the Save and Load buttons in the Color Range dialog box to save and reuse the current settings.

Creating selections from slices (ImageReady)

If you create a slice in ImageReady, it can be converted into a selection.

To create a selection from a slice:

1 Select a slice. (See "Selecting slices" on page 276.)

2 Choose Select > Create Selection from Slice.

Adjusting pixel selections

You can adjust and refine your pixel selections using the selection tools and a variety of commands in the Select menu.

In addition, you can apply geometric transformations to change the shape of a selection border.

 For more information, see "Transforming objects in two dimensions" in online Help.

Moving, hiding, or inverting a selection

You can move a selection border around an image, hide a selection border, and invert a selection so that the previously unselected part of the image is selected.

To move a selection border:

1 Using any selection tool, select new selection (■) from the options bar, and position the pointer inside the selection border. The pointer changes to indicate that you can move the selection (▸:::).

2 Drag the border to enclose a different area of the image. You can drag a selection border partly beyond the canvas boundaries. When you drag it back, the original border reappears intact. You can also drag the selection border to another image window.

To control the movement of a selection:

• To constrain the direction to multiples of 45°, begin dragging, and then hold down Shift as you continue to drag.

• To move the selection in 1-pixel increments, use an arrow key.

• To move the selection in 10-pixel increments, hold down Shift, and use an arrow key.

To hide or show selection edges:

Do one of the following:

• Choose View > Show Extras. This command also shows or hides: (Photoshop) selection edges, target path, slices, and notes, or (ImageReady) selection edges, slices, image maps, text bounds, text baseline, and text selection. (See "Working with Extras" on page 77.)

• Choose View > Show > Selection Edges. This toggles the view of the selection edges and affects the current selection only. The selection edges reappear when you make a different selection.

To select the unselected parts of an image:

Choose Select > Inverse.

You can use this option to select an object placed against a solid-colored background. Select the background using the magic wand tool and then inverse the selection.

Adjusting selections manually

You can use the selection tools to add to or subtract from existing pixel selections.

Before manually adding to or subtracting from a selection, set the feather and anti-aliased values in the options bar to the same settings used for the original selection. (See "Softening the edges of a selection" on page 147.)

To adjust selections numerically, see "Adjusting selections numerically" in online Help.

To add to a selection or select an additional area:

1 Make a selection.

2 Using any selection tool, do one of the following:

• Select the Add to Selection option (🖿) in the options bar, and drag.

• Hold down Shift (a plus sign appears next to the pointer), and drag to add another selection.

To subtract from a selection:

1 Make a selection.

2 Using any selection tool, do one of the following:

• Select the Subtract from Selection option (🖿) in the options bar, and drag to intersect with other selections.

• Hold down Alt (Windows) or Option (Mac OS) (a minus sign appears next to the pointer), and drag to subtract another selection.

To select only an area intersected by other selections:

1 Make a selection.

2 Using any selection tool, do one of the following:

• Select the Restrict Selection option (🖿) in the options bar, and drag.

• Hold down Alt+Shift (Windows) or Option+Shift (Mac OS) (a cross appears next to the pointer), and drag over the portion of the original selection that you want to select.

Softening the edges of a selection

You can smooth the hard edges of a selection by anti-aliasing and by feathering.

Anti-aliasing Smooths the jagged edges of a selection by softening the color transition between edge pixels and background pixels. Since only the edge pixels change, no detail is lost. Anti-aliasing is useful when cutting, copying, and pasting selections to create composite images.

Anti-aliasing is available for the lasso, polygonal lasso, magnetic lasso, rounded rectangle marquee, elliptical marquee, and magic wand tools. (Select a tool to display its options bar.) You must specify this option before using these tools. Once a selection is made, you cannot add anti-aliasing.

Feathering Blurs edges by building a transition boundary between the selection and its surrounding pixels. This blurring can cause some loss of detail at the edge of the selection.

You can define feathering for the marquee, lasso, polygonal lasso, or magnetic lasso tool as you use the tool, or you can add feathering to an existing selection. Feathering effects become apparent when you move, cut, copy, or fill the selection.

To use anti-aliasing:

1 Select the lasso, polygonal lasso, magnetic lasso, rounded rectangle marquee, elliptical marquee, or magic wand tool.

2 Select Anti-aliased in the options bar.

To define a feathered edge for a selection tool:

1 Select any of the lasso or marquee tools.

2 Enter a Feather value in the options bar. This value defines the width of the feathered edge and can range from 1 to 250 pixels.

To define a feathered edge for an existing selection:

1 Choose Select > Feather.

2 Enter a value for the Feather Radius, and click OK.

Note: A small selection made with a large feather radius may be so faint that its edges are invisible and thus not selectable. If a message appears stating "No pixels are more than 50% selected," either decrease the feather radius or increase the selection's size. Or click OK to accept the mask at its current setting and create a selection where you cannot see the edges.

*A. Original selection B. Feather: 0 C. Feather: 10
D. Feather: 30*

Moving, copying, and pasting selections and layers

You can move or copy selections and layers within or between images—and also between images in other applications.

Moving selections and layers within an image

The move tool lets you drag a selection or layer to a new location in the image. With the Info palette open, you can track the exact distance of the move.

To specify move tool options:

1 Select the move tool (▸₊).

2 Select any of the following in the options bar:

• Auto Select Layer to select the topmost layer that has pixels under the move tool, rather than the selected layer.

• Show Bounding Box to display the bounding box around the selected item.

• If multiple items are selected, you can choose one of the alignment options.

To move a selection or layer:

1 Select the move tool (▸₊).

To activate the move tool when another tool is selected, hold down Ctrl (Windows) or Command (Mac OS). (This technique does not work with the pen tool (✎), freeform pen (✎‸), direct selection tool (▸), hand tool (✋), or anchor point tools (✎⁺) (✎⁻) (⌐).) Hold down Command (Mac OS) to activate the move tool when using the shape tools (▢) (▭) (○) (⬠) (＼) (✳).

2 Do one of the following:

• Move the pointer inside the selection border, and drag the selection to a new position. If you have selected multiple areas, all move as you drag.

• Select the layer you want to move. Then drag the layer to a new position.

Copying selections or layers

You can use the move tool to copy selections as you drag them within or between images, or you can copy and move selections using the Copy, Copy Merged, Cut, and Paste commands. Dragging with the move tool saves memory because the Clipboard is not used as it is with the Copy, Copy Merged, Cut, and Paste commands.

• The Copy command copies the selected area on the active layer.

• The Copy Merged command makes a merged copy of all the visible layers in the selected area.

• The Paste command pastes a cut or copied selection into another part of the image or into another image as a new layer.

(Photoshop) The Paste Into command pastes a cut or copied selection inside another selection in the same image or different image. The source selection is pasted onto a new layer, and the destination selection border is converted into a layer mask. (See "Hiding portions of a layer" on page 237.)

Keep in mind that when a selection or layer is pasted between images with different resolutions, the pasted data retains its pixel dimensions. This can make the pasted portion appear out of proportion to the new image. Use the Image Size command to make the source and destination images the same resolution before copying and pasting. (See "Determining a recommended resolution for an image (Photoshop)" on page 99.)

Depending on your color management settings and the color profile associated with the file (or imported data), you may be prompted to specify how to handle color information in the file (or imported data). For more information, see "About color management policies" on page 125.

To copy a selection:

1 Select the area you want to copy.

2 Choose Edit > Copy or Edit > Copy Merged.

To copy a selection while dragging:

1 Select the move tool (▸₊), or hold down Ctrl (Windows) or Command (Mac OS) to activate the move tool.

2 Hold down Alt (Windows) or Option (Mac OS), and drag the selection you want to copy and move.

When copying between images, drag the selection from the active image window into the destination image window. If nothing is selected, the entire active layer is copied. As you drag the selection over another image window, a border highlights the window if you can drop the selection into it.

To create multiple copies of a selection within an image:

1 Select the move tool (▸₊), or hold down Ctrl (Windows) or Command (Mac OS) to activate the move tool.

2 Copy the selection:

• Hold down Alt (Windows) or Option (Mac OS), and drag the selection.

• To copy the selection and offset the duplicate by 1 pixel, hold down Alt or Option, and press an arrow key.

• To copy the selection and offset the duplicate by 10 pixels, press Alt+Shift (Windows) or Option+Shift (Mac OS), and press an arrow key.

As long as you hold down Alt or Option, each press of an arrow key creates a copy of the selection and offsets it by the specified distance from the last duplicate.

To paste one selection into another (Photoshop):

1 Cut or copy the part of the image you want to paste.

2 Select the part of the image into which you want to paste the selection. The source selection and the destination selection can be in the same image or in two different Photoshop images.

3 Choose Edit > Paste Into. The contents of the source selection appear masked by the destination selection.

In the Layers palette, the layer thumbnail for the source selection appears next to the layer mask thumbnail for the destination selection. The layer and layer mask are unlinked—that is, you can move each one independently.

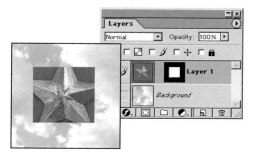

Source selection pasted into destination selection.

For more information on editing layer masks, see "Applying and discarding layer masks" on page 242.

4 Select the move tool (⊹), or hold down the Ctrl (Windows) or Command (Mac OS) key to activate the move tool. Then drag the source contents until the part you want appears through the mask.

5 To reveal more or less of the image underlying the layer, click the layer mask thumbnail in the Layers palette, select a painting tool, and edit the mask:

• To hide more of the image underlying the layer, paint the mask with black.

• To reveal more of the image underlying the layer, paint the mask with white.

• To partially reveal the image underlying the layer, paint the mask with gray.

6 If you are satisfied with your results, you can choose Layer > Merge Down to merge the new layer and layer mask with the underlying layer and make the changes permanent.

Using drag and drop to copy between applications

The drag-and-drop feature lets you copy and move images between Photoshop or ImageReady and other applications.

In Windows, the application must be OLE-compliant. To duplicate an entire image by dragging and dropping, use the move tool to drag the image. To copy an OLE object that contains.psd data, use the OLE Clipboard. (See your Windows documentation.)

In Mac OS, the application must support Mac OS Drag Manager, and you must be running System 8.5, 8.6, or 9.0.

Dragging vector artwork from Adobe Illustrator or from other applications that use the Illustrator Clipboard rasterizes the artwork—the mathematically defined lines and curves of the vector art are converted into the pixels or bits of a bitmap image. To copy the vector artwork as a path in Photoshop, hold down Ctrl (Windows) or Command (Mac OS) as you drag from Adobe Illustrator. To copy type, you must first convert it to outlines.

Using the Clipboard to copy between applications

You can often use the Cut or Copy command to copy selections between Photoshop or ImageReady and other applications. The cut or copied selection remains on the Clipboard until you cut or copy another selection.

In some cases, the contents of the Clipboard are converted to a *raster* image. Photoshop prompts you when vector artwork will be rasterized.

Note: *The image is rasterized at the resolution of the file into which you paste it.*

To change the Export Clipboard preference (Photoshop):

1 Choose Edit > Preferences > General.

2 Select Export Clipboard to save any Photoshop contents on the Clipboard when you exit from Photoshop. If you leave this deselected, the contents are deleted when you exit from the program.

3 Click OK.

To paste PostScript artwork from another application:

1 In the supporting application, select your artwork, and choose Edit > Copy. Applications that produce PostScript artwork include Adobe Illustrator (versions 5.0 through 8.0), Adobe Dimensions®, and Adobe Streamline™.

For more information, see "About file formats" in online Help.

2 In Photoshop or ImageReady, select the image into which you'll paste the selection.

3 Choose Edit > Paste.

4 (Photoshop) In the dialog box, select from the following options:

• Paste as Pixels to have the artwork rasterized as it is pasted. Rasterizing converts mathematically defined vector artwork to pixels.

• Paste as Paths to paste the copy as a path in the Paths palette. When copying type from Illustrator, you must first convert it to outlines.

• Paste as Shape Layer to create a new shape layer that uses the path as a layer clipping path.

5 If you chose Paste as Pixels in the previous step, you can choose Anti-alias in the options bar to make a smooth transition between the edges of the selection and the surrounding pixels. (See "Softening the edges of a selection" on page 147.)

Note: *You can use the Matting commands if you have already merged data and are trying to re-extract the rasterized data. (See "Removing fringe pixels from a selection (Photoshop)" on page 154.)*

6 Click OK (Photoshop).

Working with snap

Snap helps with precise placement of selection edges, crops, slices, drawing tools, paths, and objects by aligning them with guides, slices, document bounds and (Photoshop) a grid. Snap can be turned on for any combination of options from the Snap To submenu.

To choose options from the Snap To submenu:

Choose View > Snap To, and choose from the submenu:

• Guides, Slices, and Document Bounds in any combination to snap to these options.

(Photoshop) You can also choose the Grid option from the Snap To submenu.

• All to turn snap on for all available options in the submenu.

• None to turn snap off for all options.

To activate or suppress snap:

Choose View > Snap.

When snap is chosen, activated options in the Snap To submenu display a check mark. When snap is suppressed, a dot (Windows) or a dash (Mac OS) appears next to chosen options in the Snap To submenu.

Note: Suppressing snap only temporarily disables snap for the options chosen in the Snap To submenu. The submenu options next to dots (Windows) or dashes (Mac OS) remain chosen for snapping.

To turn on an option from a list of suppressed Snap To options:

1 With snap suppressed, choose View > Snap To. The Snap To submenu opens with a dot (Windows) or a dash (Mac OS) next to options for which snap is chosen but suppressed.

2 Choose an option next to a dot (Windows) or a dash (Mac OS) to turn on snap for that option only. This automatically turns snap off for all other options.

Saving and loading selections

Selections can be saved and loaded for reuse. (See "Saving a mask selection" on page 200.)

To save a selection:

Choose Select > Save Selection.

To load a saved selection (Photoshop):

1 Choose Select > Load Selection, then enter the options in the Load Selection dialog window.

2 Click OK to load selection. (See "Loading a selection into an image" on page 201.)

To load a saved selection (ImageReady):

Choose Select > Load Selection, then choose an option from the submenu.

Deleting selections

To delete a selection, choose Edit > Clear, or press Backspace (Windows) or Delete (Mac OS). To cut a selection to the Clipboard, choose Edit > Cut.

Deleting a selection on a background or on a layer with the Lock Transparency option selected in the Layers palette replaces the original location with the background color. Deleting a selection on a layer without Lock Transparency selected replaces the original area with the layer transparency.

Removing fringe pixels from a selection (Photoshop)

When you move or paste an anti-aliased selection, some of the pixels surrounding the selection border are included with the selection. This can result in a fringe or halo around the edges of the pasted selection. These Matting commands let you edit unwanted edge pixels:

• Defringe replaces the color of any fringe pixels with the colors of nearby pixels containing pure colors (those without background color). For example, if you select a yellow object on a blue background and then move the selection, some of the blue background is selected and moved with the object. Defringe replaces the blue pixels with yellow ones.

• Remove Black Matte and Remove White Matte are useful when you want to paste a selection anti-aliased against a white or black background onto a different background. For example, anti-aliased black text on a white background has gray pixels at the edges, which are visible against a colored background.

> *You can also remove fringe areas by using the Advanced Blending sliders in the Layer Styles dialog box to remove, or make transparent, areas from the layer. In this case, you would make the black or white areas transparent. Alt-click (Windows) or Option-click (Mac OS) on the sliders to separate them; separating the sliders allows you to remove fringe pixels and retain a smooth edge.*

To decrease a fringe on a selection:

1 Choose Layer > Matting > Defringe.

2 Enter a value in the Width text box for the distance to search for replacement pixels. In most cases, a distance of 1 or 2 pixels is enough.

3 Click OK.

To remove a matte from a selection:

Choose Layer > Matting > Remove Black Matte or Layer > Matting > Remove White Matte.

1 Adjust the view as needed:

• To magnify an area, select the zoom tool (🔍) in the dialog box, and click in the preview image. To zoom out, hold down Alt (Windows) or Option (Mac OS) as you click.

• To view a different area, select the hand tool in the dialog box, and drag in the preview image.

Extracting objects from their background (Photoshop)

The Extract command provides a sophisticated way to isolate a foreground object and erase its background on a layer. Even objects with wispy, intricate, or undefinable edges may be clipped from their backgrounds with a minimum of manual work.

Note: *For simpler cases, you can instead use the background eraser tool.*

To extract an object, you use tools in the Extract dialog box. First you draw a highlight that marks the edges of the object, and define the object's interior. Then you can preview the extraction and redo it or touch up the result as needed. When you extract the object, Photoshop erases its background to transparency. Pixels on the edge of the object lose their color components derived from the background, so they can blend with a new background without producing a color halo.

You can add back opacity to the background and create other effects by using the Edit > Fade command after an extraction.

 For more information, see "Blending filter effects (Photoshop)" in online Help.

To extract an object from its background:

1 In the Layers palette, select the layer containing the object you want to extract. If you select a background layer, it becomes a normal layer after the extraction.

To avoid losing the original image information, duplicate the layer or make a snapshot of the original image state.

Note: *If the layer contains a selection, the extraction erases the background only in the selected area.*

2 Choose Image > Extract.

You use tools in the Extract dialog box to specify which part of the image to extract. You can resize the dialog box by dragging its lower right corner.

3 Specify options for tools in the dialog box (you can change these settings at any time):

• For Brush Size, enter a value, or drag the slider to specify the width of the edge highlighter, eraser, cleanup, and edge touchup tools.

• For Highlight, choose a preset color option, or choose Other to specify a custom color for the highlight.

• For Fill, choose a preset color option, or choose Other to specify a custom color for the area covered by the fill tool.

• If you are highlighting a well-defined edge, select Smart Highlighting. This option helps you keep the highlight on the edge, and applies a highlight that is just wide enough to cover the edge, regardless of the current brush size. Smart Highlighting can greatly improve the extraction when the object and background have similar colors or have textures.

4 Adjust the view as needed:

• To magnify an area, select the zoom tool (⌕) in the dialog box, and click in the preview image. To zoom out, hold down Alt (Windows) or Option (Mac OS) as you click.

• To view a different area, select the hand tool in the dialog box, and drag in the preview image.

5 Define the edge of the object you want to extract:

• To draw a highlight that marks the edge, select the edge highlighter tool (✐) in the dialog box, and drag so that the highlight slightly overlaps both the foreground object and its background.

Use Smart Highlighting to trace sharper edges. Use a large brush to cover wispy, intricate edges where the foreground blends into the background, such as hair or trees.

💡 *If you use Smart Highlighting to mark an object edge that is near another edge, decrease the brush size if conflicting edges pull the highlight off the object edge. If the object edge has a uniform color on one side and high-contrast edges on the other side, keep the object edge within the brush area but center the brush on the uniform color.*

• If the object has a well-defined interior, make sure that the highlight forms a complete enclosure. You do not need to highlight areas where the object touches the image boundaries. If the object lacks a clear interior, highlight the entire object.

• To base the highlight on a selection saved in an alpha channel, choose the alpha channel from the Channel menu. The alpha channel should be based on a selection of the edge boundary. If you modify a highlight based on a channel, the channel name in the menu changes to Custom.

• To erase the highlight, select the eraser tool (✐) in the dialog box, and drag over the highlight. To erase the entire highlight, press Alt+Backspace (Windows) or Option+Delete (Mac OS).

6 Define the foreground area:

• If the object has a well-defined interior, select the fill tool (🖌) in the dialog box. Click inside the object to fill its interior. (Clicking a filled area with the fill tool removes the fill.)

• If the object is especially intricate or lacks a clear interior, make sure that the highlight covers the entire object, and then select Force Foreground. Select the eyedropper tool (🖋) in the dialog box, and click inside the object to sample the foreground color, or click in the Color text box and use a color picker to select the foreground color. This technique works best with objects that contain tones of a single color.

7 Click Preview to preview the extracted object, or skip to step 10 to extract the object without a preview.

Selected area highlighted and filled, and extracted object

Zoom in as needed, and set any preview options:

• Use Show menu options to switch between previews of the original and extracted images.

• Use Display menu options to preview the extracted object against a colored matte background or as a grayscale mask. To display a transparent background, choose None.

• Select Show Highlight or Show Fill to display the object's highlight or fill.

8 If necessary, repeat the extraction to improve the results (when you are finished, you can perform final touch-ups as described in step 9):

• To perform another extraction after adjusting the highlight and fill, repeat steps 5, 6, and 7.

• To perform another extraction with new extraction settings, change the Smooth, Force Foreground, or Color settings, and repeat step 7.

Note: *To specify the amount of smoothing of the extracted object, drag the Smooth slider or enter a value. It is usually best to begin with a zero or small value to avoid unwanted blurring of details. If there are sharp artifacts in the extraction result, you can increase the Smooth value to help remove them in the next extraction.*

9 Touch up the extraction results as needed:

• To erase background traces in the extracted area, use the cleanup tool (🖊). The tool subtracts opacity and has a cumulative effect. You can also use the cleanup tool to fill gaps in the extracted object. Hold down Alt (Windows) or Option (Mac OS) while dragging to add back opacity.

• To edit the edge of the extracted object, use the edge touchup tool (🖊). The tool sharpens edges and has a cumulative effect. If there is no clear edge, the edge touchup tool adds opacity to the object or subtracts opacity from the background.

10 Click OK to apply the final extraction. On the layer, all pixels outside the extracted object are erased to transparency.

Note: *For best results in cleaning up stray edges, use the cleanup and edge touchup tools in the Extract dialog box. You can also clean up after an extraction by using the background eraser and history brush tools in the toolbox.*

6

Chapter 6: Drawing and Editing

The drawing tools let you create and edit vector shapes. You can work with shapes in shape layers and as paths; you can also create rasterized shapes, which can be edited with the painting tools. The drawing tools provide an easy way to create buttons, navigation bars, and other items used on Web pages.

Other tools and commands let you transform and retouch an image.

About drawing and painting

When creating graphics on a computer, there is a distinction between painting and drawing. *Painting* involves changing the colors of pixels using a painting tool. You can apply colors gradually, with soft edges and transitions, and manipulate individual pixels using powerful filter effects. However, once you apply a brush stroke, there is no simple way to select the entire brush stroke and move it to a new location in the image.

For more information on painting, see "Painting" in online Help.

Drawing, on the other hand, involves creating shapes that are defined as geometric objects (also called *vector objects*). For example, if you draw a circle using the ellipse tool, the circle is defined by a specific radius, location, and color. You can quickly select the entire circle and move it to a new location, or you can edit the outline of the circle to distort its shape. (See "About bitmap images and vector graphics" on page 91.)

Working with shapes provides several advantages:

• Shapes are object-oriented—you can quickly select, resize, and move a shape, and you can edit a shape's outline (called a *path*) and attributes (such as line weight, fill color, and fill style). You can use shapes to make selections and create libraries of custom shapes with the Preset Manager.

• Shapes are resolution-independent—they maintain crisp edges when resized, printed to a PostScript printer, saved in a PDF file, or imported into a vector-based graphics application.

Drawing shapes and paths

The pen tools and shape tools provide several options for creating shapes and paths:

• You can create a shape on a new layer. The shape is automatically filled with the current foreground color; however, you can easily change the fill to a different color, a gradient, or a pattern. The shape's outline is stored in a layer clipping path, which appears in the Paths palette.

• In Photoshop, you can create a new work path. A work path is a temporary path that is not part of your image until you apply it in some way. You can save a work path in the Path palette for later use.

• When using the shape tools, you can create a rasterized shape on an existing layer. The shape is automatically filled with the current foreground color. After you create a rasterized shape, you cannot edit it as a vector object.

About the drawing tools in Photoshop and ImageReady

Keep in mind the following differences when using the drawing tools in Photoshop and ImageReady:

• The pen tools, polygon tool, and custom shape tool are available only in Photoshop.

• In Photoshop, you can use the drawing tools to create a work path; in ImageReady, you can't create a work path.

• In Photoshop, you can draw multiple shapes in a layer and specify how overlapping shapes interact. In ImageReady, you can only draw one shape in a layer.

• In Photoshop, you can edit shapes after you draw them. In ImageReady, you can move and transform shapes, but you can't edit them.

Creating shape layers

You create a *shape layer* using a shape tool or a pen tool. Technically, a shape layer is a fill layer with a layer clipping path; the fill layer defines the color of the shape, while the layer clipping path defines the geometric outline of the shape. You can change the color and other attributes of a shape by editing its fill layer and applying layer styles to it. You can change the outline of a shape by editing its layer clipping path. (See "Using adjustment layers or fill layers (Photoshop)" on page 242 and "Editing a layer clipping path (Photoshop)" on page 240.)

To create a new shape layer:

1 Specify a foreground color.

2 Select the rectangle tool (□), rounded rectangle tool (▢), ellipse tool (○), or line tool (\); additionally, in Photoshop, select the polygon tool (◇), custom shape tool (✳), pen tool (✿), or freeform pen tool (✿).

3 In the options bar, click the Create New Shape Layer button (⬚), and set the following options:

• Choose a layer style from the Layer Style pop-up palette to apply a predefined layer style to the shape.

• Choose a layer blending mode from the Mode menu.

• Specify a layer opacity using the Opacity text box or slider.

• (Photoshop) If you're using the custom shape tool, select a predefined shape from the Shape pop-up palette. (See "Using pop-up palettes" on page 62.)

• Set additional, tool-specific options. (See "Setting shape tool options" on page 164, "Drawing with the pen tool" on page 167, and "Drawing with the freeform pen tool" on page 169.)

4 If you're using a shape tool, drag in the image to draw the shape. If you're using a pen tool, click or drag in the image to draw the shape. (See "Using the pen tools (Photoshop)" on page 166.)

5 (Photoshop) To create multiple shape components in the same shape layer, continue drawing shapes:

• Choose a shape area option to determine what happens at the intersection of overlapping shapes. (See "Drawing overlapping shapes (Photoshop)" on page 171.)

• Select a different tool in the toolbox to switch between drawing tools. When using a shape tool, you can also select a different shape tool in the options bar.

6 (Photoshop) Click the OK button (✔) in the options bar, or press Enter or Return, to dismiss the drawing tools.

Creating a work path (Photoshop)

A *work path* is a temporary path that appears in the Paths palette and defines the outline of a shape. You can use paths in several ways:

• You can use a path as a layer clipping path to hide areas of a layer. (See "Hiding portions of a layer" on page 237.)

• You can convert a path to a selection to use a shape as the basis for selecting pixels in an image. (See "Converting between paths and selection borders (Photoshop)" on page 180.)

• You can edit a path to change its shape. (See "Editing paths (Photoshop)" on page 172.)

• You can designate a path as a clipping path for an entire image, which is useful when exporting images to page-layout or vector-editing applications.

Create a new path in the Paths palette before you begin drawing to automatically save the work path as a named path.

To create a new work path:

1 Select the rectangle tool (□), rounded rectangle tool (◯), ellipse tool (◯), polygon tool (◇), line tool (╲), custom shape tool (✳), pen tool (♠), or freeform pen tool (♠).

2 In the options bar, click the Create New Work Path button (▨), and set additional, tool-specific options. (See "Setting shape tool options" on page 164, "Drawing with the pen tool" on page 167, and "Drawing with the freeform pen tool" on page 169.)

If you're using the custom shape tool, select a predefined shape from the Shape pop-up palette. (See "Using pop-up palettes" on page 62.)

3 If you're using a shape tool, drag in the image to draw the path. If you're using a pen tool, click or drag in the image to draw the path. (See "Using the pen tools (Photoshop)" on page 166.)

4 To create multiple components in the path, continue drawing:

• Choose a shape area option to determine what happens at the intersection of overlapping path segments and components. (See "Drawing overlapping shapes (Photoshop)" on page 171.)

• Select a different tool in the toolbox to switch between drawing tools. When using a shape tool, you can also select a different shape tool in the options bar.

5 Click the OK button (✓) in the options bar, or press Enter or Return, to dismiss the drawing tools.

To reselect the work path, select Work Path in the Paths palette. (See "Using the Paths palette (Photoshop)" on page 171.)

Creating rasterized shapes

As the name implies, rasterized shapes are not vector objects. Creating a rasterized shape is the same as making a selection and filling it with the foreground color. You cannot edit a rasterized shape as a vector object.

To create a rasterized shape:

1 Select a layer. You cannot create a rasterized shape on a vector-based layer (a shape layer or a type layer).

2 Specify a foreground color.

3 Select the rectangle tool (▭), rounded rectangle tool (▢), ellipse tool (○), or line tool (╲); additionally, in Photoshop, select the polygon tool (◇) or custom shape tool (✳).

4 In the options bar, click the Create Filled Region button (▭), and set the following options:

• Choose a layer blending mode from the Mode menu.

• Specify a layer opacity using the Opacity text box or pop-up slider.

• Select Anti-aliased to blend the shape's edge pixels with the surrounding pixels.

• Set additional, tool-specific options. (See "Setting shape tool options" on page 164, "Drawing with the pen tool" on page 167, and "Drawing with the freeform pen tool" on page 169.)

5 Drag in the image to define the shape. Continue drawing shapes as desired. You can switch between shape tools by selecting a different tool in the toolbox or options bar.

Using the shape tools

You use the shape tools to draw lines, rectangles, rounded rectangles, and ellipses in an image. In Photoshop, you can also draw polygons and create custom shape libraries to reuse and share custom shapes.

(Photoshop) Select a shape in the options bar, and click the inverted arrow to display options for the selected shape.

Setting shape tool options

Each shape tool provides specific options; for example, you can set options that allow you to draw a rectangle with fixed dimensions or a line with arrowheads.

To set tool-specific options:

1 Select a shape tool.

2 In the options bar, set the following options. In Photoshop, click the inverted arrow (▾) next to the shape buttons to view additional options.

Arrowheads Start and End Renders a line with arrowheads. Select Start, End, or both to specify on which end of the line arrows are rendered. In ImageReady, click Shape to define the shape of the arrowhead; in Photoshop, the shape options appear in the pop-up dialog box. Enter values for Width and Length to specify the proportions of the arrowhead as a percentage of the line width (10% to 1000% for Width, and 10% to 5000% for Length). Enter a value for the concavity of the arrowhead (from –50% to +50%). The concavity value defines the amount of curvature on the widest part of the arrowhead, where the arrowhead meets the line.

Note: In Photoshop, you can also edit an arrowhead directly using the vector selection and drawing tools.

Circle (Photoshop) Constrains an ellipse to a circle.

Corner Radius (ImageReady) Specifies the corner radius for rendering a rounded rectangle.

Defined Proportions (Photoshop) Renders a custom shape based on the proportions with which it was created.

Defined Size (Photoshop) Renders a custom shape based on the size at which it was created.

Fixed Size Renders a rectangle, rounded rectangle, ellipse, or custom shape as a fixed shape based on the values you enter in the Width and Height text boxes.

From Center (Photoshop) Renders a rectangle, rounded rectangle, ellipse, or custom shape from the center.

Indent Sides By (Photoshop) Renders a polygon as a star. Enter a percentage in the text box to specify the portion of the star's radius taken up by the points. A 50% setting creates points that are half the total radius of the star; a larger value creates sharper, thinner points; a smaller value creates fuller points.

Proportional (Photoshop) Renders a rectangle, rounded rectangle, or ellipse as a proportional shape based on the values you enter in the Width and Height text boxes.

Radius (Photoshop) For rounded rectangles, specifies the corner radius. For polygons, specifies the distance from the center of a polygon to the outer points.

Sides (Photoshop) Specifies the number of sides in a polygon.

Smooth Corners or Smooth Indents (Photoshop) Renders a polygon with smooth corners or indents.

Snap to Pixels (Photoshop) Snaps edges of a rectangle or rounded rectangle to the pixel boundaries.

Square (Photoshop) Constrains a rectangle or rounded rectangle to a square.

Unconstrained (Photoshop) Lets you set the width and height of a rectangle, rounded rectangle, ellipse, or custom shape by dragging.

Weight Determines the width of a line in pixels.

Manipulating a shape while dragging

You can use the following modifier keys to manipulate a shape while dragging:

• Hold down Shift to constrain a rectangle or rounded rectangle to a square, to constrain an ellipse to a circle, or to constrain the line angle to a multiple of 45°.

• Hold down Alt (Windows) or Option (Mac OS) to draw from the center of the shape.

• Hold down the spacebar to move the shape without changing its size or proportions.

Adding shapes to an existing shape layer (Photoshop)

After you create a shape layer, you can add new shapes to it at any time. You can also use the path component selection tool and the direct selection tool to move, resize, and edit shapes. For complete information on using the path component selection tool and the direct selection tool, see "Editing paths (Photoshop)" on page 172.

To add to an existing shape layer:

1 Select a layer in the Layers palette.

2 Select a drawing tool, and set its options. (See "Creating shape layers" on page 162.)

3 Before you draw, specify a shape area option in the options bar. (See "Drawing overlapping shapes (Photoshop)" on page 171.)

4 When you have finished adding shapes, click the OK button (☑) in the options bar, or press Enter or Return, to dismiss the drawing tools.

Saving custom shapes

After you create a shape, you can save it as a custom shape. The saved shape appears in the Shape pop-up palette. For information about working with pop-up palettes, see "Using pop-up palettes" on page 62.

To save a shape or path as a custom shape (Photoshop):

1 In the Paths palette, select a path—either a layer clipping path for a shape layer, a work path, or a saved path.

2 Choose Edit > Define Custom Shape, and in the Shape Name dialog box, enter a name for the new custom shape. The new shape appears in the Shape pop-up palette.

3 To save the new custom shape as part of the current library, or to save a new library, select Save Shapes from the pop-up palette menu.

You can also use the Preset Manager to manage libraries of custom shapes. (See "Managing libraries with the Preset Manager (Photoshop)" on page 85.)

Using the pen tools (Photoshop)

You can create or edit straight lines, curves, or freeform lines and shapes using the pen tools. The pen tools can be used in conjunction with the shape tools to create complex shapes.

Drawing with the pen tool

The pen tool lets you create straight lines and smooth flowing curves with greater precision than is possible with the freeform pen tool. For most users, the pen tool provides the best control and greatest accuracy for drawing.

To draw with the pen tool:

1 Select the pen tool ( ).

2 In the options bar, click either the Create New Shape Layer button ( ) or the Create New Work Path button ( ). (See "Drawing shapes and paths" on page 161.)

3 Set the following tool-specific options:

• Rubber Band to preview path segments as you draw. After you define at least one anchor point for a path, Photoshop displays the next proposed segment as you move the pointer in the image. The segment doesn't become permanent until you click.

• Auto Add/Delete to automatically add or delete anchor points while you draw.

4 Position the pen pointer where you want to begin to draw, and click to define the first anchor point. The anchor point remains selected (solid) until you define the next point.

5 Choose a shape area option to determine what happens at the intersection of overlapping path segments and components. (See "Drawing overlapping shapes (Photoshop)" on page 171.)

6 Click or drag to set anchor points for additional segments. (See "Drawing straight segments with the pen tool" on page 167 and "Drawing curves with the pen tool" on page 168.)

7 Complete the path component:

• To end an open path component, click the pen tool in the toolbox, or Ctrl-click (Windows) or Command-click (Mac OS) away from the path.

• To close a path component, position the pen pointer over the first anchor point. A small loop appears next to the pen tip when it is positioned correctly. Click to close the path.

For more information on closed and open paths, see "About anchor points, direction lines, direction points, and components" on page 172.

8 Draw additional path components if desired.

9 Click the OK button ( ) in the options bar, or press Enter or Return, to dismiss the drawing tools.

Drawing straight segments with the pen tool

The simplest segment you can draw with the pen tool is a straight segment, made by clicking to create anchor points.

To draw straight segments:

1 Position the pen pointer where you want the straight segment to begin, and click to define the first anchor point. The anchor point remains selected (solid) until you define the next point.

2 Click again where you want the first segment of the straight line to end, or Shift-click to constrain the angle of the segment to a multiple of 45°.

3 Continue clicking to set anchor points for additional segments. The last anchor point is always a solid square, indicating it is selected. Previously defined anchor points become hollow squares as you add further anchor points. If the Auto Add/Delete option is selected, you can click an existing point to delete it.

Drawing curves with the pen tool

You create curves by dragging the pen tool in the direction you want the curve to go. Keep these guidelines in mind when drawing curves:

• Always drag the first direction point in the direction of the bump of the curve, and drag the second direction point in the opposite direction to create a single curve. Dragging both direction points in the same direction creates an "S" curve.

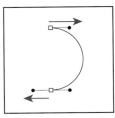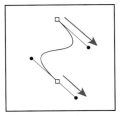

Drag in the opposite direction to create a smooth curve. Drag in the same direction to create an "S" curve.

• When drawing a series of smooth curves, draw one curve at a time, placing anchor points at the beginning and end of each curve, not at the tip of the curve. Use as few anchor points as possible, placing them as far apart as possible.

For more information on how paths are constructed, see "About anchor points, direction lines, direction points, and components" on page 172.

To draw a curve:

1 Position the pointer where you want the curve to begin, and hold down the mouse button. The first anchor point appears, and the pointer changes to an arrowhead.

2 Drag in the direction you want the curve segment to be drawn. As you drag, the pointer leads one of two direction points. Hold down the Shift key to constrain the tool to multiples of 45°, and release the mouse button once you have positioned the first direction point.

The length and slope of the direction line determine the shape of the curve segment. You can adjust one or both sides of the direction line later.

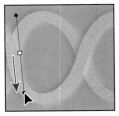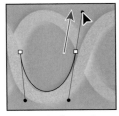

Drag in the direction of the curve to set the first anchor point. Drag in the opposite direction to complete the curve segment.

3 Position the pointer where you want the curve segment to end, and drag in the opposite direction to complete the segment.

4 Do one of the following:

• To draw the next segment of a smooth curve, position the pointer where you want the next segment to end, and drag away from the curve.

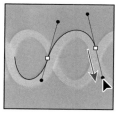

*Drag away from the curve
to create the next segment.*

• To change the direction of the curve sharply, release the mouse button, then Alt-drag (Windows) or Option-drag (Mac OS) the direction point in the direction of the curve. Release Alt (Windows) or Option (Mac OS) and the mouse button, reposition the pointer where you want the segment to end, and drag in the opposite direction to complete the curve segment.

• To break out the direction lines of an anchor point, Alt-drag (Windows) or Option-drag (Mac OS) the lines.

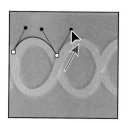 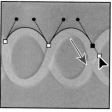

*Alt-drag or Option-drag the direction point toward the curve.
Release the key, and drag in the opposite direction.*

Drawing with the freeform pen tool

The freeform pen tool lets you draw as if you were drawing with a pencil on paper. Anchor points are added automatically as you draw. You do not determine where the points are positioned, but you can adjust them once the path is complete.

The magnetic pen is an option of the freeform tool that lets you draw a path that snaps to the edges of defined areas in your image. You can define the range and sensitivity of the snapping behavior, as well as the complexity of the resulting path. The magnetic pen and magnetic lasso tools share many of the same options.

To draw with the freeform pen tool:

1 Select the freeform pen tool ( ).

2 In the options bar, click either the Create New Shape Layer button ( ) or the Create New Work Path button ( ). (See "Drawing shapes and paths" on page 161.)

3 Set the following tool-specific options:

• Curve Fit to control how sensitive the final path is to the movement of your mouse or stylus. Enter a value between 0.5 and 10.0 pixels. A higher value creates a simpler path with fewer anchor points.

• Auto Add/Delete to automatically add or delete anchor points while you draw.

4 Drag the pointer in the image. As you drag, a path trails behind the pointer. When you release the mouse, a work path is created.

5 Choose a shape area option to determine what happens at the intersection of path segments and components. (See "Drawing overlapping shapes (Photoshop)" on page 171.)

6 To continue the existing freehand path, position the freeform pen pointer on an endpoint of the path, and drag. If the Auto Add/Delete option is selected, you can click an existing point to delete it.

7 To complete the path, release the mouse. To create a closed path, drag over the initial point of the path (a circle appears next to the pointer when it is aligned), and release the mouse. For more information on closed and open paths, see "About anchor points, direction lines, direction points, and components" on page 172.

8 Draw additional path components if desired.

9 Click the OK button (☑) in the options bar, or press Enter or Return, to dismiss the drawing tools.

To draw using the magnetic pen options:

1 To convert the freeform pen tool to the magnetic pen tool (), select Magnetic in the options bar. Then specify the following options by clicking the magnetic options button ():

• For Width, enter a pixel value between 1 and 40. The magnetic pen detects edges only within the specified distance from the pointer.

• For Contrast, enter a percentage value between 0 and 100 to specify the contrast between pixels required to be considered an edge. Use a higher value for low contrast images.

• For Frequency, enter a value between 0 and 100 to specify the rate at which the pen sets anchor points. A higher value anchors the path in place more quickly.

• If you are working with a stylus tablet, select or deselect Stylus Pressure. When this option is selected, an increase in stylus pressure causes the width to decrease.

2 Click in the image to set the first fastening point.

3 To draw a freehand segment, move the pointer or drag along the edge you want to trace.

The most recent segment of the border remains active. As you move the pointer, the active segment snaps to the strongest edge in the image, connecting the pointer to the last fastening point. Periodically, the magnetic pen adds fastening points to the border to anchor previous sections.

4 If the border doesn't snap to the desired edge, click once to add a fastening point manually and to keep the border from moving. Continue to trace the edge and add fastening points as needed. If needed, press Delete to remove the last fastening point.

5 To dynamically modify the properties of the magnetic pen, do one of the following:

• Alt-drag (Windows) or Option-drag (Mac OS) to draw a freehand path.

• Alt-click (Windows) or Option-click (Mac OS) to draw straight segments.

• Press the [key to decrease the magnetic pen width by 1 pixel; press the] key to increase the pen width by 1 pixel. Press Caps Lock to display the current pen width.

6 Complete the path:

• Press Enter or Return to end an open path.

• Double-click to close the path with a magnetic segment.

• Hold down Alt (Windows) or Option (Mac OS), and double-click to close the path with a straight segment.

7 Draw additional path components if desired. Choose a shape area option to determine how overlapping path components intersect. (See "Drawing overlapping shapes (Photoshop)" on page 171.)

8 Click the OK button (✔) in the options bar, or press Enter or Return, to dismiss the drawing tools.

Drawing overlapping shapes (Photoshop)

In Photoshop, you can draw multiple shapes in a layer or modify a path using one or more of the drawing tools. You can specify how overlapping shapes, path segments, and path components interact using the shape area options.

To specify how overlapping areas interact:

1 Create a new shape layer or work path, select an existing layer in the Layers palette, or select an existing path in the Paths palette.

2 Before drawing subsequent shapes, path segments, or path components, choose the shape tool or pen tool you want to use, and choose one of the following options in the options bar:

• Add to Shape Area (▣) to add the new area to the existing shapes or path.

• Subtract from Shape Area (▣) to remove the overlapping area from the existing shapes or path.

• Intersect Shape Area (▣) to restrict the area to the intersection of the new area and the existing shapes or path.

• Exclude Shape Area (▣), to exclude the overlap area in the consolidated new and existing areas.

Using the Paths palette (Photoshop)

The Paths palette lists the name and a thumbnail image of each saved path, the current work path, and the current layer clipping path. Decreasing the size of thumbnails or turning them off lets you list more paths in the palette, and turning thumbnails off can improve performance. To view a path, you must first select it in the Paths palette.

To display the Paths palette:

Choose Windows > Show Paths, or click the Paths palette tab.

To select or deselect a path in the palette:

Do one of the following:

• To select a path, click the path name in the Paths palette. Only one path can be selected at a time.

• To deselect a path, click in the blank area of the Paths palette, choose Turn Off Path from the Paths palette menu, or click the OK button (☑) in the options bar if you are using the shape or pen tools.

To change the size of path thumbnails:

1 Choose Palette Options from the Paths palette menu.

2 Select a size, or select None to turn off the display of thumbnails.

To change a path's stacking order:

1 Select the path in the Paths palette.

2 Drag the path up or down in the Paths palette. When the heavy black line appears in the desired location, release the mouse button.

Note: You cannot change the order of layer clipping paths in the Paths palette.

Editing paths (Photoshop)

A path is composed of one or more *path components*—collections of one or more anchor points jointed by segments.

Because they take up less disk space than pixel-based data, paths can be used for long-term storage of simple masks. Paths can also be used to clip sections of your image for export to an illustration or page-layout application. (See "Using image clipping paths" on page 369.)

About anchor points, direction lines, direction points, and components

A path consists of one or more straight or curved segments. *Anchor points* mark the endpoints of the path segments. On curved segments, each selected anchor point displays one or two *direction lines*, ending in *direction points*. The positions of direction lines and points determine the size and shape of a curved segment. Moving these elements reshapes the curves in a path.

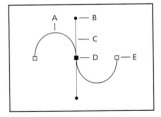

*A. Curved line segment B. Direction point
C. Direction line D. Selected anchor point
E. Unselected anchor point*

A path can be *closed*, with no beginning or end (for example, a circle), or *open*, with distinct *endpoints* (for example, a wavy line).

Smooth curves are connected by anchor points called *smooth points*. Sharply curved paths are connected by *corner points*.

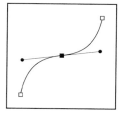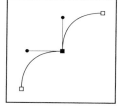

Smooth point, and corner point

When you move a direction line on a smooth point, the curved segments on both sides of the point adjust simultaneously. By comparison, when you move a direction line on a corner point, only the curve on the same side of the point as the direction line is adjusted.

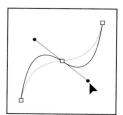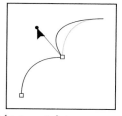

Adjusting a smooth point, and a corner point

A path does not have to be all one connected series of segments. It can contain more than one distinct and separate *path component*. Each shape in a shape layer is a path component, as described by the layer's clipping path.

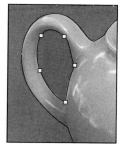

Separate path components selected

Selecting paths (Photoshop)

You can select path segments and path components by clicking with the path component selection tool or the direct selection tool.

Selecting a shape or segment displays all of the anchor points on the selected portion, including any direction lines and direction points if the selected segment is curved. Direction points appear as filled circles, selected anchor points as filled squares, and unselected anchor points as hollow squares.

To select a path:

1 Do one of the following:

• To select a path component (including a shape in a shape layer), select the path component selection tool (▶), and click anywhere inside the path component. If a path consists of several path components, only the path component under the pointer is selected.

To display the bounding box along with the selected path component, select Show Bounding Box in the options bar.

• To select a path segment, select the direct selection tool (▷), and click one of the segment's anchor points or drag a marquee over part of the segment.

Drag a marquee to select segments.

2 To select additional components or segments, select the path component selection tool or the direct selection tool, then hold down Shift while selecting additional paths or segments.

💡 *When the direct selection tool is selected, you can select the entire path or path component by Alt-clicking (Windows) or Option-clicking (Mac OS) inside the path. To activate the direct selection tool when any other tool is selected, position the pointer over an anchor point, and press Ctrl (Windows) or Command (Mac OS).*

To change the overlap mode for the selected path component:

Using the path component selection tool, drag a marquee to select existing path areas, then choose a shape area option in the options bar. (See "Drawing overlapping shapes (Photoshop)" on page 171.)

To show or hide the selected path component:

Do one of the following:

• Choose View > Show > Target Path.

• Choose View > Show Extras. This command also shows or hides a grid, guides, selection edges, annotations, and slices.

Moving, reshaping, and deleting path segments

You can move, reshape, or delete individual segments in a path, and you can add or delete anchor points to change the configuration of segments.

Note: *You can also apply a transformation, such as scaling, rotating, flipping, or distorting, to a segment.*

To move a straight segment:

1 Select the direct selection tool (▷), and select the segment you want to adjust. To adjust the angle or length of the segment, select an anchor point.

2 Drag the selected segment to its new position.

To move a curved segment:

1 Select the direct selection tool (⟨⟩), and select the points or segments you want to move. Be sure to select both points anchoring the segment.

2 Drag the selected anchor points or segments to new positions. Hold down Shift as you drag to constrain the movement to multiples of 45°.

Select points anchoring a curve. Then drag to move the curve.

To reshape a curved segment:

1 Select the direct selection tool (⟨⟩), and select the curved segment you want to adjust. Direction lines appear for that segment.

2 Adjust the curve:

• To adjust the position of the segment, drag the segment.

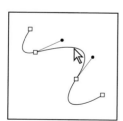

Click to select the curve segment. Then drag to adjust.

• To adjust the shape of the segment on either side of a selected anchor point, drag the anchor point or the direction point. Hold down Shift as you drag to constrain movement to multiples of 45°.

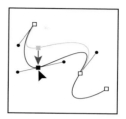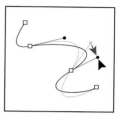

Drag the anchor point, or drag the direction point.

To delete a segment:

1 Select the direct selection tool (⟨⟩), and select the segment you want to delete.

2 Press Backspace (Windows) or Delete (Mac OS) to delete the selected segment. Pressing Backspace or Delete again erases the rest of the path component.

Moving, reshaping, copying, and deleting path components

You can reposition a path component (including a shape in a shape layer) anywhere within an image. You can copy components within an image or between two Photoshop images. Using the path component selection tool, you can merge overlapping components into a single component. All vector objects, whether they are described by a saved path, a work path, or a layer clipping path, can be moved, reshaped, copied, or deleted.

You can also use the Copy and Paste commands to duplicate vector objects between a Photoshop image and an image in another application, such as Adobe Illustrator.

To move a path or path component:

1 Select the path name in the Paths palette, and use the path component selection tool (➤) to select the path in the image. To select multiple path components, Shift-click each additional path component to add it to the selection.

2 Drag the path to its new location. If you move any part of a path beyond the canvas boundaries, the hidden part of the path is still available.

Note: If you drag a path so that the move pointer is over another open image, the path will be copied to that image.

To reshape a path component:

1 Select the path name in the Paths palette, and use the direct selection tool (➤) to select an anchor point in the path.

2 Drag the point or its handles to a new location. (See "Adding, deleting, and converting anchor points" on page 177.)

To merge overlapping path components:

1 Choose the path component selection tool (➤) and click Combine in the options bar to create a single component from all overlapping components in the layer.

To copy a path component or path:

Do any of the following:

• To copy a path component as you move it, select the path name in the Paths palette, and use the path component selection tool (➤) to select the path component in the image. Alt-drag (Windows) or Option-drag (Mac OS) the path.

• To copy a path without renaming it, drag the path in the Paths palette to the New Path button (▣) at the bottom of the palette.

• To copy and rename a path, Alt-drag (Windows) or Option-drag (Mac OS) the path in the Paths palette to the New Path button at the bottom of the palette. Or select the path to copy, and choose Duplicate Path from the Paths palette menu. Enter a new name for the path in the Duplicate Path dialog box, and click OK.

To copy path components between two Adobe Photoshop files:

1 Open both images.

2 Use the path component selection tool (➤) to select the entire path or the path components in the source image you want to copy.

3 To copy the path component, do any of the following:

• Drag the path component from the source image to the destination image. The path component is copied to the active path in the Paths palette.

• Drag the path component from the source image's Paths palette into the destination image. The path is copied to the active path in the Paths palette.

- In the source image, select the path's name in the Paths palette and choose Edit > Copy to copy the path. In the destination image, choose Edit > Paste. You can also use this method to combine paths in the same image.

- To paste the path into the center of the destination image, in the source image, choose Edit > Copy to copy the path. In the destination image, choose Edit > Paste.

Aligning and distributing path components

You can both align and distribute path components that are described in a single path. For example, you can align the left edges of several shapes contained in a single layer or distribute several components in a work path along their horizontal centers.

Note: You cannot align shapes that are on separate layers or that are stored in separate paths.

To align or distribute components:

1 Using the path component selection tool (▶), drag a marquee to select the components you want to align, then select one of the alignment options from the options bar.

- Top (ⷮⷧ) to align the top edges of the selected components.

- Vertical Center (ⷫ) to align the vertical centers of the selected components.

- Bottom (ⷮ) to align the bottom edges of the selected components.

- Left (ⷮ) to align the left edges of the selected components.

- Horizontal Center (ⷧ) to align the horizontal centers of the selected components.

- Right (ⷧ) to align the right edges of the selected components.

2 Select the components you want to distribute, then select one of the distribute options from the options bar.

- Top (ⷮ) to distribute the top edges of the selected components.

- Vertical Center (ⷫ) to distribute the vertical centers of the selected components.

- Bottom (ⷮ) to distribute the bottom edges of the selected components.

- Left (ⷮ) to distribute the left edges of the selected components.

- Horizontal Center (ⷫ) to distribute the horizontal centers of the selected components.

- Right (ⷫ) to distribute the right edges of the selected components.

Adding, deleting, and converting anchor points

The add anchor point and delete anchor point tools let you add and delete anchor points on a shape. The convert direction point tool lets you convert a smooth curve to a sharp curve or to a straight segment, and vice versa. If you have selected Auto Add/Delete in the options bar for the pen tool or freeform pen tool, when you click a line segment, a point is added, and when you click an existing point, it is deleted.

To add an anchor point:

1 Select the add anchor point tool (🖋⁺), and position the pointer on the path where you want the anchor point added (a plus sign appears next to the pointer).

2 Do one of the following:

• To add an anchor point without changing the shape of the segment, click the path.

• To add an anchor point and change the shape of the segment, drag to define direction lines for the anchor point.

• To change an anchor point to a corner point, Alt-click (Windows) or Option-click (Mac OS) the anchor point.

To delete an anchor point:

1 Select the delete anchor point tool (🖋⁻), and position the pointer on the anchor point you want deleted (a minus sign appears next to the pointer).

2 Delete the anchor point:

• Click the anchor point to delete it and to reshape the path to fit the remaining anchor points.

• Drag the anchor point to delete it and to change the shape of the segment.

To convert between a smooth point and a corner point:

1 Select the convert anchor point tool (⌐), and position the pointer over the anchor point you want changed.

💡 *To activate the convert anchor point tool while the direct selection tool is selected, position the pointer over an anchor point, and press Ctrl+Alt (Windows) or Command+Option (Mac OS).*

2 Convert the point:

• To convert a smooth point to a corner point without direction lines, click the smooth anchor point.

• To convert a smooth point to a corner point with direction lines, make sure the direction lines are visible. Then drag a direction point to break the pair of direction lines.

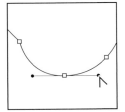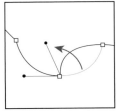

Drag direction point to break direction lines.

• To convert a corner point to a smooth point, drag away from the corner point to make direction lines appear.

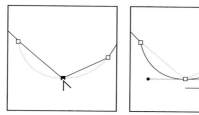

Click to create a corner point. Drag to create a smooth point.

Managing paths (Photoshop)

When you use a pen or shape tool to create a work path, the new path appears as the Work Path in the Paths palette. The Work Path is temporary; you must save it to avoid losing its contents. If you deselect the Work Path without saving it and start drawing again, a new path will replace the existing one.

When you use a pen or shape tool to create a new shape layer, the new path appears as a layer clipping path in the Paths palette. Layer clipping paths are linked to their parent layer; you must select the parent layer in the Layers palette in order to list the clipping path in the Paths palette. You can remove a clipping path from a layer and convert a clipping path to a rasterized mask. (See "Editing a layer clipping path (Photoshop)" on page 240.)

Paths saved with an image appear when you open it again. In Windows, the Photoshop, JPEG, DCS, EPS, PDF, and TIFF formats support paths. In Mac OS, all available file formats support paths.

Note: *Paths in formats other than those listed here generally don't survive a transition from Mac OS to Windows and back to Mac OS.*

To create a new path in the Paths palette:

Do one of the following:

• To create a path without naming it, click the New Path button (⬚) at the bottom of the Paths palette.

• To create and name a path, make sure no work path is selected. Choose New Path from the Paths palette menu, or Alt-click (Windows) or Option-click (Mac OS) the New Path button at the bottom of the palette. Enter a name for the path in the New Path dialog box, and click OK.

To save a work path:

Do one of the following:

• To save without renaming, drag the *Work Path* name to the New Path button (⬚) at the bottom of the Paths palette.

• To save and rename, choose Save Path from the Paths palette menu, enter a new path name in the Save Path dialog box, and click OK.

To rename a saved path:

1 Double-click the path's name in the Paths palette.

2 Enter a new name in the Rename Path dialog box, and click OK.

Note: You cannot rename a layer clipping path. If you double-click a layer clipping path, you'll make a copy of it.

3 If you have created a copy of a layer clipping path by double-clicking it, you can enter a new name for it in the Save Path dialog box.

To delete a path:

1 Select the path name in the Paths palette.

2 Do one of the following:

• Drag the path to the Trash button (🗑) at the bottom of the Paths palette.

• Choose Delete Path from the Paths palette menu.

• Click the Trash button at the bottom of the Paths palette, and click Yes.

💡 *To delete a path without being asked to confirm, Alt-click (Windows) or Option-click (Mac OS) the Trash button at the bottom of the Paths palette.*

Converting between paths and selection borders (Photoshop)

Because of their smooth outlines, you can convert paths into precise selection borders. You also can convert selection borders into paths, using the direct selection tool for fine-tuning.

Converting paths to selection borders

You can define any closed path as a selection border. A closed path that overlaps a selected area can be added to, subtracted from, or combined with the current selection.

To convert a path to a selection border using the current Make Selection settings:

1 Select the path in the Paths palette or select it in the image using the direct selection tool (⬙).

2 To convert the path, do one of the following:

• Click the Load Path as a Selection button (▱) at the bottom of the Paths palette.

• Ctrl-click (Windows) or Command-click (Mac OS) the path thumbnail in the Paths palette.

To convert a path to a selection border and specify settings:

1 To combine the path with a selection, first make the selection using a selection tool.

2 Select the path in the Paths palette or select it in the image using the direct selection tool (⬙).

3 Start converting the path:

• Alt-click (Windows) or Option-click (Mac OS) the Load Path as a Selection button (⬚) at the bottom of the Paths palette.

• Choose Make Selection from the Paths palette menu.

4 In the Make Selection dialog box, select a Rendering option:

• Feather Radius to define how far inside and outside the selection border the feather edge extends. Enter a value in pixels.

• Anti-aliased to create a finer transition between the pixels in the selection and the surrounding pixels. Make sure the Feather Radius is set to 0.

For more information on these options, see "Softening the edges of a selection" on page 147.

5 Select an Operation option:

• New Selection to select only the area defined by the path.

• Add to Selection to add the area defined by the path to the original selection.

• Subtract from Selection to remove the area defined by the path from the original selection.

• Intersect with Selection to select the area common to both the path and the original selection. If the path and selection do not overlap, nothing is selected.

6 Click OK.

Converting selection borders to paths

Any selection made with a selection tool can be defined as a path.

The Make Work Path command eliminates any feathering applied to the selection. It can also alter the shape of the selection, depending on the complexity of the path and the tolerance value you choose in the Make Work Path dialog box.

To convert a selection to a path:

1 Make the selection.

2 Start converting the selection:

• Alt-click (Windows) or Option-click (Mac OS) the Make Work Path (⬚) button at the bottom of the Paths palette.

• Choose Make Work Path from the Paths palette menu.

• Click the Make Work Path button. This converts the selection using the current settings (you can skip steps 3 and 4).

3 Enter a Tolerance value or use the default value in the Make Work Path dialog box.

Tolerance values can range from 0.5 to 10 pixels and determine how sensitive the Make Work Path command is to slight changes in the selection shape. The higher the tolerance value, the fewer the anchor points used to draw the path and the smoother the path. If the path is used as a clipping path and you have problems printing the image, use a higher tolerance value. (See "Printing image clipping paths" on page 370.)

4 Click OK. The converted selection appears as a work path at the bottom of the Paths palette.

Adding color to paths (Photoshop)

You can add color values to a path by filling or stroking it. Filling a path is the same as creating a rasterized shape using the shape tools. (See "Creating rasterized shapes" on page 164.)

For more information, see "Filling paths with color" and "Stroking to paint path borders" in online Help.

Transforming and retouching

You can transform images in many ways. For example, you can redefine an image's perspective; manipulate areas of an image as if the pixels in those areas had been melted; scale, rotate, or flip a selection or image in two dimensions; and transform an object in three dimensions. You can also apply filters to create special effects.

Tools for retouching an image include the clone stamp, pattern stamp, smudge, blur, sharpen, dodge, burn, and sponge tools.

For more information on transforming and retouching an image, see "Transforming and retouching" in online Help. For information on filters, see "Applying filters for special effects" in online Help.

7

Chapter 7: Using Channels and Masks

Each image in Adobe Photoshop has channels that store information about the image's color. You can create additional channels to store spot colors for printing with special inks and to store masks for sophisticated selections.

About channels

Photoshop uses special grayscale channels to store an image's color information and information about spot colors. If an image has multiple layers, each layer has its own set of color channels.

Color information channels are created automatically when you open a new image. The image's color mode (not its number of layers) determines the number of color channels created. For example, an RGB image has four default channels: one for each of the red, green, and blue colors plus a composite channel used for editing the image.

You can create *alpha channels* to store selections as 8-bit grayscale images. You use alpha channels to create and store masks, which let you manipulate, isolate, and protect specific parts of an image. Saved selections in alpha channels can be loaded in ImageReady. (See "Loading a selection into an image" on page 201.)

In addition, you can create *spot color channels* to specify additional plates for printing with spot color inks. An image can have up to 24 channels, including all color and alpha channels.

The file size required for a channel depends on the pixel information in the channel. (See "About image size and resolution" on page 92.) Certain file formats, including TIFF and Photoshop formats, compress channel information and can save space. (See "Managing channels (Photoshop)" on page 187.) The uncompressed size of a file, including alpha channels and layers, appears as the rightmost value in the status bar at the bottom of the window when Document Sizes is chosen from the pop-up menu.

Note: As long as you save a file in a format supporting the image's color mode, the color channels are preserved. Alpha channels are preserved only when you save a file in Adobe Photoshop, PDF, PICT, TIFF, or Raw formats. DCS 2.0 format only preserves spot channels. Saving in other formats may cause channel information to be discarded. (See "About file formats" on page 364.)

Using the Channels palette (Photoshop)

The Channels palette lets you create and manage channels and monitor the effects of editing. The palette lists all channels in the image—composite channel first (for RGB, CMYK, and Lab images), then individual color channels, spot color channels, and finally alpha channels. A thumbnail of the channel's contents appears to the left of the channel name; the thumbnail automatically updates as you edit the channel.

Viewing channels

You can use the palette to view any combination of individual channels. For example, you can view an alpha channel and the composite channel together to see how changes made in the alpha channel relate to the entire image. By default, individual channels are displayed in grayscale.

To display the Channels palette:

1 Choose Windows > Show Channels, or click the Channels palette tab.

2 Use the scroll bars or resize the palette to see additional channels.

When a channel is visible in the image, an eye icon (👁) appears to its left in the palette.

To show or hide a channel:

Click in the eye column next to the channel to show or hide that channel. (Click the composite channel to view all default color channels. The composite channel is displayed whenever all the color channels are visible.)

💡 *To show or hide multiple channels, drag through the eye column in the Channels palette.*

These guidelines apply to channels you display:

• In RGB, CMYK, or Lab images, you can view the individual channels in color. (In Lab images, only the *a* and *b* channels appear in color.)

• If more than one channel is active, the channels always appear in color.

• In alpha channels, selected pixels appear as white; unselected pixels appear as black (partially transparent or selected pixels appear as gray). These are the channel default options.

• If you display an alpha channel at the same time as color channels, the alpha channel appears as a transparent color overlay, analogous to a printer's rubylith or a sheet of acetate. To change the color of this overlay or set other alpha channel options, see "Creating alpha channels (Photoshop)" on page 200.

Changing the display of the palette

You can show the individual color channels in color (rather than grayscale) in the Channels palette and specify the size of the thumbnails. Using thumbnails is the most convenient way of tracking channel contents; however, turning off the display of thumbnails can improve performance.

To show color channels in color:

1 Choose Edit > Preferences > Display & Cursors.

2 Select Color Channels in Color, and click OK.

To resize or hide channel thumbnails:

1 Choose Palette Options from the Channels palette menu.

2 Select a display option:

• Click a thumbnail size. Smaller thumbnails reduce the space required by the palette—helpful when you're working on smaller monitors.

• Click None to turn off the display of thumbnails.

3 Click OK.

Selecting and editing channels

You can select one or more channels in the Channels palette. The names of all selected, or *active*, channels are highlighted. Any editing changes you make apply to the active channels.

To select a channel:

Click the channel name. Shift-click to select (or deselect) multiple channels.

To edit a channel:

Use a painting or editing tool to paint in the image. Paint with white to add to the channel; paint with black to remove from the channel; paint with a lower opacity or a color to add to the channel with lower opacities.

Managing channels (Photoshop)

You can rearrange channels, duplicate a channel within or between images, split a channel into separate images, merge channels from separate images into one new image, and delete alpha and spot channels when you're finished with them.

Changing the order of channels

The default color channels normally appear at the top of the Channels palette, followed by the spot color channels, and then the alpha channels. You cannot move the default channels, but you can rearrange spot and alpha channels to suit the way you work.

Spot colors are overprinted in the order they appear in the Channels palette.

To change the order of alpha or spot channels:

Drag the channel up or down. When the heavy black line appears in the position you want, release the mouse button.

Note: You can move spot channels above the default color channels only if the image is in Multichannel mode. You cannot move alpha channels above color channels.

Duplicating channels

You might duplicate an image's channel to make a backup before editing the channel. Or you might duplicate alpha channels to a new image to create a library of selections to load into the current image one by one—thus keeping the file smaller.

If you are duplicating alpha channels between images, the channels must have identical pixel dimensions. (See "Creating new images" on page 100.)

Note: You cannot duplicate a channel to a Bitmap-mode image.

To duplicate a channel using the Duplicate command:

1 In the Channels palette, select the channel to duplicate.

2 Choose Duplicate Channel from the Channels palette menu.

3 Type a name for the duplicate channel.

4 For Document, do one of the following:

• Choose a destination. Only images with pixel dimensions the same as the current image are available. To duplicate the channel in the same file, select the channel's current file.

• Choose New to copy the channel to a new image, creating a multichannel image containing a single channel. Type a name for the new image.

5 To reverse the selected and masked areas in the duplicate channel, select Invert.

6 Click OK.

To duplicate a channel by dragging:

1 In the Channels palette, select the channel you want to duplicate.

2 Do one of the following:

• To duplicate a channel within an image, drag the channel into the image window or onto the New Channel button (⊡) at the bottom of the palette.

• To duplicate a channel to another image, make sure that the destination image is open. Then drag the channel into the destination image window.

Splitting channels into separate images

You can split the channels of a flattened image into separate images. The original file is closed, and the individual channels appear in separate grayscale image windows. The title bars in the new windows show the original filename plus the channel abbreviation (Windows) or full name (Mac OS). Any changes since the last save are retained in the new images and lost in the original.

Splitting channels is useful when you want to retain individual channel information in a file format that doesn't preserve channels.

Note: Only flattened images can be split. (See "Flattening all layers" on page 248.)

To split channels into separate images:

Choose Split Channels from the Channels palette menu.

Merging channels

Multiple grayscale images can be combined into a single image. Some grayscale scanners let you scan a color image through a red filter, a green filter, and a blue filter to generate red, green, and blue images. Merging lets you combine the separate scans into a single, color image.

Note: You can also blend the data in one or more channels into an existing or new channel. (See "Mixing color channels (Photoshop)" on page 190.)

The images you want to merge must be in Grayscale mode, have the same pixel dimensions, and be open. (See "Changing the pixel dimensions of an image" on page 97.) The number of grayscale images you have open determines the color modes available when merging channels. For example, you can't merge the split channels from an RGB image into a CMYK image, because CMYK requires four channels and RGB requires only three.

Note: If you are working with DCS files that have accidentally lost their links (and so cannot be opened, placed, or printed), open the channel files, and merge them into a CMYK image. Then resave the file as a DCS EPS file.

To merge channels:

1 Open the grayscale images containing the channels you want to merge, and make one of the images active.

You must have more than one image opened for the Merge Channels option to be available.

2 Choose Merge Channels from the Channels palette menu.

3 For Mode, choose the color mode you want to create. If an image mode is unavailable, it is dimmed. The number of channels appropriate for the mode appears in the Channels text box.

4 If necessary, enter a number in the Channels text box.

If you enter a number that is incompatible with the selected mode, Multichannel mode is automatically selected. This creates a a multichannel image with two or more channels.

5 Click OK.

6 For each channel, make sure the image you want is open. If you change your mind about image type, click Mode to return to the Merge Channels dialog box.

7 If merging into a multichannel image, click Next, and repeat step 6 to select the remaining channels.

Note: All channels of a multichannel image are alpha channels.

8 When you are finished selecting channels, click OK.

The selected channels are merged into a new image of the specified type, and the original images are closed without any changes. The new image appears in an untitled window.

Note: You cannot split and recombine (merge) an image with spot color channels. The spot color channel will be added as an alpha channel.

Deleting channels

You may want to delete spot or alpha channels you no longer need before saving an image. Complex alpha channels can substantially increase the disk space required for an image.

To delete a channel with no confirmation:

1 Select the channel in the Channels palette.

2 Do one of the following:

• Alt-click (Windows) or Option-click (Mac OS) the Trash button (🗑).

• Drag the channel name in the palette to the Trash button.

• Choose Delete Channel from the Channels palette menu.

To delete a channel with confirmation:

1 Select the channel in the Channels palette.

2 Click the Trash button (🗑) at the bottom of the palette. Then click Yes.

When deleting a channel from a file with layers, regardless of the method you use, Photoshop prompts you first to flatten the visible layers and discard hidden layers (if any) before deleting the channel. This is done because removing a color channel converts the image to Multichannel mode, which does not support layers.

Mixing color channels (Photoshop)

The Channel Mixer command lets you modify a color channel using a mix of the current color channels. With this command, you can do the following:

• Make creative color adjustments not easily done with the other color adjustment tools.

• Create high-quality grayscale images by choosing the percentage contribution from each color channel.

• Create high-quality sepia-tone or other tinted images.

• Convert images to and from some alternative color spaces, such as YCbCr.

• Swap or duplicate channels.

To mix color channels:

1 In the Channels palette, select the composite color channel.

2 Choose Image > Adjust > Channel Mixer.

3 For Output Channel, choose the channel in which to blend one or more existing (or *source*) channels. (See "Restricting blending to channels (Photoshop)" on page 223).

4 Drag any source channel's slider to the left to decrease the channel's contribution to the output channel or to the right to increase it, or enter a value between –200% and +200% in the text box. Using a negative value inverts the source channel before adding it to the output channel.

5 Drag the slider or enter a value for the Constant option. This option adds a channel of varying opacity to the output channel—negative values act as a black channel, positive values act as a white channel.

6 Select Monochrome to apply the same settings to all the output channels, creating a color image that contains only gray values.

Use the Channel Mixer with the Monochrome option applied to control the amount of detail and contrast in the images you plan to convert to grayscale.

If you select and then deselect the Monochrome option, you can modify the blend of each channel separately, creating a handtinted appearance.

7 Click OK.

Adding spot colors (Photoshop)

Spot colors are special premixed inks used instead of, or in addition to, the process color (CMYK) inks. Each spot color requires its own plate on the press. (Because a varnish requires a separate plate, it is considered a spot color, too.) For information on printing spot color plates, see "Printing color separations" on page 389.

If you are planning to print an image with spot colors, you need to create spot channels to store the colors.

Note: To export spot channels, save the file in DCS 2.0 format or PDF. (See "Saving files in Photoshop EPS or DCS format (Photoshop)" on page 359.)

About spot colors

Note the following when working with spot colors:

• For spot color graphics that have crisp edges and knock out the underlying image, consider creating the additional artwork in a page-layout or illustration application.

• To apply spot color as a tint throughout an image, convert the image to Duotone mode and apply the spot color to one of the duotone plates. You can use up to four spot colors, one per plate. (See "Printing color separations" on page 389.)

• The names of the spot colors print on the separations.

• Spot colors are overprinted on top of the fully composited image. Each spot color is overprinted in the order it appears in the Channels palette.

• You cannot move spot colors above a default channel in the Channels palette except in Multi-channel mode.

• Spot colors cannot be applied to individual layers.

• If you print an image that includes spot color channels to a composite printer, the spot colors print out as extra pages.

• You can merge spot channels with color channels, splitting the spot color into its color channel components. Merging spot channels lets you print a single-page proof of your spot color image on a desktop printer.

Creating spot channels

You can create a new spot channel or convert an existing alpha channel to a spot channel.

To create a new spot channel:

1 Choose Window > Show Channels to display the Channels palette.

2 To fill a selected area with a spot color, make or load a selection.

3 Do one of the following to create a channel:

• Ctrl-click (Windows) or Command-click (Mac OS) the New Channel button (▣) in the Channels palette.

• Choose New Spot Channel from the Channels palette menu.

If you made a selection, that area is filled with the currently specified spot color.

4 Click the color box, and choose a color.

For more information, see "Using the Adobe Color Picker" in online Help.

If you select a custom color, your print service provider can more easily provide the proper ink to reproduce the image.

For more information, see "Choosing custom colors (Photoshop)" in online Help.

5 For Solidity, enter a value between 0% and 100%.

This option lets you simulate on-screen the solidity of the printed spot color. A value of 100% simulates an ink that completely covers the inks beneath (such as a metallic ink); 0% simulates a transparent ink that completely reveals the inks beneath (such as a clear varnish). You can also use this option to see where an otherwise transparent spot color (such as a varnish) will appear.

Note: The Solidity and color choice options affect only the on-screen preview. They have no effect on the printed output.

6 To enter a name for the spot channel, choose a custom color in step 4, and the channel automatically takes the name of that color.

Be sure to name spot colors so they'll be recognized by other applications reading your file. Otherwise the file might not print.

7 Click OK.

To convert an alpha channel to a spot channel:

1 Double-click the alpha channel in the Channels palette.

2 If needed, rename the channel.

3 Select Spot Color.

4 Click the color box, and choose a color in the Color Picker dialog box.

For more information, see "Using the Adobe Color Picker" in online Help.

5 Click OK. The areas of the channel containing grayscale values are converted to spot color.

6 Choose Image > Adjust > Invert to apply the color to the selected area of the channel.

Modifying spot channels

You can edit a spot channel to add or remove color in it, change a spot channel's color or on-screen color solidity, and merge a spot channel with the image's color channels.

For information on rearranging, duplicating, or deleting spot channels, see "Managing channels (Photoshop)" on page 187.

To edit a spot channel:

1 Select the spot channel in the Channels palette.

2 Use a painting or editing tool to paint in the image. Paint with black to add more spot color at 100% opacity; paint with gray to add spot color with lower opacity.

Note: Unlike the Solidity option in the Spot Channel Options dialog box, the Opacity option in the painting or editing tool's options determines the actual density of ink used in the printed output.

To change a spot channel's options:

1 Do one of the following:

• Double-click the spot channel name in the Channels palette.

• Select the spot channel in the Channels palette, and choose Channel Options from the palette menu.

2 Click the color box, and choose a color.

For more information, see "Using the Adobe Color Picker" in online Help.

By selecting a custom color, your print service can more easily provide the proper ink to reproduce the image.

For more information, see "Choosing custom colors (Photoshop)" in online Help.

3 For Solidity, enter a value between 0% and 100%.

This option lets you simulate on-screen the solidity of the printed spot color. A value of 100% simulates an ink that completely covers the inks beneath (such as a metallic ink); 0% simulates a

transparent ink that completely reveals the inks beneath (such as a clear varnish). You can also use this option to see where an otherwise transparent spot color (such as a varnish) will appear.

Note: The Solidity option affects only the on-screen preview. It has no effect on the printed output.

4 Click OK.

To merge spot channels:

1 Select the spot channel in the Channels palette.

2 Choose Merge Spot Channel from the palette menu.

The spot color is converted to and merged with the color channels. The spot channel is deleted from the palette.

Merging spot channels flattens layered images. The merged composite reflects the preview spot color information, including the Solidity settings. For example, a spot channel with a solidity of 50% will produce different merged results than the same channel with a solidity of 100%.

In addition, the resulting merged spot channels usually don't reproduce the same colors as the original spot channels, because CMYK inks can't represent the range of colors available from spot color inks.

Adjusting overlapping spot colors

To prevent overlapping spot colors from either printing over or knocking out the underlying spot color, remove one of the spot colors where they overlap.

Use a printed sample of the overprinted inks to adjust your screen display to help you predict how colors will look when printed.

Note: In some cases, such as varnish and bump plates, you may want colors to overprint.

To adjust overlapping spot colors:

1 In the Channels palette, select the spot channel with the color you want to print.

2 Choose Select > Load Selection.

💡 *To quickly select an image in a channel, hold down Ctrl (Windows) or Command (Mac OS), and click the channel in the Channels palette.*

3 For Channel, choose the spot channel from step 1, and click OK.

4 To create a trap when knocking out the underlying color, choose Select > Modify > Expand or Contract, depending on whether the overlapping spot color is darker or lighter than the spot color beneath it. For more information on trapping, see "Creating color traps" on page 384.

5 In the Channels palette, select the underlying spot channel that contains areas you want to knock out. Press Backspace (Windows) or Delete (Mac OS).

💡 *This method can be used to knock out areas from any channels under a spot color, such as the CMYK channels.*

6 If a spot color in one channel overlaps more than one other spot color, repeat this process for each channel that contains areas you want removed.

Using channel calculations to blend layers and channels (Photoshop)

You can use the blending effects associated with layers to combine channels within and between images into new images using the Apply Image command (on single and composite channels) and the Calculations command (on single channels). These commands offer two additional blending modes not available in the Layers palette—Add and Subtract. Although it's possible to create new combinations of channels by copying channels into layers in the Layers palette, you may find it quicker to use the calculation commands to blend channel information.

The calculation commands perform mathematical operations on the corresponding pixels of two channels (the pixels with identical locations on the image) and then combine the results in a single channel. Two concepts are fundamental to understanding how the calculation commands work.

• Each pixel in a channel has a brightness value from 0 (off or black) to 255 (on or white). The Calculations and Apply Image commands manipulate these values to produce the resulting composite pixels.

• These commands overlay the pixels in two or more channels. Thus, the images used for calculations must have the same pixel dimensions. (See "Changing image size and resolution" on page 95 for information on adjusting an image's pixel dimensions.)

Using the Apply Image command

The Apply Image command lets you blend one image's layer and channel (the *source*) with a layer and channel of the active image (the *destination*).

To use the Apply Image command:

1 Open the source and destination images, and select the desired layer and channel in the destination image. The pixel dimensions of the images must match for image names to appear in the Apply Image dialog box.

Note: If the color modes of the two images differ (for example, one image is RGB and the other is CMYK), you can copy a single channel to another channel between images, but you cannot copy a composite channel to a composite channel in another image.

2 Choose Image > Apply Image.

3 Choose the source image, layer, and channel you want to combine with the destination. To use all layers in the source image, select Merged for Layer.

4 Select Preview to preview the results in the image window.

5 Select Invert to use the negative of the channel contents in the calculation.

6 For Blending, choose a blending option.

For information on the Add and Subtract options, see "About the Add and Subtract blending modes" on page 196.

For information on other blending options, see "Selecting a blending mode" in online Help.

7 Enter an opacity to specify the effect's strength.

8 Select Preserve Transparency to apply the results only to opaque areas in the result layer.

9 Select Mask if you want to apply the blending through a mask. Then choose the image and layer containing the mask. For Channel, you can choose any color or alpha channel to use as the mask. You can also use a mask based on the active selection or the boundaries of the chosen layer (Transparency). Select Invert to reverse the masked and unmasked areas of the channel. (See "Using channel calculations to blend layers and channels (Photoshop)" on page 194.)

10 Click OK.

Using the Calculations command

The Calculations command lets you blend two individual channels from one or more source images. You can then apply the results to a new image or to a new channel or selection in the active image. You cannot apply the Calculations command to composite channels.

To use the Calculations command:

1 Open the source image or images. The pixel dimensions of the images must match for image names to appear in the Calculations dialog box.

2 Choose Image > Calculations.

3 Select Preview to preview the results in the image window.

4 Choose the first source image, layer, and channel. To use all the layers in the source image, choose Merged for Layer.

5 Select Invert to use the negative of the channel contents in the calculation. For Channel, choose Gray to get the same effect as would be obtained by converting the image to a grayscale image.

6 Choose the second source image, layer, and channel, specifying further options as described in step 5.

7 For Blending, choose a blending mode.

For information on the Add and Subtract modes, see "About the Add and Subtract blending modes" on page 196.

For information on other blending modes, see "Selecting a blending mode" in online Help.

8 Enter an opacity to specify the effect's strength.

9 Select Mask if you want to apply the blending through a mask. Then choose the image and layer containing the mask. For Channel, you can choose any color or alpha channel to use as the mask. You can also use a mask based on the active selection or the boundaries of the chosen layer (Transparency). Select Invert to reverse the masked and unmasked areas of the channel.

10 For Result, specify whether to place the blending results in a new document, or in a new channel or selection in the active image.

11 Click OK.

About the Add and Subtract blending modes

The Add and Subtract blending modes are available only for the Apply Image and Calculations commands.

Add Adds the pixel values in two channels. This is a good way to combine nonoverlapping images in two channels.

Because higher pixel values represent lighter colors, adding channels with overlapping pixels lightens the image. Black areas in both channels remain black (0 + 0 = 0). White in either channel results in white (255 + any value = 255 or greater).

Add mode divides the sum of the pixel values by the Scale amount and then adds the Offset value to the sum. For example, if you wanted to find the average of the pixels in two channels, you would add them, divide by 2, and enter no Offset value.

The Scale factor may be any number between 1.000 and 2.000. Entering a higher Scale value darkens the image.

The Offset value lets you lighten or darken the pixels in the destination channel by any brightness value between +255 and −255. Negative values darken the image; positive values lighten the image.

Subtract Subtracts the pixel values in the source channel from the corresponding pixels in the target channel. As with Add mode, the result is then divided by the Scale factor and added to the Offset value.

The Scale factor may be any number between 1.000 and 2.000. The Offset value lets you lighten or darken the pixels in the destination channel by any brightness value between +255 and −255.

About masks (Photoshop)

Masks let you isolate and protect areas of an image as you apply color changes, filters, or other effects to the rest of the image. When you select part of an image, the area that is not selected is "masked" or protected from editing. You can also use masks for complex image editing such as gradually applying color or filter effects to an image.

In addition, masks let you save and reuse time-consuming selections as alpha channels. (Alpha channels can be converted to selections and then used for image editing.) Because masks are stored as 8-bit grayscale channels, you can refine and edit them using the full array of painting and editing tools.

When a mask channel is selected in the Channels palette, foreground and background colors appear as grayscale values. (See "Creating temporary masks in Quick Mask mode (Photoshop)" on page 197.)

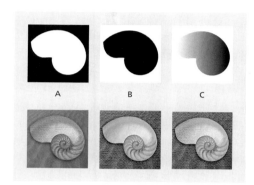

A. Opaque mask used to protect the background and color the shell. **B.** *Opaque mask used to protect the shell and color the background.* **C.** *Semitransparent mask used to color the background and part of the shell.*

In Photoshop, you can create masks, all stored at least temporarily as grayscale channels, in the following ways:

• Quick Mask mode lets you create and view a temporary mask for an image. Temporary masks are useful when you don't want to save the mask for later use. (See "Creating temporary masks in Quick Mask mode (Photoshop)" on page 197.)

• Alpha channels let you save and load a selection to be used as a mask. (See "Storing masks in alpha channels" on page 199.)

• Layer masks and layer clipping paths let you produce a mix of soft and hard masking edges on the same layer. By making changes to the layer mask or the layer clipping path, you can apply a variety of special effects. (See "Hiding portions of a layer" on page 237.)

Creating temporary masks in Quick Mask mode (Photoshop)

Quick Mask mode lets you edit any selection as a mask without using the Channels palette and while viewing your image. The advantage of editing your selection as a mask is that you can use almost any Photoshop tool or filter to modify the mask. For example, if you create a rectangular selection with the marquee tool, you can enter Quick Mask mode and use the paintbrush to extend or contract the selection, or you can use a filter to distort the edges of the selection. You can also use selection tools, because the quick mask is not a selection.

Start with a selected area and use Quick Mask mode to add to or subtract from it to make the mask. Alternatively, create the mask entirely in Quick Mask mode. Color differentiates the protected and unprotected areas. When you leave Quick Mask mode, the unprotected areas become a selection.

A temporary Quick Mask channel appears in the Channels palette while you work in Quick Mask mode. However, you do all mask editing in the image window.

To create a temporary mask:

1 Using any selection tool, select the part of the image you want to change.

2 Click the Quick Mask mode button ( ) in the toolbox.

Selected area, and Quick Mask mode applied

A color overlay (similar to a rubylith) covers and protects the area outside the selection. The original selection is left unprotected by this mask. By default, Quick Mask mode colors the protected area using a red, 50% opaque overlay.

3 To edit the mask, select a painting or editing tool from the toolbox, or select a filter or adjustment command from the menu bar. By default, painting with black adds to the mask,

shrinking the selection. Painting with white removes areas from the mask, expanding the selection. Painting with gray or another color creates a semitransparent area, useful for feathering or anti-aliased effects.

4 Click the Standard mode button ( ) in the toolbox to turn off the quick mask and return to your original image. A selection border now surrounds the unprotected area of the quick mask.

If a feathered mask is converted to a selection, the boundary line runs halfway between the black pixels and the white pixels of the mask gradient. The selection boundary indicates the pixels transition from being less than 50% selected to more than 50% selected.

5 Apply the desired changes to the image. Changes affect only the selected area.

6 Choose Select > Deselect to deselect the selection, or save the selection.

To change the Quick Mask options:

1 Double-click the Quick Mask mode button ( ) in the toolbox.

2 Choose from the following display options:

• Masked Areas (the default) to have masked (protected or unselected) areas appear black (opaque) and to have selected areas appear white (transparent). Painting with black increases the masked, protected area; painting with white increases the selected area.

With this option, the Quick Mask button in the toolbox appears as a white circle on a gray background ( ).

• Selected Areas to have masked or protected areas appear white (transparent) and to have selected areas appear black (opaque). Painting with white increases the masked, protected area; painting with black increases the selected area.

With this option, the Quick Mask button in the toolbox appears as a gray circle on a white background (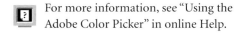).

To toggle between the Masked Areas and Selected Areas options for quick masks, Alt-click (Windows) or Option-click (Mac OS) the Quick Mask mode button.

3 To choose a new mask color, click the color box, and choose a new color.

For more information, see "Using the Adobe Color Picker" in online Help.

4 To change the opacity, enter a value between 0% and 100%.

Both the color and opacity settings affect only the appearance of the mask and have no effect on how underlying areas are protected. Changing these settings may make the mask more easily visible against the colors in the image.

5 Click OK.

You can convert this temporary mask to a permanent alpha channel by switching to standard mode and choosing Select > Save Selection.

Storing masks in alpha channels

In addition to the temporary masks of Quick Mask mode, you can create more permanent masks by storing them in *alpha channels*. This allows you to use the masks again in the same image or in a different image.

You can create an alpha channel in Photoshop and then add a mask to it. You can also save an existing selection in a Photoshop or ImageReady image as an alpha channel that will appear in the Channels palette in Photoshop.

About alpha channels (Photoshop)

An alpha channel has these properties:

• Each image (except 16-bit images) can contain up to 24 channels, including all color and alpha channels.

• All channels are 8-bit grayscale images, capable of displaying 256 levels of gray.

• You can specify a name, color, mask option, and opacity for each channel. (The opacity affects the preview of the channel, not the image.)

• All new channels have the same dimensions and number of pixels as the original image.

• You can edit the mask in an alpha channel using the painting and editing tools.

Creating alpha channels (Photoshop)

You can create a new alpha channel and then use painting or editing tools to add the mask to it.

To create an alpha channel using current options:

1 Click the New Channel button (▣) at the bottom of the Channels palette. The new channel is named according to the sequence in which it was created.

2 Use a painting or editing tool to paint in the image. Paint with black to add to the channel; paint with white to remove from the channel; paint with a lower opacity or a color to add to the channel with lower opacities.

To create an alpha channel and specify options:

1 Do one of the following:

• Alt-click (Windows) or Option-click (Mac OS) the New Channel button (▣) at the bottom of the palette.

• Choose New Channel from the Channels palette menu.

2 Type a name for the channel.

3 Select display options for the channel, as described in steps 2 through 4 of the procedure for changing Quick Mask options in "Creating temporary masks in Quick Mask mode (Photoshop)" on page 197. Alpha channel options are identical to Quick Mask options.

4 Click OK. A new channel appears at the bottom of the Channels palette and is the only channel visible in the image window.

5 Click the eye icon (👁) next to a color channel or the composite color channel to display the image with a color overlay.

6 Use a painting or editing tool to paint in the image. Paint with black to add to the new channel, paint with white to remove from the new channel, or paint with a lower opacity or a color to add to the new channel with lower opacities.

Saving a mask selection

You can save any selection as a mask in a new or existing alpha channel.

To save a selection to a new channel with default options (Photoshop):

1 Select the area or areas of the image that you want to isolate.

2 Click the Save Selection button (▢) at the bottom of the Channels palette. A new channel appears, named according to the sequence in which it was created.

To save a selection to a new or existing channel:

1 Select the area or areas of the image that you want to isolate.

2 Choose Select > Save Selection.

3 In the Save Selection dialog box, choose a destination image for the selection in the Document menu.

By default, the selection is placed in a channel in your active image. You can choose to save the selection to a channel in another open image with the same pixel dimensions or to a new image.

4 In the Channel menu, choose a destination channel for the selection.

By default, the selection is saved in a new channel. You can choose to save the selection to any existing channel in the selected image or to a layer mask if the image contains layers.

5 If you're saving the selection to an existing channel, select how to combine the selections:

• Replace Channel to replace the current selection in the channel.

• Add to Channel to add the selection to the current channel contents.

• Subtract from Channel to delete the selection from the channel contents.

• Intersect with Channel to keep the areas of the new selection that intersect with the channel contents.

6 Click OK.

In Photoshop, you can select the channel in the Channels palette to see the saved selection displayed in grayscale. A selection saved in ImageReady will appear in a new or existing channel in the Photoshop Channels palette.

Modifying alpha channels (Photoshop)

You can edit an alpha channel to add or remove color in it, and you can specify settings for the masking colors and opacity.

See "Managing channels (Photoshop)" on page 187 for information on rearranging, duplicating, or deleting alpha channels.

To edit an alpha channel:

Use a painting or editing tool to paint in the image. Paint with black to add to the channel, paint with white to remove from the channel, or paint with a lower opacity or a color to add to the channel with lower opacities.

To change an alpha channel's options:

1 Do one of the following:

• Select the channel in the Channels palette, and choose Channel Options from the palette menu.

• Double-click the channel name in the Channels palette.

2 Enter a new name for the channel.

3 Choose display options, as described in steps 2 through 4 of the procedure on Quick Mask options in "Creating temporary masks in Quick Mask mode (Photoshop)" on page 197.

See "Modifying spot channels" on page 192 for information on changing Spot Color channel options.

Note: *You cannot modify options for the default color channels.*

Loading a selection into an image

You can reuse a previously saved selection by loading it into an image. In Photoshop, you can also load the selection into an image when you have finished modifying an alpha channel.

To load a saved selection using shortcuts (Photoshop):

Do one of the following in the Channels palette:

• Select the alpha channel, click the Load Selection button (⬚) at the bottom of the palette, and then click the composite color channel near the top of the palette.

• Ctrl-click (Windows) or Command-click (Mac OS) the channel containing the selection you want to load.

• To add the mask to an existing selection, press Ctrl+Shift (Windows) or Command+Shift (Mac OS), and click the channel.

• To subtract the mask from an existing selection, press Ctrl+Alt (Windows) or Command+Option (Mac OS), and click the channel.

• To load the intersection of the saved selection and an existing selection, press Ctrl+Alt+Shift (Windows) or Command+Option+Shift (Mac OS), and select the channel.

To load a saved selection into an image (Photoshop):

1 Choose Select > Load Selection. For Document, the active filename is selected.

2 For Channel, choose the channel containing the selection you want to load.

3 Click Invert to make the nonselected areas selected and vice versa.

4 If the destination image already has a selection, indicate how to combine the selections. (For information on these options, see "Saving a mask selection" on page 200.)

5 Click OK.

To load a saved selection into an image (ImageReady):

Choose Select > Load Selection, then choose an option from the submenu.

To load a selection from another image (Photoshop):

1 Open the two images you want to use.

Note: The images must have identical pixel dimensions. (See "Changing the pixel dimensions of an image" on page 97.)

2 Make the destination image active, and choose Select > Load Selection.

3 For Document, choose the source image.

4 For Channel, choose the channel containing the selection you want to use as a mask.

5 Click Invert if you want to make the nonselected areas selected and vice versa.

6 If the destination image already has a selection, indicate how to combine the selections. (For information on these options, see "Saving a mask selection" on page 200.)

7 Click OK.

8

Chapter 8: Using Layers

When you create, import, or scan an image in Adobe Photoshop or Adobe ImageReady, the image consists of a single layer. You can add more layers to the image, allowing you to organize your work into distinct levels.

About layers

A new image in Photoshop or ImageReady has a single layer. In Photoshop, this layer is called the *background layer* and is analogous to the base layer of a painting. You cannot change the position of the background layer in the stacking order (it is always at the bottom of the stacking order); nor can you apply a blending mode or opacity to a background layer (unless you first convert it to a normal layer).

Layers allow you to make changes to an image without altering your original image data. For example, you might store photographs or elements of photographs on separate layers and then combine them into one composite image. Think of layers as sheets of acetate stacked one on top of the other. Where there is no image on a layer (that is, in places where the layer is transparent),

you can see through to the layers below. All layers in a file have the same resolution, start with the same number of channels, and have the same image mode (RGB, CMYK, or Grayscale).

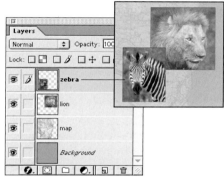

The zebra is on the topmost layer.

Transparent areas on a layer let you see through to the layers below.

You can draw, edit, paste, and reposition elements on one layer without disturbing the others. Until you combine, or *merge*, the layers, each layer remains independent of the others in the image. This means you can experiment freely with graphics, type, opacities, and blending modes. Photoshop and ImageReady support normal layers and text layers. Additionally, Photoshop supports adjustment and fill layers. You can apply sophisticated effects to layers using masks, layer clipping paths, and layer styles. In ImageReady, you can also use layers to create rollover states and animations.

When you transfer a layered image between Photoshop and ImageReady, all layers, layer masks, layer clipping paths, layer styles, and adjustment layers are preserved. Although adjustment layers and fill layers can be applied and edited only in Photoshop, they can be viewed in ImageReady. Layer clipping paths can be created with either Photoshop or ImageReady, but Photoshop provides more support for editing them.

About layer sets

Layer sets help you organize and manage contiguous layers. You can expand a layer set to display the layers it contains or collapse it to reduce clutter. You can also use layer sets to apply masks to groups of layers.

Layer sets function like layers; you can view, select, duplicate, move, or change the stacking order of layers in a set the same way you do layers. You can easily move layers into and out of layer sets, or create new layers within a layer set; however, you cannot nest layers, that is, create or move one layer set within another. Additionally, you cannot apply a layer effect to a layer set or use a layer set as the base for a clipping group.

Using the Layers palette

You can use the Layers palette to create, hide, display, duplicate, merge, link, lock, and delete layers. The Layers palette lists all layers and layer sets in an image, starting with the topmost layer. A thumbnail of the layer's contents appears next to the layer name. The thumbnail is updated as you edit. You can make changes only to the *active* layer, and only one layer can be active at a time. When you move or transform the active layer, those changes also affect any layers linked to it. Additionally, you can fully or partially lock layers to protect their contents.

You can also use the Layers palette to apply layer masks and layer clipping paths to a layer. You can also apply layer styles to a layer and create adjustment layers or fill layers. You can use a clipping group to act as a mask for a group of layers or to specify a blending mode for a group of layers.

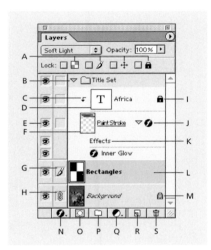

A. Layer lock options (from left to right): Transparency, Image, Position, All B. Layer set C. Clipping group D. Text layer E. Show/Hide F. Base of clipping group G. Paintbrush icon H. Link/Unlink I. Fully locked layer J. Show/Hide layer style K. Effects bar L. Selected layer M. Partially locked layer N. New layer styles O. New layer mask P. New layer set Q. New adjustment or fill layer R. New layer S. Trash

Viewing the Layers palette

You can use the Windows menu to display the Layers palette, and use the palette tab to bring it to the front of the group of palettes.

To view the Layers palette:

1 Choose Window > Show Layers, or click the Layers palette tab.

2 Use the scroll bars, or resize the palette to see additional layers.

3 Click the arrow (▷) to expand or collapse layer sets and layer effects such as drop shadows, glows, beveling, and embossing. (See "Using layer styles" on page 226.)

Viewing and selecting layers

With the Layers palette, you can control whether or not a layer, layer set, or layer effect is visible; whether or not a preview or *thumbnail* of a layer's contents is displayed; and also how transparency is displayed. Turning off thumbnails can improve performance and save monitor space. You can also color code layers to easily locate related layers or serve as a reminder of changes you need to make. Select a layer to make it the active layer; changes you make affect the active layer.

To show or hide a layer, layer set, or layer effect:

Do one of the following:

• In the Layers palette, click the eye icon (👁) next to a layer, layer set, or layer effect to hide that layer, layer set, or layer effect. Click in the column again to redisplay the layer, layer set, or layer effect.

• Drag through the eye column to show or hide multiple layers or layer effects. You can drag through the eye column next to the layers or layer sets to show or hide them. You can also drag through the eye column next to layer effects applied to a layer to show or hide them.

• Alt-click (Windows) or Option-click (Mac OS) the eye icon for a layer to display just that layer. Alt-click (Windows) or Option-click (Mac OS) in the eye column again to redisplay all the layers.

Only visible layers are printed. Making layers temporarily invisible can improve performance.

Note: You can make the active layer invisible. Keep in mind, however, that changes still affect the layer.

To select a layer:

Do one of the following:

• In the Layers palette, click a layer or layer set to make it active.

• Select the move tool (▸₊), right-click (Windows) or Control-click (Mac OS) in the image, and choose the layer you want from the context menu. The context menu lists all the layers that contain pixels under the current pointer location. (For information on selecting layers interactively with the move tool, see "Moving selections and layers within an image" on page 149.)

The name of the active layer appears in the title bar of the image window, and a paintbrush (✏) appears next to the layer in the Layers palette.

To change the display of layer thumbnails:

1 Choose Palette Options from the Layers palette menu.

2 Select a display option:

• Click a thumbnail size. Smaller thumbnails reduce the space required by the palette—helpful when you're working on smaller monitors.

• Click None to turn off the display of thumbnails.

3 Click OK.

Layer sets do not have thumbnails.

To change the transparency display:

You can specify how transparent areas of a document are displayed while you are editing it.

1 Do one of the following:

• (Photoshop) Choose Edit > Preferences > Transparency & Gamut.

• (ImageReady) Choose Edit > Preference > Transparency.

By default, the transparent areas of a document appear as a checkerboard pattern.

2 For Grid Size, choose a new size for the pattern. Choose None to show the transparent areas in the layer as white.

3 For Grid Colors, choose an option:

• Light, Medium, or Dark to specify a gray pattern.

• Any other color from the list to display the checkerboard in that color.

• Custom to choose a color that does not appear in the list. Then click either of the color selection boxes to specify a custom color.

4 (Photoshop) Select Use Video Alpha to enable Photoshop to send transparency information to your computer's video board. This option requires hardware support—make sure that your computer's video board allows images to be overlaid on top of a live video signal. Selecting this option without hardware support produces unpredictable results.

5 Click OK.

Changing the stacking order of layers

The stacking order determines whether a layer or layer set appears in front of or behind other layers. Note that you cannot drag a layer set into another layer set or drag layer effects below the background. For more information about the stacking order in layers, see "Grouping layers into sets" on page 213.

To change the order of a layer:

1 In the Layers palette, select the layer or layer set that you want to move.

2 Choose Layer > Arrange, and choose an option from the submenu:

• Bring to Front to make the layer the topmost layer.

• Bring Forward to move the layer one level up in the stacking order.

• Send Backward to move the layer one level down in the stacking order.

• Send to Back to make the layer the bottommost layer in the image (except for the background).

To change the order of layers by dragging:

1 In the Layers palette, select the layer or the layer set you want to move.

2 Drag the layer up or down in the Layers palette. When the highlighted line appears in the desired position, release the mouse button.

Note: *By default, the background cannot be moved from the bottom of the layer list unless it is first converted to a layer. (See the procedure to convert a background into a layer in "Adding layers" on page 210.)*

Linking layers

By linking two or more layers, you can move their contents together. You can link layers outside a layer set to each other, to a layer within a layer set, or to the entire layer set. You can also link a layer in a layer set to a layer contained in another layer set or to a layer that is not part of a layer set. Once you link to a layer set, the layers within the layer set are implicitly linked.

By linking layers and layer sets, you can move their contents together. You can also perform the following tasks on linked layers and layers in a set:

• Apply transformations.

 For more information, see "Transforming objects in two dimensions" in online Help.

• Align layer contents. (See "Moving and aligning the contents of layers" on page 214.)

• Merge layers. (See "Merging layers" on page 247.)

• Create clipping groups. (See "Creating clipping groups" on page 218.)

• Create layer sets from linked layers. (See "Linking layers" on page 209.)

• Rasterize linked layers. (See "Simplifying layers" on page 245.)

To link layers:

1 Select a layer or layer set in the Layers palette.

2 Click in the column immediately to the left of any layers you want to link to the selected layer. A link icon (⊗) appears in the column. When you link to a layer set, the layers contained in the layer set are implicitly linked and display a dimmed link icon (⊗).

To unlink layers:

In the Layers palette, click the link icons to remove them.

Creating a layered image

You can create a maximum of 8000 combined layers, layer sets, and layer effects per image, each with its own blending mode and opacity. However, the amount of memory in your system may limit the number of layers possible in a single image. Because each layer, layer set, and layer effect takes up part of that maximum value, a realistic maximum value would be closer to 1000 layers.

Note: Images created using the Transparent option in the New dialog box are created without a background. Images with no background—even if they only contain a single layer—are considered to be layered images. Thus, like all layered images, they can only be saved in Photoshop, PDF, or TIFF format.

Adding layers

Newly added layers and layer sets appear above the selected layer in the Layers palette. You can add layers to an image in a variety of ways:

• By creating new layers or converting selections into layers.

• By converting a background to a layer or adding a background to an image.

• By placing, dragging and dropping, or pasting selections or entire images into the image. (See "Duplicating layers" on page 211.)

• By creating type using the type tool. (See "Creating type" on page 251.)

• By using the shape or pen tools to create a new layer that contains a layer clipping path. (See "Drawing shapes and paths" on page 161.)

To add a new layer or layer set using default options:

Click the New Layer button (⊡) or New Layer Set button (▢) at the bottom of the Layers palette. The layer defaults to Normal mode with 100% opacity and is named according to its order of creation. The layer set defaults to Pass Through mode.

To add a new layer or layer set and specify options:

1 Do one of the following:

• Alt-click (Windows) or Option-click (Mac OS) the New Layer button or New Layer Set button at the bottom of the Layers palette.

• Ctrl-click (Windows) or Command-click (Mac OS) the New Layer button or New Layer Set button at the bottom of the Layers palette to add a layer below the currently selected layer.

2 Name the layer, and select mode, opacity, and, in some cases, fill options. (See "Specifying layer properties" on page 219.) Then click OK.

You can also use the New Layer and New Layer Set commands in the Layer menu and the Layers palette menu to add layers.

To convert a selection into a new layer:

1 Make a selection.

2 Do one of the following:

• Choose Layer > New > Layer Via Copy to copy the selection into a new layer.

• Choose Layer > New > Layer Via Cut to cut the selection and paste it into a new layer.

The selection contents appear in the same position relative to the image boundaries.

To convert a background into a layer:

1 Do one of the following:

• Choose Layer > Layer from Background.

• Double-click Background in the Layers palette.

2 Enter a name, opacity, and mode for the layer. (See "Specifying layer properties" on page 219.)

3 Click OK.

To add a background to an image (Photoshop):

1 Add a layer. (See "Adding layers" on page 210.)

2 Choose Layer > New > Background from Layer to create a background layer from the selected layer.

You cannot change the stacking order of the background or apply a blending mode or opacity.

Duplicating layers

You can duplicate any layer (including the background) or any layer set within the same image. You can also duplicate any layer or layer set from one image to another.

When duplicating between images, keep in mind that the resulting size of the duplicated layer depends on the resolution of the destination image. For example, if the source image has a lower resolution than the destination image, the duplicated layer will appear smaller in the destination image and when printed. (See "About image size and resolution" on page 92.)

To duplicate and name a layer in an image:

1 Select the layer or layer set in the Layers palette.

2 Press Alt (Windows) or Option (Mac OS) and drag the layer name in the layers palette to the New Layer button (▣) or the New Layer Set button (▭) at the bottom of the palette.

3 (Photoshop) Name the duplicate layer or layer set, and click OK.

You can also duplicate layers using the commands in the Layer menu and the Layers palette menu.

To duplicate a layer or layer set without naming:

Drag the layer name in the Layers palette to the New Layer button (▣) or New Layer Set button (▭) at the bottom of the palette. The new layer is named according to its order of creation.

To copy a layer or layer set between images:

1 Make sure that both the source and destination images are open.

2 In the Layers palette of the source image, select the name of the layer or layer set that you want to copy.

3 Do one of the following:

• For layers, drag the layer's name from the Layers palette into the destination image.

• Use the move tool (►+) to drag the layer or layer set from the source image to the destination image. The copied layer appears in the destination image where you release the mouse button (and above the active layer in the Layers palette). If the layer you're dragging is larger than the destination image, only part of the layer is visible, but its contents remain available. Use the move tool to drag other sections of the layer into view.

♀ *Hold down Shift as you drag a layer to copy it in the same position it occupied in the source image (if the source and destination images have the same pixel dimensions) or to the center of the destination image (if the source and destination images have different pixel dimensions).*

To copy a layer's contents and paste them into another image:

1 Choose Select > All to select all of the pixels on the layer that fall inside the canvas boundaries.

2 Choose Edit > Copy.

Select a target layer in the destination image, and choose Edit > Paste. The contents of the clipboard are centered in the image. (Only the information inside the canvas boundaries is copied.)

To copy multiple layers or layer sets into another image:

1 Make sure that both the source and destination images are open, and select one of the layers or layer sets you want to copy.

2 If not already linked, in the Layers palette, click in the column immediately to the left of any additional layers you want to move. The link icon appears in the column.

3 Use the move tool (►+) to drag the linked layers or layer set from the source image to the destination image.

To duplicate a layer into another image or a new image:

1 If you are duplicating a layer or layer set to an existing image, open both the source and destination images.

2 In the source document's Layers palette, select the name of the layer you want to duplicate.

3 Choose Layer > Duplicate Layer or Layer > Duplicate Layer Set.

4 Type a name for the duplicate layer.

5 For Document, choose a destination for the layer. To create a new document for the layer, choose New, and type a name for the new document.

6 Click OK.

An image created by duplicating a layer has no background layer.

Grouping layers into sets

Layers can be grouped into layer sets. Layer sets allow you to easily move the layers as a group, apply attributes or a mask to the group, or collapse the group to reduce clutter. Layer sets also allow you to set up blending options for the entire set.

By default, the blending mode of a layer set is Pass Through, which means that the layer set has no blending properties of its own. Layers inside a layer set in Pass Through mode appear the same as they would outside of the layer set. When you choose a different blending mode for a layer set, you effectively change the order in which the entire image is composited. All of the layers in the layer set are composited first. The composited layer set is then treated as a single image, and blended with the rest of the image using the selected blending mode. Thus, if you choose a blending mode other than Pass Through for the layer set, none of the adjustment layers or layer blending modes inside the layer set will apply to layers outside the set.

To create a new layer set from linked layers:

Choose Layer > New > Layer Set from Linked.

For additional methods of creating layer sets, see "Adding layers" on page 210.

To drag a layer into a set:

Do one of the following:

• If the destination layer set is collapsed, drag a layer to the layer set folder (🗀) or the layer set name. When the layer set folder and name are highlighted, release the mouse button. The layer is placed at the bottom of the layer set.

• If the destination layer set is expanded, drag a layer to the desired location within the layer set. When the highlighted line appears in the desired location, release the mouse button.

To drag a layer out of a set:

Do one of the following:

• Drag the layer up or down in the Layers palette. When the highlighted line appears in the desired location, release the mouse button.

• To drag a layer to a position directly below a layer set, drag below the layer set and to the left of the layers contained within the layer set. If the layer set is collapsed, drag the layer below the layer set and make sure the layer set folder and name is not highlighted before you release the mouse button.

To collapse or expand a layer set:

Do one of the following:

• Click the triangle (▷) to expand the layer set and display the layers contained within the layer set.

• Click the inverted triangle (▽) to collapse the layer set and display only the layer set name.

• To collapse or expand effects applied to layers contained within a layer set, hold Alt (Windows) or Option (Mac OS) when clicking the triangle to expand or collapse the set.

Moving and aligning the contents of layers

Moving a layer or layer set on an image moves its contents. You can reposition a layer using the move tool, or you can align and distribute a linked group of layers using the Align Linked or Distribute Linked commands.

You can also lock a layer to prevent the contents from being moved on an image. However, a locked layer can be moved above or below other layers. (See "Locking layers" on page 217.)

Moving the contents of layers

You can reposition the contents of individual layers, layer sets, or linked layers within an image's boundaries unless the layer or layer set is locked or partially locked to prevent movement. (See "Locking layers" on page 217.)

To reposition the contents of a layer in an image:

1 In the Layers palette, select the layer or layer set whose contents you want to move.

2 Select the move tool (⊹). To activate the move tool when most other tools are selected, hold down Ctrl (Windows) or Command (Mac OS). (When a drawing tool is selected, holding down Ctrl or Command switches to the path component selection tool or direct selection tool. When using the slice tool, holding down Ctrl or Command switches to the slice selection tool, and when using the hand tool, holding down Ctrl or Command switches to the zoom tool.)

3 Drag anywhere in the image to move the selected layer into the desired position. To constrain the direction of movement to a multiple of 45°, hold down Shift as you drag.

💡 *To reposition the contents of the layer in 1-pixel increments when the move tool is selected, press the arrow keys on the keyboard. To move the contents of the layer in 10-pixel increments (or to move one frame if you're editing a filmstrip file), press Shift and an arrow key.*

To reposition the contents of multiple layers:

1 In the Layers palette, link the layers or layer sets you want to move. (See "Linking layers" on page 209.)

2 Use the move tool (⊹) to move the linked layers in the image window.

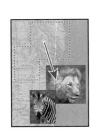
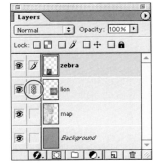

Lion and zebra layers linked and moved

Aligning and distributing the contents of linked layers

The Align Linked commands let you align the contents of linked layers to the contents of the active layer or to a selection border. The Distribute Linked commands let you position the contents of linked layers at evenly spaced intervals. You can also align and distribute the contents of layers using the alignment and distribution options on the move tool's options bar. (See "Aligning and distributing path components" on page 177.)

Before you can align or distribute the contents of layers in a set, you must link them.

To align linked layers:

1 To align layers to a selection border, make a selection.

2 In the Layers palette, specify the layers you want to align:

• To align a single layer to a selection, select the layer.

• To align multiple layers to a selection or to the active layer, link together the layers to be aligned, then select one of the linked layers.

For more information, see "Linking layers" on page 209.

3 Choose Layer > Align Linked (or Align To Selection if you made a selection), and choose an option from the submenu:

• Top Edges to align the topmost pixel on the linked layers to the topmost pixel on the active layer or the topmost edge of the selection border.

• Vertical Centers to align the vertical centermost pixel on the linked layers to the vertical centermost pixel on the active layer or the vertical center of the selection border.

• Bottom Edges to align the bottommost pixel on the linked layers to the bottommost pixel on the active layer or the bottommost edge of the selection border.

• Left Edges to align the leftmost pixel on the linked layers to the leftmost pixel on the active layer or the leftmost edge of the selection border.

• Horizontal Centers to align the horizontal centermost pixel on the linked layers to the horizontal centermost pixel on the active layer or the horizontal center of the selection border.

• Right Edges to align the rightmost pixel on the linked layers to the rightmost pixel on the active layer or the rightmost edge of the selection border.

To distribute linked layers:

1 In the Layers palette, link together three or more layers.

For more information, see "Linking layers" on page 209.

2 Choose Layer > Distribute Linked, and choose an option from the submenu:

• Top Edges to space the linked layers evenly starting from the top pixel on each layer.

• Vertical Centers to space the linked layers evenly starting from the vertical centermost pixel on each layer.

• Bottom Edges to space the linked layers evenly starting from the bottom pixel on each layer.

• Left Edges to space the linked layers evenly starting from the leftmost pixel on each layer.

• Horizontal Centers to space the linked layers evenly starting from the horizontal centermost pixel on each layer.

• Right Edges to space the linked layers evenly starting from the rightmost pixel on each layer.

Note: Photoshop aligns and distributes only those layers whose pixels have greater than 50% opacity. For example, the Align Linked > Top Edges command aligns to the topmost pixel on the active layer that is more than 50% opaque.

Editing layers

A newly created layer is transparent. You can change the colors of pixels in a layer using the painting and editing tools, and then apply layer styles and filters to modify the layer's image data. All painting and editing occurs on the active layer (and in the active channel).

Sampling from all layers

By default, when working with the magic wand, smudge, blur, sharpen, clone stamp, or pattern stamp tool, you are applying color sampled only from pixels on the active layer. This means you can smudge or sample in a single layer even when other layers are visible, and you can sample from one layer and paint in another one.

Alternatively, you can choose to paint using sampled data from all the visible layers. For example, you can use the clone stamp tool to clone an area containing pixels from all the visible layers and layer sets.

To sample from all visible layers:

1 Click the magic wand tool (✎), smudge tool (👆), blur tool (◊), sharpen tool (△), paint bucket tool (🖐), or clone stamp tool (🎂).

2 Select Use All Layers in the options bar.

Note: When you are using tools that sample image data, painting or editing in a new layer where there are no pixels produces the best results when Use All Layers is selected.

Filling a new layer with a neutral color

Some filters (such as the Lighting Effects filter) cannot be applied to layers with no pixels. Selecting Fill with Neutral Color in the New Layer dialog box resolves this problem by first filling the layer with a preset, neutral color. If no effect is applied, filling with a neutral color has no effect on the remaining layers. The Fill with Neutral Color option is not available for layers that use the Normal, Dissolve, Hue, Saturation, Color, or Luminosity modes. (See "Adding layers" on page 210.)

Note: Not all filters produce a visible effect when applied to a layer filled with a neutral color.

Specifying opacity

You can change the opacity of a layer or layers in a set using the Opacity option in the Layers palette. At 0% opacity, a layer is completely transparent; at 100% opacity, a layer is completely opaque.

Note: You cannot change the opacity of a background layer or a locked layer.

To specify opacity for a layer:

In the Layers palette, enter a value in the Opacity text box, or drag the Opacity pop-up slider.

You can also specify opacity in the Layer Styles dialog box (Photoshop) and in the Layer Options dialog box (ImageReady). (See "Using the Layer Style dialog box (Photoshop)" on page 220 and "Specifying layer properties" on page 219.)

Specifying layer blending modes

You use layer blending modes to determine how the pixels in a layer or set of layers are blended with underlying pixels in the image. By applying modes to layers, you can create a variety of special effects.

For a description of each blending mode, see "Setting options for painting and editing tools" in online Help.

When working with layer sets, you can use Pass Through blending. *Pass Through* blending allows the blending modes and adjustments of the layers within the set to interact with the layers outside the set. (For more information on Pass Through mode, see "Grouping layers into sets" on page 213.)

Note: *There is no Clear blending mode for layers. In addition, the Color Dodge, Color Burn, Darken, Lighten, Difference, and Exclusion modes are unavailable for Lab images.*

To specify a blending mode for a layer:

In the Layers palette, choose an option from the Blend Mode menu.

You can also specify a blending mode in the Layer Styles dialog box (Photoshop) and in the Layer Options dialog box (ImageReady). (See "Using the Layer Style dialog box (Photoshop)" on page 220 and "Specifying layer properties" on page 219.)

Locking layers

You can lock layers and layer sets to make certain properties of a layer unchangeable. When a layer is locked, a lock displays to the right of the layer name. The lock is solid when the layer is fully locked so that no editing is possible; it is hollow when partially locked. For example, a layer is partially locked when you lock the layer position so its contents cannot be moved using the move tool. Locked layers can be moved to a different location within the stacking order of the Layers palette, but they cannot be deleted. When a layer is fully locked, you cannot edit the pixels, move the image, or change the opacity, blending mode, or layer style applied to that layer.

You can lock transparency to confine your painting and editing to those areas of a layer already containing pixels. For example, you may want to edit an object (adding special effects, changing color) without adding pixels to the transparent area outside the object. You can also lock the image to prevent inadvertent pixel changes or movement of the image and yet still allow the blending mode, opacity, or layer style to be edited. For example, you can edit the layer mask of a layer with locked pixel data. This is very useful when doing montages.

To lock all properties including blending mode, opacity, and layer style, for layers or layer sets:

Select the layer or layer set, and select Lock (🔒) in the Layers palette to automatically lock all properties for layers or layer sets.

When Lock is selected, the dimmed lock icon (🔒) displays next to all of the layers in a layer set except for layers that have their own individual lock options set.

You can also use the commands in the Layer menu and Layers palette menu to lock all properties.

To partially lock a layer or layer set:

Select a layer and in the Layers palette, select one or more desired lock options:

• Transparency (🔲) to prevent editing of transparent pixels. This option is equivalent to Preserve Transparency in earlier versions of Photoshop.

• Image (🖌) to prevent the painting tools from modifying the image, but not any mask that might be applied to the layer. This option also prevents moving the image.

• Position (✛) to disable the move tool.

You can also use the commands in the Layer menu and Layers palette menu to set Lock options.

To lock all properties for linked layers including blending modes, opacity, and layer style:

Select a linked layer, and select Lock (🔒) in the Layers palette to automatically lock all properties.

You can also use the commands in the Layer menu and Layers palette menu to lock linked layers.

To partially lock linked layers:

1 Select a linked layer, and do one of the following to lock selected properties:

2 Choose Layers > Lock All Linked Layers, or choose Lock All Linked Layers from the Layers palette menu, and in the Lock All Link Layers dialog box, set the following Lock options:

• Transparency (🔲) to prevent editing of transparent pixels.

• Image (🖌) to prevent the painting tools from modifying the image, but not any mask that might be applied to the layer. This option also prevents moving the image.

• Position (✛) to disable the move tool.

To confine editing to the opaque portions of a layer:

Select the layer, a linked layer, or layer set in the Layers palette and select Lock Transparency (🔲) in the Layers palette.

You can also use the commands in the Layer menu and Layers palette menu to lock transparency.

Note: For type layers, Lock Transparency and Lock Image is selected by default and cannot be turned off.

Creating clipping groups

In a clipping group, the bottommost layer, or *base layer*, acts as a mask for the entire group. For example, you might have a shape on one layer, a texture on the overlying layer, and some text on the topmost layer. If you define all three layers as a clipping group, the texture and the text appear only through the shape on the base layer, and take on the opacity of the base layer.

Note that only successive layers can be included in a clipping group. The name of the base layer in the group is underlined, and the thumbnails for the overlying layers are indented. Additionally, the overlying layers display a clipping group icon. The Blend Clipped Layers As Group option in the Layer Style dialog box (Photoshop) or the Layer Options palette (ImageReady) determines whether the blending mode of the base affects the whole group or just the base.

Clipping group with Layer 1 and lion layers

To create a clipping group:

1 Do one of the following:

• Hold down Alt (Windows) or Option (Mac OS), position the pointer over the line dividing two layers in the Layers palette (the pointer changes to two overlapping circles (·⊛)), and click.

• Select a layer in the Layers palette, and choose Layer > Group with Previous.

• Link together the desired layers in the Layers palette. (See "Linking layers" on page 209.) Then choose Layer > Group Linked.

The clipping group is assigned the opacity and mode attributes of the bottommost layer in the group.

To remove a layer from a clipping group:

Do one of the following:

• Hold down Alt (Windows) or Option (Mac OS), position the pointer over the line separating two grouped layers in the Layers palette (the pointer changes to two overlapping circles (·⊛)), and click.

• In the Layers palette, select a layer in the clipping group, and choose Layer > Ungroup. This command removes the selected layer and any layers above it from the clipping group.

To ungroup all layers in a clipping group:

1 In the Layers palette, select the base layer in the clipping group.

2 Choose Layer > Ungroup.

Specifying layer properties

The Layer Properties dialog box (Photoshop) and the Layer Options dialog box (ImageReady) provide options for changing a layer or layer set's name and its color code in the palette.

In ImageReady, you can also set some of the same options in the Layer Options palette. To show the Layer Options palette, choose Window > Show Layer Options/Styles, or click the Layer Options palette tab.

To choose properties for a layer or layer set:

1 Do one of the following:

• (Photoshop) Alt-double-click (Windows) or Option-double-click (Mac OS) the layer name.

• (ImageReady) Double-click the layer.

• Double-click the layer set name.

• (Photoshop) Choose Layer > Layer Properties, or choose Layer Properties from the Layers palette menu.

• (ImageReady) Choose Layer > Layer Options, or choose Layer Options from the Layers palette menu.

2 To change the name of the layer as it appears in the Layers palette, type a new name.

3 To change the color code of the layer in the palette, choose a color from the menu.

4 (ImageReady) Select a blend mode and opacity if desired. (See "Specifying opacity" on page 216 and "Specifying layer blending modes" on page 217.)

5 (ImageReady) To group this layer with the previous layer, select Group with Previous Layer.

6 (ImageReady) Select one or more of the Lock options if needed. (See "Locking layers" on page 217.)

7 (Photoshop) For layer sets, select the appropriate Channel options. (See "Restricting blending to channels (Photoshop)" on page 223.)

8 Click OK.

Using the Layer Style dialog box (Photoshop)

The Layer Style dialog box allows you to set blending options and apply layer effects. To create a custom style using the Layer Styles dialog box in Photoshop, click an effect name in the effects list on the left side of the dialog box, then set options on the right. As you select names from the left column, the options on the right change. You can select or deselect options from the Styles panel to create your desired result.

To use the Layer Style dialog box:

1 Do one of the following:

• Choose a layer effect from the Layer > Layer Style submenu.

• Double-click a layer name or thumbnail in the Layers palette.

• Click the layer styles button (⊘) at the bottom of the Layers palette, and select an effect from the list.

2 To select a predefined style, click the Styles panel on the left side of the dialog box and select a style from the palette. If needed, you can load additional style libraries using the pop-up palette menu.

3 To create a style based on one effect, click an effect name in the Styles panel to display the options for that effect.

4 Edit the options as desired. (See "Using the Layer Style dialog box (Photoshop)" on page 220.)

5 Click OK.

To display the Advanced Blending options:

Double-click a layer name or layer thumbnail. You can also use the Layer menu or the Layers palette menu.

Setting layer blending options

The blending options in the Layer Styles dialog box (Photoshop) and the Layer Options palette (ImageReady) let you change a layer's opacity and blending with the pixels underneath.

Keep in mind that a layer's opacity and blending mode interact with the opacity and mode of the tools you use to paint and edit the pixels on the layer. For example, suppose you are working on a layer that uses the Dissolve mode and an opacity of 50%. If you paint on this layer using the paintbrush tool set to Normal mode with an opacity of 100%, the paint will appear in Dissolve mode with a 50% opacity because this is the maximum the layer can display. On the other hand, suppose you are working on a layer created using Normal mode and 100% opacity. If you use the eraser tool with an opacity of 50%, only 50% of the paint will disappear as you erase.

Setting layer blending options

Photoshop provides general and advanced blending options in the Layer Style dialog box. Advanced blending options allow you to customize layer styles and blend selected contents from multiple layers.

ImageReady provides a subset of the blending options available in Photoshop in the Layer Options palette.

To set blending options (Photoshop):

1 Open the Layer Styles dialog box as described in "Using the Layer Style dialog box (Photoshop)" on page 220.

2 In the General Blending section, do the following:

• Select a mode from the Blend Mode pop-up menu. (See "Specifying layer blending modes" on page 217.)

• Set the opacity using the opacity slider or text box. (See "Specifying opacity" on page 216.)

3 In the Advanced Blending section, do the following:

• Set a fill opacity using the Fill Opacity slider or text box.

• To restrict blending, deselect one or more Channel options.

• Choose a knockout option from the Knockout pop-up menu.

• Select additional knockout options.

• Set a range for the blending operation.

4 To turn off previewing as you choose layer options, deselect Preview in the Layer Style dialog box.

5 Click OK.

To set blending options (ImageReady):

1 Choose Windows > Show Layer Options/Style to display the Layer Options palette. If no options appear in the palette, choose Show Options from the Layer Options palette menu or click the Show Options button (⬍) to view all of the options.

2 Do the following:

• Set a fill opacity using the Fill Opacity slider or text box.

• Choose a knockout option from the Knockout pop-up menu.

• Select additional knockout options.

Specifying fill opacity

In addition to setting opacity for a layer, which affects any layer styles and blending modes applied to the layer, you can specify a fill opacity for layers. Fill opacity affects only the fill of pixels painted in a layer or shapes drawn on a layer without affecting the opacity of the layer effect (bevel, drop shadow, and so on) that has been applied. For example, you can use Fill opacity to cause a bevel effect to appear to be super-imposed directly on an underlying layer.

To specify fill opacity for objects in a layer:

1 Do one of the following:

• (Photoshop) Double-click a layer name or layer thumbnail. (See "Using the Layer Style dialog box (Photoshop)" on page 220.)

• (ImageReady) Choose Windows > Show Layer Options/Style to display the Layer Options palette. In the Layer Options palette, if the Fill Opacity option is not showing, choose Show Options from the Layer Options palette menu or click the Show Options button (⬍) to view all of the options.

2 In the Layer Options palette (ImageReady), or the Layer Style dialog box Blending Options panel (Photoshop), enter a value for Fill Opacity.

Specifying knockout options

The knockout options allow you to specify which layers "punch through" to reveal content from other layers. For example, you can use a text layer to knock out a color adjustment layer to reveal a portion of the image using the original colors. Set the knockout option for the layer where you want the effect to start. For example, if you want text to knock out layers underneath it, set the knockout option on the text layer.

When using knockout options on a layer in a layer set, set the layer set blend mode to Pass Through, otherwise the knockout will stop at the bottom of the layer set. For more information on Pass Through mode, see "Grouping layers into sets" on page 213. You can also use knockout with clipping groups. (See "Creating clipping groups" on page 218.)

Important: *To see knockout effects, lower the fill opacity or change the blending mode of the layer.*

To specify a knockout mode:

1 Select the layer that you want to knock out other layers.

2 To display the Advanced Blending options, do one of the following:

• (Photoshop) Double-click a layer name or layer thumbnail.

• (ImageReady) Choose Windows> Show Layer Options/Style. In the Layer Options palette, if the advanced options are not showing, choose Show Options from the palette menu or click the Show Options button (⬍) to view all of the options.

3 In the Layer Options palette (ImageReady) or the Layer Style dialog box Blending Options panel (Photoshop), choose one of the knockout options:

• Shallow to knock out to the first possible stopping point such as the bottom of the layer set or clipping group containing the knockout option.

• Deep to knock out to the background layer or to the first mandatory stopping point. For example, a mandatory stopping point is the bottom of the layer set containing the layer using knockout, when the layer set uses a blend mode other than Pass Through. If there is no background layer, Deep knocks out to transparency.

4 Select additional knockout options: Blend Interior Effects as Group and Blend Clipped Layers as Group.

There are a number of options that define possible and mandatory stopping points for knockout. Layer sets and clipping groups are possible stopping points for knockout. The blending mode of a layer or layer set and the option Blend Clipped Layers as Group also affects knockout.

For layer sets containing a layer using knockout, knockout stops immediately beneath the layer set if the layer blending mode is not set to Pass Through. Otherwise, it stops before the background. Other layers can still knock through the entire layer set regardless of its blending mode. For clipping groups, knockout stops above the

base of the clipping group when Blend Clipped Layers as Group is selected. However, it stops just below the base of the clipping group when Blend Clipped Layers as Group is not selected.

Africa text with shallow knockout to lion layer and deep knockout to background

Restricting blending to channels (Photoshop)

You can restrict blending to changing only data from specified channels when blending a layer or layer set. By default, all channels are included when blending a layer or layer set. The channel selections vary based on the type of image you are editing. For example, if you are editing a RGB image, the channel choices are R, G, and B. If you are editing a CMYK image, the channel choices are C, M, Y, and K. When using an RGB image, for example, you can choose to exclude the Red channel from blending, and change in the composite image only the channel information contained in Green and Blue.

 For more information, see "About color channels" in online Help.

To exclude channels from blending:

1 Select the layer or layer set from which you want to exclude channels.

• Double-click a layer or layer set name or a layer thumbnail.

2 In the dialog box, deselect any channels that you do not want to include when the layer is blended.

Grouping blend effects

By default, layers in a clipping group are blended with the underlying layers using the blending mode of the bottommost layer in the group. However, you can choose to have the blending mode of the bottommost layer apply only to that layer, allowing you to maintain the original blending appearance of the clipped layers. For more information on clipping groups, see "Creating clipping groups" on page 218.

In addition, you can choose to have the blending mode of any layer apply to all layer effects that fall within the boundaries of that layer. Thus, you can choose to have a layer's blending mode apply to its own Inner Glow, Satin, or Overlay. Conversely, you cannot choose to apply the layer's mode to an Outer Glow or Outer Shadow, because these effects fall outside the layer's original boundaries.

To specify the scope of blend effects:

1 Select the layer that you want to affect such as the bottom layer of a clipping group.

2 To display the Advanced Blending options, do one of the following:

• (Photoshop) Select a layer and choose Layer > Layer Style > Blending Options. (See "Using the Layer Style dialog box (Photoshop)" on page 220.)

• (ImageReady) Choose Windows > Show Layer Options/Style to display the Layer Options palette. If the advanced options are not showing in the Layer Options palette, choose Show Options from the palette menu or click the Show Options button (◆) to view all of the options.

3 To blend the layers in a clipping group using only the blending option applied to the base layer, select Blend Clipped Layers as Group option. This option, which is always selected by default, causes the blending mode of the bottom layer in a clipping group to be applied to all layers within the group. Deselecting this option allows you to maintain the original blending mode and appearance of each layer in the group.

Blend Clipped Layers as Group option deselected and selected

4 To restrict blending of interior effects such as Inner Glow, Satin, and the Color, Pattern, or Gradient Overlay, select Blend Interior Effects as Group. When this option is selected, the blending mode of the layer is applied to all layer effects falling inside the layer bounds.

Blend Interior Effects as Group option deselected, and selected.

Specifying a range for blending layers (Photoshop)

The sliders in the Blending Options dialog box let you control which pixels from the active layer and which pixels from the underlying visible layers appear in the final image. For example, you can drop dark pixels out of the active layer or force bright pixels from the underlying layers to show through. You can also define a range of partially blended pixels to produce a smooth transition between blended and unblended areas.

To define a range for the blending operation:

1 In the Layer Style dialog box Blending Options panel, select a Blend If option:

• Gray to specify a blending range for all channels.

• An individual color channel (for example, red, green, or blue in an RGB image) to specify blending in that channel.

(See "Using the Layer Style dialog box (Photoshop)" on page 220.)

 For more information, see "About color channels" in online Help.

2 Use the This Layer and Underlying sliders to set the brightness range of the blended pixels—measured on a scale from 0 (black) to 255 (white). Drag the white slider to set the high value of the range. Drag the black slider to set the low value of the range.

3 To define a range of partially blended pixels, hold down Alt (Windows) or Option (Mac OS), and drag one half of a slider triangle. The two values that appear above the divided slider indicate the partial blending range.

Keep the following guidelines in mind when specifying blending ranges:

• Use the This Layer sliders to specify the range of pixels on the active layer that will blend, and therefore, appear in the final image. For example, if you drag the white slider to 235, pixels with brightness values higher than 235 will remain unblended and will be excluded from the final image.

• Use the Underlying sliders to specify the range of pixels in the underlying visible layers that will blend in the final image. Blended pixels are combined with pixels in the active layer to produce composite pixels, while unblended pixels show through overlying areas of the active layer. For example, if you drag the black slider to 19, pixels with brightness values lower than 19 will remain unblended and will show through the active layer in the final image.

Using layer styles

Layer styles affect how a layer interacts with other layers, including its blending mode and opacity. You can apply layer styles using the Styles palette, the Layers > Layer Styles menu selections, the Styles button at the bottom of the Layers palette (known as the Layer Effect button in ImageReady), or the Styles pop-up palette in the options bar of the shape and pen tools. You can manage libraries of layer styles using the Styles palette menu, the Preset Manager, or the pop-up palette menu of the shape and pen tools. (See "Managing libraries with the Preset Manager (Photoshop)" on page 85.)

Note: Use the Styles button at the bottom of the Layers palette to create a style by applying one or more layer effects to a layer.

In addition to using predefined layer styles, you can create custom layer styles. Layer styles are especially useful for enhancing type layers and layers containing layer clipping paths. Once one or more layer styles or layer effects have been applied to a layer, they become part of that layer's custom style, which can then be saved as a new layer style for ease of reuse. (See "Using the Layer Style dialog box (Photoshop)" on page 220.)

Note: You cannot apply layer styles to a background, a locked layer, or to a layer set.

Displaying layer styles

You can show or hide all layer styles in the image or in the Layers palette.

To hide or show all layer styles in the image:

Choose Layer > Layer Style > Hide All Layer Styles or Show All Layer Styles.

To expand or collapse layer styles in the Layers palette:

1 Click the triangle (▷) next to the layer styles icon (✹) to expand the list of layer effects applied to that layer.

2 Click the inverted triangle (▽) to collapse the layer effects.

3 To expand or collapse all of the layer styles applied within a layer set, hold Alt (Windows) or Option (Mac OS) and click the triangle or inverted triangle for a single layer within the set. The layer styles applied to the other layers within the layer set expand or collapse correspondingly.

Using the Styles palette

You can use the default layer styles, load libraries of layer styles, or create your own layer styles using the Styles palette. You can change the view of layer styles. Additionally, you can clear a layer style from a layer, create a new layer style, or delete a layer style from the palette. (See "Using the Layer Style dialog box (Photoshop)" on page 220.)

To display the Styles palette:

Choose Window > Show Styles, or click the Styles palette tab.

To change the view of layer styles in the Styles palette:

Choose a view from the Styles palette menu.

• (Photoshop) Select Text Only to view the layer styles as a list.

• Select Small or Large Thumbnail to view the layer styles as thumbnails.

• Select Small or (Photoshop) Large List to view the layer styles as a list, with a thumbnail of the selected layer style displayed.

Layer styles are displayed in the order created by name from top to bottom (and from left to right in thumbnail view).

To delete a layer style from the Styles palette:

Select a layer style in the Styles palette and do one of the following:

• Drag it to the trash button (🗑) at the bottom of the Styles palette.

• Press Alt (Windows) or Option (Mac OS) and click the layer style in the Styles palette.

Managing layer styles

The Styles palette and the Styles pop-up palette in the options bar for the pen and shape tools can hold many layer styles. You can easily change how they display in either palette. (The Styles palette displays in the options bar for the pen and shape tools when you choose Create New Shape Layer.) (See "Using pop-up palettes" on page 62.)

You can also load or save layer styles using the Preset Manager. (See "Managing libraries with the Preset Manager (Photoshop)" on page 85.)

Exiting Photoshop saves the contents of the current pop-up palette in the Preferences file.

Applying layer styles

Layer styles are composed of one or more layer effects. You can apply layer styles to layers in any image. Once you apply a layer effect to a layer, you have created a custom layer style composed of that single effect. You can use a layer style either to replace all of the current layer effects applied to a layer, or to add layer effects while preserving the existing layer effects. After you have applied a layer effect, you can customize it. (See "Using the Layer Style dialog box (Photoshop)" on page 220.) You can also save the resulting layer style for ease of reuse.

Layer styles are composed of a combination of one or more of the following effects:

• Drop Shadow to add a shadow that falls behind the contents on the layer.

• Inner Shadow to add a shadow that falls just inside the edges of the layer contents, giving the layer a recessed appearance.

• Outer Glow and Inner Glow to add glows that emanate from the outside or inside edges of the layer contents.

• Bevel and Emboss to add various combinations of highlights and shadows to a layer.

• Satin to apply shading to the interior of a layer that reacts to the shape of the layer, typically creating a satiny finish.

• Color, Gradient, and Pattern Overlay to overlay a color, gradient, or pattern on a layer.

• Stroke to outline the object on the current layer using color, a gradient, or a pattern. It is particularly useful on hard-edged shapes such as type.

The preset layer styles in the Styles palette, Styles pop-up palette (Photoshop), and the style libraries are composed of one or more of these layer effects and typically have been customized to create a specific result.

To apply a layer style to a layer:

1 Select a method for applying the layer style:

• Click the style thumbnail in the Styles palette to apply it to the currently selected layer in the active document. Press Shift as you drag to add the layer style while preserving layer effects on the destination layer that are not duplicated by the new layer style. (Any duplicated layer effects will be replaced by the new layer style.)

• Drag the style thumbnail from the Styles palette onto a layer in the Layers palette. Press Shift as you drag to add the layer style while preserving layer effects on the destination layer that are not duplicated by the new layer style. (Any duplicated layer effects will be replaced by the new layer style.) The layer style is applied to the layer that contains pixel data under the drop point. If there is no pixel data in that location of the image, the layer style is not applied.

• Drag the style thumbnail from the Styles palette onto pixel data in a document. The layer style is applied to the topmost layer containing pixels where the layer style is dropped. Press Shift as you drag to preserve layer effects on the destination layer that are not duplicated by the new layer style. (Any duplicated layer effects will be replaced by the new layer style.)

• Click the layer styles button (🅞) in the Layers palette and choose an effect from the list. This creates a layer style composed of that single effect.

• Choose a layer effect from the Layer > Layer Style submenu.

• (Photoshop) Double-click a layer name or thumbnail in the Layers palette and select one or more layer effects from the Layer Style dialog box Styles panel to create a layer style, and click OK.

• (Photoshop) Open the Layer Style dialog box and click on the work *Styles* (top item in the list on the left side of the dialog box). Click the style thumbnail you want to apply, and click OK.

• If you are using the shape or pen tools to create a layer clipping path, select a style from the pop-up palette in the options bar before drawing the shape.

2 You can specify options to customize the layer style. (See "Specifying options for layer styles" on page 232.)

If a layer style is dragged onto a layer without pressing Shift, the layer style replaces any existing effects on the destination layer.

To copy layer styles between layers:

1 In the Layers palette, select the source layer containing the layer style you want to copy.

2 Choose Layer > Layer Style > Copy Layer Style.

3 Do one of the following:

• To paste into a single layer, select the destination layer in the palette, and choose Layer > Layer Style > Paste Layer Style.

• To paste into multiple layers, link the destination layers. (See "Linking layers" on page 209.) Then choose Layer > Paste Layer Style to Linked.

The pasted layer style will replace the existing layer style on the destination layer or layers.

To copy layer styles between layers by dragging:

Do one of the following:

• Drag a single layer effect from one layer to another to duplicate the layer effect, or drag the Effects bar from one layer to another to duplicate the layer style.

• Drag one or more layer effects from a layer to the image to apply the resulting layer style to the highest layer in the Layers palette that contains pixels at the drop point.

Scaling layer effects (Photoshop)

A layer style may have been tuned to look best on a target resolution with features of a given size. Using Scale Effects allows you to scale the effects contained in the layer style without scaling the object to which the layer style is applied.

To scale a layer effect:

1 Select the layer in the Layers palette.

2 Choose Layer > Layer Style > Scale Effects.

3 Enter a percentage or drag the slider.

4 Select Preview to preview the changes in the image.

5 Click OK.

Removing layer styles

You can remove a layer style that you have applied to a layer.

To remove a layer style:

1 In the Layers palette, select the layer containing the layer style you want to remove.

2 Do one of the following:

• Choose the desired layer style in the Layers palette, and drag it to the Trash button.

• (Photoshop) Double-click the layer name or the layer thumbnail containing the layer style you want to remove. In the Layer Styles dialog box, deselect the layer style you want to remove.

To remove all layer effects applied to a layer:

1 In the Layers palette, select the layer containing the layer effects you want to remove.

2 Do one of the following:

• In the Layers palette, drag the Effects bar to the Trash button.

• Choose Layer > Layer Style > Clear Layer Style.

• Select the layer, then click the Clear style button ( ) at the bottom of the Styles palette.

• (ImageReady) Select an effect in the Layers palette, then choose Delete Effect or Delete All Effects from the Layers palette menu to delete that one effect or all of the effects applied to that layer.

Converting layer styles to layers

To customize or fine-tune the appearance of layer styles, you can convert the layer styles to regular image layers. Once you have converted a layer style to image layers, you can enhance the result by painting or applying commands and filters. However, you can no longer edit the layer style on the original layer, and the layer style will no longer update as you change the original image layer.

Note: The layers produced by this process may not result in artwork that exactly matches the version using layer styles. In Photoshop, you may see an alert when you create the new layers.

To convert a layer style to image layers:

1 In the Layers palette, select the layer containing the layer style you want to convert.

2 Choose Layer > Layer Style > Create Layers.

You can now modify and restack the new layers in the same way as regular layers. Some effects— for example, Inner Glow—convert to layers within a clipping group.

Customizing layer styles

You can customize a layer style by applying predefined layer styles or effects to a layer, modifying its options, and setting the blend mode and opacity for the layer. In Photoshop, you define a new layer style and customize it using the Layer Style dialog box. (See "Using the Layer Style dialog box (Photoshop)" on page 220.) In ImageReady, you define a layer style using the Styles palette or the Effects button at the bottom of the Layers palette, and customize it using a group of palettes named for each type of effect such as Drop Shadow, Inner Shadow, and so on.

Once you have customized a layer style, you can save that new layer style as a predefined layer style. You can create libraries, load, and save libraries of layer styles using the Styles palette, the Layers Style dialog box, the Style pop-up palette menu of the shape and pen tools accessed from the options bar, the Styles palette accessed by clicking the Styles panel in the Layer Style dialog box, or the Preset Manager. (See "Managing layer styles" on page 227 or "Managing libraries with the Preset Manager (Photoshop)" on page 85.)

Defining a new layer style

You can use an existing style to create a new style or apply a number of layer effects to layers, including drop shadows, glows, beveling, and embossing. When you apply one or more layer effects or a layer style to a layer, an inverted triangle (▽) and a layer styles icon (🌑) appear to the right of the layer's name in the Layers palette. Additionally, an Effects bar containing each layer effect in the layer style is displayed in an indented list below the layer name. Layer styles are linked to the layer contents. When you move or edit the contents on the layer, the layer style applied to that layer is modified correspondingly.

To define a new layer style preset:

1 Apply layer effects to a layer. (See "Using layer styles" on page 226.)

2 Select a single layer effect or a group of layer effects by doing one of the following:

• In the Layers palette, click an individual layer effect name to select it.

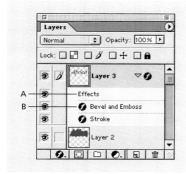

A. Effects bar **B.** *Layer styles icon*

• (Photoshop) In the Layers palette, click the Effects bar in that layer or the layer styles icon (●) next to the layer name to select the style on a layer.

• (Photoshop) Double-click a layer style or the Effects bar. In the Layer Styles dialog box, select additional types of layer effects. Click the checkbox next to a layer effect name to add it to the custom layer style, or click the name of the layer effect to select it and to display its options in the dialog box. (See "Specifying options for layer styles" on page 232.)

3 Create a new layer style by doing one of the following:

• Drag the selected layer style into the Styles palette or onto the New Item button (⊡) in the Styles palette. In Photoshop, enter a name in the New Style dialog box and select Include Layer Effects or Include Layer Blending Options. Click OK. In ImageReady, the layer style is added with a default name.

• Select the layer containing the layer style you want to add. Press Alt (Windows) or Option (Mac OS) and click the New Item button (⊡) at the bottom of the Styles palette, and name the layer style. Click OK.

• Click an empty area of the Styles palette, name the layer style and select Include Layer Effects or Include Layer Blending Options. (The cursor changes to a bucket (⬧).) Click OK.

• Choose New Style from the Styles palette menu. Enter a name in the New Style dialog box and select Include Layer Effects or Include Layer Blending Options. Click OK.

• (Photoshop) Double-click the layer containing the layer style you want to add. In the Layer Styles dialog box, click New Style. In the New Style dialog box, name the layer style and select Include Layer Effects or Include Layer Blending Options. Click OK.

If you create a new layer style using the New Item button, New Style menu command, or Layer Style dialog box, all effects on the current layer are included in the new layer style.

4 To rename a layer style, double-click the new layer style in the Styles palette, rename the layer style, and then click OK.

Editing layer styles

You can edit the layer effects that compose a layer style applied to a layer. To remove layer styles, see "Removing layer styles" on page 229.

To edit the layer style applied to a layer:

1 Do one of the following:

• Double-click the effect displayed below the layer name. Click the inverted triangle (▽) next to the layer name to display the effects contained in the layer style.

• (Photoshop) Double-click a layer name, thumbnail, or the layer styles icon (❷) next to the layer and choose an effect from the Layer Styles dialog box Styles panel.

• (ImageReady) Select the palette named for the effect you want to change.

2 Edit the options. (See "Specifying options for layer styles" on page 232.)

Specifying options for layer styles

When customizing layer styles, you can specify a number of options for each effect contained in the layer style. In Photoshop, many options can also be set by dragging. For example, when you customize a drop shadow style, you can drag the shadow to position it.

Note: In Photoshop, customize layer styles using the Layer Style dialog box. In ImageReady, you can use the palette named for the type of effect such as Drop Shadow, Inner Shadow, and so on. ImageReady provides a subset of the options provided by Photoshop.

Angle Determines the lighting angle at which the effect is applied to the layer. You can define a global angle that applies to all layer effects in the image; you can also assign a local angle that applies only to a specific layer effect. Using a global angle gives the appearance of a consistent light source shining on the image.

Anti-alias Blends the edge pixels of a contour or gloss contour. Most useful on shadows with a small size and complicated contour.

Blend Mode Determines how the layer style blends with the underlying layers, which may or may not include the active layer. For example, an inner shadow blends with the active layer because the effect is drawn on top of that layer, but a drop shadow blends only with the layers beneath the active layer. In most cases, the default mode for each effect produces the best results. (See "Specifying layer blending modes" on page 217.)

Choke Shrinks the boundaries of the matte of an Inner Shadow or Inner Glow prior to blurring.

Color Specifies the color of a shadow, glow, or highlight. You can click the color box and choose a color.

 For more information, see "Using the Adobe Color Picker" in online Help.

Contour With solid color glows, allows you to create rings of transparency. With gradient filled glows, allows you to create variations in the repetition of the gradient color and opacity. With bevel and emboss, contour allows you to sculpt the ridges, valleys, and bumps that are shaded in the embossing process. With shadows, allows you to specify the fade. (See "Creating and editing contours (Photoshop)" on page 236.)

Depth Specifies the depth of a bevel and is a ratio of size. It also specifies the depth of a pattern.

Gloss Contour creates a glossy, metal-like appearance and is applied after shading a bevel or emboss.

Gradient Specifies the gradient of a layer effect. In Photoshop, click the gradient to display the Gradient Editor or click the inverted arrow (▽) and choose a gradient from the pop-up palette. In Photoshop, you can edit a gradient or create a new gradient using the Gradient Editor. In ImageReady, click the inverted arrow (▽) next to the gradient sample and select a gradient from the list, or choose a gradient type from the pop-up list. You can edit the color or opacity in the Gradient Overlay panel the same way you do in the Gradient Editor. For some effects, you can specify additional gradient options. Reverse flips the orientation of

the gradient, Align With Layer uses the bounding box of the layer to calculate the gradient fill. Scale scales the application of the gradient. You can also use the mouse to move the center of the gradient by clicking and dragging in the image window. Style specifies the shape of the gradient.

 For more information, see "Creating gradient fills" in online Help.

Highlight or Shadow Mode Specifies the blend mode of a bevel or emboss highlight or shadow.

Jitter Varies the application of a gradient's color and opacity.

Layer Knocks Out Drop Shadow Controls the drop shadow's visibility or occlusion in a semitransparent layer.

Noise Specifies the amount of random elements in the opacity of a glow or shadow as you enter a value or drag the slider.

Opacity Sets the opacity of the layer effect as you enter a value or drag the slider.

Pattern Specifies the pattern of a layer effect. In ImageReady, click the inverted arrow (▽) next to the pattern sample and choose a pattern from the list. In Photoshop, click the pop-up palette and choose a pattern. Click the New preset button (▣) to create a new preset pattern based on the current settings. Click Snap to Origin to position the origin of the pattern with that of the document if Link With Layer is selected or to position the origin with the top left corner of the layer if it is deselected. Select Link With Layer to specify that the pattern moves with the layer as it is relocated, and drag the Scale slider or enter a value to specify the size of the pattern. You can drag a pattern in the layer to position it while in this panel. The position can be reset with the Snap to Origin button. There must be at least one pattern loaded for the pattern option to be available. You can also load patterns using the Preset Manager.

Position Specifies the position of a stroke effect as Outside, Inside, or Center.

Preview (Photoshop) Displays a preview of the layer style in the image as you change the layer effect settings. This option is in the Layer Style dialog box.

Range Controls which portion or range of the glow is targeted for the contour.

Size Specifies the amount of blur or the size of the shadow.

Soften Blurs the results of shading before compositing to reduce unwanted artifacts.

Source Specifies the glow source for an inner glow. Choose Center to apply a glow that emanates from the center of the layer contents or Edge to apply a glow that emanates from the inside edges of the layer contents.

Spread Dilates the boundaries of the matte prior to blurring. This is particularly useful on small, thin features such as cursive descenders or ascenders on type face, which tend to disappear in the presence of a large blur.

Style Specifies the style of a bevel: Inner Bevel to create a bevel on the inside edges of the layer contents, Outer Bevel to create a bevel on the outside edges of the layer contents, Emboss to create the effect of embossing the layer contents against the underlying layers, Pillow Emboss to create the effect of stamping the edges of the layer contents into the underlying layers, or Stroke Emboss to confine the emboss to the boundaries of a stroke effect applied to the layer. (Note that the Stroke Emboss effect will not be visible if no stroke is applied to the layer.)

Technique For bevel and emboss, Smooth uses a blur-based technique that is smooth and is useful on all types of mattes, whether their edges are soft or hard. It does not preserve detailed features at larger sizes. Chisel Hard uses a distance measurement technique and is primarily useful on hard-edged mattes from anti-aliased geometry such as type. It preserves detailed features more so than the Smooth technique. Chisel Soft uses a modified distance measurement technique and, while not as accurate as Chisel Hard, it is more useful on a larger range of mattes. It preserves features better than the Smooth technique.
For glows, Softer uses a blur-based technique to create a glow and is useful on all types of mattes, whether their edges are soft or hard. At larger sizes, it does not preserve detailed features. Precise uses a distance measurement technique to create a glow and is primarily useful on hard-edged mattes from anti-aliased shapes such as type. It preserves features better than does the Softer technique.

Texture Allows you to specify a pattern used to texture the bevel effect. Scale allows you to scale the size of the texture. Link With Layer specifies that the texture is to move with the layer as it is relocated. Invert inverts the texture. Depth varies the degree and direction (up/down) to which the texturing is applied. Snap to Origin controls the snap of the pattern's origin with that of the document if Link With Layer is disabled and with the top left corner of the layer if it is selected. You can also drag the texture with the mouse to position it while in this panel.

To set a global lighting angle:

To set a global lighting angle for all layers, do one of the following:

• Choose Layer > Layer Style > Global Light. In the Global Light dialog box, enter a value, or drag the angle radius to set the Angle and Altitude, and click OK.

• (Photoshop) In the Layer Style dialog box for Drop Shadow, Inner Shadow, or Bevel, select Use Global Light. For Angle, enter a value, or drag the slider, and click OK.

• (ImageReady) In the Bevel and Emboss or Drop Shadow palette, select Use Global Angle. For Angle and Altitude, enter a value or drag the angle radius.

The new lighting angle appears as the default for each layer effect that uses the global lighting angle.

To set a local lighting angle:

In the PS Layer Style dialog box for Drop Shadow, Inner Shadow, or Bevel, deselect Use Global Light. For Angle, enter a value, or drag the angle radius. Set Distance, Spread, and Size by dragging a slider or entering a value. In ImageReady, deselect Use Global Angle in the palette named for the effect such as Bevel and Emboss.

To set the quality options for glows:

1 Select a contour to shape the effects of opacity by doing one of the following:

• (Photoshop) In the Layer Style dialog box, click the inverted arrow (▽) next to the currently selected contour to view the contour display and select a contour from the pop-up palette. To edit the currently selected contour, click the contour sample. (See "Creating and editing contours (Photoshop)" on page 236.)

• (ImageReady) Click the contour in the effect palette such as the Satin palette, and select a contour name from the list.

2 Select Anti-aliased to anti-alias the effect.

3 To control the amount of Noise, Range, or Jitter, enter a value, or drag the slider. (See "Specifying options for layer styles" on page 232.)

Managing layer styles

You can select, reset, delete, or change the preview of layer styles using the Styles palette and the Styles pop-up palette menu. (See "Using pop-up palettes" on page 62.) You can also use the Preset Manager. (See "Managing libraries with the Preset Manager (Photoshop)" on page 85.)

Creating and editing contours (Photoshop)

You can use contours to shape the appearance of an effect over a given range in the Drop Shadow, Inner Shadow, Inner Glow, Outer Glow, Bevel and Emboss, and Satin effects when creating custom layer styles. For example, a Linear contour on a Drop Shadow causes the opacity to drop off in a linear transition while a Custom contour can be used to create a unique shadow transition. Custom contours created in Photoshop can be used in ImageReady.

You can select, reset, delete, or change the preview of contours in the contour pop-up palette. (See "Using pop-up palettes" on page 62.) You can also use the Preset Manager. (See "Managing libraries with the Preset Manager (Photoshop)" on page 85.) You can create custom contours,

load contours, or save contours in the Contour Editor dialog box. Exiting Photoshop saves the contents of the current pop-up palette in the Preferences file.

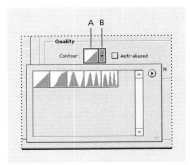

A. *Click to display the Contour Editor dialog box*
B. *Click to display the pop-up palette*

Editing contours

You can use the Contour Editor dialog box to edit the currently selected contour. After you have edited it, you can save it as a preset.

To create a custom contour:

1 Click the contour in the Layer Style dialog box.

2 Click the contour to add points and drag to adjust the contour. Or enter values for Input and Output.

3 To create a sharp corner instead of a smooth curve, select a point and click Corner.

4 To save the contour to a file, click Save and name the contour.

5 To store a contour as a preset, choose New.

6 Click OK. New contours are added at the bottom of the pop-up palette.

To load contours from the Contour Editor dialog box:

Click the contour in the Layer Style dialog box, and in the Contour Editor dialog box, choose Load. Go to the folder where the contour library you want to load is located and click Open.

To delete a contour in the Contour Editor dialog box:

Click the inverted arrow (▽) next to the currently selected contour to view the pop-up palette. Press Alt (Windows) or Option (Mac OS), and click the contour you want to delete.

Hiding portions of a layer

You can create a *layer mask* to control how different areas within a layer or layer set are hidden and revealed. By making changes to the layer mask, you can apply a variety of special effects to the layer without actually affecting the pixels on that layer. You can then apply the mask and make the changes permanent or remove the mask without applying the changes. You can save all layer masks with a layered document.

Another way to control how areas of a layer are revealed or hidden is to use a *layer clipping path*, which creates a sharp-edged mask. You can use both a layer mask and a layer clipping path on a single layer or layer set. A layer mask is resolution-dependent and is created with the painting or selection tools; a layer clipping path is resolution-independent and is created with the pen or shape tools.

In the Layers palette, both the layer mask and layer clipping path appear as an additional thumbnail to the right of the layer thumbnail. For the layer mask, this thumbnail represents the grayscale (alpha) channel created when you add the layer mask. (See "Storing masks in alpha channels" on page 199.) The layer clipping path represents the path that clips out the contents of the layer.

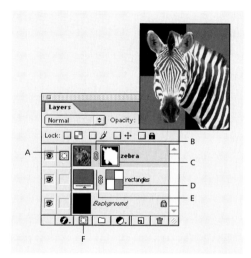

A. Layer mask selected **B.** *Layer mask link icon*
C. *Layer mask* **D.** *Layer clipping path*
E. *Layer clipping path link icon* **F.** *New Layer Mask*

Using a mask to hide or show a layer

You can obscure an entire layer or layer set, or just a selected part of it, using a mask or a layer clipping path.

To add a mask that shows or hides the entire layer:

1 Choose Select > Deselect to clear any selection borders in the image.

2 In the Layers palette, select the layer or layer set to which to add a mask.

3 Do one of the following:

• To create a mask that reveals the entire layer, click the New Layer Mask (◙) button at the bottom of the Layers palette.

• To create a mask that hides the entire layer, Alt click (Windows) or Option-click (Mac OS) the New Layer Mask button.

You can also use the Layer menu to hide or reveal an entire layer.

To add a mask that shows or hides a selection:

1 In the Layers palette, select the layer or layer set to which to add a mask.

2 To create a mask that reveals or hides the selected area of a layer, select the desired area in the image, using the selection tools, then click the New Layer Mask button (◙), and the selected area is revealed.

You can also use the Layer menu to hide or show a selection.

> After creating a layer mask, you can use the painting tools to paint black over the area of the mask you want to hide or paint white over the area you want to reveal. (See "Editing a layer mask" on page 239.)

For information on viewing the contents of the layer mask channel, see "Viewing layer masks" on page 240.

To add a layer clipping path that shows or hides the entire layer (Photoshop):

1 In the Layers palette, select the layer to which you want to add a layer clipping path.

2 Do one of the following:

• To create a layer clipping path that reveals the entire layer, choose Layer > Add Layer Clipping Path > Reveal All.

• To create a layer clipping path that hides the entire layer, choose Layer > Add Layer Clipping Path > Hide All.

To add a layer clipping path that shows the contents of a shape (Photoshop):

1 In the Layers palette, select the layer to which to add a layer clipping path.

2 Select a path or use one of the shape or pen tools to draw a work path. (See "Editing paths (Photoshop)" on page 172.)

3 Choose Layer > Add Layer Clipping Path > Current Path.

Editing a layer mask

You edit a layer mask by adding to or subtracting from the masked region.

To edit a layer mask:

1 Click the layer mask thumbnail in the Layers palette to make it active (the mask icon (◼) appears to the left of the layer thumbnail).

2 Select any of the editing or painting tools.

Because the layer mask is a grayscale alpha channel, the foreground and background colors default to grayscale values when the mask is active. As you edit, the mask thumbnail displays the changes.

3 Do one of the following:

• To subtract from the mask and reveal the layer, paint the mask with white.

Background painted with black, head painted with white, neck painted with gray

• To make the layer partially visible, paint the mask with gray.

• To add to the mask and hide the layer or layer set, paint the mask with black.

To edit the layer instead of the layer mask, select it by clicking its thumbnail in the Layers palette. The paintbrush icon (✐) appears to the left of the thumbnail to indicate that you are editing the layer.

○ *To paste a selection into a layer mask, Alt-click (Windows) or Option-click (Mac OS) the layer mask thumbnail in the Layers palette to select and display the mask channel. Choose Edit > Paste, drag the selection in the image to produce the desired masking effect, and choose Select > Deselect. Click the layer thumbnail in the Layers palette to deselect the mask channel.*

To edit a layer mask's options (Photoshop):

1 Double-click the layer mask's thumbnail in the Layers palette.

2 To choose a new mask color, click the color swatch in the Layer Mask Display Options dialog box, and choose a new color.

▣ For more information, see "Using the Adobe Color Picker" in online Help.

3 To change the opacity, enter a value between 0% and 100%.

Editing a layer clipping path (Photoshop)

A layer clipping path creates a sharp-edged shape on a layer. Typically, you can use a layer clipping path to create buttons or panels. It's useful any time you want to add a design element with clean, defined edges. Once you create a layer with a layer clipping path, you can apply one or more layer styles to it, edit them if needed, and instantly have a usable button, panel, or other Web design element. For information on how to create a layer clipping path, see "Drawing shapes and paths" on page 161. Edit a layer clipping path by clicking the layer clipping path thumbnail in the Layers palette, or the thumbnail in the Paths palette, then change the shape, using the shape and pen tools. (See "Selecting paths (Photoshop)" on page 173.) You can also convert a layer clipping path into a layer mask, which automatically rasterizes the mask.

Important: Once a layer clipping path has been rasterized, it cannot be changed back into a vector object.

To remove a layer clipping path:

1 Click the layer clipping path in the Layers palette to select it.

2 Drag the layer clipping path to the Trash button (🗑).

You can also use the Layer menu to delete a clipping path.

To convert a layer clipping path to a layer mask:

1 Click the layer clipping path in the Layers palette to select it.

2 Choose Layer > Rasterize > Layer Clipping Path.

Unlinking layers, layer masks, and layer clipping paths

By default, a layer or layer set is linked to its layer mask or layer clipping path, as indicated by the link icon between the thumbnails in the Layers palette. The layer and its layer mask or layer clipping path (or both) move together in the image when you move either one with the move tool.

You can unlink the layer from its layer mask or layer clipping path by clicking the link icon. Unlinking them lets you move them independently and shift the mask or layer clipping path boundaries separately from the layer. Unlinking a layer mask or layer clipping path can change how layer effects are calculated. To re-establish the link, click between the layer and layer mask or layer clipping path thumbnails.

Viewing layer masks

By default, the layer mask channel does not appear in the image. You can view and edit the contents of the mask or temporarily turn off its effects. You can also change the display options for the mask.

To select and display the layer mask channel:

Do one of the following:

• Alt-click (Windows) or Option-click (Mac OS) the layer mask thumbnail to view only the grayscale mask. The eye icons in the Layers palette are dimmed because all layers or layer sets are hidden. To redisplay the layers, Alt-click or Option-click the layer mask thumbnail, or click an eye icon.

• Hold down Alt+Shift (Windows) or Option+Shift (Mac OS), and click the layer mask thumbnail to view the mask on top of the layer in a rubylith masking color. Hold down Alt+Shift or Option+Shift, and click the thumbnail again to turn off the color display.

To turn off the layer mask temporarily:

1 Press Shift, and click the layer mask thumbnail in the Layers palette.

A red *X* appears over the layer mask thumbnail in the Layers palette, and the entire underlying layer or layer set appears without masking effects.

2 To turn on the mask, Shift-click the layer mask thumbnail in the Layers palette.

You can enable or disable layer masks using the Layer menu.

To change the rubylith display for a layer mask:

1 Do one of the following:

• Alt-click (Windows) or Option-click (Mac OS) the layer mask thumbnail to select the layer mask channel; then double-click the layer mask thumbnail.

• Double-click the layer mask channel in the Channels palette.

2 To choose a new mask color, in the Layer Mask Display Options dialog box, click the color swatch, and choose a new color.

For more information, see "Using the Adobe Color Picker" in online Help.

3 To change the opacity, enter a value between 0% and 100%.

Both the color and opacity settings affect only the appearance of the mask and have no effect on how underlying areas are protected. For example, you might want to change these settings to make the mask more easily visible against the colors in the image.

4 Click OK.

Viewing layer clipping paths

By default, the layer clipping path does not appear in the image. You can view and edit the path or temporarily turn off its effects. You can also change the display options for the mask.

To turn off the layer clipping path temporarily:

1 Press Shift, and click the layer mask thumbnail in the Layers palette.

A red *X* appears over the layer clipping path thumbnail in the Layers palette, and the entire underlying layer appears without masking effects.

2 To turn on the layer clipping path, Shift-click the layer clipping path thumbnail in the Layers palette.

You can also use the Layer menu to temporarily turn off a layer clipping path.

Applying and discarding layer masks

When you have finished creating a layer mask, you can either apply the mask and make the changes permanent or discard the mask without applying changes. Because layer masks are stored as alpha channels, applying and discarding layer masks can help reduce file size. (See "Storing masks in alpha channels" on page 199.)

To apply or discard a layer mask:

1 Click the layer mask thumbnail in the Layers palette.

2 To remove the layer mask and make changes permanent, click the Trash button (🗑) at the bottom of the Layers palette, then click Apply.

3 To remove the layer mask without applying the changes, click the trash button at the bottom of the Layers palette, then click Discard.

You can also apply or discard layer masks using the Layer menu.

Selecting opaque areas on a layer

By loading a layer mask, you can quickly select all the opaque areas on a layer—that is, the areas within the layer boundaries. This is useful when you want to exclude transparent areas from a selection. You can also load the boundaries of a layer mask as a selection.

To load a layer or layer mask's boundaries as a selection:

Do one of the following:

• In the Layers palette, Ctrl-click (Windows) or Command-click (Mac OS) the layer or layer mask thumbnail.

• To add the pixels to an existing selection, press Ctrl+Shift (Windows) or Command+Shift (Mac OS), and click the layer or layer mask thumbnail in the Layers palette.

• To subtract the pixels from an existing selection, press Ctrl+Alt (Windows) or Command+Option (Mac OS), and click the layer or layer mask thumbnail in the Layers palette.

• To load the intersection of the pixels and an existing selection, press Ctrl+Alt+Shift (Windows) or Command+Option+Shift (Mac OS), and click the layer or layer mask thumbnail in the Layers palette.

💡 *To move all the contents of a layer, you can use the move tool without loading a transparency mask.*

Using adjustment layers or fill layers (Photoshop)

An adjustment layer lets you experiment with color or tonal adjustments to an image without permanently modifying the pixels in the image. The color or tonal changes reside within the adjustment layer, which acts as a veil through which the underlying image layers appear.

Fill layers do not have any effect on the layers underneath them. The fill layer options are solid color, gradient, or pattern. Once you create an adjustment or fill layer, you can easily edit the settings, or dynamically replace it with a different adjustment or fill type.

When you create an adjustment layer, its effect appears on all the layers below it. This lets you correct multiple layers by making a single adjustment, rather than making the adjustment to each layer separately. Adjustment layers can be applied and edited only in Photoshop; however, they can be viewed in ImageReady. When you apply an adjustment layer to a layer set, Photoshop adds the new adjustment layer in the layer set above the existing layers.

For more information, see "Making color adjustments" in online Help.

To confine the effects of an adjustment layer to a group of layers, create a clipping group consisting of these layers. You can place the adjustment layers in or at the base of the clipping group. The adjustment will be confined to the layers inside the set. (See "Creating clipping groups" on page 218.) Alternatively, you can create a layer set, and have the set use any blending mode other than Pass Through.

Original, adjustment layer applied to zebra only, and adjustment layer applied to entire image

Creating adjustment layers or fill layers

Adjustment layers and fill layers have the same opacity and blending mode options as image layers and can be rearranged, deleted, hidden, and duplicated in the same manner. By default, adjustment layers and fill layers have layer masks, as indicated by the mask icon to the left of the layer thumbnail. If a path is active when you create the adjustment or fill layer, a layer clipping path is created instead of a layer mask. When an adjustment layer or fill layer is active, the foreground and background colors default to grayscale values so you can easily edit the mask.

Adjustment layers You can also specify a color adjustment type for an adjustment layer. Depending on your choice, the dialog box for the selected adjustment command may appear. The adjustment layer takes the name of the adjustment type and is indicated in the Layers palette by a thumbnail linked to a partially filled circle. By painting the adjustment layer, you can apply the content to just portions of the under-lying layers.

For more information, see "Making color adjustments" in online Help.

Fill layers The fill layer takes the name of the fill type and is indicated by a color, pattern, or gradient icon to the left of the thumbnail. Fill layers are primarily used with layer clipping paths. For example, when you create a new layer clipping path, it gets filled with a solid color by default. You can later choose to change it to a gradient or pattern fill layer. At times, you may also want to create a new color, pattern, or gradient layer independently of the shape tools.

For example, you can darken the lower half of an image by creating a fill gradient layer from white to black and set its blending mode to Multiply. By doing this on a fill layer, you do not have to permanently modify the original image. (See "Specifying fill layer options" on page 244.)

To create an adjustment layer or fill layer:

1 To confine the effects of the adjustment layer or fill layer to a selected area, make a selection, create a closed path and select it, or select an existing closed path. When you use a selection, you create an adjustment layer or fill layer confined by a layer mask. When you use a path, you create an adjustment layer or fill layer confined by a layer clipping path.

2 Click the New Adjustment Layer button (●) at the bottom of the Layers palette.

3 Choose the layer type you want to make.

4 Choose layer properties as desired, and then click OK. (See "Specifying layer properties" on page 219.)

5 If needed, define the contents of the layer in the dialog that appears, and click OK.

You can also create a fill or adjustment layer using the Layer menu.

To edit an adjustment layer or fill layer:

1 Double-click the adjustment layer or fill layer's thumbnail in the Layers palette.

2 Make the desired adjustments, and click OK.

Note: If an adjustment layer has no associated adjustment dialog box (for example, Invert Layer), double-click the layer's name to open the Layer Options dialog box.

For information on editing a mask, see "Editing a layer mask" on page 239. For information on editing a layer clipping path, see "Editing a layer clipping path (Photoshop)" on page 240.

To change the content of an adjustment or fill layer:

1 Select the adjustment layer or fill layer that you want to change.

2 Choose Layer > Change Layer Content and select a different fill or adjustment layer from the list.

Specifying fill layer options

You can create color, pattern, or gradient fill layers.

Color Specifies the color of a fill layer. You can click the color box and choose a color.

 For more information, see "Using the Adobe Color Picker" in online Help.

Pattern Specifies the pattern of a fill layer. You can click the pop-up palette and choose a pattern. Click Scale and enter a value or drag the slider to scale the pattern. You can edit the pattern settings, then click the New preset button (▤) to create a new preset pattern. Click Snap to Origin to position the origin of the pattern with that of the document if Link With Layer is selected or to position the origin with the top left corner of the layer if it is deselected. Select Link With Layer to specify that the pattern moves with the layer as it is relocated, and drag the Scale slider or enter a value to specify the size of the pattern. You can drag a pattern in the layer to position it while in this panel. The position can be reset with the Snap to Origin button. There must be at least one pattern loaded for the pattern option to be available. You can also load patterns using the Preset Manager.

Gradient Specifies the gradient of a fill layer. You can click the gradient to display the Gradient Editor or click the inverted arrow (▽) and choose a gradient from the pop-up palette. For some effects, you can specify additional gradient options. Reverse flips the orientation of the gradient, Align With Layer uses the bounding box of the layer to calculate the gradient fill when the document bounds are used. Dither dithers the pattern. Scale scales the application of the gradient. You can also use the mouse to move the center of the gradient by clicking and dragging in the image window. Style specifies the shape of the gradient.

 For more information, see "Creating gradient fills" in online Help.

Merging adjustment layers or fill layers

You can merge an adjustment or fill layer several ways: with the layer below it, with the layers in its own clipping group, with the layers it is linked to, with all other visible layers. You cannot, however, use an adjustment layer or fill layer as the target layer for a merge. When you merge an adjustment layer or fill layer with the layer below it, the adjustments are rasterized and become permanently applied within the merged layer. (See "Merging layers" on page 247.) You can rasterize an adjustment layer or fill layer without merging it. (See "Simplifying layers" on page 245.)

Adjustment layers whose masks contain only white values do not add significantly to the file size, so it is not necessary to merge these adjustment layers to conserve file space.

Simplifying layers

You can take layers that may be composed of multiple, generated elements and simplify them to a flat raster image that can then be edited with the painting tools. You can convert data from type layers, shapes, fill layers, linked layers, layer clipping paths, the current layer, or all layers.

To rasterize a layer:

1 Select the layer you want to rasterize.

2 Choose Layer > Rasterize and select one of the following options:

• Type to rasterize a type layer.

• Shape to rasterize a layer containing a shape.

• Layer Content (Photoshop) or Dynamic Fill Data (ImageReady) to rasterize an adjustment or fill layer.

• Layer Clipping Path to rasterize a layer containing a layer clipping path.

• Layer to rasterize multiple generated elements.

• Linked Layers to rasterize linked layers.

• All Layers to rasterize all layers in the image.

Managing layered images

Adding nontransparent layers to an image increases its file size. To conserve disk space, you can delete layers or layer sets, merge two or more layers, or flatten all layers in an image into one layer.

Tracking file size

File size is proportional to the pixel dimensions of an image and the number of layers contained in the image. Images with more pixels may produce more detail at a given printed size, but they require more disk space to store and may be slower to edit and print. You should keep track of your file sizes to make sure the files are not becoming too large for your purposes. If the file is becoming too large, reduce the number of layers in the image or change the image size.

To track file size:

Check the values in the Document Sizes box at the lower left corner of the screen (Windows) or the image window (Mac OS). (See "Displaying file and image information" on page 78.) For more information on displaying file size, see "Changing image size and resolution" on page 95.

The first (left) value indicates the size of the file if flattened. The second (right) value shows the estimated file size of the unflattened file, including any layers and channels.

To track the use of the Photoshop scratch disk (temporary disk space used for storing data when RAM is insufficient), position the pointer over the triangle at the bottom of the image window, hold down the mouse button, and choose Scratch Sizes.

Deleting a layer

Delete layers and layer sets you no longer need to reduce the size of your image file.

To delete a layer:

1 Select the layer or layer set in the Layers palette.

• Click the Trash button (🗑) at the bottom of the Layers palette, and click Yes, or drag the layer name in the Layers palette to the trash button.

• You can also delete a layer using the Layer menu or Layers palette menu.

To delete a selected layer automatically, Alt-click (Windows) or Option-click (Mac OS) the Trash button at the bottom of the Layers palette. When you Ctrl-click (Windows) or Command-click (Mac OS) the Trash button while a layer set is selected, you can specify whether only the layer set is deleted, or the set and its contents.

Merging layers

Merging layers, layer sets, layer clipping paths, clipping groups, linked layers, or adjustment layers combines several layers into one and keeps file size manageable. When you've finalized the characteristics and positioning of a layer's contents, you can merge the layer with one or more layers to create partial versions of your composite image. The intersection of all transparent areas in the merged layers remains transparent.

In addition to merging layers, you can stamp layers, which allows you to merge the contents of more than one layer into a target layer, while leaving the other layers intact. Typically, the selected layer will stamp down to the layer below it.

To merge a layer with the layer below it:

1 Make sure that the two layers or layer sets you want to merge are visible. Select the top layer or layer set of the pair in the Layers palette.

2 Choose Layer > Merge Down or Layer > Merge Layer Set.

To merge all visible linked layers:

1 Make visible all layers or layer sets you want to merge, and link them together. (See "Linking layers" on page 209.)

2 Choose Layer > Merge Linked or choose Merged Linked from the Layers palette menu.

To merge a clipping group:

1 Make visible all the layers in the group that you want to merge (any hidden layers in the group are discarded when you merge).

2 Select the base layer in the group.

3 Choose Layer > Merge Group, or choose Merge Group from the Layers palette menu.

To merge all the visible layers in an image:

1 Hide any layers or layer sets you do not want to merge. Make sure that no layers are linked.

2 Choose Layer > Merge Visible, or choose Merge Visible from the Layers palette menu.

To merge all visible layers into a new layer and create a new empty layer, hold down Alt (Windows) or Option (Mac OS), and choose Layer > Merge Visible. The original layers remain intact.

To stamp a layer or linked layers:

1 Make sure that the two layers or linked layers you want to merge are visible. Select the top layer of the pair.

2 Press Ctrl+Alt+E (Windows) or Command+Option+E (Mac OS).

3 To stamp linked layers, select one of the linked layers, and press Ctrl+Alt+E (Windows) or Command+Option+E (Mac OS). The selected layer is stamped with the contents from the other linked layers.

To stamp layer sets:

1 Make sure that the layers in the layer set you want to merge are visible. Select the layer set.

2 Press Ctrl+Alt+E (Windows) or Command+Option+E (Mac OS). A new layer named after the layer set is created above the layer set, containing an image that matches all of the contents of the layer set.

To stamp all visible layers:

1 Make sure that the layers you want to include are visible.

2 Select the layer or layer set that you want to contain the new contents, and press Shift+Ctrl+Alt+E (Windows) or Shift+Command+Option+E (Mac OS).

The selected layer is stamped with the contents of all visible layers. If a layer set is selected, a new layer named after the set is created, the original layer set is deleted, and all of the layers contained in the set remain in the Layers palette.

Flattening all layers

In a flattened image, all visible layers are merged into the background, greatly reducing file size. Flattening an image discards all hidden layers and fills the remaining transparent areas with white. In most cases, you won't want to flatten a file until you have finished editing individual layers.

Note: Converting an image between some color modes flattens the file. Be sure to save a copy of your file that includes all layers if you want to edit the original image at a later date.

To flatten an image:

1 Make sure that all the layers you want to keep the content from are visible.

2 Choose Layer > Flatten Image, or choose Flatten Image from the Layers palette menu.

Saving layered documents

You may want to save two versions of your file—a flattened version for final use and a second version with layers intact for future edits.

For more information on saving documents and determining file formats, see "Saving images" on page 357.

9

Chapter 9: Using Type

Typography gives visual form to language. Adobe Photoshop and Adobe ImageReady let you add type to images with flexibility and precision. You can create and edit type directly on-screen (instead of in a dialog box) and quickly change the font, style, size, and color of the type. You can apply changes to individual characters and set formatting options for entire paragraphs, including alignment, justification, and word-wrapping. You can create designs that include Chinese, Japanese, and Korean type (if you have the correct system software installed on your computer).

About type

Type consists of mathematically defined shapes that describe the letters, numbers, and symbols of a *typeface*. Many typefaces are available in more than one format, the most common formats being Type 1 (also called PostScript fonts), TrueType, and OpenType.

When you add type to an image, the characters are composed of pixels and have the same resolution as the image file—zooming in on characters shows jagged edges. However, Photoshop and ImageReady preserve the vector-based type outlines and use them when you scale or resize type, save a PDF or EPS file, or print the image to a PostScript printer. As a result, it's possible to produce type with crisp, resolution-independent edges.

Creating type

You can create horizontal or vertical type anywhere in an image. Depending on how you use the type tool, you can enter *point type* or *paragraph type*. Point type is useful for entering a single word or a line of characters; paragraph type is useful for entering and formatting the type as one or more paragraphs.

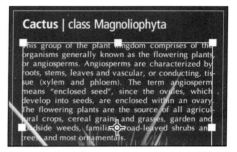

Type entered as point type (top) and in a bounding box.

When you create type, a new type layer is added to the Layers palette. In Photoshop, you can also create a selection border in the shape of the type.

Note: In Photoshop, a type layer is not created for images in Multichannel, Bitmap, or Indexed Color mode, because these modes do not support layers. In these image modes, type appears on the background and cannot be edited.

About using the type tool (Photoshop)

Clicking in an image with the type tool puts the type tool in edit mode. You can enter and edit characters when the tool is in edit mode; however, you must commit changes to the type layer before you can perform other operations. For example, you cannot select a command from the Layer menu while the type tool is in edit mode. To determine if the type tool is in edit mode, look in the options bar—if you see the OK button (✓) and Cancel button (✗), the type tool is in edit mode.

To commit changes to a type layer:

Do one of the following:

• Click the OK button (✓) in the options bar.

• Press the Enter key on the numeric keypad.

• Press Ctrl+Enter on the main keyboard (Windows) or Command+Return (Mac OS).

• Select any tool in the toolbox, or click in the Layers, Channels, Paths, Actions, History, or Styles palette.

Entering point type

When you enter point type, each line of type is independent—the length of a line grows or shrinks as you edit it, but it doesn't wrap to the next line.

To enter point type:

1 Select the type tool (T).

2 (Photoshop) Click the New Type Layer button (T) in the options bar.

3 Click an orientation button in the options bar:

• Horizontal (I) to enter type horizontally.

• Vertical (IT) to enter type vertically.

4 Click in the image to set an insertion point for the type. The small line through the I-beam marks the position of the type *baseline*. For horizontal type, the baseline marks the line on which the type rests; for vertical type, the baseline marks the center axis of the type characters.

5 Select additional type options in the options bar, Character palette, and Paragraph palette. (See "Formatting characters" on page 258 and "Formatting paragraphs" on page 265.)

6 Enter the characters you want. Press Enter on the main keyboard (Windows) or Return (Mac OS) to begin a new line.

7 (Photoshop) Commit the type layer. (See "About using the type tool (Photoshop)" on page 252.)

The type you entered appears in a new type layer.

Entering paragraph type

When you enter paragraph type, the lines of type wrap to fit the dimensions of the bounding box. You can enter multiple paragraphs and select a paragraph justification option.

You can resize the bounding box, which causes the type to reflow within the adjusted rectangle. You can adjust the bounding box while you're entering type or after you create the type layer. You can also rotate, scale, and skew type using the bounding box.

To enter paragraph type:

1 Select the type tool (T).

2 (Photoshop) Click the New Type Layer button (T) in the options bar.

3 Click an orientation option in the options bar:

• Horizontal (I) to enter type horizontally.

• Vertical (IT) to enter type vertically.

4 Do one of the following:

• Drag diagonally to define a bounding box for the type.

• Hold down Alt (Windows) or Option (Mac OS) as you click or drag to display the Text Box Size dialog box. Enter values for Width and Height, and click OK.

5 Select additional type options in the options bar, Character palette, and Paragraph palette. (See "Formatting characters" on page 258 and "Formatting paragraphs" on page 265.)

6 Enter the characters you want. Press Enter on the main keyboard (Windows) or Return (Mac OS) to begin a new paragraph. If you enter more type than can fit in the bounding box, the overflow icon (⊞) appears on the bounding box.

7 (Photoshop) If desired, resize, rotate, or skew the bounding box.

8 (Photoshop) Commit the type layer. (See "About using the type tool (Photoshop)" on page 252.)

The type you entered appears in a new type layer.

To resize or transform a type bounding box:

1 Display the bounding box handles:

• (Photoshop) With the type tool active, select the type layer in the Layers palette, and click in the text flow.

• (ImageReady) With the type tool active, select the type layer. If the bounding box handles don't appear, make sure that the Text Bounds option is selected in the View > Show submenu.

2 Drag to achieve the desired effect:

• To resize the bounding box, position the pointer over a handle—the pointer turns into a double arrow (↘)—and drag. Shift-drag to maintain the proportion of the bounding box.

• (Photoshop) To rotate the bounding box, position the pointer outside of the bounding border—the pointer turns into a curved, two-sided arrow (↰)—and drag. Shift-drag to constrain the rotation to 15° increments. To change the center of rotation, Ctrl-drag (Windows) or Command-drag (Mac OS) the center point to a new location. The center point can be outside the bounding box.

• (Photoshop) To skew the bounding box, hold down Ctrl+Shift (Windows) or Command+Shift (Mac OS) and drag a side handle. The pointer turns into an arrowhead with a small double arrow (▶₊).

• (Photoshop) To scale the type as you resize the bounding box, Ctrl-drag (Windows) or Command-drag (Mac OS) a corner handle.

Note: *You can also transform type layers using the transformation commands in the Edit menu, except for Perspective and Distort.*

To show or hide the type bounding box (ImageReady):

Do one of the following:

• Choose View > Show > Text Bounds.

• Choose View > Show Extras. This command also shows or hides selection edges, slices, image maps, text bounds, text baseline, and text selection. (See "Working with Extras" on page 77.)

Creating a type selection border (Photoshop)

When you use the type tool with the Masked Type option selected, you create a selection in the shape of the type. Type selections appear on the active layer, and can be moved, copied, filled, or stroked just like any other selection.

To create a type selection border:

1 Select the layer on which you want the selection to appear. For best results, create the type selection border on a normal image layer, not a type layer.

2 Select the type tool (T), and click the Masked Type button (⊤) in the options bar.

3 Select additional type options, and enter type at a point or in a bounding box. (See "Entering point type" on page 252 and "Entering paragraph type" on page 252.)

The type selection border appears in the image on the active layer.

Working with type layers

Once you create a type layer, you can edit the type and apply layer commands to it. You can change the orientation of the type, apply anti-aliasing, convert between point type and paragraph type, create a work path from type, or convert type to shapes. You can move, restack, copy, and change the layer options of a type layer as you do for a normal layer. You can also make the following changes to a type layer and still edit the type:

• Apply transformation commands from the Edit menu, except for Perspective and Distort. (To apply the Perspective or Distort commands, or to transform part of the type layer, you must rasterize the type layer, making the type uneditable.)

• Use layer styles.

• Use fill shortcuts. To fill with the foreground color, press Alt+Backspace (Windows) or Option+Delete (Mac OS); to fill with the background color, press Ctrl+Backspace (Windows) or Command+Delete (Mac OS).

• Warp type to conform to a variety of shapes.

Editing text in type layers

You can insert new text, change existing text, and delete text in type layers.

To edit text in a type layer:

1 Select the type tool (T).

2 Select the type layer in the Layers palette, or click in the text flow to automatically select a type layer.

3 Position the insertion point in the text, and do one of the following:

• Click to set the insertion point.

• Select one or more characters you want to edit.

4 Enter text as desired.

5 (Photoshop) Commit the changes to the type layer. (See "About using the type tool (Photoshop)" on page 252.)

Rasterizing type layers

Some commands and tools—such as filter effects and painting tools—are not available for type layers. You must rasterize the type prior to applying the command or using the tool. *Rasterizing* converts the type layer to a normal layer and makes its contents uneditable as text. A warning message appears if you choose a command or tool that requires a rasterized layer. Some warning messages provide an OK button that you can click to rasterize the layer.

To convert a type layer to a normal layer:

1 Select the type layer in the Layers palette.

2 Choose Layer > Rasterize > Type.

Changing type layer orientation

The orientation of a type layer determines the direction of type lines in relation to the document window (for point type) or the bounding box (for paragraph type). When a type layer is vertical, the type lines flow up and down; when a type layer is horizontal, the type lines flow from left to right. Don't confuse the orientation of a type layer with the direction of characters in a type line. (See "Rotating vertical type" on page 264.)

To change the orientation of a type layer:

1 Select the type layer in the Layers palette.

2 Do one of the following:

• Choose Layer > Type > Horizontal, or Layer > Type > Vertical.

• (ImageReady) Select Horizontal (I) or Vertical (I T) in the options bar.

Specifying anti-aliasing

Anti-aliasing lets you produce smooth-edged type by partially filling the edge pixels. As a result, the edges of the type blend into the background.

Anti-aliasing None, and Strong.

When creating type for online use, consider that anti-aliasing greatly increases the number of colors in the original image. This limits your ability to reduce the number of colors in the image and thus reduce the optimized file size, and may cause stray colors to appear along the edges of the type.

When file size and limiting the number of colors is most important, leaving type without anti-aliased edges may be preferable, despite the jagged edges. Also, consider using larger type than you would use for printed works. Larger type can be easier to view online and gives you more freedom in deciding whether to apply anti-aliasing to type.

Note: When you use anti-aliasing, type may be rendered inconsistently at small sizes and low resolutions (such as the resolution used for Web graphics). To reduce this inconsistency, deselect the Fractional Width option in the Character palette menu.

To apply anti-aliasing to a type layer:

1 Select the type layer in the Layers palette.

2 Choose Layer > Type, and choose an option from the submenu; or select the type tool (**T**) and choose an option from the anti-aliasing menu (ªa) in the options bar:

- None to apply no anti-aliasing.
- Crisp to make type appear more sharp.
- Strong to make type appear heavier.
- Smooth to make type appear smoother.

Converting between point type and paragraph type

You can convert point type to paragraph type to adjust the flow of characters within a bounding box. Or you can convert paragraph type to point type to make each text line flow independently from the others.

When you convert from paragraph type to point type, a carriage return is added at the end of each line of type (with the exception of the last line). When you convert point type to paragraph type, you must remove carriage returns in the paragraph type to let the characters reflow in the bounding box.

Important: When you convert paragraph type to point type, all characters that overflow the bounding box are deleted. To avoid losing text, adjust the bounding box so that all type is visible prior to conversion.

To convert between point type and paragraph type:

1 Select the type layer in the Layers palette.

2 Choose Layer > Type > Convert to Point Text, or Layer > Type > Convert to Paragraph Text.

Warping type layers

Warping allows you to distort type to conform to a variety of shapes; for example, you can warp type in the shape of an arc or a wave. The warp style you select is an attribute of the type layer—you can change a layer's warp style at any time to change the overall shape of the warp. Warping options give you precise control over the orientation and perspective of the warp effect.

Warping applies to all characters on a type layer—you cannot warp selected characters. While warping is applied to a type layer, you cannot resize or transform the bounding box for paragraph type.

Note: You cannot warp type layers that include Faux Bold formatting or use fonts that do not include outline data (such as bitmap fonts).

To warp type:

1 Select a type layer.

2 Do one of the following:

• Select the type tool (T), and click the Warp button (T..) in the options bar.

• Choose Layer > Type > Warp Text.

3 Choose a warp style from the Style pop-up menu.

4 Select the orientation of the warp effect—Horizontal or Vertical.

5 If desired, specify values for additional warping options:

• Bend to specify how much warp is applied to the layer.

• Horizontal Distortion and Vertical Distortion to apply perspective to the warp.

6 Click OK.

To unwarp type:

1 Select a type layer that has warping applied to it.

2 Select the type tool (T), and click the Warp button (T..) in the options bar; or choose Layer > Type > Warp Text.

3 Choose None from the Style pop-up menu, and click OK.

Creating a work path from type (Photoshop)

Creating a work path from type lets you work with characters as vector shapes. A *work path* is a temporary path that appears in the Paths palette. Once you create a work path from a type layer, you can save and manipulate it like any other path. (See "Selecting paths (Photoshop)" on page 173.) You cannot edit characters in the path as text; however, the original type layer remains intact and editable.

To create a work path from type:

Select a type layer, and choose Layer > Type > Create Work Path.

Converting type to shapes (Photoshop)

When you convert type to shapes, the type layer is replaced by a layer with a vector-based layer clipping path. You can edit the layer clipping path and apply styles to the layer; however, you cannot edit characters in the layer as text. (See "Editing a layer clipping path (Photoshop)" on page 240.)

To convert type to shapes:

Select a type layer, and choose Layer > Type > Convert to Shapes.

Formatting characters

Photoshop and ImageReady give you precise control over individual characters in type layers, including font, size, color, leading, kerning, tracking, baseline shift, and alignment. You can set type attributes before you enter characters or reset them to change the appearance of selected characters in a type layer.

Selecting characters

Before you can format individual characters, you must select them. You can select one character, a range of characters, or all characters in a type layer.

To select characters:

1 Select the type tool (T).

2 Select the type layer in the Layers palette, or click in the text flow to automatically select a type layer.

3 Position the insertion point in the text, and do one of the following:

• Drag to select one or more characters.

• Click in the text and then shift-click to select a range of characters.

• Choose Select > All to select all the characters in the layer.

• Double-click a word to select it. Triple-click a line to select it. Quadruple-click a paragraph to select it. Quintuple-click anywhere in the text flow to select all characters in a bounding box.

• To use the arrow keys to select characters, hold down Shift and press the Right arrow or Left arrow key. To use the arrow keys to select words, hold down Shift+Ctrl (Windows) or Shift+Command (Mac OS) and press the Right arrow or Left arrow key.

4 To select all the characters in a layer without positioning the insertion point in the text flow, select the type layer in the Layers palette, and then double-click the layer's type icon (T).

Note: In Photoshop, selecting and formatting characters in a type layer puts the type tool into edit mode. You must commit the changes before you can perform other operations. (See "About using the type tool (Photoshop)" on page 252.)

To show or hide selection highlighting (ImageReady):

Do one of the following:

• Choose View > Show > Text Selection.

• Choose View > Show Extras. This command also shows or hides selection edges, slices, image maps, text bounds, text baseline, and text selection. (See "Working with Extras" on page 77.)

Using the Character palette

The Character palette provides options for formatting characters. Some formatting options are also provided in the options bar.

To display the Character palette:

Do one of the following:

• Choose Window > Show Character.

• Click the Character palette tab.

• With the type tool selected (T), click Palettes in the options bar.

Choosing a font

A font is a complete set of characters—letters, numbers, and symbols—that share a common weight, width, and style. When you select a font, you can select the *font family* and its *type style* independently. The font family is a collection of fonts sharing an overall typeface design; for example, Times. A type style is a variant version of an individual font in the font family, for example, Regular, Bold, or Italic. The range of available type styles varies with each font. If a font doesn't include the style you want, you can apply *faux* styles—simulated versions of bold, italic, super-script, subscript, all caps, and small caps styles.

In addition to the fonts installed on your system, Photoshop uses font files in these local folders:

Windows Program Files/Common Files/ Adobe/Fonts

Mac OS System Folder/Application Support/ Adobe/Fonts

If you install a Type 1, TrueType, OpenType, or CID font into the local Fonts folder, the font appears in Adobe applications only.

To choose a font family and style:

1 Choose a font family from the Font Family pop-up menu in the Character palette or options bar. If more than one copy of a font is installed on your computer, an abbreviation follows the font name: (T1) for Type 1 fonts, (TT) for TrueType fonts, or (OT) for OpenType fonts.

In Photoshop, you can choose a font family and style by typing the desired name in the text box. As you type, the name of the first font or style beginning with that letter appears. Continue typing until the correct font or style name appears. Be sure to deselect the font name before entering new type in the image.

2 Do one of the following:

• Choose a font style from the Font Style pop-up menu in the Character palette or options bar.

• If the font family you chose does not include a bold or italic style, choose Faux Bold or Faux Italic from the Character palette menu to apply a simulated style.

Note: *You cannot apply Faux Bold formatting to warped type. (See "Warping type layers" on page 256.)*

Choosing a type size

The *type size* determines how large the type appears in the image:

• In Photoshop, the default unit of measurement for type is *points*. One PostScript point is equal to 1/72 of an inch in a 72-ppi image; however, you can switch between using the PostScript and traditional definitions of point size. You can change the default unit of measurement for type in the Units & Rulers section of the Preferences dialog box.

• In ImageReady, *pixels* are the only unit of measurement for type. This is because the ImageReady application is tailored to creating images for online media, in which pixels are the standard unit of measurement.

To choose a type size:

In the Character palette or options bar, enter or select a new value for Size ($_{\frac{1}{T}}$). To use an alternate unit of measurement, enter the unit (in, cm, pt, px, or pica) after the value in the Size text box. The value you enter is converted to the default unit of measurement.

To specify the default unit of measurement for type (Photoshop):

1 Choose Edit > Preferences > Units & Rulers.

2 Select a unit of measurement for Type.

To specify the point size definition (Photoshop):

1 Choose Edit > Preferences > Units & Rulers.

2 Select an option for Point/Pica Size. Traditional points are slightly smaller than PostScript points.

Changing the type color

The type you enter gets its color from the current foreground color; however, you can change the type color before or after you enter type. When editing existing type layers, you can change the color of individual, selected characters or all type in a layer.

To change the type color:

Do one of the following:

• Click the Color selection box in the options bar or Character palette, and select a color using the color picker. In ImageReady, you can also select an option from the Color selection box pop-up menu: Foreground Color, Background Color, Other (to use the color picker), or a color from the pop-up palette.

• Click the foreground color selection box in the toolbox, and select a color using the color picker. Or click a color in the Color palette, the Swatches palette, or the Color Table palette (ImageReady).

• Use fill shortcuts. To fill with the foreground color, press Alt+Backspace (Windows) or Option+Delete (Mac OS); to fill with the background color, press Ctrl+Backspace (Windows) or Command+Delete (Mac OS).

• Apply an overlay layer style to the type layer to apply a color, pattern, or gradient on top of the existing color. (See "Using layer styles" on page 226.) In ImageReady, you can drag a color from the toolbox color selection box, the Color palette, the Color Table palette, or the Swatches palette, and drop it onto a type layer to automatically apply a color overlay style. Applying an overlay layer style affects all character in the type layer; you cannot use this method to change the color of individual characters.

Specifying leading

The amount of space between lines of type is called *leading*. For Roman type, leading is measured from the baseline of one line of type to the baseline of the next line. The *baseline* is the invisible line on which most type lies. You can apply more than one leading amount within the same paragraph; however, the largest leading value in a line of type determines the leading value for that line.

You can use other options to set leading for Chinese, Japanese, or Korean type.

 For more information, see "Specifying how leading is measured" in online Help.

5-point type with 5-point leading, and with 10-point leading.

To change the leading:

In the Character palette, do one of the following:

• Choose the desired leading from the Leading menu ( ).

• Select the existing leading value, and enter a new value.

To change the default auto leading percentage:

1 Display the Paragraph palette.

2 Choose Justification from the palette menu.

3 For Auto Leading, specify a new default percentage.

Specifying kerning and tracking

Kerning is the process of adding or subtracting space between specific letter pairs. You can control kerning manually, or you can use automatic kerning to turn on the kerning built into the font by the font designer. *Tracking* is the process of creating an equal amount of spacing across a range of letters.

Positive kerning or tracking values move characters apart (adding to the default spacing); negative values move characters closer together (reducing the default spacing). Kerning and tracking values are measured in units that are 1/1000 of an *em space*. The width of an em space is relative to the current type size. In a 1-point font,

1 em corresponds to 1 point; in a 10-point font, 1 em corresponds to 10 points. Because kerning and tracking units are 1/1000 em, 100 units in a 10-point font are equivalent to 1 point.

Default, and tracking set to 350.

To use a font's built-in kerning information:

In the Character palette, choose Metrics (Photoshop) or Auto (ImageReady) from the Kerning menu ( ).

Note: The Metrics option replaces the Auto Kern option in previous versions of Photoshop.

To adjust kerning manually:

1 Click with the type tool (**T**) to set an insertion point between two characters.

Note: If a range of type is selected, you can't manually kern the characters. Instead, use tracking.

2 In the Character palette, enter or select a numeric value for Kerning ( ).

3 (Photoshop) Commit the changes to the type layer. (See "About using the type tool (Photoshop)" on page 252.)

To specify tracking:

In the Character palette, enter or select a numeric value for Tracking ( ).

Adjusting horizontal or vertical scale

Horizontal scale and *vertical scale* specify the proportion between the height and width of the type. Unscaled characters have a value of 100%. You can adjust scale to compress or expand selected characters in both width and height.

Note: Depending on the value you enter when you use vertical type, the horizontal scale may make the type appear narrower; the opposite is true for vertical scale.

To adjust the horizontal or vertical scale of type:

In the Character palette, enter a new percentage for Horizontal Scale (**T**) or Vertical Scale (IT).

Specifying baseline shift

Baseline shift controls the distance that type appears from its baseline, either raising or lowering the selected type to create superscripts or subscripts.

Default, and baseline shift of 10 points.

To specify baseline shift:

In the Character palette, enter or select (ImageReady) a value for Baseline Shift ( ). A positive value moves horizontal type above and vertical type to the right of the baseline; a negative value moves type below or to the left of the baseline.

Changing case

You can enter or format type as uppercase characters, either all caps or small caps. When you format type as small caps, Photoshop and ImageReady use the small caps designed as part of the font, if available. If the font does not include small caps, Photoshop and ImageReady generate faux small caps.

To change the case of type:

Choose All Caps or Small Caps from the Character palette menu. A check mark indicates that the option is selected. Selecting Small Caps will not change characters that were originally typed in uppercase.

Making characters superscript or subscript

You can enter or format type as superscript or subscript characters. Superscript characters are reduced in size and shifted above the type baseline; subscript characters are reduced in size and shifted below the type baseline. If the font does not include superscript or subscript characters, Photoshop and ImageReady generate faux superscript or subscript characters.

To specify superscript or subscript characters:

Choose Superscript or Subscript from the Character palette menu. A check mark indicates that the option is selected.

Applying underline and strikethrough

You can apply a line under horizontal type, or to the left or right of vertical type. You can also apply a line through horizontal or vertical type. The line is always the same color as the type color.

To apply an underline or strikethrough:

Choose an option from the Character palette menu:

• Underline applies an underline beneath horizontal type.

• Underline Left and Underline Right apply an underline to the left or right of vertical type. You can apply an underline to the left or right, but not to both sides.

Note: The Underline Left and Underline Right options only appear in the Character palette menu when a type layer that contains vertical type is selected.

• Strikethrough applies a horizontal line through horizontal type or a vertical line through vertical type.

A check mark indicates that an option is selected.

Using ligatures and old style numerals

When working with OpenType fonts, you can use ligatures and old style typographic numerals in your type, if the font provides them. *Ligatures* are typographic replacements for certain pairs of characters, such as "fi" and "fl." Old style numerals are shorter than regular numerals, and some old style numerals descend below the type baseline.

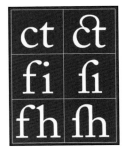

Type with Ligatures option unselected and selected.

To use ligatures or old style numerals:

Choose Ligatures or Old Style from the Character palette menu. A check mark indicates that the option is selected.

Using fractional character widths

By default, type is displayed using fractional character widths. This means that the spacing between characters varies, with fractions of whole pixels between some characters. In most situations, fractional character widths provide the best spacing for type appearance and readability.

However, for type in small sizes (less than 20 points) displayed online, fractional character widths can cause type to run together or have too much extra space, making it difficult to read.

You can turn off fractional character widths to fix type spacing in whole-pixel increments and prevent small type from running together. The fractional character width setting applies to all characters on a type layer—you cannot set the option for selected characters.

To turn fractional character widths on or off:

Choose Fractional Widths from the Character palette menu. A check mark indicates that the option is selected.

Rotating vertical type

When working with vertical type, you can rotate the direction of characters by 90°. Rotated characters appear upright; unrotated characters appear sideways (perpendicular to the type line).

Original, and type without vertical rotation.

To rotate characters in vertical type:

Choose Rotate Character from the Character palette menu. A check mark indicates that the option is selected.

Note: *You cannot rotate double-byte characters (full width characters only available in Chinese, Japanese, and Korean fonts). Any double-byte characters in the selected range will not be rotated.*

Formatting paragraphs

A paragraph is any range of type with a carriage return at the end. You use the Paragraph palette to set options that apply to entire paragraphs, such as the alignment, indentation, and space between lines of type. For point type, each line is a separate paragraph. For paragraph type, each paragraph can have multiple lines, depending on the dimensions of the bounding box.

Selecting paragraphs and showing the Paragraph palette

You can use the Paragraph palette to set formatting options for a single paragraph, multiple paragraphs, or all paragraphs in a type layer.

To select paragraphs for formatting:

Do one of the following:

• Select the type tool (**T**), and click in a paragraph to apply formatting to a single paragraph.

• Select the type tool, and make a selection within a range of paragraphs to apply formatting to multiple paragraphs.

• Select the type layer in the Layers palette to apply formatting to all paragraphs in the layer.

To show the Paragraph palette:

Choose Window > Show Paragraph, or click the Paragraph palette tab.

Aligning and justifying type

You can *align* type to one edge of a paragraph (left, center, or right for horizontal type; top, center, or bottom for vertical type) and *justify* type to both edges of a paragraph. Alignment options are available for both point type and paragraph type; justification options are only available for paragraph type.

To specify alignment:

In the Paragraph palette or options bar, click an alignment option. The options for horizontal type are:

(≡) Aligns type to the left, leaving the right edge of the paragraph ragged.

(≡) Aligns type to the center, leaving both edges of the paragraph ragged.

(≡) Aligns type to right, leaving the left edge of the paragraph ragged.

The options for vertical type are:

(ⅲ) Aligns type to the top, leaving the bottom edge of the paragraph ragged.

(▥) Aligns type to the center, leaving both the top and bottom edges of the paragraph ragged.

(▥) Aligns type to bottom, leaving the top edge of the paragraph ragged.

To specify justification for paragraph type:

In the Paragraph palette, click a justification option. The options for horizontal type are:

(≡) Justifies all lines except the last, which is left-aligned.

(≡) Justifies all lines except the last, which is centered.

(≡) Justifies all lines except the last, which is right-aligned.

(≡) Justifies all lines including the last, which is force-justified.

The options for vertical type are:

(▥) Justifies all lines except the last, which is top-aligned.

(▥) Justifies all lines except the last, which is centered.

(▥) Justifies all lines except the last, which is bottom-aligned.

(▥) Justifies all lines including the last, which is force-justified.

Indenting paragraphs

Indentation specifies the amount of space between type and the bounding box or line that contains the type. Indentation affects only the selected paragraph or paragraphs, so you can easily set different indentations for paragraphs.

To specify paragraph indentation:

In the Paragraph palette, enter a value for an indentation option:

• Left Indent (⊣≣) to indent from the left edge of the paragraph. For vertical type, this option controls the indentation from the top of the paragraph.

• Right Indent (≣⊢) to indent from the right edge of the paragraph. For vertical type, this option controls the indentation from the bottom of the paragraph.

• First Line Indent (⁻≣) to indent the first line of type in the paragraph. For horizontal type, the first line indent is relative to the left indent; for vertical type, the first line indent is relative to the top indent. To create a first line hanging indentation, enter a negative value.

Changing space above or below paragraphs

You can control the space above and below paragraphs using the paragraph spacing options.

To specify paragraph spacing:

In the Paragraph palette, enter a value for Space Before (⁻≣) and Space After (₋≣).

Specifying hanging punctuation

Hanging punctuation controls whether punctuation marks fall inside or outside the margins. If hanging punctuation is turned on for Roman fonts, periods, commas, single-quotation marks, double-quotation marks, apostrophes, hyphens, em dashes, en dashes, colons, and semicolons appear outside the margins.

To use hanging punctuation for Roman fonts:

Choose Roman Hanging Punctuation from the Paragraph palette menu. A check mark indicates that the option is selected.

Note: When you use Roman Hanging Punctuation, any double-byte punctuation marks available in Chinese, Japanese, and Korean fonts in the selected range will not hang.

 For more information, see "Using burasagari" in online Help.

Controlling hyphenation and justification

The settings you choose for hyphenation and justification affect the horizontal spacing of lines and the aesthetic appeal of type on a page. Hyphenation options determine whether words can be hyphenated and, if they can, what breaks are allowable. Justification options determine word, letter, and glyph spacing.

 For more information, see "Controlling hyphenation and justification" in online Help.

Working with composition

The appearance of type on the page depends on a complex interaction of processes called *composition*. Using the word spacing, letter spacing, glyph spacing, and hyphenation options you've selected, Photoshop and ImageReady evaluate possible line breaks and choose the one that best supports the specified parameters.

 For more information, see "Working with composition" in online Help.

Setting options for Chinese, Japanese, and Korean type (Photoshop)

Photoshop provides several options for working with Chinese, Japanese, and Korean (CJK) type. Characters in CJK fonts are often referred to as *double-byte characters*.

 For more information, see "Setting options for Chinese, Japanese, and Korean type" in online Help.

10

Chapter 10: Designing Web Pages

Adobe Photoshop and Adobe ImageReady provide you with a comprehensive environment for designing complex, image-rich Web pages. You can use the tools and techniques you're already familiar with to design Web pages that include images, text, and sophisticated effects—such as rollovers, image maps, and animations—quickly and easily. Best of all, you never have to view or edit the underlying HTML and JavaScript.

About designing Web pages with Photoshop and ImageReady

When designing Web pages using Adobe Photoshop and Adobe ImageReady, keep in mind the tools and features that are available in each application.

• Photoshop provides tools for creating and manipulating static images for use on the Web. You can divide an image into slices, add links and HTML text, optimize the slices, and save the image as a Web page.

• ImageReady provides many of the same image-editing tools as Photoshop. In addition, it includes tools and palettes for advanced Web processing and creating dynamic Web images like animations and rollovers.

Using the Web design palettes (ImageReady)

ImageReady provides the following palettes for adding advanced Web design features to images: Rollover, Slice, and Image Map.

To display the Rollover, Slice, or Image Map palette:

Do one of the following:

• Click the tab of the palette you want to display.

• Choose Window > Show Rollover, Window > Show Slice, or Window > Show Image Map.

Other factors to consider

When you save an image for use as a Web page, you can choose to generate an HTML file. This file contains information that tells a Web browser what to display when it loads the page. It can contain pointers to images (in the form of GIF, PNG, and JPEG files), HTML text, linking information, and JavaScript code for creating rollover effects.

You can integrate your Web production process by opening Photoshop files directly in Adobe GoLive 5.0. Slices, URLs, and other Web features in Photoshop files are accessible in GoLive for management and editing. You can also open Photoshop files in GoLive as page templates. Page templates display as a shaded preview and provide a visual guide for building a Web page in GoLive. For more information on using GoLive, see the *Adobe GoLive 5.0 User Guide*.

You can preview most Web effects directly in Photoshop or ImageReady. However, the appearance of an image on the Web depends on the operating system, color display system, and browser used to display the image. Be sure to preview images in different browsers, on different operating systems, and with different color bit depths. (See "Previewing an image in a browser" on page 84.)

Creating and viewing slices

A slice is a rectangular area of an image that you can use to create links, rollovers, and animations in the resulting Web page. Dividing an image into slices lets you selectively optimize it for Web viewing.

About slices

You use slices to divide a source image into functional areas. When you save the image as a Web page, each slice is saved as an independent file that contains its own settings, color palette, links, rollover effects, and animation effects. You can use slices to achieve faster download speeds. Slices are also advantageous when working with images that contain different types of data. For example, if one

area of an image needs to be optimized in GIF format to support an animation, but the rest of the image is better optimized in JPEG format, you can isolate the animation using a slice.

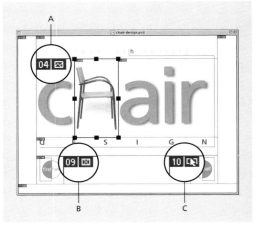

Web page divided into slices: **A.** *Image slice* **B.** *No Image slice* **C.** *Slice that contains a rollover*

You set how the Photoshop or ImageReady application generates HTML code for aligning slices—either using tables or cascading style sheets—in the Output Settings dialog box. You can also set how slice files are named. (See "Setting output options" on page 348.)

Types of slices

Slices you create using the slice tool are called *user-slices*; slices you create from a layer are called *layer-based slices*. When you create a new user-slice or layer-based slice, additional *auto-slices* are generated to account for the remaining areas of the image. In other words, auto-slices fill the space in the image that is not defined by user-slices or layer-based slices. Auto-slices are regenerated every time you add or edit user-slices or layer-based slices. User-slices, layer-based slices, and auto-slices look different—user-slices and layer-based slices are defined by a solid line, while auto-slices are defined by a dotted line.

A *subslice* is a type of auto-slice that is generated when you create overlapping slices. Subslices indicate how the image will be divided when you save the optimized file. Although subslices are numbered and display a slice symbol, you cannot select or edit them separately from the underlying slice. Subslices are regenerated every time you arrange the stacking order of slices.

Creating user-slices

You can create user-slices with the slice tool, and in ImageReady, from a selection or from guides.

To create a slice with the slice tool:

1 Select the slice tool ( ). Any existing slices automatically display in the document window.

2 Choose a style setting in the options bar:

• Normal to determine slice proportions by dragging.

• Constrained Aspect Ratio to set a height-to-width ratio. Enter whole numbers or decimals for the aspect ratio. For example, to create a slice twice as wide as it is high, enter 2 for the width and 1 for the height.

• Fixed Size to specify the slice's height and width. Enter pixel values in whole numbers.

3 Drag over the area where you want to create a slice. Shift-drag to constrain the slice to a square. Alt-drag (Windows) or Option-drag (Mac OS) to draw from the center. Use snap to align a new slice to a guide or another slice in the image. (See "Moving and resizing user-slices" on page 277.)

To create a slice from a selection (ImageReady):

1 Select a portion of the image.

2 Choose Slices > Create Slice from Selection.

ImageReady creates a user-slice based on the selection marquee. If the selection is feathered, the slice covers the full selection (including the feathered edges). If the selection is nonrectangular, the slice covers a rectangular area large enough to cover the full selection.

To create slices from guides (ImageReady):

In an image containing guides, choose Slices > Create Slices from Guides. All slices created from guides are user-slices.

When you create slices from guides, any existing slices are deleted.

Creating layer-based slices

When you create a slice from a layer, the slice area encompasses all the pixel data in the layer. If you move the layer or edit the layer's content, the slice area automatically adjusts to encompass the new pixels.

Layer-based slices are especially useful when working with rollovers. Start by placing the rollover element on a separate layer, and then create a slice from that layer. If you apply an effect to the layer—such as a drop shadow or glow—to create a rollover state, the slice automatically adjusts to encompass the new pixels. However, do not use a layer-based slice when you plan to move the layer over a large area of the image during an animation, because the slice dimension may exceed a useful size. (See "Working with rollovers (ImageReady)" on page 292.)

To create a slice from a layer:

1 Select a layer in the Layers palette.

2 Choose Layer > New Layer Based Slice.

Converting auto-slices to user-slices

You can move, duplicate, combine, divide, resize, delete, arrange, align, and distribute user-slices. You can also apply different optimization settings to user-slices. In contrast, all auto-slices in an image are linked and share the same optimization settings. This is because auto-slices are regenerated every time you create or edit a user-slice or layer-based slice.

Converting an auto-slice to a user-slice prevents it from being changed when regeneration occurs. Dividing, combining, linking, and setting options for auto-slices automatically converts them to user-slices.

To convert an auto-slice to a user-slice:

1 Select an auto-slice. In ImageReady, you can select multiple slices. (See "Selecting slices" on page 276.)

2 Do one of the following:

• (Photoshop) Click Promote to User Slice in the options bar.

• (ImageReady) Choose Slices > Promote to User-slice(s).

Converting layer-based slices to user-slices

Because a layer-based slice is tied to the pixel content of a layer, the only way to move, combine, divide, resize, and align it is to edit the layer. You can convert a layer-based slice to a user-slice to unlink it from the layer.

To convert a layer-based slice to a user-slice:

1 Select a layer-based slice. In ImageReady, you can select multiple slices. (See "Selecting slices" on page 276.)

2 Do one of the following:

• (Photoshop) Click Promote to User Slice in the options bar.

• (ImageReady) Choose Slices > Promote to User-slice(s).

Viewing slices

You can view slices in Photoshop, the Photoshop Save for Web dialog box (see "Optimizing images" on page 320), and ImageReady. The following characteristics can help you identify and differentiate between slices:

Slice lines Define the boundary of the slice. Solid lines indicate that the slice is a user-slice or layer-based slice; dotted lines indicate that the slice is an auto-slice.

Slice colors Differentiate user-slices and layer-based slices from auto-slices. By default, user-slices and layer-based slices have blue symbols, while auto-slices have gray symbols.

In addition, ImageReady and the Photoshop Save for Web dialog box use color adjustments to dim unselected slices. These adjustments are for display purposes only and do not affect the final image's color. By default, the color adjustment for auto-slices is twice the amount of that for user-slices.

Slice numbers Slices are numbered from left to right and top to bottom, beginning in the upper left corner of the image. If you change the arrangement or total number of slices, slice numbers are updated to reflect the new order.

Slice symbols Indicate whether a user-slice is an Image (▣) or No Image (▣) slice; if the slice is a layer-based slice (▣); if the slice is linked (▣); or if the slice includes a rollover effect (▣). (See "Choosing a content type" on page 281, "Linking slices (ImageReady)" on page 285, and "Working with rollovers (ImageReady)" on page 292.)

To show or hide slices:

Do one of the following:

• Turn on display of slices in the View > Show submenu, and choose View > Show Extras. This command also shows or hides: (Photoshop) selection edges, guides, a grid, target path, and notes, or (ImageReady) selection edges, image maps, text bounds, text baseline, and text selection. (See "Working with Extras" on page 77.)

• (Photoshop Save for Web dialog box and ImageReady) Click the Slices Visibility button (▦).

To change the color of slice lines (Photoshop):

1 Choose a color from the Line Color pop-up menu in the options bar.

To change the color of slice lines (ImageReady):

1 Choose Edit > Preferences > Slices.

2 Under Slice Lines, choose a color from the Line Color pop-up menu.

Changing the color of slice lines automatically changes the color of selected slice lines to a contrasting color.

To show or hide slice numbers (Photoshop):

Select Show Slice Numbers in the options bar. Slice numbers show when the option is checked.

To change the display of slice numbers and slice symbols (ImageReady):

1 Choose Edit > Preferences > Slices.

2 Under Numbers and Symbols, select a size for display symbols:

• None to display no numbers or symbols.

• The small icon to display small numbers and symbols.

• The large icon to display large numbers and symbols.

3 For Opacity, enter a value, or choose a value from the pop-up slider to change the opacity of the numbers and symbols display.

To change slice color adjustments (ImageReady):

1 Choose Edit > Preferences > Slices.

2 Enter a value, or choose a value from the Color Adjustments pop-up slider for User-slices, Auto-slices, or both. (The User-slices option controls color adjustments for both user-slices and layer-based slices.)

The value determines by how much the brightness and contrast of unselected slices are dimmed.

To display slice lines only (ImageReady):

1 Choose Edit > Preferences > Slices.

2 Under Slice Lines, select Show Lines Only to display slice lines only, and deselect color adjustments and numbers and symbols display.

Selecting and modifying slices

You can move, duplicate, combine, divide, resize, delete, arrange, align, and distribute user-slices. There are fewer options for modifying layer-based slices and auto-slices; however, you can promote a layer-based slice or an auto-slice to a user-slice at any time.

In Photoshop, you cannot divide, combine, align, or distribute slices. Jump to ImageReady to access these slice-editing capabilities.

Selecting slices

You select a slice with the slice select tool in order to apply modifications to it. In the Photoshop Save for Web dialog box and in ImageReady, you can select multiple slices.

To select a slice:

1 Select the slice select tool (🔪).

2 Click on a slice in the image. When working with overlapping slices, click the visible section of an underlying slice to select it.

💡 *To toggle between the slice tool and the slice select tool, hold down Ctrl (Windows) or Command (Mac OS).*

To select multiple slices (Photoshop Save for Web dialog box and ImageReady):

With the slice select tool (⯑), do one of the following:

• Shift-click to add slices to the selection.

• (Photoshop Save for Web dialog box) Drag across the slices you want to select in the image area.

• (ImageReady) Click in an auto-slice or outside the image area, and drag across the slices you want to select. (Clicking in a user-slice and dragging moves the slice.)

In ImageReady, you can save, load, and delete slice selections. Using slice selections lets you reselect specific slices quickly and accurately.

To save a slice selection (ImageReady):

1 Select one or more slices.

2 Choose Slices > Save Slice Selection.

3 Enter a name in the Selection Name text box, and click OK.

To load a slice selection (ImageReady):

Choose Slices > Load Slice Selection, and select the name of the slice selection you want to load from the submenu.

Note: *You must save a slice selection before you can load it.*

To delete a slice selection (ImageReady):

Choose Slices > Delete Slice Selection, and select the name of the slice selection you want to delete from the submenu. Deleting a slice selection does not delete the slices themselves.

Moving and resizing user-slices

You can move and resize user-slices in Photoshop and ImageReady, but not in the Photoshop Save for Web dialog box. You can also move and resize slices using numeric coordinates. (See "Resizing and moving slices using numeric coordinates" on page 283.)

To move or resize a user-slice:

1 Select a user-slice. In ImageReady, you can select and move multiple slices.

2 Do one of the following:

• To move a slice, move the pointer inside the slice selection border, and drag the slice to a new position. Press Shift to restrict movement to a vertical, horizontal, or 45° diagonal line.

• To resize a slice, grab a side or a corner handle of the slice, and drag to resize the slice. In ImageReady, if you select and resize adjacent slices, common edges shared by the slices are resized together.

To snap slices to a guide or another user-slice:

1 Select the options you want from the View > Snap To submenu, and choose View > Snap. (See "Working with snap" on page 152.) A check mark indicates that the option is turned on.

2 Move the selected slices as desired. The slices snap to any guide or slice within 4 pixels.

Dividing user-slices and auto-slices (ImageReady)

In ImageReady, the Divide Slice dialog box lets you divide one or more slices horizontally, vertically, or both. Duplicate slices are always user-slices, regardless of whether the original is a user-slice or an auto-slice.

Note: You cannot divide layer-based slices.

To divide slices:

1 Select one or more slices.

2 Do one of the following:

• Choose Slices > Divide Slice(s).

• Choose Divide Slice(s) from the Slice palette menu.

3 Select Preview in the Divide Slice dialog box to preview the changes.

4 In the Divide Slice dialog box, select one or both of the following options:

• Divide Horizontally Into to divide the slice lengthwise.

• Divide Vertically Into to divide the slice width-wise.

5 Define how you want to divide each selected slice:

• Select and enter a value for slices down or slices across to divide each slice evenly into the specified number of slices.

• Select and enter a value for pixels per slice to divide each slice based on the specified number of pixels. Any section of a slice that is left over is made into another slice. For example, if you divide a slice that is 100 pixels wide into three new slices each 30 pixels wide, the remaining 10-pixel-wide area becomes a new slice.

6 Click OK.

Duplicating slices

You can create a duplicate slice with the same dimensions and optimization settings as the original. If the original slice is a linked user-slice, the duplicate is linked to the same set. (See "Linking slices (ImageReady)" on page 285.) Duplicate slices are always user-slices, regardless of whether the original is a user-slice, a layer-based slice, or an auto-slice.

In ImageReady, you can also copy and paste slices within or between documents.

To duplicate a slice:

1 Select a slice. In ImageReady, you can select multiple slices.

2 Do one of the following:

• Alt-drag (Windows) or Option-drag (Mac OS) from inside the selection. (Dragging from the edge will resize a user-slice.)

• (ImageReady) Choose Slices > Duplicate Slice(s).

• (ImageReady) Choose Duplicate Slice(s) from the Slice palette menu.

The duplicate slice appears on top of the original (offset 10 pixels down and to the right) and can be moved, resized, or otherwise modified.

To copy and paste a slice (ImageReady):

1 Select one or more slices.

2 Choose Copy Slice from the Slice palette menu.

3 If you want to paste into another image, open and display that image.

4 Choose Paste Slice from the Slice palette menu. If you paste the slice into the same image as you copied it from, the pasted slice appears on top of the original.

Combining slices (ImageReady)

In ImageReady, you can combine two or more slices into a single slice. The resulting slice takes its dimensions and position from the rectangle created by joining the outer edges of the combined slices. If the combined slices are not adjacent or are of different proportions or alignments, the newly combined slice may overlap other slices.

Optimization settings for the combined slice are those of the first slice selected before the Combine Slices operation. A combined slice is always a user-slice, regardless of whether the original slices include auto-slices.

Note: *You cannot combine layer-based slices.*

To combine slices:

1 Select two or more slices.

2 Choose Slices > Combine Slices.

Arranging user-slices and layer-based slices

When slices overlap, the last slice you create is the top slice in the stacking order. You can change the stacking order to gain access to underlying slices. You can specify which slice is on the top and bottom of the stack and move slices up or down in the stacking order.

Note: *You cannot arrange the stacking order of auto-slices.*

To change the stacking order of slices:

1 Select a slice. In ImageReady, you can select multiple slices.

2 Do one of the following:

• With the slice select tool active, click a stacking order option in the options bar: Bring to Front ( ), Bring Forward ( ), Send Backward ( ), Send to Back ( ).

• (ImageReady) Choose Slices > Arrange, and choose a stacking order command from the submenu; or choose a stacking order command from the Slice palette menu.

Aligning user-slices (ImageReady)

In ImageReady, you can align user-slices with the top, bottom, left, right, or middle. Aligning user-slices can eliminate unneeded auto-slices and generate a smaller, more efficient HTML file.

Note: You cannot align layer-based slices or auto-slices.

To align user-slices:

1 Select the user-slices you want to align.

2 Do one of the following:

• With the slice select tool active, click an alignment option in the options bar: Align Top Edges (⊤□), Align Vertical Centers (⊪⊅), Align Bottom Edges (⊡□), Align Left Edges (⊫), Align Horizontal Centers (⊞), Align Right Edges (⊒).

• Choose Slices > Align, and choose a command from the submenu.

Distributing user-slices (ImageReady)

In ImageReady, you can distribute user-slices evenly along the vertical or horizontal axis. Distributing user-slices can eliminate unneeded auto-slices and generate a smaller, more efficient HTML file.

Note: You cannot distribute layer-based slices or auto-slices.

To distribute user-slices:

1 Select the user-slices you want to distribute.

2 Do one of the following:

• With the slice select tool active, click a distribute option in the options bar: Distribute Top Edges (☰), Distribute Vertical Centers (☲), Distribute Bottom Edges (☶), Distribute Left Edges (⊪⊳), Distribute Horizontal Centers (◑◐), Distribute Right Edges (◁◁).

• Choose Slices > Distribute, and choose a command from the submenu.

Deleting user-slices and layer-based slices

When you delete a user-slice or layer-based slice, auto-slices are regenerated to fill the document area.

Deleting a layer-based slice does not delete the associated layer; however, deleting the layer associated with a layer-based slice does delete the layer-based slice.

Note: You cannot delete auto-slices. If you delete all user-slices and layer-based slices in an image, one auto-slice layer will remain.

To delete a slice:

1 Select a slice. In ImageReady, you can select multiple slices.

2 Do one of the following:

• Press the Backspace key or the Delete key.

• (ImageReady) Choose Slices > Delete Slice(s), or choose Delete Slice from the Slice palette menu.

To delete all user-slices and layer-based slices:

Do one of the following:

- (Photoshop) Choose View > Clear Slices.
- (ImageReady) Choose Slices > Delete All.

Locking slices (Photoshop)

Locking slices prevents you from making changes accidentally, such as resizing or moving slices.

To lock all slices:

Choose View > Lock Slices.

Specifying slice options

Setting slice options lets you specify how the slice data will appear in a Web browser. The available options vary according to the application and the slice type you select. You can only set options for one slice at a time.

Note: Setting options for an auto-slice promotes the slice to a user-slice.

Viewing slice options

You specify slice options in the Slice Options dialog box (Photoshop) and the Slice palette (ImageReady).

To display the Slice Options dialog box (Photoshop):

Do one of the following:

- Double-click a slice with the slice select tool.
- With the slice select tool active, click the Slice Options button in the options bar. This method is available only in the main Photoshop application, not in the Photoshop Save for Web dialog box.

To display the Slice palette (ImageReady):

See "Using the Web design palettes (ImageReady)" on page 271.

Choosing a content type

Formatting and display options for a slice vary according to its content type. There are two types of slice content:

- Image slices contain image data, including rollover states. This is the default content type.
- No Image slices contain solid color or HTML text. Because No Image slices contain no image data, they download more quickly. Photoshop and ImageReady do not display No Image slice content. To view No Image slice content, preview the image in a browser. (See "Previewing an image in a browser" on page 84.)

To specify a content type:

1 Select a slice. If you are working in Photoshop, double-click the slice with the slice select tool to display the Slice Options dialog box.

2 In the Slice Options dialog box (Photoshop) or the Slice palette (ImageReady), select a slice type from the Type pop-up menu.

3 (Photoshop) Click OK.

Specifying slice names

The Name option lets you change the default name of a slice. This option is only available for Image slices. You can also change the default naming pattern for slices. (See "Setting slice naming preferences" on page 351.)

To change the name of a slice:

1 Select a slice. If you are working in Photoshop, double-click the slice with the slice select tool to display the Slice Options dialog box.

2 In the Slice Options dialog box (Photoshop) or the Slice palette (ImageReady), type a new name in the Name text box.

3 (Photoshop) Click OK.

Specifying slice background colors

The background color option lets you select a color to fill the transparent area (for Image slices) or entire area (for No Image slices) of the slice. In Photoshop, this option is available only if you activate the Slice Options dialog box from within the Save for Web dialog box.

Photoshop and ImageReady do not display the selected background color—you must preview the image in a browser to view the effect of selecting a background color. (See "Previewing an image in a browser" on page 84.)

To choose a background color:

1 Select a slice. If you are working in the Photoshop Save for Web dialog box, double-click the slice with the slice select tool to display the Slice Options dialog box.

2 In the Slice Options dialog box (Photoshop) or the Slice palette (ImageReady), select a background color from the Background/BG pop-up menu:

• (Photoshop) Select None, Matte, Eyedropper (to use the color in the eyedropper sample box), White, Black, or Other (using the color picker).

• (ImageReady) Select None, Matte, Foreground Color, Background Color, or Other (to use the color picker), or select a color from the pop-up palette.

3 (Photoshop) Click OK.

Assigning a URL to an Image slice

Assigning a URL to a slice makes the entire slice area a hotspot in the resulting Web page. When a user clicks in the hotspot, the Web browser links to the specified URL and target frame. This option is only available for Image slices.

To assign link information to an Image slice:

1 Select a slice. If you are working in Photoshop, double-click the slice with the slice select tool to display the Slice Options dialog box.

2 In the Slice Options dialog box (Photoshop) or the Slice palette (ImageReady), enter a URL in the URL text box, or choose a previously created URL from the pop-up menu. You can enter a relative URL or a full URL. If you enter a full URL, be sure to include http:// (for example, enter http://www.adobe.com, not www.adobe.com). For more information on using relative URLs and full URLs, see an HTML reference (either printed or on the Web).

3 If desired, enter the name of a target frame in the Target text box, or choose an option from the pop-up menu. A frame name must match a frame previously defined in the HTML file for the document. When a user clicks the link, the specified file displays in the new frame:

• _blank to display the linked file in a new window, leaving the original browser window open.

• _self to display the linked file in the same frame as the original file.

• _parent to display the linked file in its own original parent frameset. Use this option if the HTML document contains frames and the current frame is a child. The linked file displays in the current parent frame.

• _top to replace the entire browser window with the linked file, removing all current frames.

Note: *For more information on frames, see an HTML reference (either printed or on the Web).*

4 (Photoshop) Click OK.

Resizing and moving slices using numeric coordinates

The Dimensions options let you set the exact position and dimensions of a slice in relation to the document window. This option is not available if you access the Slice Options dialog box through the Photoshop Save for Web dialog box.

In ImageReady, if the Dimensions options aren't showing, choose Show Options from the Slice palette menu, or click the Show Options button (✦) on the palette tab to view them.

Note: *You cannot resize or move a layer-based slice using this method.*

To resize and move a slice using numeric coordinates:

1 Select a slice. If you are working in Photoshop, double-click the slice with the slice select tool to display the Slice Options dialog box.

2 In the Dimensions area of the Slice Options dialog box (Photoshop) or the Slice palette (ImageReady), change one or more of the following options:

• X to specify the distance in pixels between the left edge of the slice and the origin point of the ruler in the document window.

• Y to specify the distance in pixels between the top edge of the slice and the origin point of the ruler in the document window.

Note: *The default origin point of the ruler is the upper left corner of the image. (See "Using rulers, the measure tool, guides, and the grid" on page 74.)*

• W to specify the width of the slice.

• H to specify the height of the slice.

• Constrain Proportions to preserve the current proportions of the slice.

3 (Photoshop) Click OK.

Specifying browser messages

You can specify what messages appear in the browser using the Message and Alt options. These options are only available for Image slices.

Message Lets you change the default message in the browser's status area for a selected slice or slices. By default the slice's URL is displayed.

Alt Lets you specify an Alt tag for a selected slice or slices. The Alt text appears in place of the slice image in nongraphical browsers. It also appears in place of the image while the image is downloading and as a tool tip in some browsers.

In ImageReady, if the Message and Alt options aren't showing, choose Show Options from the Slice palette menu, or click the Show Options button (♦) on the palette tab to view them.

To specify a browser message:

1 Select a slice. If you are working in Photoshop, double-click the slice with the slice select tool to display the Slice Options dialog box.

2 In the Slice Options dialog box (Photoshop) or the Slice palette (ImageReady), type the desired text in the Message text box, Alt text box, or both.

3 (Photoshop) Click OK.

Adding HTML text to a slice

Choosing the No Image type for a slice lets you enter text that will appear in the slice area of the resulting Web page. This text is HTML text— you can format it using standard HTML tags. You can also select vertical and horizontal alignment options. For more information on specific HTML tags, see an HTML reference (either printed or on the Web).

Photoshop and ImageReady do not display HTML text in the document window; you must use a Web browser to preview the text. (See "Previewing an image in a browser" on page 84.) Keep in mind that the appearance of text is affected by the browser settings and operating system it is viewed on. Be sure to preview HTML text in different browsers, with different browser setting, and on different operating systems to see how text will appear on the Web.

Note: Be careful not to enter more text than can be displayed in the slice area. If you enter too much text, it will extend into neighboring slices and affect the layout of your Web page.

To add HTML text to a slice:

1 Select a slice. If you are working in Photoshop, double-click the slice with the slice select tool to display the Slice Options dialog box.

2 In the Slice Options dialog box (Photoshop) or the Slice palette (ImageReady), select No Image from the Type pop-up menu.

3 Type the desired text in the provided text box. You can use standard HTML tags to format the text.

4 (Photoshop Save for Web dialog box and ImageReady) If desired, select options in the Cell Alignment section of the dialog box.

Horizontal alignment options:

• Default to use the browser's default for horizontal alignment.

• Left to align the text to the left side of the slice area.

• Center to align the text to the center of the slice area.

• Right to align the text to the right side of the slice area.

Vertical alignment options:

• Default to use the browser's default for vertical alignment.

• Top to align the text to the top of the slice area.

• Baseline to set a common baseline for the first line of text in cells in the same row (of the resulting HTML table). Each cell in the row must use the Baseline option.

• Middle to center the text vertically in the slice area.

• Bottom to align the text to the bottom of the slice area.

5 (Photoshop) Click OK.

Optimizing slices

You can optimize Image slices using the Save for Web dialog box (Photoshop) or the Optimize palette (ImageReady).

All Image slices use the optimization settings of the entire image until you apply new settings. If you select multiple slices with different optimization settings, only the controls that are relevant to all of the selected slices are visible. If settings for a control differ among slices, the control is blank. Any settings you choose are applied to all selected slices.

In ImageReady, you can also copy optimization settings from one slice to another within a document, or from a slice in one view to a slice in another view in 2-Up or 4-Up view.

To optimize a slice:

Select one or more Image slices, and specify options in the Optimize panel/palette. (See "Optimizing images" on page 320.)

To copy optimization settings between slices (ImageReady):

1 Select the slice that uses the optimization settings you want to copy.

2 Drag the Droplet icon ( ) from the Optimize palette onto the slice to which you want to apply the optimization settings.

Linking slices (ImageReady)

Linking slices lets you share optimization settings between slices. You must use ImageReady to link slices; however, you can apply settings to linked slices in either the Save for Web dialog box (Photoshop) or the Optimize palette (ImageReady). When you apply optimization settings to a linked slice, all slices in the set are updated.

Linked slices in GIF and PNG-8 format share a color palette and dither pattern. The dither pattern is applied across adjacent slice boundaries to prevent the appearance of seams between the slices. (See "Previewing and controlling dithering" on page 341.)

To link slices:

1 Select two or more slices you want to link.

Note: *If the first slice you select is a user-slice, any auto-slices you link to the first slice become user-slices. If the first slice you select is an auto-slice, any user-slices you select are linked to the auto-slice group.*

2 Choose Slices > Link Slices.

Each linked set of user-slices is assigned a different color for the slice display graphics in the upper left corner of the slice. This helps to identify all the slices in one set.

To unlink user-slices:

Do one of the following:

• To unlink a user-slice, select the slice, and then choose Slices > Unlink Slices.

• To unlink all user-slices in a set, select a slice in the set, and choose Slices > Unlink Set.

• To unlink all user-slices in an image, choose Slices > Unlink All.

Creating and viewing image maps (ImageReady)

Image maps enable you to link an area of an image to a URL. You can set up multiple linked areas—called image map areas—in an image, with links to text files; other images; audio, video, or multimedia files; other pages in the Web site; or other Web sites. You can also create rollover effects in image map areas.

The main difference between using image maps and using slices to create links is in how the source image is exported as a Web page. Using image maps keeps the exported image intact as a single file, while using slices causes the image to be exported as a separate file. Another difference between image maps and slices is that image maps enable you to link circular, polygonal, or rectangular areas in an image, while slices enable you to link only rectangular areas. If you need to link only rectangular areas, using slices may be preferable to using an image map.

Note: *To avoid unexpected results, do not create image map areas in slices that contain URL links—either the image map links or the slice links may be ignored in some browsers.*

Creating image maps

You can create image map areas using an image map tool or a layer.

Tool-based image map areas Are created using an image map tool—you drag in the image to define the image map area. You can view and set options for tool-based image maps in the Image Map palette.

Layer-based image map areas Are created from a layer—the layer's content defines the shape of the image map area. If you edit the layer's content, the image map area automatically adjusts to encompass the new pixels. You can view and set options for layer-based image map areas in the Image Map palette, however you cannot use the Duplicate or Align commands. To access these commands, or to move or resize the image map area by dragging, you can convert a layer-based image map area to a tool-based image map area.

If you plan to add a rollover effect to an image map area, it is often preferable to use a layer-based image map area rather than a tool-based image map area. For example, if you create a rollover button that displays a glow effect in the Over state, a layer-based image map area will automatically adjust to encompass the pixels that are produced by the glow.

Important: If you overlap image map areas, the topmost area is active.

To create an image map area using an image map tool:

1 Select the rectangle image map tool (⟨⟩), the circle image map tool (⟨⟩), or the polygon image map tool (⟨⟩) in the toolbox.

2 For the rectangle or circle image map tool, select Fixed Size to specify set values for the image map area's dimensions. Enter pixel values in whole numbers.

3 Do one of the following to define the image map area:

• With the rectangle or circle image map tool, drag over the area you want to define. Shift-drag to constrain the area to a square. Alt-drag (Windows) or Option-drag (Mac OS) to drag an image map area from its center.

• With the polygon image map tool, click in the image to set the starting point. Position the pointer where you want the first straight segment to end, and click. Continue clicking to set endpoints for subsequent segments. Hold down Shift to constrain the segment to 45° increments. To close the border, double-click, or position the pointer over the starting point (a closed circle appears next to the pointer) and click.

To create an image map area from a layer:

1 In the Layers palette, choose a layer from which to create an image map area. (To use multiple layers in one image map area, first merge the layers.)

2 Choose Layer > New Layer Based Image Map Area.

Converting layer-based image maps to tool-based image maps

Because a layer-based image map area is tied to the pixel content of a layer, the only way to move, resize, or align it is to edit the layer. You can convert a layer-based image map area to a tool-based image map area to unlink it from the layer.

To convert a layer-based image map area to a tool-based image map area:

1 Select a layer-based image map area using the image map select tool (image). (See "Selecting image maps" on page 289).

2 Choose Promote Layer Based Image Map Area from the Image Map palette menu. If the layer contains multiple, non-overlapping areas of pixel content, multiple tool-based image map areas are produced.

Viewing image maps

When you select the image map select tool, image map areas show automatically. You can also show or hide image map areas using the Image Map Visibility button.

Image map preferences determine how image map areas appear in the document window. You can set preferences for image map lines, line color, and color adjustments.

To show or hide image map areas:

Do one of the following:

• Click the Image Map Visibility button (image) in the toolbox.

• Choose View > Show > Image Maps.

• Choose View > Show Extras. This command also shows or hides selection edges, slices, text bounds, text baseline, and text selections. (See "Working with Extras" on page 77.)

To set image map display preferences:

1 Choose Edit > Preferences > Image Maps.

2 To change the color of image map lines, choose a color from the Line Color pop-up menu. Changing the color of image map lines also changes the line color of selected image map areas to a contrasting color.

3 To change the strength of image map color adjustments, enter a value, or choose a value from the Image Map Overlay pop-up slider. The value determines the extent of color adjustments that dim the brightness and contrast of unselected image map areas.

4 To display image map lines only and deselect color adjustment display, select Show Lines Only.

5 To show a bounding box for circular image map areas, select Show Bounding Box.

Selecting and modifying image maps (ImageReady)

You can move, arrange, align, and duplicate tool-based image map areas using the Image Map palette. There are fewer options for modifying layer-based image map areas because they are tied to the pixel content of the associated layer; however, you can select, arrange, and delete layer-based image map areas as you do tool-based image map areas.

Selecting image maps

You select image map areas with the image map select tool.

To select an image map area:

1 Select the image map select tool ( ).

2 Click on an image map area in the image. Shift-click to add areas to the selection.

You can also select multiple image map areas by clicking outside an image map area and dragging across the image map areas you want to select.

Moving and resizing tool-based image maps

You can move and resize tool-based image map areas by dragging. You can also move and resize rectangular and circular image map areas using numeric coordinates.

Note: *To move or resize a layer-based image map area, move or edit the layer.*

To move a tool-based image map area:

1 Select one or more image map areas you want to move.

2 Position the pointer inside the image map area, and drag it to a new position. Press Shift to restrict movement to a vertical, horizontal, or 45° diagonal line.

To resize a tool-based image map area:

1 Select an image map area you want to resize.

2 Drag a handle on the image map border to resize the image map area.

To resize and move a tool-based image map area using numeric coordinates:

1 Select a rectangular or circular image map area.

2 In the Dimensions area of the Image Map palette, change one or more of the following options:

• X to specify the distance in pixels between the left edge of a rectangular image map area, or the center point of a circular image map area, and the origin point of the ruler in the document window.

• Y to specify the distance in pixels between the top edge of a rectangular image map area, or the center point of a circular image map area, and the origin point of the ruler in the document window.

Note: *The default origin point of the ruler is the upper left corner of the image. (See "Using rulers, the measure tool, guides, and the grid" on page 74.)*

• W to specify the width of a rectangular image map area.

• H to specify the height of a rectangular image map area.

• R to specify the radius of a circular image map area.

Changing the shape of layer-based image maps

When you create a layer-based image map area, the default image map area is a rectangle that encompasses all of the layer's pixel data. You can change the shape of the image map area by selecting a Shape option in the Image Map palette.

To change the shape of a layer-based image map area:

1 Select a layer-based image map area.

2 In the Layer Image Map section of the Image Map palette, choose an option from the shape pop-up list: Rectangle, Circle, or Polygon. If you choose Polygon, enter a value or choose a value from the Quality pop-up slider to set the number of segments in the polygon.

Duplicating tool-based image maps

You can create a duplicate image map area with the same dimensions and settings as the original tool-based image map area.

To duplicate a tool-based image map area:

1 Select one or more image map areas.

2 Do one of the following:

• Choose Duplicate Image Map Area(s) from the Image Map palette menu.

• Alt-drag (Windows) or Option-drag (Mac OS) from inside the image map area.

The duplicate image map area appears on top of the original (offset 10 pixels down and to the right) and can be moved, resized, or otherwise modified.

Arranging image maps

When image map areas overlap, the last image map area you create is the top image map area in the stacking order. You can specify which image map area is on the top and bottom of the stack and move image map areas up or down in the stacking order.

To change the stacking order of image map areas:

1 Select one or more image map areas you want to arrange. You can select a combination of tool-based image map areas and layer-based image map areas.

2 Do one of the following:

• With the image map select tool active, click a stacking order option in the options bar: Bring to Front (🖾), Bring Forward (🖾), Send Backward(🖾), Send to Back (🖾).

• Choose a stacking order command from the Image Map palette menu.

Aligning tool-based image maps

You can align tool-based image map areas to the top, bottom, left, right, and middle.

Note: *To align layer-based image map areas, first link the layers, and then choose an alignment option from the Layer > Align Linked submenu.*

To align tool-based image map areas:

1 Select the tool-based image map areas you want to align.

2 Do one of the following:

• With the image map select tool active, click an alignment option in the options bar: Align Top Edges (🖾), Align Vertical Centers (🖾), Align Bottom Edges (🖾), Align Left Edges (🖾), Align Horizontal Centers (🖾), Align Right Edges (🖾).

• Choose an alignment command from the Image Map palette menu.

Distributing tool-based image maps

You can distribute tool-based image map areas evenly along the vertical or horizontal axis.

To distribute tool-based image map areas:

1 Select the tool-based image map areas you want to distribute.

2 Do one of the following:

• With the image map select tool active, click a distribute option in the options bar: Distribute Top Edges (⬒), Distribute Vertical Centers (⬒), Distribute Bottom Edges (⬒), Distribute Left Edges (⫿⫿), Distribute Horizontal Centers (⬤⬤), Distribute Right Edges (⫿⫿).

• Choose a distribute command from the Image Map palette menu.

Deleting image maps

You can delete selected image map areas by pressing the Backspace key or the Delete key, or choosing Delete Image Map Area(s) from the Image Map palette menu.

Specifying image map options (ImageReady)

You can specify a name, a URL, a target frame, and Alt text for an image map area in the Image Map palette.

To change the name of an image map area:

1 Select an image map area.

2 In the Image Map palette, enter a new name in the Name text box.

To specify link options for an image map area:

1 Select an image map area.

2 In the Image Map palette, enter a URL for the link, or choose a previously created URL from the URL pop-up menu. You can enter a relative URL or a full URL. If you enter a full URL, be sure to include http:// (for example, enter http://www.adobe.com, not www.adobe.com). For more information on using relative URLs and full URLs, see an HTML reference (either printed or on the Web).

3 In the Image Map palette, enter the name of a target frame in the Target text box, or choose an option from the pop-up menu. A frame name must match a frame previously defined in the HTML file for the document. When a user clicks the link, the specified file displays in the new frame:

• _blank to display the linked file in a new window, leaving the original browser window open.

• _self to display the linked file in the same frame as the original file.

• _parent to display the linked file in its own original parent frameset. Use this option if the HTML document contains frames and the current frame is a child. The linked file displays in the current parent frame.

• _top to replace the entire browser window with the linked file, removing all current frames.

Note: For more information on frames, see an HTML reference (either printed or on the Web).

4 In the Image Map palette, enter text for an Alt tag in the Alt text box. The Alt text appears in place of the image map area in nongraphical browsers. In most browsers, it also appears if the user positions the mouse over the image map area.

Selecting an image map type (ImageReady)

ImageReady can create client-side and server-side image maps. In client-side image maps, the links are interpreted by the browser itself. In server-side image maps, the links are interpreted by the server. Because client-side image maps don't need to contact the server to function, they are often significantly faster to navigate. By default, ImageReady saves image maps as client-side image maps.

Important: Server-side image maps do not work in images that have multiple slices.

You select an image map type in the Output Settings dialog box. (See "Setting HTML output options" on page 349.) If you select a server-side image map, ImageReady generates a separate map file based on the server option you select. However, you'll need to update the path to the map file in your HTML file.

Working with rollovers (ImageReady)

You use the Rollover palette, in conjunction with the Layers palette, to add rollover effects to a Web page. You can display an animation as a rollover state, or you can create secondary rollovers in which moving a mouse over one area causes an image change in another area. ImageReady adds JavaScript code to the resulting HTML file to specify rollover states.

Note: When working with rollovers, it is important to preview images in a Web browser to ensure your document will function correctly for Web users. Also remember that image appearance will vary on different operating systems.

About rollovers

A *rollover* is a Web effect in which different states of an image appear when a viewer performs a mouse action—such as rolling or clicking—over an area of the Web page. A *state* is defined by a specific configuration of the Layers palette, including layer location, styles, and other formatting options.

You use a slice or image map area to define the active area for a rollover. By default, every slice or image map area has one state—the Normal state. (The Normal state corresponds to the appearance of an image when it is first loaded into a Web browser and no rollover effects have occurred.) When you add a new state to the rollover, you capture a snapshot of the slice or image map area in the previous state. You can then use the Layers palette to make changes to the image in the new state. You can also add an animation to a rollover state.

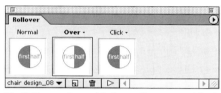

The Rollover palette with three rollover states. The dark border around the middle thumbnail indicates that the Over state is selected.

When you save an image with rollover states as a Web page, each rollover state is saved as a separate image file. By default, rollover states are named using the corresponding slice name plus the mouse action that triggers the rollover state. When you change the name of a slice, rollover states in the slice are renamed.

Working with layers in rollovers

How you work with layers is an essential part of creating rollovers. Placing the image content for a rollover on its own layer allows you to use Layers palette commands and options to create rollover effects. When creating rollovers or animations, some changes you make to a layer affect only the active state or frame, while others affect all states or frames. (See "Using layers to edit frames" on page 306.)

When creating a slice for a rollover, use a layer-based slice. This is recommended because the dimensions of a layer's content may change in the course of creating a rollover, and layer-based slices

automatically adjust to encompass the new pixels. However, do not use a layer-based slice when you plan to move the layer over a large area during an animation, because the slice dimension may exceed a useful size. (See "Creating layer-based slices" on page 273.)

You can use layer styles to create instant rollover effects. When working with layer-based slices, you can also save the series of states as a rollover style. (See "Applying and creating rollover styles" on page 296.)

Using the Rollover palette

You use the Rollover palette to create and set options for rollover states. The Rollover palette displays thumbnails for each state of a rollover. The first state in the Rollover palette is always the Normal state.

To change the thumbnail view of rollover states:

1 Choose Palette Options from the Rollover palette menu.

2 Select a thumbnail size.

3 Under Thumbnails Show, define the content of the thumbnail:

• Current Slice to show only the current slice in the thumbnail.

• Entire Document to show the entire image in the thumbnail. This view is useful when creating a secondary rollover effect.

4 Click OK.

To select a slice or image map area in the Rollover palette:

Choose a slice or image map area from the pop-up menu at the lower left corner of the Rollover palette.

Creating rollover states

When you create a rollover state, you select a mouse action which activates the state (except for the first state in a rollover, which is always the Normal state).

To create a rollover state:

1 Select the slice or image map area to which you want to add the rollover.

Note: When creating a slice or image map area for a rollover, use a layer-based slice or a layer-based image map area. This is recommended because the dimensions of a layer's content may change in the course of creating a rollover.

2 In the Rollover palette, create a new state:

• Click the New State button (☐) at the bottom of the palette.

• Choose New State from the Rollover palette menu.

The new rollover state is identical to the state immediately preceding it, until you make modifications to the image using the Layers palette.

3 Use the default rollover state assigned by ImageReady, or select a rollover state from the pop-up menu above the rollover thumbnail:

• Over to define the rollover state when the Web viewer rolls over the slice or image map area with the mouse while the mouse button is not pressed. (Over is automatically selected for the second rollover state.)

• Down to define the rollover state when the Web viewer presses the mouse button on the slice or image map area. (This state appears as long as the viewer keeps the mouse button pressed down on the area.)

• Click to define the rollover state when the Web viewer clicks the mouse on the slice or image map area. (This state appears after the viewer clicks the mouse and remains until the viewer activates another rollover state.)

• Out to define the rollover state when the Web viewer rolls the mouse out of the slice or image map area. (The Normal state usually serves this purpose.)

• Up to define the rollover state when the Web viewer releases the mouse button over the slice or image map area. (The Over state usually serves this purpose.)

Note: Different Web browsers, or different versions of a browser, may process clicks and double-clicks differently. For example, some browsers leave the slice in the Click state after a click, and in the Up state after a double-click; other browsers use the Up state only as a transition into the Click state, regardless of single- or double-clicking. To ensure your Web page will function correctly, be sure to preview rollovers in various Web browsers.

• Custom to define a new rollover state. (You must create JavaScript code and add it to the HTML file for the Web page in order for the Custom rollover option to function. See a JavaScript manual for more information.)

• None to preserve the current state of the image for later use as a rollover state. (A state designated as None will not be displayed on the Web page.)

The Rollover States pop-up menu displays only the rollover states that have not yet been used for the selected slice or image map area (with the exception of the None and Custom states, which are always available and can be used repeatedly). You can redefine rollover states as you work (with the exception of the Normal state).

4 Modify the image for the rollover state using the Layers palette.

Previewing rollover states

You can preview rollover states directly in the ImageReady document window by switching to rollover preview mode. This preview is consistent with Internet Explorer 5.0 for Windows. To preview the rollover effect in your computer's default Web browser, click the Preview in Default Browser button in the toolbox. (See "Previewing an image in a browser" on page 84.)

To use rollover preview mode:

1 Click the Rollover Preview button (🐾) in the toolbox, or click the Play button (▷) in the Rollover palette.

2 In the document window, perform the action that activates the rollover state. For example, position the mouse over the rollover slice or image map area to preview the Over state. Then click the slice or image map area to preview the Click state.

To exit rollover preview mode:

Select any tool in the toolbox (including the Rollover Preview button), or click the Play button in the Rollover palette.

Adding animation to rollover states

You use the Animation palette, in conjunction with the Rollover palette, to add an animation to a rollover state.

When working with a layer-based slice or a layer-based image map area, moving the layer in the Normal state repositions the layer in every rollover state. However, moving the layer in a rollover state other than the Normal state repositions the layer only in the current state.

To add an animation to a rollover state:

1 In the Rollover palette, create a new rollover state or select the thumbnail for a rollover state in which you want to display an animation.

2 In the Animation palette, create frames for the animation. (See "Creating animations" on page 301.)

Note: *Adding an animation to the Normal state will cause the animation to appear when the image is loaded in a Web browser.*

Applying and creating rollover styles

Rollover styles simplify rollover creation by allowing you to turn a layer into a rollover effect with a single click. A rollover style includes all the attributes of a rollover, including its states and layer effects. When you apply a rollover style to a layer, the layer becomes a layer-based slice.

To apply a rollover style to a layer:

1 Select a layer in the Layers palette.

2 Choose Window > Show Styles, or click the Styles palette tab, to display the Styles palette.

3 Click the thumbnail for the rollover style you want to apply. Rollover style thumbnails have a triangle in the upper left corner.

To create a rollover style:

1 Create or select a layer-based slice. (See "Creating layer-based slices" on page 273.)

Note: You must use a layer-based slice in order to create a rollover style.

2 In the Rollover palette, create the desired rollover states. Apply the effects to each state using predefined styles in the Styles palette or by manually setting layer effects in the Layers palette.

3 In the Styles palette, click the New Style button ( ), or choose New Style from the palette menu.

4 Enter a name for the style, set style options, and click OK. The Include Rollover States option must be selected in order to create a rollover style.

The new rollover style appears in the Styles palette. The thumbnail preview displays the effects in the Normal state.

Matching layers across rollover states

When you use Layers palette commands to create effects for a rollover state, the changes apply only to the active state. However, you can use the Rollover palette to apply layer changes to all states in a rollover or all rollover states associated with an image. For more information about working with layers when creating rollovers, see "Using layers to edit frames" on page 306.

To match layer changes across rollover states:

1 In the Layers palette, select the layer containing the element you want to match across states.

2 In the Rollover palette, choose an option from the palette menu:

• Match Layer Across States to apply layer attributes for the selected state to all states in the current rollover.

• Match Layer Across All Rollovers to apply layer attributes for the selected state to all states in all rollovers associated with the current image.

Copying and pasting rollover states

You can copy a rollover state and paste it into another state in the current rollover or into a state in another rollover. Layers in the source state replace layers in the destination state.

You can also copy frames from the Animation palette and paste them into the Rollover palette as states, or copy states from the Rollover palette and paste them into the Animation palette as frames.

Note: Copy commands in the Animation palette and the Rollover palette use an internal clipboard available to these commands only. Copying frames or rollover states does not overwrite the primary ImageReady clipboard.

To copy and paste rollover states:

1 Select a rollover state, and choose Copy Rollover State from the Rollover palette menu.

2 Select a rollover state in which to paste the copied state:

• Select a state in the current rollover.

• Open or display another rollover, and select a state.

3 Choose Paste Rollover State from the Rollover palette menu.

Deleting rollover states

You can delete individual states or all states in a rollover.

To delete rollover states:

• To delete one state, select a rollover state, and either click the Trash button (🗑) on the Rollover palette or choose Delete State from the Rollover palette menu.

• To delete all states in a rollover, choose Delete Rollover from the Rollover palette menu.

Creating Web photo galleries (Photoshop)

You use the Web Photo Gallery command to automatically generate a Web photo gallery from a set of images. A Web photo gallery is a Web site that features a home page with thumbnail images and gallery pages with full-size images. Each page contains links that allow visitors to navigate the site. For example, when a visitor clicks a thumbnail image on the home page, a gallery page with the associated full-size image loads.

Photoshop provides a variety of styles for your gallery, which you can select using the Web Photo Gallery command. If you are an advanced user who has knowledge of HTML, you can also customize a style by editing a set of HTML template files or create a new style.

For more information, see "Customizing and creating Web photo gallery styles" in online Help.

To create a Web photo gallery:

1 Choose File > Automate > Web Photo Gallery.

2 Under Files, click Source. Then select the folder containing the images that you want to appear in the gallery, and click OK. Select Include All Subdirectories to include images inside any subfolders of the selected folder.

3 Click Destination. Then select the destination folder that you want to contain the images and HTML pages for the gallery, and click OK.

4 For Styles, choose a style for the gallery. A preview of the home page for the chosen style appears in the dialog box.

5 To set options for the banner that appears on each page in the gallery, choose Banner from the Options pop-up menu. Then do the following:

• For Site Name, enter the title of the gallery.

• For Photographer, enter the name of the person or organization that deserves credit for the photos in the gallery.

• For Date, enter the date that you want to appear on each page of the gallery. By default, Photoshop uses the current date.

• For Font and Font Size, choose options for the banner text.

6 To set options for the gallery pages, choose Gallery Images from the Options pop-up menu. Then do the following:

• For Border Size, enter the width of the border around the image in pixels.

• To have Photoshop resize the source images for placement on the gallery pages, select Resize Images. Then choose an option for the image size from the pop-up menu or enter a size in pixels. For JPEG Quality, choose an option from the pop-up menu, enter a value between 0 and 12, or drag the slider. A higher value results in better image quality but larger file size.

7 To set options for the home page, choose Gallery Thumbnails from the Options pop-up menu. Then do the following:

• For Caption, select Use Filename to display the filename under each thumbnail.

• Select Use File Info Caption to display caption text from the File Info dialog box under each thumbnail and on each gallery page. For more information, see "Adding title and copyright information to HTML files" on page 351.

• For Font and Font Size, choose options for the thumbnail text.

• For Size, choose an option for the thumbnail size from the pop-up menu or enter a value in pixels for the width of each thumbnail.

• For Columns and Rows, enter the number of columns and rows that you want to be used to display the thumbnails on the home page. This option doesn't apply to galleries that use the Horizontal Frame Style or Vertical Frame Style.

• For Border Size, enter the width of the border around each thumbnail in pixels.

8 To set options for colors of elements in the gallery, choose Customize Colors from the Options pop-up menu. To change the color of a particular element, click its color swatch, and then select a new color using the Color Picker. The Background option lets you change the background color of each page. The Banner option lets you change the background color of the banner.

9 Click OK to create the gallery.

Photoshop places the following HTML and JPEG files in your destination folder:

• A home page for your gallery named index.htm. Open this file in any Web browser to preview your gallery.

• JPEG images inside an images subfolder.

• HTML pages inside a pages subfolder.

• JPEG thumbnail images inside a thumbnails subfolder.

11

Chapter 11: Creating Animations (ImageReady)

Adobe ImageReady provides a powerful, easy way to create multiple-frame animations from a single document.

Using the Animation and Layers palettes, you can create, edit, copy, paste, and rearrange frames in a sequence. You can use the powerful Tween feature to quickly create new frames that vary a layer's opacity, position, or layer effects, and create the illusion of a single element in a frame moving or fading in or out. You can also optimize the animation, specify looping and repeat options for playback, and flatten frames into layers. The number of frames you can create is limited only by the amount of memory available to ImageReady on your system.

Working with layers is an essential part of creating animations in ImageReady. Placing each element of an animation on its own layer enables you to change the position and appearance of the element across a series of frames, using the Layers palette commands and options.

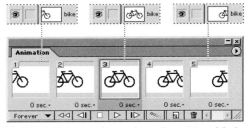

The bicycle image is on its own layer; the position of the layer changes in each frame of the animation.

About animation

An animation is a sequence of images, or *frames*, that is displayed over time. Each frame varies slightly from the preceding frame, creating the illusion of movement when the frames are viewed in quick succession.

Creating animations

You use the Animation palette, in conjunction with the Layers palette, to create animation frames from an original, multilayer image. You can assign a delay time to each frame, use the Tween command to generate new frames, and specify looping for the animation.

Keep in mind that an image can have multiple animations that are associated with different rollover states. For example, adding an animation to the Normal rollover state causes the animation to play when the Web page is first loaded by a Web browser. Adding an animation to another rollover state causes the animation to play only when the Web user performs the specified action (such as placing the mouse over the rollover or clicking on the rollover). Before creating an animation, check the Rollover palette to ensure that the desired state is selected. (See "Working with rollovers (ImageReady)" on page 292.)

Using the Animation palette

The Animation palette lets you create, view, and set options for the frames in an animation. You can change the thumbnail view of frames in the Animation palette—using smaller thumbnails reduces the space required by the palette and displays more frames in a given palette width.

To display the Animation palette:

Choose Window > Show Animation, or click the Animation palette tab.

To change the thumbnail view of frames:

1 Select Palette Options from the Animation palette menu.

2 Select a thumbnail size, and click OK.

Adding frames

Adding frames is the first step in creating an animation. If you have an image open in ImageReady, the Animation palette displays the image as the first frame in a new animation. Each frame you add starts as a duplicate of the preceding frame. You then make changes to the frame using the Layers palette.

Note: Always create and edit frames in Original view. While you can view frames in an optimized view, the editing options are very limited.

To add a frame to an animation:

1 If you want to add the animation to a rollover state, select the desired state in the Rollover palette. (See "Using the Rollover palette" on page 293.)

2 In the Animation palette, do one of the following:

• Click the New Frame button (🖻).

• Select New Frame from the Animation palette menu.

Selecting frames

Before you can work with a frame, you must select it as the current frame. The contents of the current frame appear in the document window.

You can select multiple frames, either contiguous or discontiguous, to edit them or apply commands to them as a group. When multiple frames are selected, only the current frame appears in the document window.

In the Animation palette, the current frame is indicated by a narrow border (inside the shaded selection highlight) around the frame thumbnail. Selected frames are indicated by a shaded highlight around the frame thumbnails.

To select the current frame:

Do one of the following:

• In the Animation palette, click the thumbnail of the frame you want to select as the current frame.

• In the Animation palette or the Layers palette, click the Forward button (ı▷) to select the next frame in the series as the current frame.

• In the Animation palette or the Layers palette, click the Backward button (◁ı) to select the previous frame in the series as the current frame.

• In the Animation palette, click the Rewind button (◁◁) to select the first frame in the series as the current frame.

To select multiple frames:

In the Animation palette, do one of the following:

• To select contiguous multiple frames, Shift-click a second frame. The second frame and all frames between the first and second are added to the selection.

• To select discontiguous multiple frames, Ctrl-click (Windows) or Command-click (Mac OS) additional frames to add those frames to the selection.

• To select all frames, choose Select All Frames from the Animation palette menu.

To deselect a frame in a multiframe selection:

Ctrl-click (Windows) or Command-click (Mac OS) a frame to deselect it.

Rearranging and deleting frames

You can change the position of frames in an animation and reverse the order of selected contiguous frames. You can also delete selected frames or the entire animation.

To change the position of a frame:

1 Select the frame you want to move. Ctrl-click (Windows) or Command-click (Mac OS) to add frames to the selection.

2 Drag the selection to the new position.

Note: If you drag multiple discontiguous frames, the frames are placed contiguously in the new position.

To reverse the order of contiguous frames:

1 Select the contiguous frames you want to reverse.

2 Choose Reverse Frames from the Animation palette menu.

To delete selected frames:

Do one of the following:

• Select Delete Frame(s) from the Animation palette menu.

• Click the Trash button (🗑) in the Animation palette, and click Yes to confirm the deletion.

• Drag the selected frame or frames onto the Trash button.

To delete an entire animation:

Select Delete Animation from the Animation palette menu.

Copying and pasting frames

To understand what happens when you copy and paste a frame, think of a frame as a duplicate version of an image with a given layer configuration. When you copy a frame, you copy the configuration of layers (including each layer's visibility setting, position, and other attributes). When you paste a frame, you apply that layer configuration to the destination frame.

To copy and paste layers between frames:

1 Select one or more frames.

2 Choose Copy Frame(s) from the Animation palette menu.

3 Select a destination frame or frames in the current animation or another animation.

4 Choose Paste Frame(s) from the Animation palette menu.

5 Select a Paste Method:

• Replace Frames to replace the selected frames with the copied frames. When you paste frames into the same image, no new layers are added to the image; rather, the attributes of each existing layer in the destination frames are replaced by those of each copied layer. When you paste frames between images, new layers are added to the image; however, only the pasted layers are visible in the destination frames (the existing layers are hidden).

• Paste Over Selection to add the contents of the pasted frames as new layers in the image. When you paste frames into the same image, using this option doubles the number of layers in the image. In the destination frames, the newly pasted layers are visible, and the original layers are hidden. In the nondestination frames, the newly pasted layers are hidden.

• Paste Before Selection or Paste After Selection to add the copied frames before or after the destination frame. When you paste frames between images, new layers are added to the image; however, only the pasted layers are visible in the new frames (the existing layers are hidden).

6 Select Link Added Layers if you want to link pasted layers in the Layers palette. Use this option when you need to reposition the pasted layers as a unit.

7 Click OK.

Tweening frames

You use the Tween command to automatically add or modify a series of frames between two existing frames—varying the layer attributes (position, opacity, or effect parameters) evenly between the new frames to create the appearance of movement. For example, if you want to fade out a layer, set the opacity of the layer in the starting frame to 100%; then set the opacity of the same layer in the ending frame to 0%. When you tween between the two frames, the opacity of the layer is reduced evenly across the new frames.

The term "tweening" is derived from "in betweening," the traditional animation term used to describe this process. Tweening significantly reduces the time required to create animation effects such as fading in or fading out, or moving an element across a frame. You can edit tweened frames individually after you create them.

Using tweening to animate warped text: Specify different warping effects in two frames of the animation, then use the Tween command to generate the intermediate frames.

To create frames using tweening:

1 To apply tweening to a specific layer, select it in the Layers palette.

2 Select a single frame or multiple contiguous frames.

If you select a single frame, you choose whether to tween the frame with the previous frame or the next frame. If you select two contiguous frames, new frames are added between the frames. If you select more than two frames, existing frames between the first and last selected frames are altered by the tweening operation. If you select the first and last frames in an animation, these frames are treated as contiguous, and tweened frames are added after the last frame. (This tweening method is useful when the animation is set to loop multiple times.)

Note: *You cannot select discontiguous frames for tweening.*

3 Do one of the following:

• Click the Tween button ( ) in the Animation palette.

• Select Tween from the Animation palette menu.

4 Specify the layer or layers to be varied in the added frames:

• All Layers to vary all layers in the selected frame or frames.

• Selected Layer to vary only the currently selected layer in the selected frame or frames.

5 Specify layer attributes to be varied:

• Position to vary the position of the layer's content in the new frames evenly between the beginning and ending frames.

• Opacity to vary the opacity of the new frames evenly between the beginning and ending frames.

• Effects to vary the parameter settings of layer effects evenly between the beginning and ending frames.

6 If you selected a single frame in step 2, choose where to add frames from the Tween With menu:

• Next Frame to add frames between the selected frame and the following frame.

• First Frame to add frames between the last frame and first frame. This option is only available if you select the last frame in the Animation palette.

• Previous Frame to add frames between the selected frame and the preceding frame.

• Last Frame to add frames between the first frame and last frame. This option is only available if you select the first frame in the Animation palette.

7 Enter a value, or use the Up or Down Arrow key to choose the number of frames to add. (This option is not available if you selected more than two frames. In this case, the tweening operation alters the existing frames between the first and last frames in the selection.)

8 Click OK.

Specifying looping

You select a looping option to specify how many times the animation sequence repeats when played.

To specify looping:

1 Click the looping option selection box at the lower left corner of the Animation palette.

2 Select a looping option: Once, Forever, or Other.

3 If you selected Other, enter a value in the Set Loop Count dialog box, and click OK.

Specifying delay for frames

You can specify a *delay*—the time that a frame is displayed—for single frames or for multiple frames in an animation. Delay time is displayed in seconds. Fractions of a second are displayed as decimal values. For example, one-quarter second is specified as .25.

To specify a delay time:

1 Select one or more frames.

2 In the Animation palette, click on the Delay value below the selected frame to view the Delay pop-up menu.

3 Specify the delay:

• Choose a value from the pop-up menu. (The last value used appears at the bottom of the menu.)

• Choose Other, enter a value in the Set Frame Delay dialog box, and click OK.

If you selected multiple frames, specifying a delay value for one frame applies the value to all frames.

Note: Delay time may not be accurate during an animation preview in ImageReady. For an accurate preview of delay time, preview animations in a browser.

Working with layers in animations

Working with layers is the key to creating animations in ImageReady. Each new frame starts out as a duplicate of the preceding frame—you edit the frame by adjusting its layers. You can apply layer changes to a single frame, a group of frames, or the entire animation.

Using layers to edit frames

The information in this section applies to rollover states as well as to animation frames.

When you work with layers in a frame, you can create or copy selections in the layer; adjust color and tone; change the layer's opacity, blending mode, or position; add layer effects; and perform editing tasks as you would with layers in any image. Using layer attributes to create animation effects is very simple, and it allows you to save an animation file in Photoshop format for later reediting.

Keep in mind that some changes you make to layers affect only the active frame, while others affect all frames:

Frame-specific changes Affect only the selected frames in the Animation palette. Changes you make to a layer using Layers palette commands and options—including a layer's opacity, blending mode, visibility, position, and layer effects—are frame-specific.

Global changes Affect all frames in an animation. Changes you make to the layer's pixel values, using painting and editing tools, color and tone adjustment commands, filters, type, and other image-editing commands, affect every frame in which the layer is included.

When you work with layer masks and layer clipping paths, changes in position, state (enabled or disabled), and link state are frame-specific, whereas changes in pixel or vector content affect all frames.

Adding layers to frames

When you create a new layer, it is visible in all frames of an animation. To hide a layer in a specific frame, select the frame in the Animation palette, and then hide the desired layer in the Layers palette.

You can use the Add Layer to New Frames option to automatically add a new layer to the image every time you create a frame. The new layer is visible in the new frame but hidden in other frames. Using this options saves time when you are creating an animation that requires you to add a new visual element to each frame.

To add a new layer every time you create a frame:

Choose Add Layer to New Frames from the Animation palette menu. A check mark indicates that the option is turned on.

Showing and hiding layers in frames

When you show or hide a layer in a frame, the visibility of the layer changes for that frame only. For example, if you use a multilayer image to create a three-frame animation, and you hide the top layer in the second frame, that layer will still be visible in first and third frames.

Matching layers across frames

When you use Layers palette commands to edit a layer, the changes apply only to the selected frame. To apply layer changes to all frames in an animation, use the Match Layer Across Frames command.

You can also use the Paste Frames command to apply layer changes to other frames. (See "Copying and pasting frames" on page 304.)

To match layer changes across frames:

1 In the Layers palette, select the layer containing the element you want to match across frames.

2 In the Animation palette, choose Match Layer Across Frames from the palette menu. The layer attributes for the selected frame are applied to all frames in the animation.

Setting the frame disposal method

The frame disposal method specifies whether to discard the current frame before displaying the next frame. You select a disposal method when working with animations that include background transparency in order to specify whether the current frame will be visible through the transparent areas of the next frame.

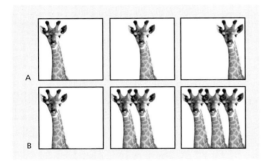

A. *Frame with background transparency with Restore to Background option* **B.** *Frame with background transparency with Do Not Dispose option*

The Disposal Method icon indicates whether the frame is set to Do Not Dispose (✤) or Restore to Background (⋰). (No icon appears when disposal method is set to Automatic.)

To choose a disposal method:

1 Select a frame or frames for which you want to choose a disposal method.

2 Right-click (Windows) or Ctrl-click (Mac OS) the frame thumbnail to view the Disposal Method context menu.

3 Choose a disposal method:

• Automatic to determine a disposal method for the current frame automatically, discarding the current frame if the next frame contains layer transparency. For most animations, the Automatic option yields the desired results and is, therefore, the default option.

Note: Choose the Automatic disposal option when using the Redundant Pixel Removal optimization option, to enable ImageReady to preserve frames that include transparency.

• Do Not Dispose to preserve the current frame as the next frame is added to the display. The current frame (and preceding frames) may show through transparent areas of the next frame. To accurately preview an animation using the Do Not Dispose option, preview the animation in a browser.

• Restore to Background to discard the current frame from the display before the next frame is displayed. Only a single frame is displayed at any time (and the current frame will not appear through the transparent areas of the next frame).

Flattening frames into layers

You can flatten animation frames into layers. A single, composite layer is created for each frame, containing all of the layers in the frame. The original layers in the frame are hidden but preserved (the original layers will be available if they are needed for another frame).

Note: If you save an animation as a GIF, the animation frames are flattened and the original layers are lost. You should save the original file in Photoshop file format to preserve layers for reediting.

To flatten frames into layers:

In the Animation palette, choose Flatten Frames into Layers from the palette menu.

Viewing animations

Viewing an animation lets you preview the frames in timed sequence. You can preview an animation in ImageReady or in a Web browser.

To view an animation in ImageReady:

1 Click the Play button (▷) in the Animation palette. The animation is displayed in the document window. The animation repeats indefinitely unless you specified another repeat value in the Play Options dialog box. (See "Specifying looping" on page 306.)

2 To stop the animation, click the Stop button (☐).

3 To rewind the animation, click the Rewind button (◁◁).

To preview an animation in a browser:

1 Click the Preview in Default Browser tool (🦢), (🔣) in the toolbox, or choose File > Preview In and select a browser from the submenu.

2 Use the browser's Stop and Reload commands to stop or replay the animation.

Optimizing animations

You can apply optimization settings to animated images just as you do to nonanimated images. (See "Optimizing images" on page 320.) You should always optimize an animation in GIF format because GIF is the only format in ImageReady that supports the display of animated images on the Web.

Note: While you can optimize an image that includes animation in JPEG or PNG format, these formats do not support animation. The resulting Web page will display only the first frame of the animation.

In addition to the standard optimization options for GIF format, you can optimize frames to include only areas that change from frame to frame. (This greatly reduces the file size of the animated GIF.) ImageReady also applies a special dithering technique to animations to ensure that dither patterns are consistent across all frames and to prevent flickering during playback. Due to these additional optimization functions, ImageReady may require more time to optimize an animated GIF than to optimize a standard GIF.

To optimize an animated image:

1 Choose Optimize Animation from the Animation palette menu.

2 Set the following options:

• Bounding Box to crop each frame to the area that has changed from the preceding frame. Animation files created using this option are smaller but are incompatible with GIF editors that do not support the option. (This option is selected by default and is recommended.)

• Redundant Pixel Removal to make transparent all pixels in a frame that are unchanged from the preceding frame. This option is selected by default and is recommended. The Transparency option in the Optimize palette must be selected for redundant pixel removal to work. (See "Making transparent and matted images" on page 339.)

Important: Set the frame disposal method to Automatic when using the Redundant Pixel Removal option. (See "Setting the frame disposal method" on page 308.)

3 Click OK.

4 Apply optimization settings, as described in "Optimizing images" on page 320.

When optimizing the colors in an animation, use the Adaptive, Perceptual, or Selective palette. This insures that the colors are consistent across frames. (See "Generating a color table" on page 330.)

Viewing animated images in Photoshop

When you open a file containing an animation in Photoshop, only the frame that was selected when you saved the file in ImageReady is displayed. You cannot edit the animation frames separately, play the animation, or save the animation as an animated GIF.

If you add a new layer to the file while in Photoshop, the layer is added to all frames of the animation. However, the new layer will only appear in the selected frame when you reopen the file in ImageReady. If you change the stacking order of layers while in Photoshop, the stacking order of layers will be changed when you reopen the file in ImageReady.

Saving animations

You can save an animation as a series of GIF files or as a QuickTime™ movie.

Saving animations as animated GIFs

Animations that you view in a Web browser are called *animated GIFs*. When you save an optimized document containing an animation, you can choose to generate an HTML file that contains code for displaying the animated GIF in a Web page. The resulting Web page can contain just the animated GIF or additional Web features, such as links and rollovers, depending on the source document.

To save an animation as an animated GIF:

1 Optimize the animation, as described in "Optimizing animations" on page 309.

2 Save the image, as described in "Saving optimized images" on page 347.

Saving animations as QuickTime movies

You can save an animation as a QuickTime movie. The resulting file is viewable in the QuickTime player and can be opened in other applications that support QuickTime movie format.

To save an animation as a QuickTime movie:

1 Choose File > Export Original.

2 Select QuickTime Movie from the format pop-up menu.

Note: On Windows, QuickTime Movie format is only available when QuickTime is installed on your computer.

3 Type a filename, and choose a location for the file.

4 Click Save.

5 If desired, adjust the compression settings, and click OK.

Opening and importing files as animations

You can use the animation features in ImageReady to edit animated GIFs, multilayered Photoshop files, and QuickTime movies.

Opening animated GIFs

You can open an existing animated GIF in ImageReady using the File > Open command. The file is opened as a stack of layers. Each layer corresponds to one frame. In each frame, the layer for that frame is visible, and the layers for the other frames are hidden.

Opening existing animated GIF files in ImageReady is useful primarily for applying optimization settings to the files. The one-layer-per-frame structure of imported animated GIF files may make it impractical to edit animation frames in other ways.

Opening Photoshop files as animations

You can easily create animated GIFs from existing one-layer-per-frame images in Adobe Photoshop file format or from a group of single-layer images.

You can make each layer in a multilayer Photoshop file a separate frame in the Animation palette. The layers are placed in the Animation palette in their stacking order, with the bottom layer becoming the first frame.

You can also import a folder of files and use each file as a frame in ImageReady. Files can be in any format that ImageReady supports. Each file becomes a frame in the Animation palette. The files are placed in the Animation palette in alphabetical order by image filename.

To open a multilayer Photoshop file as frames:

1 Choose File > Open, and select the Photoshop file to open.

2 Select Make Frames From Layers in the Animation palette menu.

Each layer in the image appears as a frame in the Animation palette. The bottom layer in the Photoshop image is frame 1 in the Animation palette.

To import a folder of files as frames:

1 Place the files to be used as frames into a folder. Make sure that the folder contains only those images that are to be used as frames. The resulting animation will display more successfully if all files are the same pixel dimensions.

To have frames appear in the correct order in the animation, name the files in alphabetical or numeric order, with the file to be used as frame 1 the first in order. (You can also change the order of the frames in the Animation palette after you import the files.)

2 Choose File > Import > Import Folder As Frames, and choose the folder to be imported.

The files appear in the Animation palette as frames and in the Layers palette as layers, with each layer assigned to a separate frame. The image that is first alphabetically or numerically by filename is frame 1 in the Animation palette and the bottom layer in the Layers palette.

Opening QuickTime movies as animations

You can open movies in MOV, AVI, and FLIC formats to view and edit in ImageReady.

To open QuickTime-compatible movies:

1 Choose File > Open, and select the movie to open.

2 Select the range of frames to import:

• From Beginning to End to open the full file.

• Selected Range Only to open selected frames. Drag the slider below the movie thumbnail to specify the starting point for the range, then Shift-drag to specify the ending point. (A black bar on the slider indicates the range you select.)

3 Select Limit to Every <number> Frame to specify which frames to include from the selected range. (You can use this option with either Range option.)

4 Click Open.

12

Chapter 12: Optimizing Images for the Web

Creating small graphics files is key to distributing images on the World Wide Web. With smaller files, Web servers can store and transmit images more efficiently, and viewers can download images more quickly. Likewise, when preparing images for CD-ROM or other multimedia viewing, it's important to make the image files as small as possible. This conserves file storage space and decreases the amount of RAM needed for image display.

About optimization

Optimization is the process of fine- tuning the display quality and file size of an image for use on the Web or other online media. Adobe Photoshop and Adobe ImageReady give you an effective range of controls for compressing the file size of an image while optimizing its online display quality. You can optimize images in the three major graphic file formats used on the Web: GIF (Graphics Interchange Format), JPEG (Joint Photographic Experts Group), and PNG-8 or PNG-24 (Portable Network Graphics, with 8-bit or 24-bit color).

There are two methods of optimizing images:

• For basic optimization, the Photoshop Save As command lets you save an image as a GIF, JPEG, or PNG file. Depending on the file format, you can specify image quality, background transparency or matting, color display, and downloading method. However, any Web features—such as slices, links, animations, and rollovers—that you've added to a file are not preserved.

For complete information on using the Save As command to save an image as a GIF, JPEG, or PNG file, see "Saving images" on page 357.

• For precise optimization, you can use the optimization features in Photoshop or ImageReady to preview optimized images in different file formats and with different file attributes. You can view multiple versions of an image simultaneously and modify optimization settings as you preview the image to select the best combination of settings for your needs. You can also specify background transparency and matting, select options to control dithering, and resize the image to specified pixel dimensions or a specified percentage of the original size.

When you save an optimized file using the Save for Web (Photoshop) or Save Optimized (ImageReady) command, you can choose to generate an HTML file for the image. This file contains all the necessary code to display your image—as well as links, rollovers, and animations—in a Web browser.

Viewing images during optimization

In Photoshop, you must choose File > Save for Web to view and work with optimized images. In ImageReady, you can view and work with optimized images at any time in the document window.

Choosing a display option

Display options in Photoshop and ImageReady enable you to switch easily between optimized and original (non-optimized) versions of an image and view up to four versions of an optimized image simultaneously.

To select a display option for viewing images:

Click a tab at the top of the image:

• Original to view the image with no optimization.

• Optimized to view the image with the current optimization settings applied.

• 2-Up to view two versions of the image side by side.

• 4-Up to view four versions of the image side by side.

Working in 2-Up and 4-Up view

When you choose 2-Up or 4-Up view, Photoshop or ImageReady determines a layout for the images based on the aspect ratio (width/height ratio) of the image. Images can appear in vertical layout, horizontal layout, or 2 x 2 layout (two rows and two columns). 2 x 2 layout is available for 4-Up view only.

You can select a version of the image in 2-Up or 4-Up view to apply new optimization settings. You can automatically *repopulate* 2-Up and 4-Up views—generate new optimized versions of the image based on the selected version. You can also revert an optimized version to the original version of the image.

In ImageReady, you can change the default optimizations in Optimization Preferences. (See "Setting optimization preferences (ImageReady)" on page 345.)

To select a view:

Click the view you want to select. A black frame indicates the selected version.

To repopulate optimized versions of an image in 2-Up or 4-Up view:

1 Select an optimized version of the image in the 2-Up or 4-Up view.

2 In the Optimize panel of the Save for Web dialog box (Photoshop) or the Optimize palette (ImageReady), select Repopulate Views from the menu.

Photoshop and ImageReady generate smaller optimized versions of the image based on the optimization settings of the selected version. The selected version and the original version, if present, are not altered during repopulation. For this reason, the Repopulate Views option works with 2-Up view only if the original version of the image is not present.

To restore an optimized version of an image to the original version:

1 Select an optimized version of the image in the 2-Up or 4-Up view.

2 In the Optimize panel/palette, choose Original from the Settings pop-up menu.

Navigating in a view

If the entire image is not visible in the view area, you can navigate to bring another area of the image into view. This is particularly useful when working in 2-Up or 4-Up view. In ImageReady, you can also use the Fit on Screen command to view the entire image in the available space.

To navigate in a view:

1 Do one of the following:

• Select the hand tool in the Save for Web dialog box (Photoshop) or the toolbox (ImageReady).

• Hold down the spacebar.

2 Drag in the view area to pan over the image.

To display the entire image in the view area (ImageReady):

Choose View > Fit on Screen.

Viewing optimization annotations

In 2-Up and 4-Up view, an annotation area appears by default below each optimized image, showing its optimization settings. In Photoshop, the annotation area always shows; in ImageReady, you can hide or show the annotation area.

To hide or show optimization annotations in 2-Up and 4-Up views (ImageReady):

Choose View > Hide Optimization Info or View > Show Optimization Info.

Choosing a file format for optimization

The file format you choose for an optimized image is determined by the color, tonal, and graphic characteristics of the original image. In general, continuous-tone images such as photographs should be compressed as JPEG files. Illustrations with flat color or sharp edges and crisp detail, such as type, should be compressed as GIF or PNG-8 files.

PNG-24 file format is suitable for continuous-tone images. However, PNG-24 files are often much larger than JPEG files of the same image. PNG-24 format is recommended only when working with a continuous-tone image that includes multilevel transparency. (Multilevel transparency is supported by the PNG-24 format but not the JPEG format. See "Making transparent and matted images" on page 339.)

A photograph suitable for compression as a JPEG or PNG-24 image, and artwork suitable for compression as a GIF or PNG-8 image

Choose a format that contains sufficient pixel depth to display the color information in the image. (See "About bit depth" on page 116.) PNG-8 and GIF files support 8-bit color. JPEG and PNG-24 files support 24-bit color. Depending on the format, you can specify image quality, background transparency or matting, color display, and downloading method.

The appearance of an image on the Web also depends on the computer platform, color display system, operating system, and browser used to display the image. Preview images in different browsers on different platforms to see how the images will appear on the Web.

About JPEG format

The JPEG format supports 24-bit color and preserves the broad range and subtle variations in brightness and hue found in photographs and other continuous-toned images. JPEG is supported by most browsers.

JPEG compresses file size by selectively discarding data. Because it discards data, JPEG compression is referred to as *lossy*. A higher quality setting results in less data being discarded, but the JPEG compression method can degrade sharp detail in an image, particularly in images containing type or vector art.

Note: *Artifacts, such as wave-like patterns or blocky areas of banding, are created each time you save an image in JPEG format. These artifacts accumulate each time you resave the image to the same JPEG file; therefore, you should always save JPEG files from the original image, not from a previously saved JPEG.*

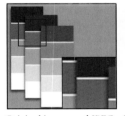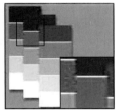

Original image, and JPEG with Low quality setting

You can create a *progressive* JPEG file, in which a low-resolution version of the image appears in a browser while the full image is downloading.

The JPEG format does not support transparency. When you save an image as a JPEG file, transparent pixels are filled with the Matte color, as specified in the Optimize palette. If you know the background color of the Web page where you will place the image, you can match the Matte color to the Web page background color to simulate the effect of background transparency. If your image contains transparency and you do not know the Web page background color, or if the background will be a pattern, you should use a format that supports transparency (GIF, PNG-8, or PNG-24).

About GIF format

The GIF format uses 8-bit color and efficiently compresses solid areas of color while preserving sharp detail, such as that in line art, logos, or illustrations with type. You also use the GIF format to create animated images. GIF is supported by most browsers.

The GIF format uses LZW compression, which is a *lossless* compression method. However, because GIF files are limited to 256 colors, optimizing an original 24-bit image as an 8-bit GIF can result in the loss of color information. In addition, Photoshop and ImageReady allow you to apply *lossy* compression to a GIF file. Using the Lossy option yields significantly smaller files by sacrificing some image quality.

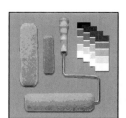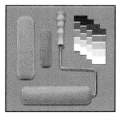
GIF image with 0% dither, and with 100% dither

You can reduce the number of colors in a GIF image and choose options to control the way colors dither in the application or in a browser. GIF supports background transparency and background matting, in which you blend the edges of the image with a Web page background color.

About PNG-8 format

The PNG-8 format uses 8-bit color. Like the GIF format, PNG-8 efficiently compresses solid areas of color while preserving sharp detail, such as that in line art, logos, or illustrations with type.

Because PNG-8 is not supported by all browsers, it may be advisable to avoid this format for situations in which your image must be accessible to the widest possible Web viewing audience. For more information on browser support for PNG, see your browser's documentation.

PNG-8 files use more advanced compression schemes than GIF, and can be 10–30% smaller than GIF files of the same image, depending on the image's color patterns. Although PNG-8 compression is considered lossless, optimizing an original 24-bit image as an 8-bit PNG file can result in the loss of color information.

Note: *With certain images, especially those with very few colors and very simple patterns, GIF compression can create a smaller file than PNG-8 compression. View optimized images in GIF and PNG-8 format to compare file size.*

As with the GIF format, you can reduce the number of colors in the image and choose options to control the way colors dither in the application or in the browser. The PNG-8 format supports background transparency and background matting, in which you blend the edges of the image with a Web page background color.

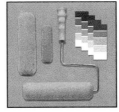

PNG-8 with 0% dither, and with 100% dither

About PNG-24 format

The PNG-24 format supports 24-bit color. Like the JPEG format, PNG-24 preserves the broad range and subtle variations in brightness and hue found in photographs. Like the GIF and PNG-8 formats, PNG-24 preserves sharp detail, such as that in line art, logos, or illustrations with type.

The PNG-24 format uses the same lossless compression method as the PNG-8 format. For that reason, PNG-24 files are usually larger than JPEG files of the same image. PNG-24 browser support is similar to that for PNG-8.

In addition to supporting background transparency and background matting, the PNG-24 format supports multilevel transparency. Multilevel transparency allows you to preserve up to 256 levels of transparency to blend the edges of an image smoothly with any background color. However, multilevel transparency is not supported by all browsers.

Optimizing images

To optimize an image for the Web, you select a file format and other options in the Optimize panel (Photoshop) or the Optimize palette (ImageReady). You can apply different optimization settings to different slices in an image. You can also use alpha channels to selectively optimize an image within a slice or across slice boundaries.

Viewing optimization options

Optimization options appear in the Optimize panel (Photoshop) and the Optimize palette (ImageReady). These options vary depending on the file format you select.

To view the Optimize panel/palette:

Do one of the following:

• (Photoshop) Choose File > Save for Web. The Optimize panel is displayed on the right side of the dialog box, beneath the Output Settings button.

• (ImageReady) Choose View > Show Optimize or click the Optimize palette tab. To show all the optimization options, click the Show Options control (✦) on the Optimize palette tab or choose Show Options from the Optimize palette menu.

Using named optimization settings

You can save optimization settings as a named set and apply the settings when working with other images. Settings that you save appear in the Settings pop-up menu in the Optimize panel/palette. Photoshop and ImageReady also include several predefined named settings.

When you adjust optimization settings so that they no longer match a named set, the Settings menu displays the term "Unnamed." When you select multiple slices with different optimization settings, the Settings menu option is blank.

To save optimization settings:

1 Choose Save Settings from the Optimize panel/palette menu.

2 Name the settings and choose a location where they will be saved. By default, named settings are saved in the Optimized Settings folder, inside the Presets folder in the Adobe Photoshop folder.

3 Click OK.

To apply named optimization settings to an image:

1 Select a view in which to apply the optimization setting.

2 Select the slice or slices you want to apply the optimization setting to. (See "Selecting slices" on page 276.)

3 Choose a named optimization set from the Settings pop-up menu.

To edit a named set of optimization settings:

1 Choose the named set from the Settings pop-up menu.

2 Adjust the settings as desired in the Optimize panel /palette.

(The Settings menu displays the term "Unnamed," since the settings no longer match a named set.)

3 Choose Save Settings from the Optimize panel/palette menu, and save the settings with the name of the original set.

4 Click OK, and then click Replace.

To delete named optimization settings:

1 In the Optimize panel/palette, select a named set of optimization settings from the Settings pop-up menu.

2 Choose Delete Settings from the Optimize panel/palette menu.

Setting optimization options for JPEG format

JPEG is the standard format for compressing continuous-tone images such as photographs. (See "About JPEG format" on page 318.)

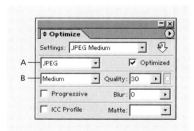

ImageReady Optimize palette JPEG options, with hidden options shown:
A. File Format menu B. Quality menu

In ImageReady, you can control which options show in the Optimize palette by clicking the Show Options control (✦) on the Optimize palette tab. To show all options, choose Show Options from the Optimize palette menu.

To optimize an image in JPEG format:

1 Select a view in which to apply the optimization setting.

2 Select the slice or slices to which you want to apply the optimization setting. (See "Selecting slices" on page 276.)

3 In the Optimize panel/palette, choose JPEG from the File Format menu.

4 Do one of the following to specify the image quality:

• Choose an option from the Quality menu.

• Drag the Quality pop-up slider.

• Enter a value in the Quality text box.

The higher the Quality setting, the more detail the compression algorithm preserves. However, using a high Quality setting results in a larger file size than using a low Quality setting. View the optimized image at several quality settings to determine the best balance of quality and file size.

5 To vary the Quality setting across the selected slices using an alpha channel, click the channel button (▨). In the Modify Quality Setting dialog box, choose an alpha channel from the pop-up menu, set a quality range, and click OK. (See "Using channels to modify JPEG quality" on page 327.)

6 To create an enhanced JPEG with a slightly smaller file size, select Optimized. The Optimized JPEG format is recommended for maximum file compression; however, some older browsers do not support this feature.

7 Select Progressive to create an image that displays progressively in a Web browser. The image will display as a series of overlays, enabling viewers to see a low-resolution version of the image before it downloads completely. The Progressive option requires use of the Optimized JPEG format.

Progressive JPEGs require more RAM for viewing, and are not supported by some browsers.

8 To apply a blur to the image to smooth rough edges, enter a value for Blur or drag the pop-up slider.

The Blur option applies an effect identical to that of the Gaussian Blur filter and allows the file to be compressed more, resulting in a smaller file size. A setting of 0.1 to 0.5 is recommended.

9 To preserve the ICC profile of the image with the file, select ICC Profile.

ICC profiles are used by some browsers for color correction. The ICC profile option preserves ICC profiles embedded by Photoshop. This option is only available after you've saved an image with an ICC profile—it is not available for unsaved images. (See "Setting up color management" on page 124).

10 If the original image contains transparency, select a Matte color that matches the background of your Web page. (See "Making transparent and matted images" on page 339.)

Setting optimization options for GIF and PNG-8 formats

GIF is the standard format for compressing images with flat color and crisp detail, such as line art, logos, or illustrations with type. (See "About GIF format" on page 319.) Like the GIF format, PNG-8 efficiently compresses solid areas of color while preserving sharp detail; however, not all Web browsers can display PNG-8 files. (See "About PNG-8 format" on page 319.)

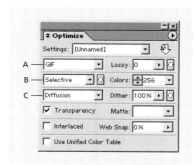

ImageReady Optimize palette GIF options, with hidden options shown:
A. *File Format menu* **B.** *Color Reduction Algorithm menu* **C.** *Dither Algorithm menu*

In ImageReady, you can control which options show in the Optimize palette by clicking the Show Options control (✦) on the Optimize palette tab. To show all options, choose Show Options from the Optimize palette menu.

To optimize an image in GIF or PNG-8 format:

1 Select a view in which to apply the optimization setting.

2 Select the slice or slices to which you want to apply the optimization setting. (See "Selecting slices" on page 276.)

3 In the Optimize panel/palette, choose GIF or PNG-8 from the File Format menu.

4 For GIF format only: Drag the Lossy slider or enter a value to allow for lossy compression. Lossy compression reduces file size by selectively discarding data—a higher Lossy setting results in more data being discarded.

You can often apply a Lossy value of 5–10, and sometimes up to 50, without degrading the image. File size can often be reduced 5%–40% using the Lossy option.

Note: *You cannot use the Lossy option with the Interlaced option, or with Noise or Pattern Dither algorithms.*

5 For GIF format only: To vary the Lossy setting across the selected slices using an alpha channel, click the channel button (⊡) next to the Lossy text box. In the Modify Lossiness Setting dialog box, choose an alpha channel from the pop-up menu, set a lossiness range, and click OK. (See "Using channels to modify GIF lossiness" on page 328.)

6 Select a color reduction algorithm. (See "Generating a color table" on page 330.)

7 To modify the color reduction using an alpha channel, click the channel button (▣) next to the Color Reduction Algorithm text box. In the Modify Color Reduction dialog box, choose an alpha channel from the pop-up menu, and click OK. (See "Using channels to modify color reduction" on page 329.)

8 To specify the maximum number of colors in the color palette, select a number from the Colors pop-up menu, enter a value in the text box, or use the arrows to change the number of colors. If the image contains fewer colors than the number specified, the color table will contain only the number of colors in the image.

You can choose the Auto option when working with a fixed color palette. This option determines the number of colors in the color table based on the frequency of colors in the image. Choose Auto if you want Photoshop or ImageReady to determine the optimal number of colors in the color table.

9 Select a Dither option and amount. For information on dither, see "Previewing and controlling dithering" on page 341.

10 To vary the Dither setting across the selected slices using an alpha channel, click the channel button (▣) next to the Dither text box. In the Modify Dither Setting dialog box, choose an alpha channel from the pop-up menu, set a dither range, and click OK. (See "Using channels to modify dithering" on page 329.)

11 If the image contains transparency, choose an option for preserving or filling transparent pixels:

• Select Transparency (the default setting) to preserve fully transparent pixels as transparent. (Partially transparent pixels are filled with the Matte color or converted to fully transparent or fully opaque pixels, depending on the Matte option you choose.)

• Deselect Transparency to fill fully and partially transparent pixels with the Matte color.

For more information on setting transparency and Matte color, see "Making transparent and matted images" on page 339.

12 Select Interlaced to create an image that displays as low-resolution versions in a browser while the full image file is downloading. Interlacing can make downloading time seem shorter and assures viewers that downloading is in progress.

13 To automatically shift colors to the closest Web palette equivalents (and prevent the colors from dithering in a browser), drag the Web Snap slider or enter a value to specify a tolerance level for colors to be shifted. A higher value shifts more colors. See "Previewing and controlling dithering" on page 341.

14 To apply a unified color table across all rollover states, select Use Unified Color Table.

Setting optimization options for PNG-24 format

PNG-24 format is suitable for compressing continuous-tone images. However, PNG-24 files are often much larger than JPEG files of the same image. PNG-24 format is recommended only when working with a continuous-tone image that includes multilevel transparency. (See "About PNG-24 format" on page 320.)

To optimize an image in PNG-24 format:

1 Select a view in which to apply the optimization setting.

2 Select the slice or slices to which you want to apply the optimization setting. (See "Selecting slices" on page 276.)

3 In the Optimize panel/palette, choose PNG-24 from the File Format menu in the Optimize panel/palette.

4 Select Interlaced to create an image that displays low-resolution versions in a browser while the full image file is downloading. Interlacing can make downloading time seem shorter, and assures viewers that downloading is in progress.

5 If the image contains transparency, choose an option for preserving or filling transparent pixels:

• Select Transparency (the default setting) to preserve transparent pixels as transparent.

• Deselect Transparency to fill transparent pixels with the Matte color.

Optimizing by file size

You can optimize an image or slice to an approximate file size. This feature enables you to quickly achieve a desired file size without having to test different optimization settings.

To optimize a file according to a specified file size:

1 Select Optimize to File Size from the Optimize panel/palette menu.

2 Select a Start With option:

• Current Settings to use current optimization settings.

• Auto Select GIF/JPEG to automatically generate a GIF or JPEG. (Photoshop or ImageReady selects GIF or JPEG format, depending on an analysis of colors in the image.)

3 Select a Slices option:

• Current Slice to optimize the selected slice to approximately the specified file size.

• All Slices Separately to optimize each slice in the image to approximately the specified file size.

• All Slices Together to optimize the sum of the size of all slices to approximately the specified file size. The total value is apportioned to individual slices based on each slice's relative size. For example, if you select three slices, one of which is twice as large as the other two, the large slice is optimized to 50% of the specified file size, and each of the other slices is optimized to 25% of the specified file size.

4 Specify a value for Desired File Size.

5 Click OK.

Resizing the image during optimization (Photoshop Save For Web dialog box)

When optimizing an image in the Photoshop Save For Web dialog box, you can resize the image to specified pixel dimensions or to a percentage of the original size.

Note: You can also resize an image by choosing Image > Image Size. (See "Changing the pixel dimensions of an image" on page 97.)

To change the pixel dimensions of an image during optimization:

1 Click the Image Size tab in the Save For Web dialog box.

2 To maintain the current proportions of pixel width to pixel height, select Constrain Proportions.

3 Enter values for Width, Height, or Percent. The New Size text field displays the new file size for the image.

4 Choose an interpolation method from the Quality pop-up menu:

• Jagged (Nearest Neighbor) for the faster, but less precise, method. This method is recommended for use with illustrations containing non-anti-aliased edges, to preserve hard edges and produce a smaller file.

• Smooth (Bicubic) for the slower, but more precise, method, resulting in smoother tonal gradations.

For more information on interpolation, see "About resampling" on page 96.

5 Click Apply.

Controlling optimization (ImageReady)

By default, Photoshop and ImageReady automatically regenerate the optimized image when you click the Optimized, 2-Up, or 4-Up tab at the top of the document (if you have modified the image since the last optimization), when you change optimization settings with the optimized image displayed, or when you edit the original image.

In ImageReady, you can turn off auto-regeneration so that the last version of the optimized image remains in the image window until you manually reoptimize the image or reactivate auto-regeneration. This feature is useful if you want to edit the image without pausing for reoptimization with each modification. You can also cancel optimization while it's in progress, and preserve the previous image.

When auto-regeneration is turned off, the Regenerate button (△) appears in the lower-right corner of each optimized image view. A regeneration alert symbol also appears in the Color Table palette if the optimized image is in GIF or PNG-8 format, indicating that the color table is out of date.

To turn Auto Regenerate on or off:

In the Optimize palette, choose Auto Regenerate from the palette menu. A check mark indicates that the option is turned on.

To manually optimize an image:

Choose a method for optimizing:

• Click the Regenerate button (△) in the lower-right corner of the optimized image (if it appears).

• Choose Regenerate from the Optimize palette menu.

Note: *Manually optimizing an image does not turn auto-regeneration on.*

The Regenerate option is available only when the optimized image is out of date (when Auto Regenerate is turned off and the image or its optimization settings are modified, or when optimization has been canceled).

To cancel optimization:

Click the Stop button next to the progress bar at the bottom of the image window.

Using weighted optimization

Weighted optimization lets you smoothly vary optimization settings across an image using an alpha channel. This technique produces higher-quality results in critical image areas without sacrificing file size. With weighted optimization, you can produce gradual variations in GIF dithering, lossy GIF settings, and JPEG compression. Weighted optimization also lets you favor colors in selected image areas when you generate a color table.

About alpha channels and weighted optimization

Alpha channels lets you store selections as grayscale images called *masks*. In a mask, selected areas appear white, deselected areas appear black, and partially selected areas appear as shades of gray. When you use an alpha channel to apply optimization settings, the white areas of the mask describe the highest level of image quality, while the black areas for the mask describe the lowest level of image quality. (The level of optimization in gray areas of the mask decreases by a linear scale.)

Weighted optimization is available for specific settings in the Optimize panel/palette, as indicated by the channel button (⊡). This button has a dark background (⊡) when a channel is selected and appears dimmed (⊡) when no channels are available. To access the weighted optimization dialog box, simply click the channel button.

To create a channel for use during optimization:

Do one of the following:

• (Photoshop) Save a selection as a mask, or create a new alpha channel and use the painting and editing tools to modify it. (See "Storing masks in alpha channels" on page 199.)

• (ImageReady) Use a selection tool to select an area of the image. Either save the selection using the Select > Save Selection command, or choose the Save Selection command from the Channel pop-up menu in the weighted optimization dialog box.

Using channels to modify JPEG quality

When you use an alpha channel to optimize the range of quality in a JPEG image, white areas of the mask yield the highest quality, and black areas of the mask yield the lowest quality. You can adjust the maximum and minimum level of quality in the Modify Quality Setting dialog box.

To use a channel to modify JPEG quality:

1 In the Optimize panel/palette, choose a JPEG setting from the Settings menu, or choose JPEG from the file format menu.

2 Click the channel button (⬚) to the right of the Quality text box.

3 In the Modify Quality Setting dialog box, choose the desired channel from the Channel menu. In ImageReady, you can choose Save Selection to create a new alpha channel based on the current selection.

4 To preview the results of the weighted optimization, select the Preview option.

5 Define the quality range:

• To set the highest level of quality, drag the right (white) tab on the slider, enter a value in the Maximum text box, or use the arrows to change the current value.

• To set the lowest level of quality, drag the left (black) tab on the slider, enter a value in the Minimum text box, or use the arrows to change the current value.

6 Click OK.

Using channels to modify GIF lossiness

When you use an alpha channel to optimize the amount of lossiness (or quality reduction) in a GIF image, white areas of the mask yield the highest quality, and black areas of the mask yield the lowest quality. You can adjust the maximum and minimum level of quality reduction in the Modify Lossiness Setting dialog box.

To use a channel to modify GIF lossiness:

1 In the Optimize panel/palette, choose a GIF setting from the Settings menu, or choose GIF from the file format menu.

2 Click the channel button (⬚) to the right of the Lossy text box.

3 In the Modify Lossiness Setting dialog box, choose the desired channel from the Channel menu. In ImageReady, you can choose Save Selection to create a new alpha channel based on the current selection.

4 To preview the results of the weighted optimization, select the Preview option.

5 Define the quality range:

• To set the highest level of quality, drag the left (white) tab on the slider, enter a value in the Minimum text box, or use the arrows to change the current value.

• To set the lowest level of quality, drag the right (black) tab on the slider, enter a value in the Maximum text box, or use the arrows to change the current value.

Note: *Lossiness is a reduction in quality; therefore, the highest level of image quality is defined by the Minimum value, and the lowest level of image quality is defined by the Maximum value. This is the opposite of the JPEG quality setting.*

6 Click OK.

Using channels to modify dithering

When you use an alpha channel to optimize the amount of dithering in a GIF or PNG-8 image, white areas of the mask yield the most dithering, and black areas of the mask yield the least dithering. You can adjust the maximum and minimum levels of dithering in the Modify Quality Setting dialog box.

To use a channel to modify dithering:

1 In the Optimize panel/palette, choose a GIF or PNG-8 setting from the Settings menu, or choose GIF or PNG-8 from the file format menu.

2 Click the channel button (⊠) to the right of the Dither text box.

3 In the Modify Quality Setting dialog box, choose the desired channel from the Channel menu. In ImageReady, you can choose Save Selection to create a new alpha channel based on the current selection.

4 To preview the results of the weighted optimization, select the Preview option.

5 Define the dithering range:

• To set the highest percentage of dithering, drag the right (white) tab on the slider, enter a value in the Maximum text box, or use the arrows to change the current percentage.

• To set the lowest percentage of dithering, drag the left (black) tab on the slider, enter a value in the Minimum text box, or use the arrows to change the current percentage.

6 Click OK.

Using channels to modify color reduction

When you use an alpha channel to optimize the colors in a GIF or PNG-8 image, the white areas of the mask determine what areas of the image are the most important when calculating the color table. White areas of the channel indicate to the color reduction algorithm which pixels are highly important, whereas black areas of the channel indicate which pixels are less important.

To use a channel to modify color reduction:

1 In the Optimize panel/palette, choose a GIF or PNG-8 setting from the Settings menu, or choose GIF or PNG-8 from the file format menu.

2 Choose a color reduction algorithm and specify the maximum number of colors.

3 Click the channel button (⊠) to the right of the Color Reduction Algorithm pop-up menu.

4 In the Modify Color Reduction dialog box, choose the desired channel from the Channel menu. In ImageReady, you can choose Save Selection to create a new alpha channel based on the current selection.

5 To preview the results of the weighted optimization, select the Preview option.

6 Click OK.

Optimizing colors in GIF and PNG-8 images

Decreasing the number of colors in an image is a key factor in optimizing GIF and PNG-8 images. A reduced range of colors will often preserve good image quality while dramatically reducing the file space required to store extra colors.

The color table gives you precise control over the colors in optimized GIF and PNG-8 images (as well as original images in indexed color mode). With a maximum of 256 colors, you can add and delete colors in the color table, shift selected colors to Web-safe colors, and lock selected colors to prevent them from being dropped from the palette.

Viewing a color table

The color table for a slice appears in the Color Table panel in the Save for Web dialog box (Photoshop) or the Color Table palette (ImageReady).

Note: In ImageReady, be careful not to confuse the Color Table panel/palette with the Color palette or Swatches palette. You use the Color Table panel/palette to optimize colors; you use the Color palette and Swatches palette to select colors.

To view the color table for an optimized slice:

1 (ImageReady) Choose Window > Show Color Table.

2 Select a slice that is optimized in GIF or PNG-8 format. (See "Selecting slices" on page 276.) The color table for the selected slice appears in the Color Table panel/palette.

If an image has multiple slices, the colors in the color table may vary between slices (you can link the slices first to prevent this from happening). If you select multiple slices that use different color tables, the color table is empty and its status bar displays the message "Mixed."

Generating a color table

You can change the palette—or set of colors—in the color table by selecting a color reduction option in the Optimize panel/palette. There are three categories of options:

• Dynamic options use a color reduction algorithm to build a palette based on the colors in the image and the number of colors specified in the optimization setting. The colors in the palette are regenerated every time you change or reoptimize the image. Perceptual, Selective, and Adaptive are dynamic options.

• Fixed options use a set palette of colors. In other words, the set of available colors is constant, but the actual colors in the palette will vary depending on the colors in the image. Web, Mac OS, Windows, Black & White, and Grayscale tables are fixed options.

• The Custom option uses a color palette that is created or modified by the user. If you open an existing GIF or PNG-8 file, it will have a custom color palette.

To select a color reduction algorithm:

Choose an option from the Color Reduction Algorithm pop-up menu (below the file format menu in the Optimize panel/palette):

Perceptual Creates a custom color table by giving priority to colors for which the human eye has greater sensitivity.

Selective Creates a color table similar to the Perceptual color table, but favoring broad areas of color and the preservation of Web colors. This color table usually produces images with the greatest color integrity. Selective is the default option.

Adaptive Creates a custom color table by sampling colors from the spectrum appearing most commonly in the image. For example, an image with only the colors green and blue produces a color table made primarily of greens and blues. Most images concentrate colors in particular areas of the spectrum.

Web Uses the standard 216-color color table common to the Windows and Mac OS 8-bit (256-color) palettes. This option ensures that no browser dither is applied to colors when the image is displayed using 8-bit color. (This palette is also called the Web-safe palette.) If your image has fewer colors than the total number specified in the color palette, unused colors are removed.

Using the Web palette can create larger files, and is recommended only when avoiding browser dither is a high priority. See "Previewing and controlling dithering" on page 341.

Custom Preserves the current color table as a fixed palette that does not update with changes to the image.

Mac OS Uses the Mac OS system's default 8-bit (256-color) color table, which is based on a uniform sampling of RGB colors. If your image has fewer colors than the total number specified in the color palette, unused colors are removed.

Windows Uses the Windows system's default 8-bit (256-color) color table, which is based on a uniform sampling of RGB colors. If your image has fewer colors than the total number specified in the color palette, unused colors are removed.

Other color tables appear in the menu if you have saved them previously. (See "Loading and saving color tables" on page 336.)

You can use an alpha channel to influence the generation of color tables. (See "Using channels to modify color reduction" on page 329.)

To regenerate a color table (ImageReady):

Choose Rebuild Color Table from the Color Table palette menu. Use this command to generate a new color table when the Auto Regenerate option is off. (See "Controlling optimization (ImageReady)" on page 326.)

Sorting the color table

You can sort colors in the color table by hue, luminance, or popularity, making it easier to see an image's color range and locate particular colors.

To sort a color table:

Choose a sorting order from the Color Table palette menu:

- Unsorted. Restores the original sorting order.

- Sort By Hue, or by the location of the color on the standard color wheel (expressed as a degree between 0 to 360). Neutral colors are assigned a hue of 0, and located with the reds.

- Sort By Luminance, or by the lightness or brightness of a color.

- Sort By Popularity, or by the colors' frequency of occurrence in the image.

Adding new colors to the color table

You can add colors that were left out in building the color table. Adding a color to a dynamic table replaces the color in the palette closest to the new color. Adding a color to a fixed or Custom table adds an additional color to the palette. (See "Generating a color table" on page 330.)

To add a new color:

1 Deselect all colors in the color table (see "Selecting colors" on page 333).

2 Choose a color:

- Click the color selection box in the Save for Web dialog box (Photoshop) or the toolbox (ImageReady), and choose a color from the color picker.

- Select the eyedropper tool (🖊) in the Save for Web dialog box (Photoshop) or the toolbox (ImageReady) and click in the image.

- (ImageReady) Select the eyedropper tool (🖊), click in the image, hold the mouse down, and drag anywhere on the desktop. You can use this option to select a color displayed in another application, such as a color in a Web page displayed in a browser.

- (ImageReady) Select a color from the Color palette or the Swatches palette.

3 Do one of the following:

- Click the New Color button (🔲) in the Color Table panel/palette.

- Select New Color from the Color Table palette menu.

- (ImageReady) Drag the color from the color selection box, Color palette, or Swatches palette to the Color Table palette.

💡 *To switch the color table to a Custom palette, hold down Ctrl (Windows) or Command (Mac OS) when you add the new color.*

The new color appears in the color table with a small white square in the lower right corner, indicating that the color is locked. (See "Locking colors in the color table" on page 335.)

Including transparency in a color table

The color table includes a transparency swatch (⬚)
if the original image contains transparent pixels.
You can use the matting option to fill transparent
pixels with a solid color, or you can preserve transparent pixels when optimizing the image in GIF or
PNG format. (See "Making transparent and
matted images" on page 339.)

*Note: When optimizing an animated image,
the color table may include a transparency swatch
even if the image does not contain transparent pixels.
This is a result of using the Redundant Pixel
Removal optimization option in the Animation
palette. (See "Optimizing animations" on
page 309.)*

Including black and white in a color table

You can add black and white to the color table
when the image does not include these colors.
Including black and white is useful when
preparing files for multimedia authoring applications, such as Adobe After Effects.

To add black or white to the color table for an image:

1 Choose black or white as the foreground color.

For more information, see "Choosing
foreground and background colors" in
online Help.

2 Add the color to the color table as described in
"Adding new colors to the color table" on
page 332.

Selecting colors

You select colors directly in the optimized image
or in the color table. In ImageReady, you can select
a color from another application, such as a Web
page displayed in a browser.

To select a color from the optimized image:

1 Select the eyedropper tool (✎) in the Save for
Web dialog box (Photoshop) or the toolbox
(ImageReady).

2 Click a color in the image. A white border (▣)
appears around that color in the color table.
Shift-click to select additional colors.

**To select a color from another application
(ImageReady):**

(ImageReady) Select the eyedropper tool, click in
the image, hold the mouse down, and drag
anywhere on the desktop. You can use this option
to select a color displayed in another application,
such as a color in a Web page displayed in a
browser.

To select a color directly in the color table:

Click the color in the Color Table panel/palette.

To select a contiguous group of colors, press Shift
and click another color. All colors in the rows
between the first and second selected colors are
selected.

To select a discontiguous group of colors, press
Ctrl (Windows) or Command (Mac OS) and click
each color that you want to select.

To select colors based on a selection in the image (ImageReady):

1 Make a selection in the image using the selection tools or the Select menu commands.

2 Choose Select All From Selection from the Color Table palette menu.

To select all colors:

Choose Select All Colors from the Color Table palette menu.

To select all Web-safe colors:

Choose Select All Web Safe Colors from the Color Table palette menu.

To select all non-Web-safe colors:

Choose Select All Non-Web Safe Colors from the Color Table palette menu.

To view selected colors in an image (ImageReady):

Select the optimized image. Then click and hold a selected color in the Color Table palette to temporarily invert the color in the optimized image, enabling you to see which areas of the image contain the color.

To view a contiguous group of colors, press Shift and click and hold another color. All colors in the rows between the first and second selected colors are inverted.

To view a discontiguous group of colors, press Ctrl (Windows) or Command (Mac OS) and click each color that you want to select, and hold the mouse button down on any color in the group.

To deselect all colors:

Choose Deselect All Colors from the Color Table palette menu.

Editing colors

You can change a selected color in the color table to any other RGB color value. When you regenerate the optimized image, the selected color changes to the new color wherever it appears in the image.

To edit a color:

1 Double-click the color in the color table to display the default color picker.

2 Select a color.

A small black diamond (◼) appears in the center of each edited color. The edited color replaces the original color in the image.

Note: Editing a color also locks it—a white square appears in the lower right corner of the color. (See "Locking colors in the color table" on page 335.)

Shifting to Web-safe colors

To protect colors from dithering in a browser, you can shift the colors to their closest equivalents in the Web palette. This ensures that the colors won't dither when displayed in browsers on either Windows or Macintosh operating systems capable of displaying only 256 colors. (See "Previewing and controlling dithering" on page 341.)

To shift colors to the closest Web palette equivalent:

1 Select one or more colors in the optimized image or color table. (See "Selecting colors" on page 333.)

2 Do one of the following:

• Click the Web Shift button (⊛) in the Color Table panel/palette.

• Choose Web Shift/Unshift Selected Colors from the Color Table palette menu.

A small white diamond (◻) appears in the center of a Web-shifted color and in all Web-safe colors.

To revert Web-shifted colors to their original colors:

Do one of the following:

• Select a Web-shifted color in the color table and click the Web Shift button (⊛) in the Color Table panel/palette.

• Choose Unshift All Colors from the Color Table palette menu.

To specify tolerance for shifting colors automatically to the closest Web palette equivalents:

In the Optimize panel/palette, enter a value for Web Snap or drag the pop-up slider. A higher value shifts more colors. (See "Previewing and controlling dithering" on page 341.)

(In ImageReady, click the Show Options control (⬥) on the Optimize palette tab or choose Show Options from the Optimize palette menu to view the Web Snap option.)

Locking colors in the color table

You can lock selected colors in the color table to prevent them from being dropped when the number of colors is reduced and to prevent them from dithering in the application.

Note: *Locking colors does not prevent them from dithering in a browser. (See "Previewing and controlling dithering" on page 341.)*

To lock a color:

1 Select one or more colors in the color table. (See "Selecting colors" on page 333.)

2 Lock the color:

• Click the Lock button (🔒).

• Choose Lock/Unlock Selected Colors from the Color Table palette menu.

A white square (◻) appears in the lower right corner of each locked color.

Note: *If the selected colors include both locked and unlocked colors, all colors will be locked.*

To unlock a color:

1 Click the locked color to select it.

2 Unlock the color:

• Click the Lock button (🔒).

• Choose Lock/Unlock Selected Colors from the Color Table palette menu.

The white square disappears from the color swatch.

Deleting colors from the color table

You can delete selected colors from the color table to decrease the image file size. When you delete a color, areas of the optimized image that previously included that color are rerendered using the closest color remaining in the palette.

When you delete a color, the color table automatically changes to a Custom palette. This is because the Adaptive, Perceptual, and Selective palettes automatically add the deleted color back into the palette when you reoptimize the image—the Custom palette does not change when you reoptimize the image.

To delete selected colors:

1 Select one or more colors in the color table. (See "Selecting colors" on page 333.)

2 Delete the color:

• Click on the Trash button (🗑).

• Choose Delete Color from the Color Table palette menu.

Loading and saving color tables

You can save color tables from optimized images to use with other images and to load color tables created in other applications. Once you load a new color table into an image, the colors in the optimized image are changed to reflect the colors in the new color table.

To save a color table:

1 Select Save Color Table from the Color Table palette menu.

2 Name the color table and choose a location where it will be saved. By default, the color table file is given the extension .act (for Adobe Color Table).

If you want to access the color table when selecting Optimization options for a GIF or PNG image, save the color table in the Optimized Colors folder, inside the Presets folder in the Adobe Photoshop folder.

3 Click Save.

To load a color table:

1 Select Load Color Table from the Color Table palette menu.

2 Navigate to a file containing the color table you want to load—either an Adobe Color Table (.act) file, or a GIF file (to load the file's embedded color table).

3 Click Open.

Using master palettes (ImageReady)

You can create a master palette to use with a group of GIF or PNG-8 images that will be placed on a CD-ROM or other multimedia storage medium. When you include the master palette with a batch of images, all images display using the same colors.

To build a master palette, you add colors from a set of images and then build and save the master palette. To create a master palette for a batch of images, you add colors to the palette from other optimized images.

To create and apply a master palette:

1 With an image displayed, choose Image > Master Palette > Clear Master Palette (if available). Clearing the master palette ensures that colors from previous images are not included in the new palette.

2 Open an image whose colors you want to include in a master palette.

3 Choose Image > Master Palette > Add To Master Palette. All color information for the current image is added to the master palette.

4 Repeat steps 2 and 3 for all images whose colors you want to include in the master palette.

5 In the Optimize palette, select optimization settings for the master palette.

6 Choose Image > Master Palette > Build Master Palette to create a new color table from the color information of images used in steps 2, 3, and 4.

7 Choose Image > Master Palette > Save Master Palette.

8 Name the master palette and choose a location where it will be saved. By default, the master palette file is given the extension .act (for Adobe Color Table).

If you want to access the color table when selecting Optimization options for a GIF or PNG image, save the master palette in the Optimized Colors folder, inside the Presets folder in the Adobe Photoshop folder.

9 Click Save.

10 To apply the master palette to the image or images for which it was created, open the image or images and select the master palette:

• If the master palette appears in the Color Reduction Algorithm menu in the Optimize palette, select the master palette from this menu. (The Color Reduction Algorithm menu includes all palettes saved in the Optimized Colors folder, inside the Presets folder in the Adobe Photoshop folder.)

• Load the master palette, as described in "Loading and saving color tables" on page 336.

Working with hexadecimal values for color

You can view colors as hexadecimal values in the Info palette. In addition, you can copy colors as hexadecimal values to the Clipboard and paste them into an HTML document.

Viewing hexadecimal values for colors in the Info palette

In Photoshop, hexadecimal values for colors are displayed in the Info palette when you select Web Color Mode for one or both color readouts. In ImageReady, hexadecimal values for colors are displayed automatically in the right side of the Info palette, next to RGB color values. The Photoshop and ImageReady Info palettes also display other information, depending on the tool being used.

To view hexadecimal color values in the Info palette:

1 Choose Window > Show Info or click the Info palette tab to view the palette.

2 (Photoshop) Choose Palette Options from the palette menu. Under First Color Readout or Second Color Readout, choose Web Color from the Mode menu and click OK.

3 Position the pointer over the color you want to view hexadecimal values for.

Copying colors as hexadecimal values

You can copy colors as hexadecimal values from files in Photoshop or ImageReady, using the context menu with the eyedropper tool, or using menu commands. In Photoshop, you copy a color as a hexadecimal value while in the main work area (not the Save for Web dialog box).

To copy a color as a hexadecimal value using the eyedropper tool:

1 Select the eyedropper tool ( ) in the toolbox.

2 Select a color to copy:

• Right-click (Windows) or Control-click (Mac OS) a color in the image to select the color and view the eyedropper tool context menu.

• (ImageReady) Click the color in the image which you want to copy. The color you click becomes the foreground color. With the eyedropper tool still over the image, right-click (Windows) or Control-click (Mac OS) to view the eyedropper tool context menu.

3 Choose Copy Color as HTML (Photoshop) or Copy Foreground Color as HTML (ImageReady) from the eyedropper tool context menu.

The selected color is copied to the Clipboard as a hexadecimal value. To paste the color into an HTML file, choose Edit > Paste with the HTML file displayed in your HTML editing application. You can insert the code for any HTML element that allows a color property.

To copy a color as a hexadecimal value using menu commands:

1 Select a color to copy.

2 Copy the color:

• (Photoshop) Choose Copy Color As HTML from the Color palette menu.

• (ImageReady) Choose Edit > Copy Foreground Color as HTML.

The foreground color is copied to the Clipboard as a hexadecimal value. To paste the color into an HTML file, open a destination application and choose Copy > Paste with the HTML file displayed.

To copy a color as a hexadecimal value by dragging (ImageReady):

Drag the Foreground Color from the toolbox or a selected color from the Color Table palette or the Swatches palette into the HTML file in the destination application.

Note: *This feature is not supported by all text and HTML editing applications.*

Making transparent and matted images

Transparency makes it possible to place a nonrectangular graphic object against the background of a Web page. Background transparency, supported by GIF and PNG formats, preserves transparent pixels in the image. These pixels allow the Web page background to show through in a browser.

Background matting, supported by GIF, PNG, and JPEG formats, simulates transparency by filling or blending transparent pixels with a matte color that you choose to match the Web page background on which the image will be placed. Background matting works better if the Web page background will be a solid color, and if you know what that color will be.

The original image must contain transparent pixels in order for you to create background transparency or background matting in the optimized image. You can create transparency when you create a new layer.

Note: *You can use the magic eraser tool to easily create transparency in an image. In Photoshop, you can also use the background eraser tool.*

Preserving transparency in GIF and PNG images

GIF format and PNG-8 format support one level of transparency—pixels can be fully transparent or fully opaque, but not partially transparent. PNG-24 format, on the other hand, supports multilevel transparency, letting you preserve up to 256 levels of transparency in an image.

To preserve background transparency in a GIF or PNG image:

1 Open or create an image that contains transparency.

2 In the Optimize panel/palette, select GIF, PNG-8, or PNG-24 from the File Format menu.

3 Select Transparency.

4 For GIF and PNG-8 format, decide how you want to treat partially transparent pixels in the original image. You can blend partially transparent pixels with a matte color, or you can create hard-edged transparency. (See "Creating background matting in GIF and PNG images" on page 339 and "Creating hard-edged transparency in GIF and PNG-8 images" on page 340.)

Creating background matting in GIF and PNG images

When you know the Web page background color on which an image will be displayed, you can use the matting feature to fill or blend transparent pixels with a matte color that matches the Web page background. The Web page background must be a solid color, not a pattern.

The results of matting GIF and PNG-8 images depend on the Transparency option. If you select Transparency, only the partially transparent pixels, such as those at the edge of an anti-aliased image, are matted. When the image is placed on a Web page, the Web background shows through the transparent pixels, and the edges of the image blend with the background. This feature prevents the halo effect that results when an anti-aliased image is placed on a background color that differs from the image's original background. This feature also prevents the jagged edges that result with GIF hard-edged transparency.

If you deselect Transparency, fully transparent pixels are filled with the matte color, and partially transparent pixels are blended with the matte color.

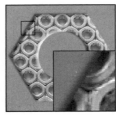

GIF with Transparency option selected, and with Transparency option deselected

To create a matted GIF or PNG image:

1 Open or create an image that contains transparency.

2 In the Optimize panel/palette, select GIF, PNG-8, or PNG-24 from the File Format menu.

3 For GIF and PNG-8 format, select of deselect the Transparency option as desired.

4 Select a color from the Matte pop-up menu:

• (Photoshop) Select Eyedropper (to use the color in the eyedropper sample box), White, Black, or Other (using the color picker).

• (ImageReady) Select Foreground Color, Background Color, or Other (using the color picker), or select a color from the Matte pop-up palette.

Creating hard-edged transparency in GIF and PNG-8 images

When working with GIF or PNG-8 files, you can create hard-edged transparency, in which all pixels that are more than 50% transparent in the original image are fully transparent in the optimized image, and all pixels that are more than 50% opaque in the original image are fully opaque in the optimized image. Use hard-edged transparency when you don't know the background color of a Web page or when the Web page background is a pattern. However, keep in mind that hard-edged transparency can cause jagged edges in the image.

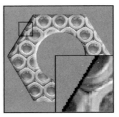

GIF with hard-edged transparency, and displayed in browser (inset at 300% magnification)

To create hard-edged transparency in a GIF or PNG-8:

1 Open or create an image that contains transparency.

2 In the Optimize panel/palette, select GIF or PNG-8 from the File Format menu.

3 Select Transparency.

4 Select None from the Matte pop-up menu to make all pixels with greater than 50% transparency fully transparent, and all pixels with 50% or less transparency fully opaque.

Creating background matting in JPEG images

When creating a JPEG from an original image that contains layer transparency, you must matte the image against a matte color. Since the JPEG format does not support transparency, blending with a matte color is the only way to create the appearance of background transparency in a JPEG. Fully transparent pixels are filled with the matte color, and partially transparent pixels are blended with the matte color. When the JPEG is placed on a Web page with a background that matches the matte color, the image appears to blend with the Web page background.

To create a matted JPEG image:

1 Open or create an image that contains transparency.

2 In the Optimize panel/palette, select JPEG from the file format menu.

3 Select a color from the Matte pop-up menu:

• (Photoshop) Select None, Eyedropper (to use the color in the eyedropper sample box), White, Black, or Other (using the color picker).

• (ImageReady) Select None, Foreground Color, Background Color, or Other (using the color picker), or select a color from the Matte pop-up palette.

Note: *When you select None, white is used as the matte color.*

Previewing and controlling dithering

Most images viewed on the Web are created using 24-bit color displays (millions of colors mode), but many Web browsers are used on computers using only 8-bit color displays (256-color mode), so that Web images often contain colors not available to many Web browsers. Computers use a technique called dithering to simulate colors not available in the color display system. Dithering creates adjacent pixels of different colors to give the appearance of a third color. For example, a red color and a yellow color may dither in a mosaic pattern to produce the illusion of an orange color that does not appear in the color palette.

When optimizing images, keep in mind that two kinds of dithering can occur:

• *Application dither* occurs in GIF and PNG-8 images when Photoshop or ImageReady attempts to simulate colors that appear in the original image but not in the color palette you specify for the optimized image. You can control the application dither that Photoshop or ImageReady applies to an optimized image.

You can choose a dithering pattern to be applied to the image. In addition, you can create customized dither patterns for GIF or PNG-8 images using the DitherBox filter. (See "Creating and applying custom dither patterns" on page 344.)

Note: Applying a dithering pattern is not recommended for JPEG or PNG-24 images.

• *Browser dither* occurs when a Web browser using an 8-bit color display (256-color mode) attempts to simulate colors that appear in an optimized image but not in the color palette used by the browser. Browser dither can occur with GIF, PNG, or JPEG images and can occur in addition to application dither in GIF or PNG-8 images. You can control the amount of browser dither by shifting selected colors in the image to Web-safe colors. Options in the color picker, the Color palette in Photoshop or ImageReady, and the Color Table panel (Photoshop) or the Color Table palette (ImageReady) let you specify Web-safe colors when choosing a color.

Previewing and controlling application dither

You can preview application dither in GIF and PNG-8 images. The Dither Algorithm pop-up menu lets you choose a dithering method for the image. Images with primarily solid colors may work well with Dither set to none. Images with continuous-tone color (especially color gradients) may require dithering to prevent color banding.

To control application dither:

1 Choose an option from the Dither Algorithm pop-up menu:

• No Dither applies no application dither to the image.

• Pattern applies a halftone-like square pattern to simulate any colors not in the color table.

• Diffusion applies a random pattern that is usually less noticeable than Pattern dither. The dither effects are diffused across adjacent pixels. Diffusion dither may cause detectable seams to appear across slice boundaries. Linking slices diffuses the dither pattern across all linked slices, and eliminates the seams.

• Noise applies a random pattern similar to the Diffusion dither method, but without diffusing the pattern across adjacent pixels. No seams appear with the Noise dither method.

2 If you chose Diffusion as the dithering algorithm, drag the Dither slider or enter a value to select a dithering percentage.

The Dither percentage controls the amount of dithering that is applied to the image. A higher dithering percentage creates the appearance of more colors and more detail in an image, but can also increase the file size. For optimal compression, use the lowest percentage of application dither that provides the color detail you require.

You can use an alpha channel to vary the Dither percentage across an image. This technique produces higher-quality results in critical image areas without sacrificing file size. (See "Using channels to modify dithering" on page 329.)

Previewing browser dither

You can preview browser dither directly in Photoshop or ImageReady, or in a browser that uses an 8-bit color display (256-color mode).

To preview browser dither:

With an optimized file displayed, preview dither in the respective application:

• (Photoshop) Choose Browser Dither from the document panel menu in the Save for Web dialog box. (To view the menu, click on the triangle near the upper right corner of the document panel.)

• (ImageReady) Choose View > Preview > Browser Dither. A check mark next to the command indicates that it is turned on. Choose View > Preview > Browser Dither again to turn the command off.

To preview browser dither in a browser:

1 Set your computer's color display to 8-bit color (256 colors). See your computer operating system's documentation for information on changing the color display.

2 Do one of the following:

• Launch your browser and open an optimized image directly in the browser.

• With an optimized image displayed, click the Preview in Browser button in the toolbox.

Minimizing browser dither

Using colors in the Web palette ensures that colors won't dither when displayed in browsers on either Windows or Macintosh operating systems capable of displaying at least 256 colors.

You have several options for choosing Web-safe colors:

• When creating an original image, you can use the color picker, Color palette, and Swatches palette to choose Web-safe colors.

 For more information, see "Using Web-safe colors" in online Help.

• In optimized GIF and PNG-8 images, you can shift existing colors to Web-safe colors using the color table. (See "Shifting to Web-safe colors" on page 334.)

Creating and applying custom dither patterns

You can use the DitherBox filter to create a custom dither pattern for a selected RGB color. You can then fill a selection or a layer in an image with the dither pattern. You can save custom dither patterns in groups called *collections*, and use the dither patterns with other images.

To create and apply a custom dither pattern:

1 With an image displayed in the document window (Photoshop) or in Original view (ImageReady), use the eyedropper tool (✎) to select a foreground color that you want to simulate with a customized dither pattern. (The foreground color becomes the basis for the custom dither pattern in DitherBox.)

Note: *In Photoshop, you create custom dither patterns while in the main Photoshop work area (not in the Save for Web dialog box). Make sure the image is in RGB color mode. See Photoshop online Help for information on color modes.*

2 Use the selection tools or the Layers palette to select an area or a layer in the image that you want to fill with the custom dither pattern.

3 Choose Filter > Other > DitherBox.

The RGB swatch in the DitherBox dialog box displays the current foreground color. To choose another RGB color on which to base the dither pattern, click the RGB swatch, select a new color in the color picker, and then press the arrow button (▱) to transfer it to the pattern box.

4 Choose one of the following from the color palette pop-up menu in the DitherBox dialog box:

• Web Safe Colors to create a dither pattern using colors from the Web palette.

• Load to load another color palette and create a dither pattern using those colors. Then navigate to the color palette and open it.

Note: *If you use non-Web palette colors in a custom dither pattern, the colors will dither in a browser using an 8-bit color display. Using non-Web colors is recommended only for non-Web display.*

By default, a new dither pattern you create is saved in the current dither pattern collection.

5 Select a pixel pattern for the custom dither pattern from the pattern list, between 2 and 8 pixels square.

6 Click the arrow button (▱) to display the dither pattern that most closely matches the selected RGB color in the Pattern preview box. If no dither patterns are currently saved in a collection in the DitherBox filter, the Pattern preview box displays the dither pattern that matches the RGB color.

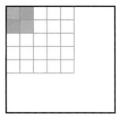

Dither pattern

7 To edit the custom dither pattern, do one of the following:

• To add a color to the dither pattern, click a color in the color palette. Then select the pencil tool (✐) in the DitherBox dialog box and click in the dither pattern grid to add the color.

• To delete a color from the dither pattern, select the eraser tool (✐) in the DitherBox dialog box and click the color in the dither pattern grid.

The Pattern preview box displays the changes you make to the dither pattern.

8 When you are satisfied with the dither pattern, click Fill to fill the selected area or layer in the current image.

The custom dither pattern is applied to the image, and the DitherBox dialog box closes.

To apply a previously saved custom dither pattern to an image:

1 With an image displayed in Photoshop or ImageReady, select an area or a layer in the image that you want to fill with the custom dither pattern.

2 Choose Filter > Other > DitherBox.

3 Select the collection containing the dither pattern you want to use from the Collection pop-up menu.

4 Select the dither pattern you want to use from the Collection contents list.

5 Click Fill.

The dither pattern is applied to the image, and the DitherBox dialog box closes.

To edit dither pattern collections:

Do one of the following in the DitherBox dialog box:

• To rename a collection, select the collection from the Collection pop-up menu. Then select Rename from the Collection pop-up menu. Enter a new name for the collection, and click OK.

• To create a new collection, select New from the Collection pop-up menu. Enter a name for the collection, and click OK.

• To delete a collection and all of its contents, select the collection from the Collection pop-up menu, and then select Delete from the Collection pop-up menu.

Setting optimization preferences (ImageReady)

You can set preferences in ImageReady to determine the default optimization settings and the default configuration of panels in 2-Up and 4-Up views.

To set optimization preferences:

1 Choose Edit > Preferences > Optimization.

2 Choose an option in the Default Optimization section:

• Previous Settings to automatically apply the last used optimization settings.

• Auto Selected GIF or JPEG to automatically optimize the image as a GIF or JPEG. ImageReady selects GIF or JPEG based on an analysis of the image.

• Named Setting and select an option from the Named Settings pop-up menu to apply that setting.

3 Under 2-Up Settings or 4-Up Settings, specify settings for the 1st, 2nd, 3rd, and 4th panes (3rd and 4th panes apply to 4-Up view only):

• Original to display the original image in the specified pane. (This option is available for the first pane only.)

• Current to display the image with current Optimize palette settings in the specified pane. (This option is available for all panes.)

• Auto to display a smaller optimized version of the image generated automatically by ImageReady, based on the current Optimize palette settings. (This option is available for the second, third, and fourth panes.)

• Select one of the twelve named settings to display the optimized image with those settings. (This option is available for the second, third, and fourth panes.)

4 Click OK.

Using a droplet to automate optimization settings (ImageReady)

You can save Optimize palette settings for use on individual images or batches of images by creating a *droplet*, a small application that applies the optimization settings to an image or batch of images that you drag over the droplet icon. You can drag a droplet to the desktop or save it to a location on disk. When you create the droplet you can choose where the images will be saved. When you drag an image over it, the droplet launches ImageReady if the program is not currently running.

Note: You can also drag a droplet onto the ImageReady Actions palette to create an action step, or you can drag a droplet onto a slice to apply the optimization settings to the slice.

To create a droplet for automating Optimize palette settings:

1 With an image displayed in the image window, choose a compression format and compression options in the Optimize palette.

2 Create a droplet:

• Drag the droplet icon (⛵) from the Optimize palette onto the desktop.

The droplet is named with a brief description of the compression settings, including file format and color palette or quality setting information. You can rename the droplet as you do other desktop icons.

• Click the droplet icon on the Optimize palette. Name the droplet, choose a location where the droplet will be saved, and click Save.

• Choose Create Droplet from the Optimize palette menu. Name the droplet, choose a location where the droplet will be saved, and click Save.

To use a droplet:

1 Drag a single image or a folder of images onto the droplet icon.

As the images are processed, a progress bar appears.

2 Do any of the following to control the processing:

• To temporarily pause the processing, click Pause. You can then click Resume to continue the processing.

• To cancel the processing, click Stop.

• Let the process finish on its own.

Saving optimized images

There are several ways to save an optimized image for use on the Web:

HTML and Images You can generate all files required to use your image as a Web page. This includes an HTML file and separate image files for the slices in the source image. The HTML file includes code for any Web effects—such as hypertext links, image maps, rollovers, and animations—in the document. The image files use the format and options specified in the optimization setting.

Images only You can save your image with the format and options specified in the optimization setting. If the source image contains multiple slices, each slice is saved as a separate file.

HTML only You can save the HTML code, but not the image data, for your image. In ImageReady, you can also create an HTML file using the Copy HTML command. This command lets you copy the HTML code for an optimized image to the Clipboard, and paste the HTML code into an HTML file. If you subsequently make changes to the source image, you can use the Update HTML command to update the HTML file.

When saving an optimized image with slices, you can choose to save all slices, or only the selected slices.

To save an optimized image:

1 (Photoshop) Choose File > Save for Web.

2 Select a view and apply optimization settings as described in "Optimizing images" on page 320.

3 Do one of the following:

• (Photoshop) Click OK in the Save For Web dialog box.

• (ImageReady) Choose File > Save Optimized to save the file in its current state. If you previously saved the optimized file using the File > Save Optimized command, applying the command again saves the file with the filename and Save options specified in the first save operation. The Save dialog box does not appear.

• (ImageReady) Choose File > Save Optimized As to save an alternate version of the file with a different filename.

4 Type a filename, and choose a location for the resulting file or files.

5 Select a Save As Type option:

• HTML and Images to generate an HTML file and save each slice as a separate image file.

• Images Only to save each slice in the image as a separate file.

• HTML Only to generate an HTML file but not save any image files.

6 To set preferences for saving image files and HTML files, click Output Settings. (See "Setting output options" on page 348.)

7 (ImageReady) Select Include GoLive Code to reformat HTML and JavaScript code so that rollovers will be fully editable in Adobe GoLive. Code is reformatted in the style used by GoLive (and may create a larger HTML file).

You need not generate an HTML file to open a Web page in GoLive 5.0. Simply save the Web page as a Photoshop (PSD) file, and then import the file directly into GoLive. For more information, see the Adobe GoLive 5.0 User Guide.

8 Choose an option for slices from the pop-up menu:

• All Slices to save all slices in the image.

• Selected Slices to save only the selected slices. If you select this option in conjunction with the HTML and Images option, ImageReady or Photoshop generates the HTML code based on the outermost bounds of the selected slices, and generates auto-slices as needed to create a complete HTML table.

Note: You must select the desired slices before starting this procedure.

• A slice selection to save only the slices in the selection. You must save a slice selection in order for this option to appear in the menu. (See "Selecting slices" on page 276.)

9 Click Save.

To copy HTML code to the Clipboard (ImageReady):

Choose Edit > Copy HTML Code, and choose an option for copying code from the submenu:

• Copy All Slices to copy HTML code for all slices in the document.

• Copy Selected Slices to copy HTML code for selected slices only.

• Copy Preloads to copy the JavaScript portion of the HTML code for slices in the document.

ImageReady generates and formats HTML code based on settings in the Output Options dialog box. Be sure to specify HTML options, such as whether to use tables or cascading style sheets, before you copy and paste HTML code. (See "Setting HTML output options" on page 349.)

To paste the ImageReady HTML code into an HTML document, open the HTML document in the destination application and choose Edit > Paste.

To update HTML code for an image (ImageReady):

1 Choose File > Update HTML.

2 Select the HTML file into which you pasted HTML code for the image.

3 Select Save Images to save the image file when you update the HTML code for the image.

4 Click Save.

Setting output options

Output settings give you control over the files that are generated when you save an optimized image as a Web page; you can specify how HTML files are formatted and how image files are named. Output settings also include options for naming slices and creating background images.

Using the Output Settings dialog box

The Output Settings dialog box contains four sets of options: HTML, Background, Saving Files, and Slices. You can save output settings as a file and reload them to apply the same settings to a different file.

To display the Output Settings dialog box:

Do one of the following:

• (Photoshop) Click Output Settings in the Save for Web dialog box. Use this method if you want to load and save settings.

• (ImageReady) Choose the desired preferences set from the File > Output Settings submenu. Use this method if you want to load and save settings.

• When you save an optimized image, click Output Settings in the Save Optimized As dialog box. The Save and Load options are not available when you use this method to access the Output Settings dialog box.

To switch to a different set of output options:

Do one of the following:

• Select the set from the pop-up menu below the Settings menu.

• Click Next to display the next set in the menu list; click Prev to display the previous set.

To save output settings in a file:

1 In the Output Settings dialog box, set the options as desired, and click Save.

2 Type a filename and choose a location for the saved file. By default, output settings are saved in the Optimized Output Settings folder, inside the Presets folder in the Adobe Photoshop folder.

3 Click Save.

To load output settings:

1 Click Load in the Output Settings dialog box.

2 Select a *.iros file and click Open.

Setting HTML output options

You can set the following options in the HTML set:

Tags Case Select the capitalization to be used for tags: all uppercase, initial cap, or all lowercase. Setting tags and attributes to all uppercase helps the code stand out in the file.

Attributes Case Select the capitalization to be used for tag attributes: all uppercase, initial cap, second initial cap, or all lowercase.

Indent Select a method for indenting lines of code: using the authoring application's tab settings, using a specified number of spaces, or using no indentation.

Line Endings Select a platform for line ending compatibility.

Always Quote Attributes To place quotation marks around all tag attributes. Placing quotation marks around attributes is required for compatibility with certain early browsers and for strict HTML compliance. However, always quoting attributes is not recommended. Quotation marks are used when necessary to comply with most browsers, even if this option is deselected.

Include Comments To add explanatory comments to the HTML code.

Include GoLive Code To reformat HTML and JavaScript code so that rollovers will be fully editable in Adobe GoLive. Code is reformatted in the style used by GoLive (and may create a larger HTML file).

Generate CSS To generate a Cascading Style Sheet.

Referenced Select an option for referencing slice position in the HTML file when using CSS:

• By ID to position each slice using styles that are referenced by a unique ID.

• Inline to include style elements in the declaration of the block element <DIV> tag.

• By Class to position each slice using classes that are referenced by a unique ID.

Generate Table To align slices using an HTML table.

Empty Cells Select an option for filling empty table data cells (slices set to No Image). Select GIF, IMG W&H to use a one-pixel GIF with width and height values specified on the IMG tag. Select GIF, TD W&H to use a one-pixel GIF with width and

height values specified on the TD tag. Select NoWrap, TD W&H to place a nonstandard NoWrap attribute on the table data and also place width and height values specified on the TD tags.

TD W&H Select an option for including width and height attributes for table data: Always, Never, or Auto (the recommended setting).

Spacer Cells Select an option for adding one row and one column of empty spacer cells around the generated table: Always, Never, or Auto (the recommended setting). Adding spacer cells is necessary with table layouts in which slice boundaries do not align, to prevent the table from breaking apart in some browsers.

Image Map Type (ImageReady only) Select an option for generating image map code:

• Client-Side to include all required code for the image map in the image's HTML file.

• NCSA Server-Side to create a separate .map file in addition to the HTML file, using NCSA specifications.

• CERN Server-Side to create a separate .map file in addition to the HTML file, using CERN specifications.

• Client & NCSA to create both a client-side and server-side compatible image map, using NCSA specifications.

• Client & CERN to create both a client-side and server-side compatible image map, using CERN specifications.

Note: Contact your Internet service provider to find out whether to use NCSA or CERN specification for server-side image maps.

Image Map Placement (ImageReady only) Select a placement option for the image map declaration (the <MAP> tag) in the HTML file:

• Top to place the image map declaration at the top of the HTML body section.

• Body to place the image map declaration above the <IMG SRC> tag for the associated slice.

• Bottom to place the image map declaration at the bottom of the HTML body section.

Setting file saving options

You can set the following options in the Saving Files set:

File Naming Select elements from the pop-up menus or enter text into the fields to be combined into the default names for all files. Elements include document name, slice name, rollover state, trigger slice, file creation date, slice number, punctuation, and file extension. Some options are relevant only if the file contains slices or rollover states.

The fields let you change the order and formatting of the filename parts (for example, letting you indicate rollover state by an abbreviation instead of the full word).

File Name Compatibility Select one or multiple options to make the filename compatible with Windows (permits longer filenames), Macintosh, and UNIX operating systems.

Copy Background Image When Saving
To preserve a background image that has been specified in the Background preferences set. (See "Creating background images" on page 352.)

Put Images In Folder To specify a folder name where optimized images are saved (available only with documents containing multiple slices).

Include Copyright To include copyright information with the image. You add copyright information for an image in the Image Info dialog box. See "Adding title and copyright information to HTML files" on page 351.

Setting slice naming preferences

You can specify the default naming pattern for slices in the Slices set. Select elements from the pop-up menus or enter text into the fields to be combined into the default names for all slices. Elements include document name, the word "slice," numbers or letters designating slices or rollover states, slice creation date, punctuation, or "none."

Adding title and copyright information to HTML files

You can add title and copyright information to an HTML file by entering information in the File Info dialog box (Photoshop) or the Image Info dialog box (ImageReady). Title information displays in the Web browser's title bar; copyright information is not displayed in the browser, but can be used in a case of copyright infringement to verify copyright.

To enter information about an image:

1 Do one of the following:

• (Photoshop) Choose File > File Info.

• (ImageReady) Choose File > Image Info.

2 Enter a title that will appear in the Web browser's title bar:

• (Photoshop) Choose Caption from the Section pop-up menu, and enter the desired text in the Caption text box.

• (ImageReady) Enter the desired text in the Page Title text box.

3 Enter copyright information:

• (Photoshop) Choose Copyright & URL from the Section pop-up menu, and enter the desired text in the Copyright Notice text box.

• (ImageReady) Enter the desired text in the Copyright text box.

4 Click OK.

Creating background images

Many Web pages contain tiled background images created from a single graphic repeated as needed to fill the entire page. In ImageReady, you can create an HTML file that will display the current image as a tiled background in a Web browser. You can also create an HTML file that will display another image or a solid color as a background behind the current image. ImageReady includes the <body background> tag for the background image and the <body bgcolor> tag for the background color in the HTML file.

In addition, you can prepare an image to be used as a tiled background using the Tile Maker filter, which blends the edges of an image to create a seamless background. You can also use the Tile Maker filter to create a kaleidoscopic background, in which an image is flipped horizontally and vertically to create an abstract design.

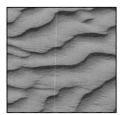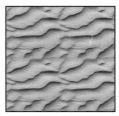

Original image, and image prepared using Blend Edges displayed as tiled background

Original image, and image prepared using Kaleidoscope Tile displayed as tiled background

To specify the current image as a background image:

1 Open the Output Settings dialog box and select the Background option set. (See "Using the Output Settings dialog box" on page 349.)

2 For View As, select Background.

3 To select a solid color background to be displayed while the background image is downloading, or to be displayed through any transparent areas in the background image, click the Color box and choose a color using the color picker. Alternatively, click the triangle next to the Color box and select None, Foreground Color, Background Color, or Other (using the color picker), or select a color from the pop-up palette.

4 Click OK.

To specify a background to be used with the current image:

1 Open the Output Settings dialog box and select the Background preference set. (See "Setting output options" on page 348.)

2 For View As, select Image.

3 Select a background:

• To select a background image, click Choose and select an image to be used as a background behind the current image.

• To select a solid color background, click the Color box and choose a color using the color picker. Alternatively, click the triangle next to the Color box and select None, Foreground Color, Background Color, or Other (using the color picker), or select a color from the pop-up palette.

If you select a background image and a background color, the background color displays while the background image is downloading. It also displays through any transparent areas in the background image.

To prepare an image for use as a tiled background image (ImageReady):

1 With an image displayed, use the marquee tool (⬚) to select an area in an image to be used as a tiled background.

2 Choose Filter > Other > Tile Maker.

3 Choose one of the following:

• Blend Edges to use the selection as a tiled background. Then enter a percent value in the Width text box to specify how much of the edge to blend, usually between 5% and 15%, with a maximum of 20%.

Select Resize Tile to Fill Image to resize the blended tile to fill the original selection. Deselect this option to create a tile that is smaller than the original selection, reduced by the amount specified in Width.

• Kaleidoscope Tile to flip and duplicate the selection horizontally and vertically and blend the edges, to create an abstract design that will be tiled on a Web page background.

4 Click OK.

5 Choose Image > Crop to crop the image to the selected area. This is not required if you use the entire image to create a tile.

13

Chapter 13: Saving and Exporting Images

Adobe Photoshop and Adobe ImageReady support a variety of file formats to suit a wide range of output needs. You can save or export your image to any of these formats. You can also use special Photoshop features to add information to files, set up multiple page layouts, and place images in other applications.

Saving images

The saving options that are available to you vary between Photoshop and ImageReady. Keep in mind that the primary focus of ImageReady is producing images for the Web. If ImageReady doesn't provide the file format or option you need, you can jump to Photoshop.

You can use the following commands to save images:

• Save to save changes you've made to the current file. In Photoshop, the file is saved in the current format; in ImageReady, the Save command always saves to PSD format.

• Save As to save an image with a different location or filename. In Photoshop, the Save As command lets you save an image in a different format and with different options. The available options vary depending on the format you choose. In ImageReady, the Save As command always saves to PSD format.

• (ImageReady) Export Original to flatten the layers in a copy of the original image and save the copy in a variety of file formats. Some information (such as slices and optimization settings) is not preserved when an original image is saved to file formats other than Photoshop.

• Save for Web (Photoshop) and Save Optimized (ImageReady) to save an optimized image for the Web. (See "Optimizing images" on page 320 and "Saving optimized images" on page 347.)

Saving files

You can save a file with its current filename, location, and format or with a different filename, location, format, and options. You can also save a copy of a file while leaving the current file open on your desktop.

To save changes to the current file:

Choose File > Save.

To save a file with a different name and location:

1 Choose File > Save As.

2 Type a filename, and choose a location for the file.

3 Click Save.

To save a file in a different file format:

1 Do one of the following:

• (Photoshop) Choose File > Save As.

• (ImageReady) Choose File > Export Original.

2 Choose a format from the format pop-up menu.

Note: In Photoshop, if you choose a format that does not support all features of the document, a warning appears at the bottom of the dialog box. If you see this warning, it is recommended that you save a copy of the file in Photoshop format or in another format that supports all of the image data.

3 Specify a filename and location.

4 (Photoshop) Select saving options. (See "Setting file saving options (Photoshop)" on page 358.)

5 Click Save.

With some image formats, a dialog box appears. (See "Saving files in Photoshop EPS or DCS format (Photoshop)" on page 359, "Saving files in GIF format (Photoshop)" on page 361, "Saving files in JPEG format (Photoshop)" on page 361, "Saving files in Photoshop PDF format (Photoshop)" on page 362, "Saving files in PNG format (Photoshop)" on page 363, and "Saving files in TIFF format" on page 364.)

To copy an image without saving it to your hard disk, use the Duplicate command. (See "Duplicating images" on page 73.) To store a temporary version of the image in memory, use the History palette to create a snapshot. (See "Making a snapshot of an image (Photoshop)" on page 72.)

Setting file saving options (Photoshop)

You can set a variety of file saving options in the Save As dialog box. The availability of options depends on the image you are saving and the selected file format. For example, if an image doesn't contain multiple layers, or if the selected file format doesn't support layers, the Layers option is dimmed.

As a Copy Saves a copy of the file while keeping the current file open on your desktop.

Alpha Channels Saves alpha channel information with the image. Disabling this option removes the alpha channels from the saved image.

Layers Preserves all layers in the image. If this option is disabled or unavailable, all visible layers are flattened or merged (depending on the selected format).

Annotations Saves annotations with the image.

Spot Colors Saves spot channel information with the image. Disabling an option removes spot colors from the saved image.

Use Proof Setup, ICC Profile (Windows), or Embed Color Profile (Mac OS) Creates a color-managed document. (See "Embedding profiles in saved documents" on page 134.)

Thumbnail (Windows) Saves thumbnail data for the file. In order to select or deselect this option, you must choose Ask When Saving for the Image Previews option in the Preferences dialog box. (See "Setting preferences for saving files (Photoshop)" on page 366.)

Image Previews options (Mac OS) Saves thumbnail data for the file. Thumbnails display in the Open dialog box. You can set these image preview options: Icon to use the preview as a file icon on the desktop, Full Size to save a 72-ppi version for use in applications that can only open low-resolution Photoshop images, Macintosh Thumbnail to display the preview in the Open dialog box, and Windows Thumbnail to save a preview that can display on Windows systems. Keep in mind that Windows thumbnails increase the size of files as delivered by Web servers.

Use Lower Case Extensions (Windows) Makes the file extension lowercase.

File Extension options (Mac OS) Specifies the format for file extensions. Select Append to add the format's extension to a filename and Use Lower Case to make the extension lowercase.

Important: *To display image preview and file extension options when saving files in Mac OS, select Ask When Saving for the Image Previews option and the Append File Extension option in the Preferences dialog box. (See "Setting preferences for saving files (Photoshop)" on page 366.)*

Saving files in Photoshop EPS or DCS format (Photoshop)

You can use Encapsulated PostScript (EPS) format to share Photoshop files effectively with many graphic, illustration, and page-layout programs. Desktop Color Separations (DCS) format, a version of the standard EPS format, lets you save color separations of CMYK or multichannel files. You use DCS 2.0 format to export images containing spot channels.

To print EPS and DCS files, you must use a PostScript printer.

To save a file in Photoshop EPS or DCS format:

1 Choose File > Save As, and choose Photoshop EPS, Photoshop DCS 1.0, or Photoshop DCS 2.0 from the format list.

2 Specify a filename and location, select saving options (as described in "Setting file saving options (Photoshop)" on page 358), and click Save.

3 For Preview, choose a low-resolution preview type. To share an EPS file between Windows and Mac OS systems, use a TIFF preview. An 8-bit preview option results in better display quality but larger file size than does a 1-bit preview option. You must save a preview of an EPS image to view the image in the destination application.

Note: *To use the JPEG preview option in Mac OS, you must have QuickTime installed.*

4 If you are saving to DCS format, follow these guidelines when choosing a DCS option:

• DCS 1.0 format creates five files: one for each color channel in the CMYK image and a fifth master file corresponding to the composite channel. You can choose to include a 72-ppi grayscale or color version of the composite image in the master file. By printing the low-resolution composite from the destination application, you can proof the image. If you plan to print directly to film or want to reduce file size, choose No Composite PostScript. To view the composite file, you must keep all five files in the same folder.

• DCS 2.0 format retains spot channels in the image. You can choose between saving color channel information as multiple files (as for DCS 1.0) or as a single file. The single-file option saves disk space. You can also include a 72-ppi grayscale or color composite with the image.

5 Specify an encoding method when printing to a PostScript output device:

• ASCII to use the most generic encoding method. Use ASCII encoding if you're printing from a Windows system, or if you experience printing errors or other difficulties.

• Binary to use a faster encoding method that produces a smaller output file and leaves the original data intact. Use Binary encoding if you're printing from a Mac OS system. However, some page-layout applications and some commercial print spooling and network printing software may not support binary Photoshop EPS files.

• JPEG to use the fastest encoding method. JPEG encoding compresses the file by discarding some image data, thus reducing the quality of your printed output; for the best printed results, choose maximum quality compression. Files with JPEG encoding can be printed only on Level 2 (or later) PostScript printers and may not separate into individual plates.

6 Select Include Halftone Screen and Include Transfer Function to save the image's halftone information (including the frequencies and angles of the screens) and transfer function information.

The PostScript language interpreter in some applications can use these screen settings when color separations are generated. You can also choose the Override Printer's Default Functions option in the Transfer Functions dialog box.

For more information, see "Compensating for dot gain in film using transfer functions" in online Help.

7 To display white areas in the image as transparent, select Transparent Whites. This option is available only for images in Bitmap mode.

8 If you are saving to EPS format, select PostScript Color Management to instruct the printer to convert the file data to the printer's color space. Select this option only if you have not already converted the file to the printer's color space. However, do not select PostScript Color Management if you're planning to place the image into another color-managed document. Doing so may disrupt color management in your page layout application.

Note: Only PostScript Level 3 printers support PostScript Color Management for CMYK images. To print a CMYK image using PostScript Color Management on a Level 2 printer, convert the image to Lab mode before saving in EPS format.

9 If the image contains vector graphics (such as shapes and type), select Include Vector Data to preserve vector data in the file. However, saved vector data in EPS and DCS files is only available to other applications; when you reopen the file in Photoshop, the vector data will be rasterized.

10 Select Image Interpolation if you want to anti-alias the printed appearance of a low-resolution image.

11 Click OK.

Saving files in GIF format (Photoshop)

You can use the Save As command to save RGB, indexed-color, grayscale, or Bitmap-mode image directly in GIF format. When saving an RGB image, Photoshop automatically displays the Indexed Color dialog box, letting you choose indexed-color conversion settings as the image is saved to GIF.

Note: You can also save an image as one or more GIF files using the Save for Web command (Photoshop) or the Save Optimized command (ImageReady). For more information on optimizing images, see "Choosing a file format for optimization" on page 317 and "Optimizing images" on page 320.

To save a file in GIF format:

1 Choose File > Save As, and choose CompuServe GIF from the format list.

2 Specify a filename and location, select saving options (as described in "Setting file saving options (Photoshop)" on page 358), and click Save.

3 For RGB images, the Indexed Color dialog box appears. Specify conversion options as described in "Conversion options for indexed-color images (Photoshop)" in online Help and click OK.

4 Select a row order for the GIF file and click OK:

• Normal to create an image that displays in a browser only when it is fully downloaded.

• Interlaced to create an image that displays as low-resolution versions in a browser while the full image file is downloading. Interlacing can make downloading time seem shorter and assures viewers that downloading is in progress. However, interlacing also increases file size.

Saving files in JPEG format (Photoshop)

You can use the Save As command to save CMYK, RGB, and grayscale images in JPEG format. Unlike GIF format, JPEG retains color information in an RGB image but compresses file size by selectively discarding data.

Note: You can also save an image as one or more JPEG files using the Save for Web command (Photoshop) or the Save Optimized command (ImageReady). For more information on optimizing images, see "Choosing a file format for optimization" on page 317 and "Optimizing images" on page 320.

To save a file in JPEG format:

1 Choose File > Save As, and choose JPEG from the format list.

2 Specify a filename and location, select saving options (as described in "Setting file saving options (Photoshop)" on page 358), and click Save.

3 If the image contains transparency, select a Matte color to simulate the appearance of background transparency. (See "Making transparent and matted images" on page 339.)

4 Do one of the following to specify the image quality:

• Choose an option from the Quality menu.

• Drag the Quality pop-up slider.

• Enter a value between 1 and 12 in the Quality text box.

5 Select a format option:

• Baseline ("Standard") to use a format recognizable to most Web browsers.

• Baseline Optimized to optimize the color quality of the image and produce a slightly smaller file size. This option is not supported by all Web browsers.

• Progressive to create an image that displays gradually as it is downloaded—in a series of scans (you specify how many) showing increasingly detailed versions of the entire image. Progressive JPEG images files are slightly larger in size, require more RAM for viewing, and are not supported by all applications and Web browsers.

6 To view the estimated download time of the image, select a modem speed from the Size pop-up menu. (The Size preview is only available when Preview is selected.)

Note: Some applications may not be able to read a CMYK file saved in JPEG format. In addition, if you find that a Java application cannot read your JPEG file (in any color mode), try saving the file without a thumbnail preview.

7 Click OK.

Saving files in Photoshop PDF format (Photoshop)

You can use the Save As command to save RGB, indexed-color, CMYK, grayscale, Bitmap-mode, Lab color, and duotone images in Photoshop PDF format.

To save a file in Photoshop PDF format:

1 Choose File > Save As and choose Photoshop PDF from the format list.

2 Specify a filename and location, select saving options (as described in "Setting file saving options (Photoshop)" on page 358), and click Save.

3 Select an encoding method. (See "About file compression" on page 365.)

Note: Bitmap-mode images are automatically encoded using CCITT compression—the PDF Options dialog box does not appear.

4 Select Save Transparency if you want to preserve transparency when the file is opened in another application. When reopening the file in Photoshop or ImageReady, transparency is always preserved, regardless of whether you select or deselect this option.

5 Select Image Interpolation if you want to anti-alias the printed appearance of a low-resolution image.

6 If the image contains vector graphics (such as shapes and type), select Include Vector Data to preserve vector data in the PDF file. Including vector data maintains resolution-independent edges for all type and paths and ensures smoother output. When Include Vector Data is selected, you can select the following options:

• Embed Fonts to embed all fonts that are used in the image. This ensures that the original font is used for display and printing on computers that do not have the font installed. Bitmap fonts, fonts that don't allow PDF embedding, substitute fonts, type that uses the faux bold style, and warped type cannot be embedded. Selecting the Embed Fonts option increases the size of the saved file.

• Use Outlines for Text to save the text as paths instead of as a PDF text object. Select this option if embedding the font results in a file that is too large, if you plan to open the file in an application that cannot read PDF files with embedded fonts, or if a font fails to display or print correctly. Text saved as outlines is not searchable or selectable in a PDF viewer (such as Adobe Acrobat). You can, however, edit the text when you reopen the PDF file in Photoshop. If you deselect Use Outlines for Text, text is saved as a PDF text object, which causes a PDF viewer to draw the text with the font information available in the file. If the font is not embedded in the file (using the Embed Fonts option), the PDF viewer may substitute a font or use a faux font.

7 Click OK.

Saving files in PNG format (Photoshop)

You can use the Save As command to save RGB, indexed-color, grayscale, and Bitmap-mode images in PNG format.

Note: *You can also save an image as one or more PNG files using the Save for Web command (Photoshop) or the Save Optimized command (ImageReady). For more information on optimizing images, see "Choosing a file format for optimization" on page 317 and "Optimizing images" on page 320.*

To save a file in PNG format:

1 Choose File > Save As and choose PNG from the format list.

2 Specify a filename and location, select saving options (as described in "Setting file saving options (Photoshop)" on page 358), and click Save.

3 Select an Interlace option:

• None to create an image that displays in a Web browser only after downloading is complete.

• Adam7 to create an image that displays low-resolution versions in a browser while the full image file is downloading. Interlacing can make downloading time seem shorter and assures viewers that downloading is in progress. However, interlacing also increases file size.

4 Select a Filter option:

• None to compress the image without a filter. This option is recommended for indexed-color and Bitmap-mode images.

• Sub to optimize the compression of images with even horizontal patterns or blends.

• Up to optimize the compression of images with even vertical patterns.

• Average to optimize the compression of low-level noise by averaging the color values of adjacent pixels.

• Paeth to optimize the compression of low-level noise by reassigning adjacent color values.

• Adaptive to apply the filtering algorithm—Sub, Up, Average, or Paeth—best-suited for the image. Select Adaptive if you are unsure of which filter to use.

5 Click OK.

Saving files in TIFF format

TIFF is a flexible bitmap image format supported by virtually all paint, image-editing, and page-layout applications.

To save a file in TIFF format (Photoshop):

1 Choose File > Save As, and choose TIFF from the format list.

2 Specify a filename and location, select saving options (as described in "Setting file saving options (Photoshop)" on page 358), and click Save.

3 Select a compression method. (See "About file compression" on page 365.) Keep in mind that some applications cannot open TIFF files that are saved with JPEG or ZIP compression. If you plan to open the TIFF file in an application other than Photoshop, LZW compression is recommended.

4 Select a byte order to determine file compatibility with IBM PC or Macintosh computers.

5 Select Save Image Pyramid to create a pyramid data structure that contains multiresolution information. The highest resolution is the image's resolution when you save it.

Note: Photoshop doesn't provide options for opening multiresolution files; however, Adobe InDesign and some image servers provide support for opening multiresolution formats.

6 Select Save Transparency if you want to preserve transparency when the file is opened in another application. When reopening the file in Photoshop or ImageReady, transparency is always preserved, regardless of whether you select this option.

7 Click OK.

To save a file in TIFF format (ImageReady):

1 Choose File > Export Original, and choose TIFF from the format list.

2 Specify a filename and location, and click Save.

3 Select a compression method, and click OK. (See "About file compression" on page 365.)

About file formats

You can use various file formats to get images into and out of Photoshop and ImageReady. Graphic file formats differ in the way they represent graphic information (as pixels or as vectors), in how they compress image data, and in which Photoshop and ImageReady features they support.

For more information on choosing file formats when opening or saving images, see "Opening and importing images" on page 101 and "Saving images" on page 357. For information on choosing a Web optimization format, see "Choosing a file format for optimization" on page 317.

Note: If a supported file format does not appear in the appropriate dialog box or submenu, you may need to install the format's plug-in module.

For more information about specific file formats and plug-in modules, see "About file formats" in online Help.

About file compression

Many image file formats use compression techniques to reduce the storage space required by bitmap image data. Compression techniques are distinguished by whether they remove detail and color from the image. *Lossless* techniques compress image data without removing detail; *lossy* techniques compress images by removing detail. The following are commonly used compression techniques:

• Run Length Encoding (RLE) is a lossless compression technique supported by Photoshop and some common Windows file formats.

• Lemple-Zif-Welch (LZW) is a lossless compression technique supported by TIFF, PDF, GIF, and PostScript language file formats. This technique is most useful in compressing images that contain large areas of single color, such as screenshots or simple paint images.

• Joint Photographic Experts Group (JPEG) is a lossy compression technique supported by JPEG, TIFF, PDF, and PostScript language file formats. JPEG compression provides the best results with continuous-tone images, such as photographs.

When you choose JPEG compression, you specify the image quality by choosing an option from the Quality menu, dragging the Quality pop-up slider, or entering a value between 1 and 12 in the Quality text box. For the best printed results, choose maximum-quality compression. Files with JPEG encoding can be printed only on Level 2 (or later) PostScript printers and may not separate into individual plates.

• CCITT encoding is a family of lossless compression techniques for black-and-white images that is supported by the PDF and PostScript language file formats. (CCITT is an abbreviation for the French spelling of International Telegraph and Telekeyed Consultive Committee.)

• ZIP encoding is a lossless compression technique supported by the PDF and TIFF file formats. Like LZW, ZIP compression is most effective for images that contain large areas of single color.

• (ImageReady) PackBits is a lossless compression technique that uses a run-length compression scheme. PackBits is supported by the TIFF file format in ImageReady only.

Adding file information (Photoshop)

Adobe Photoshop supports the information standard developed by the Newspaper Association of America (NAA) and the International Press Telecommunications Council (IPTC) to identify transmitted text and images. This standard includes entries for captions, keywords, categories, credits, and origins. The captions and keyword entries can also be searched by some third-party image browsers.

In Windows, you can add file information to files saved in Photoshop, TIFF, JPEG, EPS, and PDF formats. In Mac OS, you can add file information to files in any format.

 For more information, see "Adding file information (Photoshop)" in online Help.

Adding digital copyright information

You can add copyright information to Photoshop images and notify users that an image is copyright-protected via a digital watermark that uses Digimarc PictureMarc technology. The watermark—a digital code added as noise to the image—is generally imperceptible to the human eye. The watermark is durable in both digital and printed forms, surviving typical image edits and file format conversions—and is still detectable when the image is printed and then scanned back into a computer.

Embedding a digital watermark in an image lets viewers obtain complete contact information about the creator of the image. This feature is particularly valuable to image creators who license their work to others. Copying an image with an embedded watermark also copies the watermark and any information associated with it.

For more information on embedding digital watermarks, see "Adding digital copyright information" in online Help.

Setting preferences for saving files (Photoshop)

In Photoshop, you can set preferences for saving image previews, using file extensions, and maximizing file compatibility.

To set file saving preferences:

Choose Edit > Preferences > Saving Files, and set the following options:

Image Previews Choose an option for saving image previews: Never Save to save files without previews, Always Save to save files with specified previews, or Ask When Saving to assign previews on a file-by-file basis.

In Mac OS, you can select one or more of the following preview types (to speed the saving of files and minimize file size, select only the previews you need):

• Icon to use the preview as a file icon on the desktop.

• Macintosh Thumbnail to display the preview in the Open dialog box.

ADOBE PHOTOSHOP 6.0 **367**
User Guide

• Windows Thumbnail to save a preview that can display on Windows systems.

• Full Size to save a 72-ppi version of the file for use in applications that can only open low-resolution Photoshop images. For non-EPS files, this is a PICT preview.

File Extension (Windows) Choose an option for the three-character file extensions that indicate a file's format: Use Upper Case to append file extensions using uppercase characters or Use Lower Case to append file extensions using lowercase characters.

Append File Extension (Mac OS) File extensions are necessary for files that you want to use on or transfer to a Windows system. Choose an option for appending extensions to filenames: Never to save files without file extensions, Always to append file extensions to filenames, or Ask When Saving to append file extensions on a file-by-file basis. Select Use Lower Case to append file extensions using lowercase characters.

In Mac OS, to append a file extension to the current file only, hold down Option as you choose a file format from the Save As or Save a Copy dialog box.

Maximize Backwards Compatibility Select this option to maximize file compatibility with previous versions of Photoshop and with other applications (including previous versions of

ImageReady). This includes saving merged data for applications that don't support Photoshop layers and saving a rasterized version of each layer for applications that don't support vector data.

Note: Selecting Maximize Backwards Compatibility results in larger file sizes and increases the length of time required to save files.

To display a preview file icon (Windows only):

1 Save the file in Photoshop format with a thumbnail preview.

2 Right-click the file on the desktop (or in any Windows or Photoshop dialog box that displays a file list), and choose Properties from the context menu that appears.

3 Click the Photoshop Image tab.

4 Select an option for generating thumbnails, and click OK.

Preview icons appear on the desktop and in file lists (when the view is set to Large Icons).

Creating multiple-image layouts (Photoshop)

You can export multiple images automatically as contact sheets and picture packages using Automate commands.

Creating contact sheets

By displaying a series of thumbnail previews on a single page, contact sheets let you easily preview and catalog groups of images. You can automatically create and place thumbnails on a page using the Contact Sheet II command.

Note: Make sure that the images are closed before applying this command.

To create a contact sheet:

1 Choose File > Automate > Contact Sheet II.

2 Click Choose to specify the folder containing the images you want to use. Select Include All Subdirectories to include images inside any subfolders of the chosen folder.

3 Under Document, specify the dimensions, resolution, and color mode for the contact sheet, using the menus to specify measurement units.

4 Under Thumbnails, specify layout options for the thumbnail previews:

• For Place, choose whether to arrange thumbnails horizontally (from left to right, then top to bottom) or vertically (from top to bottom, then left to right).

• Enter the number of columns and rows that you want per contact sheet. The maximum dimensions for each thumbnail are displayed to the right, along with a visual preview of the specified layout.

• Select Use Filename As Caption to label the thumbnails using their source image filenames. Use the menu to specify a caption font.

5 Click OK to create the contact sheet.

Creating picture packages

With the Picture Package command, you can place multiple copies of a source image on a single page, similar to the photo packages traditionally sold by portrait studios. You can choose from a variety of size and placement options to customize your package layout.

You can customize and create new layouts for picture packages. For more information, see "Customizing picture package layouts" in online Help.

To create a picture package from a single image:

1 Choose File > Automate > Picture Package.

2 Specify the source image you want to use:

• Click Choose to specify a saved image file as the source.

• Select Use Frontmost Document to use the image currently active in Photoshop as the source.

3 For Layout, choose a preset layout option. Layout dimensions are measured in inches, and a preview of the chosen layout appears in the dialog box.

4 Enter a resolution value for the package layout, using the menu to specify resolution units.

5 Choose a color mode appropriate to the package layout.

6 Click OK to create the package layout.

Placing Photoshop images in other applications (Photoshop)

Photoshop provides a number of features to help you use images in other applications. You can use image clipping paths to define transparent areas in images you place in page-layout applications. In addition, Mac OS users can embed Photoshop images in many word-processor files.

💡 *For assistance with image clipping paths, choose Help > Export Transparent Image. This interactive wizard helps you prepare images with transparency for export to a page-layout application.*

Using image clipping paths

When printing a Photoshop image or placing it in another application, you may want only part of the image to appear. For example, you may want to print or show a foreground object and exclude its rectangular background. An *image clipping path* lets you isolate the foreground object and make everything outside the object transparent when the image is printed or placed in another application. This lets you place an image into another file without obscuring the other file's background.

Image imported into Illustrator without image clipping path, and with image clipping path

To save a path as an image clipping path:

1 Draw and save a path or convert an existing selection into a path.

2 Choose Clipping Path from the Paths palette menu.

3 For Path, choose the path you want to save.

4 For good results with most images, leave the flatness value blank to print the image using the printer's default value. If you experience printing errors, enter a new flatness value.

Values can range from 0.2 to 100. In general, a flatness setting from 8 to 10 is recommended for high-resolution printing (1200 dpi to 2400 dpi), a setting from 1 to 3 for low-resolution printing (300 dpi to 600 dpi).

The PostScript interpreter creates curved segments by linking a series of straight line segments. The flatness setting for a clipping path determines how closely the straight line segments approximate the curve. The lower the flatness value, the greater is the number of straight lines used to draw the curve and the more accurate the curve.

5 Click OK.

If you plan to print the file using process colors, convert the file to CMYK mode. (See "Converting between color modes (Photoshop)" on page 117.)

6 Save the file:

• To print the file using a PostScript printer, save in Photoshop EPS, DCS, or PDF format.

• To print the file using a non-PostScript printer, save in TIFF format and export to Adobe InDesign or to Adobe PageMaker 5.0 or later.

Note: If you import an EPS or DCS file with a TIFF preview into Adobe Illustrator, the image clipping path transparency may not display properly. This affects the on-screen preview only; it does not affect the printing behavior of the image clipping path on a PostScript printer.

Printing image clipping paths

Sometimes an imagesetter has difficulty interpreting image clipping paths, or a printer finds the image clipping path too complex to print, resulting in a Limitcheck error or a general PostScript error. Sometimes you can print a complex path on a low-resolution printer without difficulty but run into problems when printing the same path on a high-resolution printer. This is because the lower-resolution printer simplifies the path, using fewer line segments to describe curves than does the high-resolution printer.

You can simplify an image clipping path in the following ways:

• By manually reducing the number of anchor points on the path. (See "Adding, deleting, and converting anchor points" on page 177.)

• By increasing the tolerance setting used to create the path. (See the following procedure.)

To simplify an image clipping path with the tolerance setting:

1 Select the path in the Paths palette, and click the Make Selection button (⊡) at the bottom of the palette to convert the path to a selection.

2 Click the Trash button (🗑) at the bottom of the palette to delete the original path.

3 Choose Make Work Path from the Paths palette menu, and increase the tolerance setting (4 to 6 pixels is a good starting value).

4 Name and save the work path. Then choose Clipping Path from the Paths palette menu.

Exporting paths to Adobe Illustrator

The Paths to Illustrator command lets you export Photoshop paths as Adobe Illustrator files. This makes it easier to work with combined Photoshop and Illustrator artwork or to use Photoshop features on Illustrator artwork. For example, you may want to export a pen tool path and stroke it to use as a trap with a Photoshop clipping path you are printing in Illustrator. You can also use this feature to align Illustrator text or objects with Photoshop paths.

To use the Paths to Illustrator command:

1 Draw and save a path or convert an existing selection into a path.

2 Choose File > Export > Paths to Illustrator.

3 Choose a location for the exported path, and enter a filename.

4 Click Save.

5 Open the path in Adobe Illustrator as a new file. You can now manipulate the path or use the path to align Illustrator objects.

Note that the crop marks in Adobe Illustrator reflect the dimensions of the Adobe Photoshop image. The position of the path within the Photoshop image is maintained, provided you don't change the crop marks or move the path.

Object linking and embedding (OLE) (Windows only)

Photoshop is an OLE 2.0 server, which means it supports embedding or linking an image in an OLE container application (usually a word-processor or page-layout program). For example, you can insert Photoshop files and selections into other OLE applications such as Adobe PageMaker and Microsoft Word using copy and paste or other methods.

For more information, see "Object linking and embedding (OLE) (Windows only)" in online Help.

14

Chapter 14: Printing (Photoshop)

Printing is the process of sending your image to an output device. You can print on paper or film (positive or negative), to a printing plate, or directly to a digital printing press.

About printing

Whether you are providing an image to an outside service bureau or just sending a quick proof to a desktop printer, knowing a few basics about printing will make the print job go more smoothly and help ensure that the finished image appears as intended.

Types of printing When you print a file, the Adobe Photoshop application sends your image to a printing device, either to be printed directly onto paper or to be converted to a positive or negative image on film. In the latter case, the film can be used to create a master plate for printing by a mechanical press.

Types of images The simplest types of images, such as line art, use only one color in one level of gray. A more complex image, such as a photograph, has color tones that vary within the image. This type of image is known as a *continuous-tone image.*

Halftoning To create the illusion of continuous tones when printed, images are broken down into a series of dots. This process is called *halftoning.* Varying the sizes of the dots in a halftone screen creates the optical illusion of variations of gray or continuous color in the image.

Color separation Artwork that will be commercially reproduced and that contains more than a single color must be printed on separate master plates, one for each color. This process is called *color separation.* In Photoshop, you can adjust how the various plates are generated and create traps.

Quality of detail The detail in a printed image results from a combination of resolution and screen frequency. The higher an output device's resolution, the finer (higher) a screen ruling you can use.

A valuable resource for all aspects of print publishing, from early planning through prepress, is the *Print Publishing Guide*, an Adobe Press book. For information on purchasing Adobe Press books, visit the Adobe Web site at www.adobe.com or contact your local book distributor.

Printing images

To print any type of image, you first select general printing options and then specify settings for a particular image type. You can preview how the image and selected options will appear on the printed page and adjust the position and scale of the image.

Photoshop provides three printing-related dialog boxes: Print Options, Page Setup, and Print. Some printing options may appear in multiple dialog boxes depending on your printer, print drivers, and operating system. For example, you may be able to access output options in both the Print Options and Page Setup dialog boxes.

Note: *You cannot print images directly from ImageReady. If you have an image open in ImageReady and need to print it, use the Jump To command to open the image in Photoshop. Keep in mind that ImageReady images open at screen resolution (72 ppi); this resolution may not be high enough to produce a high-quality print.*

To print an image with its current print options:

Do one of the following:

• Choose File > Print, and click Print or OK.

• Hold down Alt (Windows) or Option (Mac OS) and choose File > Print One.

Note: *By default, Adobe Photoshop prints a composite of all visible layers and channels. To print an individual layer or channel, make it the only visible layer or channel before choosing the Print command.*

To select print options:

1 Choose File > Page Setup, and select an installed printer from the pop-up list at the top of the dialog box. (You can also select an installed printer in the Print dialog box.)

2 Select a paper size and orientation in the Page Attributes section of the Page Setup dialog box.

3 Choose File > Print Options to do the following:

• Adjust the position and scale of the image in relation to the selected paper size and orientation. (See "Positioning and scaling images" on page 377.)

• Set output options. (See "Setting output options" on page 378.)

• Select halftone screen attributes. (See "Selecting halftone screen attributes" on page 379.)

• Set other printing options. (See "Printing part of an image" on page 382, "Choosing a print encoding method" on page 382, and "Printing vector graphics" on page 382.)

• Set color management options. (See "Using color management when printing" on page 382.)

4 Click OK to save the print options for the image, or click Print to print the image. Hold down Alt (Windows) or Option (Mac OS) and click Print One to print the image without displaying the Print dialog box.

To preview the current image position and options:

Position the pointer over the file information box (at the bottom of the application window in Windows or the document window in Mac OS) and hold down the mouse button.

Positioning and scaling images

You can adjust the position and scale of an image in the Print Options dialog box and preview how the image will be printed on the selected paper. The shaded border at the edge of the paper represents the margins of the selected paper; the printable area is white.

The base output size of an image is determined by the document size settings in the Image Size dialog box. (See "Changing the print dimensions and resolution of an image (Photoshop)" on page 97.) Scaling an image in the Print Options dialog box changes the size and resolution of the printed image only. For example, if you scale a 72 ppi image to 50% in the Print Options dialog box, the image will print at 144 ppi; however, the document size settings in the Image Size dialog box will not change.

Many printer drivers, such as AdobePS and LaserWriter, provide a scaling option in the Page Setup dialog box. This scaling affects the size of all page marks, such as crop marks and captions, whereas the scaling percentage in the Print Options dialog box affects only the size of the printed image (and not the size of page marks).

Important: *The Print Options dialog box may not reflect accurate values for Scale, Height, and Width if you set a scaling percentage in the Page Setup dialog box. To avoid inaccurate scaling, specify scaling in the Print Options dialog box rather than the Page Setup dialog box; do not enter a scaling percentage in both dialog boxes.*

To reposition an image on the paper in the Print Options dialog box:

Do one of the following:

• Click Center Image to center the image in the printable area.

• Enter values for Top and Left to position the image numerically.

• Drag the image in the preview area.

To scale the print size of an image in the Print Options dialog box:

Do one of the following:

• Click Scale to Fit Media to fit the image within the printable area of the selected paper.

• Enter values for Height and Width to rescale the image numerically.

• Select Show Bounding Box, and drag a bounding box handle in the preview area to achieve the desired scale.

Setting output options

You can select a variety of page marks and other output options in the Output section of the Print Options dialog box. Depending on your printer and print drivers, these options may also appear in the Page Setup dialog box. The advantage of using the Print Options dialog box is that you can preview the selected options prior to printing.

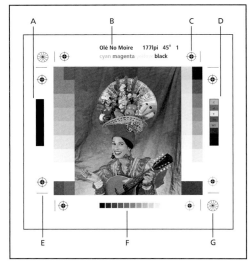

A. Black overprint color bar **B.** *Label* **C.** *Registration marks* **D.** *Progressive color bar* **E.** *Crop mark* **F.** *Gradient tint bar* **G.** *Star target*

To view output options in the Print Options dialog box:

Select Show More Options, and choose Output from the pop-up menu.

Note: Options not supported by the designated printer are dimmed.

Photoshop provides the following output options:

Background Lets you select a background color to be printed on the page outside the image area. For example, a black or colored background may be desirable for slides printed to a film recorder. To use this option, click Background, and then select a color from the Color Picker dialog box. This is a printing option only; it does not affect the image itself.

Border Lets you print a black border around an image. Type in a number and choose a unit value to specify the width of the border.

Bleed Lets you print crop marks inside rather than outside the image. Use this option when you want to trim the image within the graphic. Type a number and choose a unit value to specify the width of the bleed.

Screen Lets you set the screen frequency and dot shape for each screen used in the printing process. (See "Selecting halftone screen attributes" on page 379.)

Transfer Lets you adjust the transfer functions, traditionally used to compensate for dot gain or dot loss that may occur when an image is transferred to film. This option is recognized only when you print directly from Photoshop, or when you save the file in EPS format and print to a PostScript printer. Generally, it's best to adjust for dot gain using the settings in the CMYK Setup dialog box. Transfer functions are useful, however, when compensating for a poorly calibrated output device.

For more information, see "Compensating for dot gain in film using transfer functions" in online Help.

Interpolation Reduces the jagged appearance of a low-resolution image by automatically resampling up while printing. However, resampling may reduce the sharpness of the image quality. (See "About resampling" on page 96.) Some PostScript Level 2 (or higher) printers have interpolation capability. If your printer doesn't, this option has no effect.

Calibration Bars Prints an 11-step grayscale, a transition in density from 0 to 100% in 10% increments. With a CMYK color separation, a gradient tint bar is printed to the left of each CMY plate, and a progressive color bar to the right.

Note: Calibration bars, registration marks, crop marks, and labels will print only if the paper size is larger than the printed image dimensions.

Registration Marks Prints registration marks on the image (including bull's-eyes and star targets). These marks are used primarily for aligning color separations.

Crop Marks Prints crop marks where the page is to be trimmed. You can print crop marks at the corners, at the center of each edge, or both.

Labels Prints the filename above the image.

Caption Prints any caption text entered in the File Info dialog box. (See "Adding file information (Photoshop)" on page 366.) Caption text always prints as 9-point Helvetica plain type.

Negative Prints an inverted version of the image. Unlike the Invert command in the Image menu, the Negative option converts the output, not the on-screen image, to a negative. If you print separations directly to film, you probably want a negative, although in many countries film positives are common. Check with your print shop to determine which is required.

Emulsion Down Makes type readable when the emulsion is down—that is, when the photosensitive layer on a piece of film or photographic paper is facing away from you. Normally, images printed on paper are printed with emulsion up, with type readable when the photosensitive layer faces you. Images printed on film are often printed with emulsion down.

To determine the emulsion side, examine the film under a bright light after it has been developed. The dull side is the emulsion; the shiny side is the base. Check whether your print shop requires film with positive emulsion up, negative emulsion up, positive emulsion down, or negative emulsion down.

Selecting halftone screen attributes

Halftone screen attributes include the screen frequency and dot shape for each screen used in the printing process. For color separations, you must also specify an angle for each of the color screens. Setting the screens at different angles ensures that the dots placed by the four screens blend to look like continuous color and do not produce moiré patterns.

Halftone screens consist of dots that control how much ink is deposited at a specific location on-press. Varying their size and density creates the illusion of variations of gray or continuous color. For a process color image, four halftone screens are used: cyan, magenta, yellow, and black—one for each ink used in the printing process.

Halftone screen with black ink.

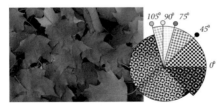

Halftone screens with process ink at different screen angles; correctly registered dots form rosettes.

In traditional print production, a halftone is produced by placing a halftone screen between a piece of film and the image and then exposing the film. In Photoshop, you specify the halftone screen attributes just before producing the film or paper output. For best results, your output device (a PostScript imagesetter, for example) should be set to the correct density limit, and your processor should be properly calibrated; otherwise, results can be unpredictable.

Before creating your halftone screens, check with your print shop for preferred frequency, angle, and dot settings. (Use the default angle settings unless your print shop specifies changes.)

Important: *Some output devices ignore the screen frequency and angle attributes you set in Photoshop. When printing custom halftone screens, it is advisable to save the image in EPS format, which embeds custom halftone screen settings in the file. In many (but not all) cases, the halftone screen settings in the EPS file will override the printer's default halftone screens.*

To define the screen attributes:

1 Choose File > Print Options.

2 Select Show More Options, choose Output from the pop-up menu, and click Screen.

3 In the Halftone Screens dialog box, choose whether to generate your own screen settings:

• Deselect Use Printer's Default Screens to choose your own screen settings.

• Select Use Printer's Default Screens to use the default halftone screen built into the printer. Photoshop then ignores the specifications in the Halftone Screens dialog box when it generates the halftone screens.

4 For a grayscale halftone, enter a screen frequency from 1 to 999.999, and choose a unit of measurement. Enter a screen angle from −180 to +180 degrees.

5 For a color separation, choose from the following options:

• To manually enter the screen frequency and angle, choose a color of the screen for Ink, and enter the frequency and angle; repeat for each color separation.

• To have Adobe Photoshop determine and enter the best frequencies and angles for each screen, click Auto. In the Auto Screens dialog box, enter the resolution of the output device and the screen frequency you intend to use, and click OK. Photoshop enters the values in the Halftone Screens dialog box. Changing these values may result in moiré patterns.

• If you are using a PostScript Level 2 (or higher) printer or an imagesetter equipped with an Emerald controller, make sure that the Use Accurate Screens option is selected in the Auto Screens dialog box (or in the Halftone Screens dialog box if you're entering the values manually). The Use Accurate Screen option lets the program access the correct angles and halftone screen frequencies for high-resolution output. If your output device is not a PostScript Level 2 (or higher) printer or is not equipped with an Emerald controller, this option has no effect.

6 For Shape, choose the dot shape you want. If you want all four screens to have the same dot shape, select Use Same Shape For All Inks.

Choosing Custom from the Shape menu displays the Custom Spot Function dialog box. You can define your own dot shapes by entering PostScript commands—useful for printing with nonstandard halftone algorithms. For information

about using PostScript language commands, see the *PostScript Language Reference* published by Addison-Wesley, or consult the imagesetter's manufacturer.

For optimal output on a PostScript printer, the image resolution should be 1.5 to 2 times the halftone screen frequency. If the resolution is more than 2.5 times the screen frequency, an alert message appears. (See "About image size and resolution" on page 92.) If you are printing line art or printing to a non-PostScript printer, see your printer documentation for the appropriate image resolutions to use.

7 Click OK.

To save halftone screen settings:

In the Halftone Screens dialog box, click Save. Choose a location for the saved settings, enter a filename, and click Save.

To save the new settings as the default, hold down Alt (Windows) or Option (Mac OS), and click the —> Default button.

To load halftone screen settings:

In the Halftone Screens dialog box, click Load. Locate and select the settings, and click Load.

To return to the original default settings, hold down Alt (Windows) or Option (Mac OS), and click <—Default.

Printing part of an image

You can use the Print Selected Area option to print a specific part of an image.

To print part of an image:

1 Use the rectangle marquee tool to select the part of an image you want to print.

2 Choose File > Print Options, select Print Selected Area, and click Print.

Choosing a print encoding method

By default, the printer driver transfers binary information to printers; however, you can choose to transfer image data using JPEG or ASCII encoding.

 For more information, see "Choosing a print encoding method" in online Help.

Printing vector graphics

If an image includes vector graphics, such as shapes and type, Photoshop can send the vector data to a PostScript printer. When you choose to include vector data, Photoshop sends the printer a separate image for each type layer and each vector shape layer. These additional images are printed on top of the base image, and clipped using their vector outline. Consequently, the edges of vector graphics print at the printer's full resolution, even though the content of each layer is limited to the resolution of your image file.

Keep in mind that including vector data likely increases the size of your print job, especially if the vector objects overlap and use transparency.

To print vector data:

Choose File > Print Options, and select Include Vector Data.

Using color management when printing

Different devices operate within different color spaces—for example, your monitor operates in a different color space than your printer, and different printers have different color spaces. The color management options in the Print Options dialog box let you change the color space of an image while printing, to get a more accurate color printout. (Depending on the designated printer and print drivers on your computer, these options may also appear in the Print dialog box.)

To use color management when printing, you first specify the source color space containing the colors you want to send to your printer. This space may be the document's current color profile (if you want the printout to match how the document appears on-screen), or it may be the current proof profile (if you want the printout to match your current soft proof). Second, you specify the color space of the printer to which you are sending the document. Specifying the printer space ensures that Photoshop has enough information to interpret and reproduce the source colors accurately on the printer.

For example, suppose your document currently uses an RGB profile, and you want to use your desktop printer to proof the colors as they will appear on an offset press. To do this, set up a proof profile for the press color space. (See "Soft-proofing colors" on page 131.) Then print the document using the proof profile as the source space and the desktop printer profile as the printer space.

To color-manage a document while printing:

1 Choose File > Print Options.

2 Select Show More Options and choose Color Management from the pop-up menu.

3 Select an option for Source Space:

• Select Document to reproduce document colors as interpreted by the profile currently assigned to the document.

• Select Proof to reproduce document colors as interpreted by the current proof profile. This option is useful for generating hard proofs of your soft-proof settings. (See "Soft-proofing colors" on page 131.)

4 Under Print Space, choose an option for Profile:

• Choose the profile that matches the color space of your printer to print using that printer space.

• Choose Same As Source to print using the source space profile. No additional conversions will be performed on the colors of the document when it is printed.

• Choose PostScript Color Management to send the document's color data, along with the source space profile, directly to a PostScript Level 2 or higher printer (Level 3 or higher for CMYK

images) and have colors managed at the level of the printer. The exact results of the color conversion can vary among printers. Choose this option only if you are printing remotely, if you are printing an RGB EPS file, or if you do not have a profile of the printer's color space. To proof a CMYK image on a PostScript Level 2 printer, choose the Lab Color option.

• Choose Printer Color Management to send the document's color data, along with the source space profile, directly to a non-PostScript printer driver and have colors managed by that driver. Choose this option only if you are printing to an RGB-based printer or if you do not have a profile of the printer's color space.

5 Under Print Space, for Intent, choose a rendering intent to use when converting colors to the destination profile space.

 For more information, see "Specifying a rendering intent" in online Help.

Printing with Adobe PressReady

If it is installed on your system, Adobe PressReady™ simplifies the color management of documents printed on inkjet printers by automatically converting the colors of documents to the correct printer color space.

 For more information, see "Printing with Adobe PressReady" in online Help.

Creating color traps

After you have converted an image to CMYK, you can adjust the color trap. Trap is the overlap needed to ensure that a slight misalignment or movement of the plates while printing does not affect the final appearance of the print job. If any distinctly different colors in your image touch, you may need to overprint them slightly to prevent tiny gaps from appearing when the image is printed. This technique is known as *trapping*. In most cases, your print shop will determine if trapping is needed and tell you what values to enter in the Trap dialog box.

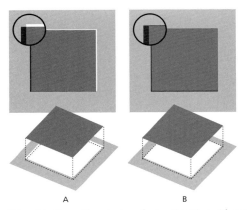

A   B

Misregistration with no trap, and misregistration with trap.

Keep in mind that trapping is intended to correct the misalignment of solid tints in CMYK images. In general, don't create traps for continuous-tone images such as photographs. Excessive trapping may generate a keyline effect (or even cross-hair lines) in the C, M, and Y plates. These problems may not be visible in the composite channel and might show up only when you output to film.

Trapping values determine how far overlapping colors are spread outward (not choked) to compensate for misregistration on the press. Adobe Photoshop uses standard rules for trapping:

- All colors spread under black.
- Lighter colors spread under darker colors.
- Yellow spreads under cyan, magenta, and black.
- Pure cyan and pure magenta spread under each other equally.

To create trap:

1 Save a version of the file in RGB mode, in case you want to reconvert the image later. Then choose Image > Mode > CMYK Color to convert the image to CMYK mode.

2 Choose Image > Trap.

3 For Width, enter the trapping value provided by your print shop. Then select a unit of measurement, and click OK. Consult your print shop to determine how much misregistration to expect.

Printing duotones

Photoshop lets you create monotones, duotones, tritones, and quadtones. Monotones are grayscale images printed with a single, nonblack ink. Duotones, tritones, and quadtones are grayscale images printed with two, three, and four inks. In these types of images, colored inks are used to reproduce tinted grays rather than different colors. This section uses the term *duotone* to refer to duotones, monotones, tritones, and quadtones.

About duotones

Duotones are used to increase the tonal range of a grayscale image. Although a grayscale reproduction can display up to 256 levels of gray, a printing press can reproduce only about 50 levels of gray per ink. This means that a grayscale image printed with only black ink can look significantly coarser than the same image printed with two, three, or four inks, each individual ink reproducing up to 50 levels of gray.

Sometimes duotones are printed using a black ink and a gray ink—the black for shadows and the gray for midtones and highlights. More frequently, duotones are printed using a colored ink for the highlight color. This technique produces an image with a slight tint to it and significantly increases the image's dynamic range. Duotones are ideal for two-color print jobs with a spot color (such as a PANTONE ink) used for accent.

Because duotones use different color inks to reproduce different gray levels, they are treated in Photoshop as single-channel, 8-bit, grayscale images. In Duotone mode, you do not have direct access to the individual image channels (as in RGB, CMYK, and Lab modes). Instead, you manipulate the channels through the curves in the Duotone Options dialog box.

To convert an image to duotone:

1 Convert the image to grayscale by choosing Image > Mode > Grayscale. Only 8-bit grayscale images can be converted to duotones.

2 Choose Image > Mode > Duotone.

3 Select Preview to view the effects of the duotone settings on the image.

4 Specify the type of image, the ink colors, the duotone curves, and the overprint colors for the duotone image.

5 Click OK.

To apply a duotone effect to only part of an image, convert the duotone image to Multichannel mode—this converts the duotone curves to spot channels. You can then erase part of the spot channel for areas that you want printed as standard grayscale. (See "Adding spot colors (Photoshop)" on page 191.)

Specifying the duotone type and ink colors

The duotone type—monotone, duotone, tritone, or quadtone—determines how many ink controls are active.

To produce fully saturated colors, print darker inks before lighter inks. The order of inks in the duotone dialog boxes affects how Photoshop applies screens, so make sure that inks are specified in descending order—darkest at the top, lightest at the bottom.

To specify the duotone type and its ink color:

1 In the Duotone Options dialog box, select Monotone, Duotone, Tritone, or Quadtone for Type.

2 Click the color box (the solid square) for an ink.

3 Use the color picker or the Custom Colors dialog box to select an ink. When you close the dialog box, the ink color appears in the color box and the color name in the text box.

 For more information, see "Using the Adobe Color Picker" in online Help.

4 If the ink is to be separated on a process color plate, name it "cyan," "magenta," "yellow," or "black."

Modifying the duotone curve

A separate duotone curve specifies how each ink is distributed across the shadow and highlight areas of the image. This curve maps each grayscale value on the original image to the actual ink percentage that will be used when the image is printed. A diagonal line indicates equal values and even distribution of ink.

To modify the duotone curve for a given ink:

1 To preview any adjustments, select the Preview option.

2 Click the curve box next to the ink color box.

The default duotone curve, a straight diagonal line across the grid, indicates that you are mapping the current grayscale value of every pixel to the same percentage value of the printing ink. At this setting, a 50% midtone pixel prints with a 50% dot of the ink, a 100% shadow with a 100% dot of the ink, and so on.

3 Adjust the duotone curve for each ink by dragging a point on the graph or by entering values for the different ink percentages.

The horizontal axis of the curve graph moves from highlights (at the left) to shadows (at the right). The density of the ink increases as you move up the vertical axis. You can specify up to 13 points on the curve. When you specify two values along the curve, Adobe Photoshop calculates intermediate values. As you adjust the curve, values are automatically entered in the percentage text boxes.

The value you type in a text box indicates the percentage of the ink color that will be used to print that percentage of the image. For example, if you enter 70 in the 100% text box, a 70% dot of that ink color will be used to print the 100% shadow areas of the image.

4 Click Save in the Duotone Curve dialog box to save curves created with this dialog box.

5 Click Load to load these curves or curves created in the Curves dialog box, including curves created using the Arbitrary Map option. (See "Saving and loading duotone settings" on page 387.)

You can use the Info palette to display ink percentages when you're working with duotone images. Set the readout mode to Actual Color to see the ink percentages that will be applied when the image is printed. These values reflect any changes you've entered in the Duotone Curve dialog box.

Specifying overprint colors

Overprint colors are two unscreened inks printed on top of each other. For example, when a cyan ink prints over a yellow ink, the resulting overprint is a green color. The order in which inks are printed, as well as variations in the inks and paper, can significantly affect the final results.

To help you predict how colors will look when printed, use a printed sample of the overprinted inks to adjust your screen display. Just remember that this adjustment affects only how the overprint colors appear on-screen, not when printed. Before adjusting these colors, make sure that you have calibrated your monitor following the instructions in "Creating an ICC monitor profile" on page 136.

To adjust the display of overprint colors:

1 Choose Image > Mode > Duotone.

2 Click Overprint Colors. The Overprint Colors dialog box displays the combinations that will result when the inks are printed.

3 Click the color swatch of the ink combination you want to adjust.

4 Select the color you want in the color picker, and click OK.

5 Repeat steps 3 and 4 until the overprint inks appear as you want them. Then click OK.

Saving and loading duotone settings

Use the Save button in the Duotone Options dialog box to save a set of duotone curves, ink settings, and overprint colors. Use the Load button to load a set of duotone curves, ink settings, and overprint colors. You can then apply these settings to other grayscale images.

The Adobe Photoshop application includes several sample sets of duotone, tritone, and quadtone curves. These sets include some of the more commonly used curves and colors and are useful as starting points for creating your own combinations.

Viewing individual printing plates

Because duotones are single-channel images, your adjustments to individual printing inks are displayed as part of the final composite image. In some cases, you may want to view the individual "printing plates" to see how the individual colors will separate when printed (as you can with CMYK images).

To view the individual colors of a duotone image:

1 After specifying your ink colors, choose Image > Mode > Multichannel.

The image is converted to a multichannel image, with each channel represented as a spot-color channel. The contents of each spot channel accurately reflect the duotone settings, but the on-screen composite preview may not be as accurate as the preview in Duotone mode.

Important: If you make any changes to the image in Multichannel mode, you will be unable to revert to the original duotone state (unless you can access the duotone state in the History palette). To adjust the distribution of ink and view its effect on the individual printing plates, make the adjustments in the Duotone Curves dialog box before converting to Multichannel mode.

2 Select the channel you want to examine in the Channels palette.

3 Choose Edit > Undo Multichannel to revert to Duotone mode.

Printing duotones

When creating duotones, keep in mind that both the order in which the inks are printed and the screen angles you use dramatically affect the final output.

Click the Auto button in the Halftone Screens dialog box to set the optimal screen angles and frequencies. (See "Selecting halftone screen attributes" on page 379.) Make sure that you select

Use Accurate Screens in the Auto Screens dialog box if you're printing to a PostScript Level 2 (or higher) printer or an imagesetter equipped with an Emerald controller.

Note: The recommended screen angles and frequencies for quadtones are based on the assumption that channel 1 is the darkest ink and channel 4 is the lightest ink.

You do not have to convert duotone images to CMYK to print separations—simply choose Separations from the Profile pop-up menu in the Color Management section of the Print Options dialog box. (See "Printing color separations" on page 389.) Converting to CMYK mode converts any custom colors to their CMYK equivalents.

Exporting duotone images to other applications

To prepare a duotone image for exporting to a page-layout application, save the image in EPS or PDF format (unless the image contains spot channels, in which case you should convert it to Multichannel mode and save it in DCS 2.0 format). Keep in mind that it's important to name custom colors so they'll be recognized by the other application. Otherwise the image won't print correctly—or might not print at all.

Printing color separations

When working with CMYK images or images with spot colors, you can print each color channel as a separate page.

Note: *If you are printing an image from another application and want to print spot channels to spot color plates, you must first save the file in DCS 2.0 format. DCS 2.0 preserves spot channels and is supported by applications such as Adobe PageMaker and QuarkXPress. (See "Saving files in Photoshop EPS or DCS format (Photoshop)" on page 359.)*

To print separations from Photoshop:

1 Choose File > Print Options.

2 Select Show More Options, and choose Color Management from the pop-up menu.

3 Choose Separations from the Profile pop-up menu.

Note: *Depending on the designated printer and print drivers on your computer, these options may also appear in the Print dialog box.*

4 Click Print. Separations are printed for each of the colors in the image.

To prepare an image with spot channels for printing from another application:

1 In the General Preferences dialog box, select Short Pantone Names. (This step is not necessary if you are exporting to Adobe Illustrator 7.0 or later, or Adobe PageMaker 6.5 or later.)

2 If the image is a duotone, convert to Multi-channel color mode.

3 Save the image in DCS 2.0 format. Be sure to deselect the Include Halftone Screen and the Include Transfer Function options. (See "Saving files in Photoshop EPS or DCS format (Photoshop)" on page 359.)

4 Open or import the image in the application you will be printing from, and set your screen angles. Make sure that you've communicated to the printer the spot color you want for each of the color plates.

15

Chapter 15: Automating Tasks

Automating tasks can save you time and ensure consistent results for many types of operations. Adobe Photoshop and Adobe ImageReady provide a variety of ways to automate tasks—using actions, droplets, the Batch command, and task-specific Automate commands.

About actions

An *action* is a series of commands that you play back on a single file or a batch of files. For example, you can create an action that applies an Image Size command to change an image to a specific size in pixels, followed by an Unsharp Mask filter that resharpens the detail, and a Save command that saves the file in the desired format.

Most commands and tool operations are recordable in actions. Actions can include stops that let you perform tasks that cannot be recorded (for example, using a painting tool). Actions can also include modal controls that let you enter

values in a dialog box while playing an action. Actions form the basis for droplets, small applications that automatically process all files that are dragged onto their icon.

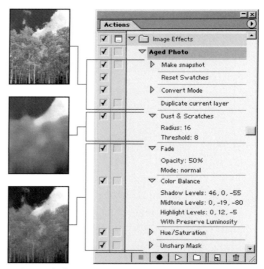

Action applied to an image

Both Photoshop and ImageReady ship with a number of predefined actions, although Photoshop has significantly more actions than ImageReady. You can use these actions as is, customize them to meet your needs, or create new actions.

Using the Actions palette

You use the Actions palette to record, play, edit, and delete individual actions. This palette also lets you save and load action files.

In Photoshop, actions are grouped into sets—you can create new sets to better organize your actions. (See "Organizing sets of actions (Photoshop)" on page 404.) In ImageReady, you cannot group actions into sets.

To display the Actions palette:

Choose Window > Show Actions, or click the Actions palette tab if the palette is visible but not active.

By default, the Actions palette displays actions in list mode—you can expand and collapse sets, actions, and commands. In Photoshop, you can also choose to display actions in button mode (as buttons in the Actions palette that play an action with a single mouse click). However, you cannot view individual commands or sets in button mode.

To expand and collapse sets, actions, and commands:

Click the triangle (▷) to the left of the set, action, or command in the Actions palette. Alt-click (Windows) or Option-click (Mac OS) to expand or collapse all actions in a set or all commands in an action.

To select actions:

Do one of the following:

• Click an action name to select a single action.

• Shift-click action names to select multiple, discontiguous actions.

• Ctrl-click (Windows) or Command-click (Mac OS) action names to select multiple, contiguous actions.

To display actions as buttons (Photoshop):

Choose Button Mode from the Actions palette menu. Choose Button Mode again to return to list mode.

Recording actions

Keep in mind the following guidelines when recording actions:

• You can record most—but not all—commands in an action.

• You can record operations that you perform with the marquee, move, polygon, lasso, magic wand, crop, slice, magic eraser, gradient, paint bucket, type, shape, notes, eyedropper, and color sampler tools—as well as those that you perform in the History, Swatches, Color, Paths, Channels, Layers, Styles, and Actions palettes.

In ImageReady, you can drag a command from the History palette to the action in the Actions palette in which you want the command recorded. You cannot drag italicized commands from the History palette to the Actions palette. (Commands in italics are nonactionable.)

• Results depend on file and program setting variables, such as the active layer or the foreground color. For example, a 3-pixel Gaussian blur won't create the same effect on a 72-ppi file as on a 144-ppi file. Nor will Color Balance work on a grayscale file.

• When recording actions that include dialog box and palette settings, keep in mind that only changed settings are recorded. For example, to record an action that sets a particular preference to its current value, you must first change that preference to some other value, and then record the action as you change the preference back to its original value.

• Modal operations and tools—as well as tools that record position—use the units currently specified for the ruler. A modal operation or tool is one that requires you to press Enter or Return to apply its effect, such as the transformation commands. Tools that record position include the marquee, slice, gradient, magic wand, lasso, path, and notes tools.

In Photoshop, when recording an action that will be played on files of different sizes, set the ruler units to percent. As a result, the action will always play back in the same relative position in the image.

• You can record the Play command listed on the Actions palette menu to cause one action to play another.

Creating a new action

When you create a new action, the commands and tools you use are added to the action until you stop recording.

To create a new action:

1 Open a file.

2 In the Actions palette, click the New Action button (🔲), or choose New Action from the palette menu.

3 Enter a name for the action.

4 (Photoshop) Choose a set from the pop-up menu.

5 If desired, set one or both of the following options:

• Assign a keyboard shortcut to the action. You can choose any combination of a Function key, the Ctrl key (Windows) or Command key (Mac OS), and the Shift key (for example, Ctrl+Shift+F3).

• (Photoshop) Assign a color for display in Button Mode.

6 Click Record. The Record button in the Actions palette turns red (●).

Important: When recording the Save As command, do not change the filename. If you enter a new filename, Photoshop records the filename and uses that filename each time you run the action. Before saving, if you navigate to a different folder, you can specify a different location without having to specify a filename.

7 Choose the commands, and perform the operations you want to record.

8 To stop recording, click the Stop button, choose Stop Recording from the Actions palette menu, or press the Escape key. To resume recording in the same action, choose Start Recording from the Actions palette menu.

Recording paths (Photoshop)

The Insert Path command lets you include a complex path (a path created with a pen tool or edited with a path selection tool) as part of an action. When the action is played back, the work path is set to the recorded path. You can insert a path when recording an action or after it has been recorded.

Note: Playing actions that insert complex paths may require significant amounts of memory. If you encounter problems, increase the amount of memory available to Photoshop.

To record a path:

1 Do one of the following:

• Start recording an action.

• Select an action's name to record a path at the end of the action.

• Select a command to record a path after the command.

2 Select an existing path from the Paths palette.

3 Choose Insert Path from the Actions palette menu.

If you record multiple Insert Path commands in a single action, each path will replace the previous one in the target file. To add multiple paths, record a Save Path command using the Paths palette after recording each Insert Path command.

Inserting stops

You can include stops in your action that let you perform a task that cannot be recorded (for example, using a painting tool). Once you've completed the task, click the Play button in the Actions palette to complete the task. You can insert a stop when recording an action or after it has been recorded.

You can also display a short message when the action reaches the stop. For example, you can remind yourself what needs to be done before continuing with the action. A Continue button can be included in the message box. This lets you check for a certain condition in the file (for example, a selection) and continue if nothing needs to be done.

To insert a stop:

1 Choose where to insert the stop:

• Select an action's name to insert a stop at the end of the action.

• Select a command to insert a stop after the command.

2 Choose Insert Stop from the Actions palette menu.

3 Type the message you want to appear.

4 If you want the option to continue the action without stopping, select Allow Continue.

5 Click OK.

Setting modal controls

A *modal control* pauses an action so that you can specify values in a dialog box or use a modal tool. You can only set modal controls for actions that launch dialog boxes or activate modal tools. If you do not set a modal control, dialog boxes do not appear when you play the action, and you cannot change the recorded values.

A modal control is indicated by a dialog box icon (▭) to the left of a command, action, or set in the Actions palette. Actions and sets in which some, but not all, available commands are modal display a red dialog box icon (▭). In Photoshop, you must be in list mode—not button mode—to set a modal control.

To set a modal control:

Do one of the following:

• Click the box to the left of the command name to display the dialog box icon. Click again to remove the modal control.

• To turn on or disable modal controls for all commands in an action, click the box to the left of the action name.

• (Photoshop) To turn on or disable modal controls for all actions in a set, click the box to the left of the set name.

Excluding commands

You can exclude commands that you don't want to play as part of a recorded action. In Photoshop, you must be in list mode—not button mode—to exclude commands.

To exclude or include a command:

1 To expand the listing of commands in an action, click the triangle to the left of the action you want to work with.

2 Click the check mark to the left of the specific command you wish to exclude; click again to include the command. To exclude or include all commands in an action, click the check mark to the left of the action name.

When you exclude a command, its check mark disappears. In addition, the check mark of the parent action turns red to indicate that some of the commands within the action are excluded.

Inserting nonrecordable commands (Photoshop)

The painting and toning tools, tool options, view commands, and window commands cannot be recorded. However, many commands that cannot be recorded can be inserted into an action using the Insert Menu Item command.

An inserted command is not executed until the action is played, so the file remains unchanged when the command is inserted. No values for the command are recorded in the action. If the command has a dialog box, the dialog box appears during playback, and the action pauses until you click OK or Cancel. You can insert a command when recording an action or after it has been recorded.

Note: When you use the Insert Menu Item command to insert a command that launches a dialog box, you cannot disable the modal control in the Actions palette.

To insert a menu item in an action:

1 Choose where to insert the menu item:

• Select an action's name to insert the item at the end of the action.

• Select a command to insert the item at the end of the command.

2 Choose Insert Menu Item from the Actions palette menu.

3 With the Insert Menu Item dialog box open, choose a command from its menu.

4 Click OK.

Specifying an output folder (ImageReady)

You can specify the folder in which images are placed after actions are performed.

Note: In Photoshop, you can set an output folder when using the Batch command to process files. (See "Using the Batch command (Photoshop)" on page 405.)

To specify an output folder:

1 Select the action for which you want to specify an output folder in the Actions palette.

2 Choose Insert Set Output Folder from the Actions palette menu.

3 Select a folder, and click OK.

Recording image size options (ImageReady)

Resizing images is a typical step in preparing irregularly sized images for use on the Web. You can automate this task by creating an action that includes the Image Size command. ImageReady provides several options that give you control over how an action resizes images.

To record Image Size options:

1 Start recording an action.

2 Choose Image > Image Size, and enter the desired image dimensions. (See "Changing the pixel dimensions of an image" on page 97.)

3 Select Action Options.

4 Choose an option from the Fit Image By menu:

• Width to constrain proportions using the new width value.

• Height to constrain proportions using the new height value.

• Width & Height to constrain proportions using either the new width value or the new height value.

• Percent to constrain proportions using the new percent value.

5 Select Do Not Enlarge to prevent images that are smaller than the new dimensions from being sized up.

6 Click OK and continue recording the action.

Inserting optimization settings for selected slices (ImageReady)

When you record a Save Optimized action step, ImageReady includes optimization settings for the entire image. You can insert optimization settings for individual slices using the Insert Set Optimization Settings command.

To insert optimization settings in an action:

1 Select the slice or slices for which you want to record optimization settings. (See "Selecting slices" on page 276.)

2 Select the action in which you want to insert the optimization settings.

3 Do one of the following:

• Choose Insert Set Optimization Settings to *current file format* from the Actions palette menu. (The command indicates the optimization file format currently applied to the selected slice.)

• Drag the droplet icon (🖐) from the Optimize palette onto the Actions palette.

Playing actions

Playing an action executes the series of commands you recorded in the active document. You can exclude specific commands from an action or play a single command. If the action includes a modal control, you can specify values in a dialog box or use a modal tool when the action pauses.

Note: In button mode, clicking a button executes the entire action—though commands previously excluded are not executed.

To play an action on a file:

1 Open the file.

2 Do one of the following:

• To play an entire action, select the action name, and click the Play button (▷) in the Actions palette, or choose Play from the palette menu.

• If you assigned a key combination to the action, press that combination to play the action automatically.

• To play part of an action, select the command from which you want to start playing, and click the Play button in the Actions palette, or choose Play from the palette menu.

To play a single command in an action:

1 Select the command you want to play.

2 Do one of the following:

• Ctrl-click (Windows) or Command-click (Mac OS) the Play button in the Actions palette.

• Press Ctrl (Windows) or Command (Mac OS), and double-click the command.

Note: Because an action is a series of commands, you can use the Edit > Undo command to undo only the last command in an action. To undo an entire action, take a snapshot in the History palette before you play an action, and then select the snapshot to undo the action.

Setting playback options (Photoshop)

Sometimes a long, complicated action does not play properly, but it is difficult to tell where the problem occurs. The Playback Options command gives you three speeds at which to play actions, so that you can watch each command as it is carried out.

When working with actions that contain audio annotations, you can specify whether or not the action will pause for audio annotations. This ensures that each audio annotation completes playing before the next step in the action is initiated.

To specify how fast actions should play:

1 Choose Playback Options from the Actions palette menu.

2 Specify a speed:

• Accelerated to play the action at normal speed (the default).

• Step by Step to complete each command and redraw the image before going on to the next command in the action.

• Pause For to enter the amount of time Photoshop should pause between carrying out each command in the action.

3 Select Pause For Audio Annotation to ensure that each audio annotation in an action completes playback before the next step in the action is initiated. Deselect this option if you want an action to continue while an audio annotation is playing.

4 Click OK.

Editing actions

After you record an action, you can edit it in a variety of ways. You can rearrange actions and commands in the Actions palette; record additional commands in an action; rerecord, duplicate, and delete commands and actions; and change action options.

Rearranging actions and commands

You can rearrange actions in the Actions palette and rearrange commands within an action to change their order of execution.

To rearrange actions:

In the Actions palette, drag the action to its new location before or after another action. When the highlighted line appears in the desired position, release the mouse button.

To rearrange commands:

In the Actions palette, drag the command to its new location within the same or another action. When the highlighted line appears in the desired position, release the mouse button.

Recording additional commands

You can add commands to an action using the Record button or the Start Recording command in the Actions palette.

To record additional commands:

1 Do one of the following:

• Select the action name to insert a new command at the end of the action.

• Select a command in the action to insert a command after it.

2 Click the Record button, or choose Start Recording from the Actions palette menu.

3 Record the additional commands.

4 Click the Stop button to stop recording.

In ImageReady, you can drag a command from the History palette to the Actions palette without clicking the Record button or choosing Start Recording from the Actions palette menu.

Rerecording and duplicating actions and commands

Rerecording an action or command lets you set new values for it. Duplicating an action or command lets you make changes to it without losing the original version.

To record an action again:

1 Select an action, and choose Record Again from the Actions palette menu.

2 For a modal tool, do one of the following:

• Use the tool differently, and Press Enter (Windows) or Return (Mac OS) to change the tool's effect.

• Press Cancel to retain the same settings.

3 For a dialog box, do one of the following:

• Change the values, and click OK to record them.

• Click Cancel to retain the same values.

To record a single command again:

1 In the Actions palette, double-click the command.

2 Enter the new values, and click OK.

To duplicate an action or command:

Do one of the following:

• Alt-drag (Windows) or Option-drag (Mac OS) the action or command to a new location in the Actions palette. When the highlighted line appears in the desired location, release the mouse button.

• Select an action or command. Then choose Duplicate from the Actions palette menu. The copied action or command appears after the original.

• Drag an action or command to the New Action button at the bottom of the Actions palette. The copied action or command appears after the original.

In Photoshop, you can duplicate sets as well as actions and commands.

Deleting actions and commands

If you no longer need an action or command, you can delete it from the Actions palette.

To delete an action or command:

1 In the Actions palette, select the action or command you want to delete.

2 Delete the action or command:

• Click the Trash button (🗑) on the Actions palette. Click OK to delete the action or command.

• Alt-click (Windows) or Option-click (Mac OS) the Trash button to delete the selected action or command without displaying a confirmation dialog box.

• Drag the action or command to the Trash button on the Actions palette to delete the selected action or command without displaying a confirmation dialog box.

• Choose Delete from the Actions palette menu.

To delete all actions in the Actions palette (Photoshop):

Choose Clear All Actions from the Actions palette menu.

Changing action options

You can change the name, keyboard shortcut, and button color (Photoshop) for an action in the Action Options dialog box.

To change action options:

1 Do one of the following:

• Double-click the action name.

• Select the action, and choose Action Options from the Actions palette menu.

2 Type a new name for the action, or change other options. For more information about action options, see "Recording actions" on page 394.

3 Click OK.

Managing actions in the Actions palette

By default, the Actions palette displays predefined actions (shipped with the application) and any actions you create. You can also load additional actions into the Actions palette.

Note: *Photoshop actions are not compatible with ImageReady, and vice versa.*

Saving and loading actions (Photoshop)

Actions are automatically saved to the Actions Palette.psp file (Windows) or the Actions Palette file (Mac OS) in the Adobe Photoshop 6 Settings folder. If this file is lost or removed, the actions you created are lost. You can save your actions to a separate actions file so that you can recover them if necessary. You can also load a variety of action sets that are shipped with Photoshop.

Note: The default location of the Adobe Photoshop 6 Settings folder varies by operating system. Use your operating system's Find command to locate this folder.

To save a set of actions:

1 Select a set.

2 Choose Save Actions from the Actions palette menu.

3 Type a name for the set, choose a location, and click Save. If you save a set of actions in the Photoshop Presets folder, the set will appear at the bottom of the Actions palette menu for easy loading.

Press Ctrl+Alt (Windows) or Command+Option (Mac OS) when you choose the Save Actions command to save the actions in a text file. You can use this file to review or print the contents of an action. However, you can't reload the text file back into Photoshop.

To load a set of actions:

1 Choose Load Actions from the Actions palette menu.

2 Locate and select the action set file. (In Windows, Photoshop action set files have the extension .atn.)

3 Click Load.

To load a preset action set:

Select an action set from the bottom section of the Actions palette menu. The name of the set indicates the type of actions it contains (for example, Buttons contains actions for creating buttons).

For more information about the contents of preset action sets, see the PDF file in the Photoshop Actions folder, inside the Presets folder in the Photoshop application folder.

To restore actions to the default set:

1 Choose Reset Actions from the Actions palette menu.

2 Click OK to replace the current actions in the Actions palette with the default set, or click Append to add the set of default actions to the current actions in the Actions palette.

Saving actions (ImageReady)

All actions you create are saved in the ImageReady Actions file in the Adobe Photoshop 6 Settings folder. ImageReady can only access actions that reside in this folder. You add actions to ImageReady by dragging actions into the ImageReady Actions folder on your computer. Because ImageReady does not include a Load Actions command, you must add files to the ImageReady Actions file manually.

Note: *The default location of the Adobe Photoshop 6 Settings folder varies by operating system. Use your operating system's Find command to locate this folder.*

You can remove actions from ImageReady by dragging the actions out of the ImageReady Actions folder or by using the Delete Action command in the Actions palette menu. Actions you remove by dragging can be saved in another folder. Actions you remove by deleting are removed permanently.

If you add or remove files from the ImageReady Actions palette, you can direct ImageReady to scan the Actions folder for changes and update the Actions palette. (ImageReady scans the Actions folder and updates the Actions palette whenever you launch the application.)

To update the Actions folder:

1 Drag an action file into or out of the ImageReady Actions folder.

2 Choose Rescan Actions Folder from the Actions palette menu.

Organizing sets of actions (Photoshop)

To help you organize your actions, you can create sets of actions and save the sets to disk. You can organize sets of actions for different types of work—such as print publishing and online publishing—and transfer sets to other computers.

Although ImageReady doesn't allow you to create sets, you can manually organize actions in the ImageReady Actions folder. For example, if the Actions palette contains too many actions, create a new folder inside the ImageReady Actions folder and move less-used actions from the ImageReady Actions folder to this new folder. The relocated actions are removed from the palette until you return them to the ImageReady Actions folder.

To create a new set of actions:

1 In the Actions palette, click the New Set button (▢), or choose New Set from the palette menu.

2 Enter the name of the set, and click OK.

To move an action to a different set:

In the Actions palette, drag the action to a different set. When the highlighted line appears in the desired position, release the mouse button.

To rename a set of actions:

1 In the Actions palette, choose Set Options from the pop-up menu.

2 Enter the name of the set, and click OK.

Using the Batch command (Photoshop)

The Batch command lets you play an action on a folder of files and subfolders. If you have a digital camera or a scanner with a document feeder, you can also import and process multiple images with a single action. Your scanner or digital camera may need an acquire plug-in module that supports actions. (If the third-party plug-in wasn't written to import multiple documents at a time, it may not work during batch-processing or if used as part of an action. Contact the plug-in's manufacturer for further information.)

When batch-processing files, you can leave all the files open, close and save the changes to the original files, or save modified versions of the files to a new location (leaving the originals unchanged). If you are saving the processed files to a new location, you may want to create a new folder for the processed files before starting the batch.

For better batch performance, reduce the number of saved history states and deselect the Automatically Create First Snapshot option in the History palette.

To batch-process files using the Batch command:

1 Choose File > Automate > Batch.

2 Choose the desired set and action from the Set and Action pop-up menus.

3 Choose a source from the Source pop-up menu:

• Folder to play the action on files already stored on your computer. Click Choose to locate and select the folder. Select Override Action "Open" Commands if you want Open commands in the action to refer to the batched files, rather than the filenames specified in the action. (Deselect Override Action "Open" Commands if the action was recorded to operate on open files or if the action contains Open commands for specific files that are required by the action.) Select Include All Subfolders to process files in subfolders. Select Suppress Color Profile Warnings to turn off display of color policy messages.

• Import to import and play the action on images from a digital camera or scanner.

• Opened Files to play the action on all open files.

4 Choose a destination for the processed files from the Destination menu:

• None to leave the files open without saving changes (unless the action includes a Save command).

• Save and Close to save the files in their current location, overwriting the original files.

• Folder to save the processed files to another location. Click Choose to specify the destination folder. Select Override Action "Save In" Commands if you want Save As commands in the action to refer to the batched files, rather than the filenames and locations specified in the action. (Deselect Override Action "Save In" Commands if the action contains Save As commands for specific files that are required by the action.)

5 If you chose Folder as the destination, specify a file-naming convention and select file compatibility options for the processed files:

• For File Naming, select elements from the pop-up menus or enter text into the fields to be combined into the default names for all files. Elements include document name, serial number or letter, file creation date, and file extension.

The fields let you change the order and formatting of the filename parts. You must include at least one field that is unique for every file (for example, filename, serial number, or serial letter) to prevent files from overwriting each other.

• For File Name Compatibility, choose Windows, Mac OS, and UNIX to make filenames compatible with Windows, Mac OS, and UNIX operating systems.

Saving files using the Batch command options always saves the files in the same format as the original files. To create a batch process that saves files in a new format, record the Save As command followed by the Close command as part of your original action. Then choose Override Action "Save In" Commands for the Destination when setting up the batch process.

6 Select an option for error processing from the Errors pop-up menu:

• Stop for Errors to suspend the process until you confirm the error message.

• Log Errors to File to record each error in a file without stopping the process. If errors are logged to a file, a message appears after processing. To review the error file, click Save As and name the error file.

To batch-process using multiple actions, create a new action and record the Batch command for each action you want to use. This technique also lets you process multiple folders in a single batch. To batch-process multiple folders, create aliases within a folder to the other folders you want to process, and select the Include All Subfolders option.

Using droplets

A *droplet* is a small application that applies an action to one or more images that you drag onto the droplet icon ( ). You can save a droplet on the desktop or to a location on disk.

Creating a droplet from an action

Actions are the basis for creating droplets—you must create the desired action in the Actions palette prior to creating a droplet. (See "Recording actions" on page 394.)

In ImageReady, you can also create droplets with the Optimize palette, so that you can apply Optimize palette settings to single images or batches of images.

To create a droplet from an action (Photoshop):

1 Choose File > Automate > Create Droplet.

2 Click Choose in the Save Droplet In section of the dialog box, and select a location to save the droplet. (The droplet icon (🐾) will appear in the selected location.)

3 Select the desired set and action from the Set and Action menus.

4 Set Play options for the droplet:

• Select Override Action "Open" Commands if you want Open commands in the action to refer to the batched files, rather than the filenames specified in the action. Deselect Override Action "Open" Commands if the action was recorded to operate on open files or if the action contains Open commands for specific files that are required by the action.

• Select Include All Subdirectories to process files in subdirectories.

• Select Suppress Color Profile Warnings to turn off display of color policy messages.

5 Select a destination for the processed files from the Destination menu:

• None to leave the files open without saving changes (unless the action included a Save command).

• Save and Close to save the files in their current location.

• Folder to save the processed files to another location. Click Choose to specify the destination folder. Select Override Action "Save In" Commands if you want Save As commands in the action to refer to the batched files, rather than the filenames and locations specified in the action. Deselect Override Action "Save In" Commands if the action contains Save As commands for specific files that are required by the action.

6 If you chose Folder as the destination, specify a file-naming convention and select file compatibility options for the processed files:

• For File Naming, select elements from the pop-up menus or enter text into the fields to be combined into the default names for all files. Elements include document name, serial number or letter, file creation date, and file extension.

• For File Name Compatibility, choose Windows, Mac OS, and UNIX to make filenames compatible with Windows, Mac OS, and UNIX operating systems.

7 Select an option for error processing from the Errors pop-up menu:

• Stop for Errors to suspend the process until you confirm the error message.

• Log Errors to File to record each error in a file without stopping the process. If errors are logged to a file, a message appears after processing. To review the error file, click Save As and name the error file.

To create a droplet from an action (ImageReady):

1 For best results, make sure that the action contains at least one Set Optimization command. To add a Set Optimization command, adjust the settings in the Optimize palette, and then drag the droplet icon ( ) from the Optimize palette onto the part of the Actions palette where you want to add that command.

If you do not add a Set Optimization command to the droplet, ImageReady will process files using the optimization settings in place at the time the droplet was created.

2 Create the droplet:

• Drag the name of the action from the Actions palette onto the desktop. The droplet has the same name as the action it was created from. You can rename the droplet as you do other desktop icons.

• Select an action, and choose Create Droplet from the Actions palette menu. Name the droplet, choose a location where the droplet will be saved, and click Save.

Creating droplets for use on different operating systems

When creating droplets that may be used in both Windows and Mac OS, keep the following compatibility issues in mind:

• When moving a droplet created in Windows to Mac OS, drag the droplet onto the Photoshop icon. Photoshop will launch and update the droplet for use in Mac OS.

• When creating a droplet in Mac OS, add .exe to the end of the droplet name. Using the .exe extension makes droplets compatible with both Windows and Mac OS.

• References to filenames are not supported between operating systems. Any action step that references a file or folder name (such as an Open command, Save command, or adjustment command that loads its settings from a file) will pause and prompt the user for a filename.

Using droplets to process files

To use a droplet, simply drag a file or folder onto the droplet icon: ( ) in Photoshop or ( ) in ImageReady. If the application you used to create the droplet is not currently running, the droplet launches it.

In ImageReady, you can control droplet processing in the following ways:

• To temporarily pause processing, click Pause. Click Resume to continue the processing.

• To cancel processing, click Stop.

Editing droplets (ImageReady)

In ImageReady, you can edit the commands in a droplet in the same ways you edit the commands in an action. You can also set batch options for a droplet before or after you create it. For example, you can set the droplet to operate in the background during execution, so that you can work in other applications while ImageReady processes images.

To edit a droplet:

1 Double-click the droplet to open the droplet window in ImageReady. The droplet window looks like a simplified version of the Actions palette.

2 Edit the droplet in the same ways you would edit an action:

• Change the order of commands by dragging them in the droplet list.

• Delete commands by dragging them to the Trash button (🗑).

• Add a command by dragging a state from the History palette to the area in which you want the command recorded in the droplet window.

To adjust droplet batch options:

1 Do one of the following:

• Before you create the droplet, select an action and choose Batch Options from the Actions palette menu.

• After you create the droplet, double-click the droplet to open the droplet window, and double-click Batch Options at the top of the droplet list.

2 Select Original (same name and folder) to save the original file with the same name and in the same folder.

3 Select Optimized to save an optimized version of the file. Then do any of the following:

• For In, choose the location in which you want to save the optimized file.

• For If Duplicate File Name, choose how and whether to append numbers or letters to indicate the optimized file in cases of duplicate filenames.

• For Modify File Name For, choose whether ImageReady appends or rewrites the filename using Windows, Mac OS, or UNIX file-naming conventions.

4 Select playback options:

• Run In Background to hide ImageReady during droplet execution, so that you can work in other applications while processing takes place. When you select Run In Background, other playback options requiring user input during processing are turned off. ImageReady appears when the droplet completes execution.

Note: ImageReady is not available for creating and modifying current images while background processing is taking place.

• Display Image to show the images as they are being processed.

• Pause Before Save to stop the processing of each image before saving it.

5 Choose error options from the Errors menu:

• Stop to suspend the process until you confirm the error message.

• Skip Step to not process steps in which errors are encountered.

• Skip File to not process files in which errors are encountered.

Using droplets to automate optimization settings (ImageReady)

You can save Optimize palette settings for use on individual images or batches of images by creating a droplet for the settings. The droplet lets you apply the compression settings to an image or batch of images that you drag onto the droplet icon.

To create a droplet for automating Optimize palette settings:

1 With an image displayed in the image window, choose a compression format and desired compression options in the Optimize palette. (See "Optimizing images" on page 320.)

2 Create a droplet:

• Drag the droplet icon (🐾) from the Optimize palette onto the desktop.

The droplet is named with a brief description of the compression settings, including file format and color palette or quality setting information. You can rename the droplet as you do other desktop icons.

• Click the droplet icon (🐾) on the Optimize palette. Name the droplet, choose a location where the droplet will be saved, and click Save.

• Choose Create Droplet from the Optimize palette menu. Name the droplet, choose a location where the droplet will be saved, and click Save.

💡 *You can add optimization settings to an action by dragging the droplet icon in the Optimize palette to the Actions palette.*

Using the Automate commands (Photoshop)

The Automate commands simplify complex tasks by combining them into one or more dialog boxes. Photoshop includes the following commands (third-party companies may provide additional commands):

• Conditional Mode Change changes the color mode of an image to the mode you specify, based on the original mode of the image. Record this command in an action to ensure that images use the correct color mode and avoid generating unwanted error messages.

• Contact Sheet produces a series of thumbnail previews on a single sheet from the files in the selected folder. (See "Creating contact sheets" on page 368.)

• Fit Image fits the current image to the width and height you specify, without changing its aspect ratio.

Note: *This will resample the image, changing the amount of data in the image.*

• Multi-Page PDF to PSD converts each page of a PDF document you select to a separate Photoshop file. (See "Opening and importing PDF files" on page 102.)

• Picture Package places multiple copies of a source image on a single page, similar to the photo packages traditionally sold by portrait studios. (See "Creating picture packages" on page 368.)

• Web Photo Gallery generates a Web site from a set of images—complete with a thumbnails index page, individual JPEG image pages, and navigable links. (See "Creating Web photo galleries (Photoshop)" on page 297.)

To use an automated command:

Choose File > Automate, and then choose any of the commands listed under it.

External automation

Photoshop supports some external automation using OLE Automation (Windows) or AppleScript (Mac OS). Using either of these methods lets you start Adobe Photoshop and execute actions externally.

Using external automation lets you perform such tasks as:

• Having another scriptable application generate a series of files, and having Photoshop batch-process them.

• Having Photoshop batch-process files and save them to your Web site.

• Writing a script that runs an action and then shuts down your computer late at night after you've gone home.

If you have further questions about OLE, contact Microsoft Corporation. For questions about AppleScript, see your Mac OS documentation or contact Apple Computer.

Index

Production Notes

This book was created electronically using Adobe FrameMaker®. Art was produced using Adobe Illustrator and Adobe Photoshop. The Minion® and Myriad® families of typefaces are used throughout this book.

Photography

The following photographers and stock agencies have supplied the photographs and artwork seen throughout this book.

CMCD, Inc.
Bike (page 91)

Definitive Stock
Bird (page 9), Hawaii (page 13), Leaf (page 14), Sailor (page 15), Venice (page 16), Cherry (page 18), Strawberry (page 21), Tree (page 25), Blaze (page 31), Cactus (page 251), Trees (page 393)

Eyewire Photography
Bison (page 156)

Mirelez/Ross, Inc.
Leaves (page 110)

Doug Menuez
Olé No Moiré (page 378)

Julieanne Kost
Coin (page 79), White flower (page 128), Flower jar (page 144), Flower (page 148), Star (page 151), Teapot (page 173,), Lion (page 205), Zebra (page 205), Giraffe (page 308), Paint brushes (page 318), Paint (page 318), Paint roller (page 319), Bolts (page 340), Sands (page 352), Clouds (page 352)

Kaoru Hollin
Bicycle illustration (page 92)

Karen Tenenbaum
Clock (page 78), Coins (page 94), Shell (page 197)

Michael Dossev
Chair (page 272)

PhotoDisc, Inc.
Soccer ball (page 369)